The Best
AMERICAN
SHORT
STORIES
of the Eighties

The Best AMERICAN SHORT STORIES

of the Eighties

Selected and
with an Introduction
by SHANNON RAVENEL

HOUGHTON MIFFLIN COMPANY
BOSTON · 1990

Shannon Ravenel is grateful to JOHANNA WOOD, *who has provided invaluable assistance and consultation, and to* BETTYE DEW, DALE PURVES, *and* JOE SCHUSTER *for their helpful criticism.*

Library of Congress Cataloging-in-Publication Data
The Best American short stories of the eighties / selected and with an introduction by Shannon Ravenel.
   p.   cm.
  ISBN 0-395-52222-6 — ISBN 0-395-52223-4 (pbk.)
   1. Short stories, American.   2. American fiction — 20th century.
I. Ravenel, Shannon.
PS648.S5B46   1990   90-30071
813'.0108'09048 — dc20   CIP

Printed in the United States of America

DOH 10 9 8 7 6 5 4 3 2 1

Contents

Introduction

THE YEAR 1990 marks the seventy-fifth anniversary of the *Best American Short Stories* series. This steadfast old friend of the short story has been published every year without interruption since its inception in 1915. It was the brainchild of a New England poet, Edward J. O'Brien, who sold the idea to a Boston publisher, Small, Maynard & Company. Dodd, Mead & Company published the series from 1926 to 1932. Then Houghton Mifflin Company took it on and has published all the subsequent volumes: those edited by O'Brien from 1933 to 1941; those of his successor, Martha Foley, from 1942 to 1977; and the "new series," with its guest editors, since 1978. Houghton Mifflin has also sponsored periodic commemorative and retrospective anthologies, the most comprehensive of which was the excellent *Fifty Best American Short Stories, 1915–1965,* edited by Martha Foley.

I have been series editor of the annual for thirteen years. As such, I was offered the opportunity to put together a retrospective anthology to celebrate a decade that has seen the American short story come — some would say come *back* — into its own. I was eager for the job, knowing that it would provide reason and time to reread and savor the introductions and my own favorite stories of the past ten years. It also gave me an excuse to wander back into the history of the anthology. I have long been curious about my two predecessors, especially about how they coped with the great volume of reading. I am chronically panicked by the rising tide of new stories published each year, and am amazed to find that neither of them seemed ever to have mentioned it — at least not in print. It is a noble tradition of non-complaint that O'Brien and Foley set, one that should be upheld.

Clearly, Edward O'Brien was an avid and voracious reader. He was also a busy literary innovator (in addition to *The Best American Short Stories,* he edited a British version of the story anthology and, for a while, a *Best Poems* series) and a frequent and opinionated commentator on the story form. But what may have been most unusual about him was his passion for statistics, certainly an unexpected trait in a poet. The legacy of his love of counting and listing is a wealth of information about the American story in its golden age of mass circulation weekly magazines. To my surprise, I discovered in O'Brien's 1919 volume (an edition with 67 pages of indexes) a list of more than 2,000 qualifying short stories—almost as many as I read in 1989. The majority of those stories appeared in the popular weekly magazines. *The Saturday Evening Post* published 308 short stories that year. *The Smart Set* published 135, *Collier's Weekly* 114, *Hearst's Magazine* 71, *The New York Tribune* 70, and *Harper's Magazine* 60. O'Brien's list of weeklies that regularly published short fiction includes more than fifty names. In those pre-TV times, determined writers could support themselves from the sale of stories to magazines that paid handsome fees indeed — for the right kinds of stories.

A far cry from the current magazine scene. Now there is only one national weekly buying and publishing short fiction, *The New Yorker.* In the few monthly magazines still able to buy and publish fiction, dwindling advertising has meant fewer pages and therefore fewer stories per issue. That once thriving mass market outlet has been replaced over the last quarter century by scores of privately funded or institutionally subsidized non-profit literary quarterlies. It is this largely unsung cultural resource, the "little magazine," that now provides the biggest and most consistent outlet for the best short story writers, only a tiny fraction of whom have any expectation of living off their writing.

In the past decade, "the renaissance of the short story" has become something of a catchphrase. I've heard little discussion, however, about exactly what this label means. If "renaissance" is taken to mean that the current new interest in the American short story heralds a rebirth of the genre's popularity among the masses to match that of the teens and twenties, then I'd say the phrase overshoots the truth. If "renaissance" refers to the story itself, then I think most readers and critics would agree that the born-again story of the 1980s has far exceeded the literary standards of its popular forebears. As evidence of the great distance the story has come, I have only to turn again to the 1919 anthology and O'Brien's introduction, in which he laments what he believed was the by-product of the magazine fiction boom: "For the past year, it has been a source of much questioning to me to determine why American fiction fails so conspicuously in presenting a national soul, why it fails to measure sincerely the heights and depths of our aspirations and failures as a nation, and why it lacks the vital elan which is so characteristic of other literatures? . . . Why is [our] national consciousness so tangled in evasion of reality?"

As an answer to his own rhetorical question, O'Brien quotes from a letter sent to him by an unnamed writer (who, unlike O'Brien, gets right to the point): "What writes itself in me is too intense for the light weight American magazines. My last story took me months to write and I had to ruin it by tacking on to it a happy ending — or starve."

O'Brien's mission was to combat commercial formularization of the literary short story. For twenty-six years, until his death in 1941, his selections for *The Best American Short Stories* were based on an unremitting insistence upon literary distinction and authorial integrity. He eschewed tales with contrived plots and happy endings in favor of stories in the classic American tradition of Irving, Poe, Hawthorne, Melville, and Crane.

His efforts paid off. The stories in his collections improved over the years, and by the time of O'Brien's death, Martha Foley was able to write in the introduction to her own first volume of the *Best*, in 1942, that "the lifelessly plotted story, with the forced happy or trick ending, is dying, slowly but surely dying." Indeed, the number of memorable stories in Foley's first collection is in contrast to the scarcity of those in O'Brien's early volumes. And when Foley compiled *Fifty Best* in 1965, she included only five stories from the first decade of the series, compared with fifteen from the 1955 to 1965 annuals.

Foley edited the series until 1977, when she died at age eighty. Her knowledge of the short story was encyclopedic. And it was not limited to just the American short story. She read and considered translations, British stories, South African stories, anything and everything that appeared in English in American and Canadian periodicals. But it was her unerring eye for literary quality in work by new writers that made her a great figure in American literature.

Martha Foley and her husband, Whit Burnett (whom she later divorced), had together founded *Story* magazine, and she co-edited it at its peak, from 1931 to 1942. When she assumed the job of editor of the *Best American* series, she offered this deceptively simple definition of the short story as the one she liked best: "A good short story is a story that is not too long and which gives the reader the feeling he has undergone a memorable experience."

The open-endedness of that definition may be the secret of Foley's success. Looking back over the thirty-six years of her editorship of the anthology, I am struck by the unfailingly high standards of the collections she assembled and by the sustained admiration of those who reviewed them. It's hard to believe that after so many years an editor wouldn't become jaded or lose touch with the times, or play favorites and begin to lose the respect of the literary critics. But to the end of her life Martha Foley maintained her critical integrity along with an extraordinarily open-minded response to new approaches to the short story. She was enthusiastic about whatever *worked*.

Martha Foley had appointed no successor, and Houghton Mifflin considered a number of ways to continue the series. They settled on a format that has changed the original procedure of selection to one intended to ensure that over time a variety of tastes will be at work in selecting the "best" stories. Because I had acted for some years as Houghton Mifflin's in-house editor of *The Best American Short Stories* and was known to cherish it, I was asked to serve as series editor in support of a different writer or critic invited to edit one annual volume. My job for the past thirteen years has been to read each year's eligible stories published in U.S. and Canadian magazines and to select 120 for the guest editor's consideration. (To be eligible, a story must be written in English by a citizen of the United States or Canada and appear first in a nationally distributed periodical. An entry cannot be an excerpt of a longer work.) I also select the stories that make up the yearly list of "100 Other Distinguished Stories," which appears at the back of each collection.

To be perfectly honest, when Houghton Mifflin proposed this procedure to me in 1977, I agreed to it secretly hoping that the complicated new system would soon be rejected in favor once again of a single ongoing editor. Of course, I wanted that editor to be me. But there is nothing like success to change the direction of one's ambitions. The plan seemed not only to work but to work extremely well. The new series, which indeed is no longer so new, has been lively and wide-ranging in taste, and readers in America have shown their approval by buying increasing numbers of the volume every year. Sales have quadrupled in the past ten years as the guest editors have, in their considerations of and introductions to each year's crop of stories, commanded wider and wider attention for the anthology itself and for the story in general. In fact, the genre does now enjoy the oft-cited renaissance. And I believe the 1980s will be known as another golden age, though for reasons very different from those which led to the story's great popularity in the teens and twenties, when writers could live off their work in a way that today's practitioners cannot. But if the present golden age is not as economically sustaining as the previous one, certainly it provides a far richer environment for the development of younger writers.

There are, of course, those who have reservations about the longevity of the current literary appetite for short stories. In 1987 Ted Solotaroff, who had served as the first guest editor of the new series, called the short story "the sun-dried tomato of the literary world," implying that readers' interest in the genre runs no deeper than the latest gourmet fad. I think indications prove otherwise. A proliferation of graduate programs in creative writing has produced not only more short story writers but more demanding readers. And there is no denying that this

growing interest in short fiction has been well served over the
past twenty-five years by those "little magazines" that have
sprung into existence. The number of literary journals is ever
growing, supported by an increasing budget for literature in the
National Endowment for the Arts, as well as by stronger state
arts councils. These journals provide, in turn, more space for
more stories to be published by those new writers and new pipe-
lines to that new audience. The increase in the number of stories being published is startling. Since I began work on *The Best
American Short Stories,* the number of eligible stories that have
found their way to me has more than doubled, from fewer than
900 in 1977 to more than 2,000 in 1989.

Another indication of the short story's resurgence in the
1980s is that collections and anthologies are being reviewed
more often in magazines and newspapers. In 1989 alone, the
New York Times Book Review turned over its front page to a short
story collection four times, and in the spring of 1988 a first
collection of stories, *Emperor of the Air* by Ethan Canin, was on
the *Times* best-seller list for seven weeks. Cropping up too are
features with titles like, "Is There a Short Story BOOM?" That
article, which appeared in *Publishers Weekly* in 1987, asked a
particularly relevant question: "Although there may be a proliferation of little magazines and presses . . . does that mean that
there is also some considerable increase in the number of great
writers of the genre?"

Every generation has its share of great writers. Ratios of one
genre's greats to another's may simply reflect the literary climate
of the times. But whatever the climate, I'm not worried about
the short story. "It is only the story that can continue beyond
the war and the warrior," said the African writer Chinua
Achebe. "It is the story that saves our progeny from blundering
like blind beggars into the spikes of the cactus fence."

The guest editors of the 1980s have been as staunch as I in
their belief in the genre. They have been as insistent as Edward
O'Brien was about literary distinction and authorial integrity,
and they have been as inclusive as Martha Foley in the broad-
ness of their definitions of what "best" short stories should be.
Margaret Atwood could have been speaking for all of them
when she cautioned against rules in writing. A rule, she said, is

a "challenge to the deviousness and inventiveness and audacity of the creative spirit." But the guest editors, all of them accomplished practitioners of the form, worked hard to select stories that best reflected their individual tastes, and all of them went to some trouble to communicate what the essentials of their tastes were. What is very welcome are the plain and emphatic statements by these ten editors of what they wanted from a short story. What follows is a selection of some of those statements, fresh and immediate redefinitions of what we've all been taught are the basic elements of the best fiction.

In contemplating their expectations of the short story's form, one guest editor approached it metaphorically, another more practically:

> It's the chamber music of literature and has the same kind of devotee.
>
> — HORTENSE CALISHER

> I want stories to startle and engage me within the first few sentences, and in their middle to widen or deepen or sharpen my knowledge of human activity, and to end by giving me a sensation of completed statement.
>
> — JOHN UPDIKE

When it came to style, two guest editors were quite direct about what they wanted:

> The most appealing short-story writer is the one who's a wastrel. He neither hoards his best ideas for something more "important" (a novel) nor skimps on his materials because this is "only" a short story . . . A spendthrift story has a strange way of seeming bigger than the sum of its parts; it is stuffed full; it gives a sense of possessing further information that could be divulged if called for. Even the sparest in style implies a torrent of additional details barely suppressed, bursting through the seams.
>
> — ANNE TYLER

> *Abjure carelessness in writing,* just as you would in life.
>
> — RAYMOND CARVER

Nobody wanted to be specific about plot or subject matter or theme, but belief in the depth of the story's responsibility was clear and of great interest:

> A good writer addresses questions over which no human authority can ever hold sway.
>
> — MARK HELPRIN

> One of the conclusions I have reached is that people want order, but some part of them craves anarchy, and writers are seen to embody both elements: in a sane, reasonable way, writers will present a situation, but the components of that situation, and the implications, can be dynamite.
>
> — ANN BEATTIE

> All I want from a good story is what children want . . . They are longing to hear a story, but only if you are longing to tell one.
>
> — MARGARET ATWOOD

> Short stories should tell us what everybody knows but what nobody is talking about. At least not publicly. Except for the short story writers.
>
> — RAYMOND CARVER

> I want stories in which the author shows frank concern, not self-protective, "sensible" detachment.
>
> — JOHN GARDNER

> The more you respect and focus on the singular and the strange, the more you become aware of the universal and the infinite.
>
> — GAIL GODWIN

And when two of the editors discussed characterization, they plainly emphasized personal involvement:

> Is it not astounding that one can love so deeply characters who are composites, portraits, or born of the thin air, especially when one has never seen or touched them, and they exist only in an imprint of curiously bent lines?
>
> — MARK HELPRIN

What is wanted then is sadness. (We're talking literature, not life. We're talking Kenny Rogers's chipped and country voice, not music.) This, it seems to me, is the absolute, ideal humor for respectable men. Sadness mind you, not grief.

— STANLEY ELKIN

In defining the elements of their own tastes, the ten guest editors remind us why it is we want to read the "best" stories and why it is that only the story can continue "beyond the war and the warrior."

This volume celebrates a decade that has seen a rich diversity of approaches to the short story form, to its style, its themes, its characterizations. I have chosen twenty stories, two from each of the past ten volumes. My purpose is to reflect not only the variety of stories written and published in the 1980s, but also the wide range of tastes at work in this new series. These stories have been sifted through my idiosyncratic process of selection. Not every reader will love every story, but as different as each one is from another, I believe that all of them meet Raymond Carver's criteria: "Short stories, like houses — or cars, for that matter — should be built to last. They should also be pleasing, if not beautiful, to look at, and everything inside them should *work*."

In the end, I cannot improve upon the words and sentiments of Martha Foley's introduction to her first volume of *The Best American Short Stories* in 1942: "When O'Brien started this anthology many years ago, the short story had fallen to a very low level. It was easy then, and quite honest, to be able to say, 'These are the very best stories published during the entire year.' Now the level of short story writing again has risen so high it is not feasible to include in any one volume all the excellent stories published . . . All that any editor can say today is: 'These are the stories I myself liked best. I hope you will agree.' "

Amen.

SHANNON RAVENEL

The Best
AMERICAN
SHORT
STORIES
of the Eighties

PETER TAYLOR

Stanley Elkin characterized this story as "almost sociology, and a
sociology that isn't even operative anymore — the stiff, cold
codes of a Memphis of the mind." He also said it was "surely a
masterpiece." At fifty-six pages, "The Old Forest" threatens the
limits of the story form in length, but as with all of Taylor's
short stories, it meets the classic criteria of focused time, place,
and event. Peter Taylor was born in Tennessee in 1917. He was
educated in schools in Nashville, Memphis, and St. Louis, and
attended Kenyon College and Vanderbilt University. He lives in
Charlottesville, Virginia.

The Old Forest

I WAS already formally engaged, as we used to say, to the girl I
was going to marry. But still I sometimes went out on the town
with girls of a different sort. And during the very week before
the date set for the wedding, in December, I was in an automobile accident at a time when one of those girls was with me. It
was a calamitous thing to have happen — not the accident itself,
which caused no serious injury to anyone, but the accident plus
the presence of that girl.

As a matter of fact, it was not unusual in those days — forty
years ago and a little more — for a well-brought-up young man
like me to keep up his acquaintance, until the very eve of his
wedding, with some member of what we facetiously and somewhat arrogantly referred to as the Memphis demimonde. (That
was merely to say with a girl who was not in the Memphis debutante set.) I am not even sure how many of us knew what the
word *demimonde* meant or implied. But once it had been applied
to such girls it was hard for us to give it up. We even learned to
speak of them individually as demimondaines — and later cor-

rupted that to demimondames. The girls were of course a considerably less sophisticated lot than any of this sounds, though they were bright girls certainly and some of them even highly intelligent. They read books, they looked at pictures, and they were apt to attend any concert or play that came to Memphis. When the old San Carlo Opera Company turned up in town, you could count on certain girls of the demimonde being present in their block of seats, and often with a score of the opera in hand. From that you will understand that they certainly weren't the innocent, untutored types that we generally took to dances at the Memphis Country Club and whom we eventually looked forward to marrying.

These girls I refer to would, in fact, very frequently and very frankly say to us that the M.C.C. (that's how we always spoke of the club) was the last place they wanted to be taken. There was one girl in particular, not so smart as some of the others perhaps and certainly less restrained in the humor she sometimes poked at the world we boys lived in, an outspoken girl, who was the most vociferous of all in her disdain for the country club. I remember one night, in one of those beer gardens that became popular in Memphis in the late thirties, when this girl suddenly announced to a group of us, "*I* haven't lost anything at the M.C.C. That's something you boys can bet your daddy's bottom dollar on." We were gathered — four or five couples — about one of the big wooden beer-garden tables with an umbrella in its center, and when she said that, all the other girls in the party went into a fit of laughter. It was a kind of giggling that was unusual for them. The boys in the party laughed, too, of course, but we were surprised by the way the girls continued to giggle among themselves for such a long time. We were out of college by then and thought we knew the world pretty well; most of us had been working for two or three years in our fathers' business firms. But we didn't see why this joke was so very funny. I suppose it was too broad for us in its reference. There is no way of knowing, after all these years, if it was too broad for our sheltered minds or if the rest of the girls were laughing at the vulgar tone of the girl who had spoken. She was, you see, a little bit coarser than the rest, and I suspect they were laughing at the way she had phrased what she said. For us boys, anyhow, it was pleasant that the demimondaines took the lighthearted view they did about not going to the M.C.C., because it was the last place most of us would have wished to take them. Our *other* girls would have known too readily who they were and would not willingly or gracefully have endured their presence. To have brought one of those girls to the club would have required, at any rate, a boy who was a much bolder and freer spirit than I was at twenty-three.

To the liberated young people of today all this may seem a corrupting factor in our old way of life — not our snobbery so much as our continuing to see those demimonde girls right up until the time of marriage. And yet I suspect that in the Memphis of today customs concerning serious courtship and customs concerning unacknowledged love affairs have not been entirely altered. Automobile accidents occur there still, for instance, the reports of which in the newspaper do not mention the name of the driver's "female companion," just as the report of my accident did not. If the driver is a "scion of a prominent local family" with his engagement to be married already announced at an M.C.C. party, as well as in the Sunday newspaper, then the account of his automobile collision is likely to refer to the girl in the car with him only as his "female companion." Some newspaper readers might, I know, assume this to be a reference to the young man's fiancée. That is what is intended, I suppose — *for* the general reader. But it would almost certainly not have been the case — not in the Memphis, Tennessee, of 1937.

The girl with me in my accident was a girl whose origins nobody knew anything about. But she was a perfectly decent sort of girl, living independently in a respectable roominghouse and working at a respectable job. That was the sort of girl about whom the Memphis newspapers felt obliged to exercise the greatest care when making any reference to her in their columns. It was as though she were their special ward. Such a girl must be protected from any blaze of publicity. Such a girl must not suffer from the misconduct of any Memphis man or group of men — even newspaper publishers. That was fine for the girl, of course, and who could possibly resent it? It was splendid for her, but I, the driver of the car, had to suffer considerable anguish just because of such a girl's presence in the car, and suffer still more because of her behavior afterward. Moreover, the response of certain older men in town to her subsequent behavior would cause me still further anguish and prolong my suffering by several days. Those men were the editors of the city's two newspapers, along with the lawyers called in by my father to represent me if I should be taken into court. There was also my father himself, and the father of my fiancée, *his* lawyer (for some reason or other), and, finally, no less a person than the mayor of Memphis, all of whom one would ordinarily have supposed to be indifferent to the caprices of such a girl. They were the civic leaders and merchant princes of the city. They had great matters on their minds. They were, to say the least, an imposing group in the eyes of a young man who had just the previous year entered his father's cotton-brokerage firm, a young man who was still learning how to operate under the pecking order of Memphis's male establishment.

The girl in question was named Lee Ann Deehart. She was a quite beautiful, fair-haired, hazel-eyed girl with a lively manner, and surely she was far from stupid. The thing she did that drew attention from the city fathers came very near, also, to changing the course of my entire life. I had known Lee Ann for perhaps two years at the time, and knew her to be more levelheaded and more reserved and self-possessed than most of her friends among the demimondaines. It would have been impossible for me to predict the behavior she was guilty of that winter afternoon. Immediately after the collision, she threw open the door on her side of the car, stepped out on the roadside, and fled into the woods of Overton Park, which is where the accident took place. And from that time, and during the next four days, she was unheard from by people who wished to question her and protect her. During that endless-seeming period of four days no one could be certain of Lee Ann Deehart's whereabouts.

The circumstances of the accident were rather complicated. The collision occurred just after three o'clock on a very cold Saturday afternoon — the fourth of December. Although at that time in my life I was already a member of my father's cotton firm, I was nevertheless — and strange as it may seem — enrolled in a Latin class out at Southwestern College, which is on the north side of Overton Park. (We were reading Horace's Odes!) The class was not held on Saturday afternoon, but I was on my way out to the college to study for a test that had been scheduled for Monday. My interest in Latin was regarded by my father and mother as one of my "anomalies" — a remnant of many "anomalies" I had annoyed them with when I was in my teens and was showing some signs of "not turning out well." It seemed now of course that I had "turned out well" after all, except that nobody in the family and nobody among my friends could understand why I went on showing this interest in Latin. I was not able to explain to them why. Any more than I was able to explain why to myself. It clearly had nothing to do with anything else in my life at that period. Furthermore, in the classroom and under the strict eye of our classics professor, a rotund, mustachioed little man hardly four feet in height (he had to sit on a large Latin dictionary in order to be comfortable at his desk), I didn't excel. I was often embarrassed by having to own up to Professor Bartlett's accusation that I had not so much as glanced at the assigned odes before coming to class. Sometimes other members of the class would be caught helping me with the translation, out in the hallway, when Professor Bartlett opened his classroom door to us. My real excuse for neglecting the assignments made by that earnest and admirable little scholar was that too many hours of my life were consumed by my job, by my courtship of the society girl I was going to marry, and by my old, bad habits of knocking about town with my boyhood cronies and keeping company with girls like Lee Ann Deehart.

Yet I had persisted with my Horace class throughout that fall (against the advice of nearly everyone, including Professor Bartlett). On that frigid December afternoon I had resolved to mend my ways as a student. I decided I would take my Horace and go out to Professor Bartlett's classroom at the college and make use of his big dictionary in preparing for Monday's test. It was something we had all been urged to do, with the promise that we would always find the door unlocked. As it turned out, of course, I was destined not to take the test on Monday and never to enter Professor Bartlett's classroom again.

It happened that just before I was setting out from home that afternoon I was filled suddenly with a dread of silence and the peculiar isolation of a college classroom building on a weekend afternoon. I telephoned my fiancée and asked her to go along with me. At the other end of the telephone line, Caroline Braxley broke into laughter. She said that I clearly had no conception of all the things she had to do within the next seven days, before we were to be married. I said I supposed I ought to be helping in some way, though until now she had not asked me so much as to help address invitations to the wedding. "No indeed," said my bride-to-be, "I want to do everything myself. I wouldn't have it any other way."

Caroline Braxley, this capable and handsome bride-to-be of mine, was a very remarkable girl, just as today, as my wife, she seems to me a very remarkable woman of sixty. She and I have been married for forty-one years now, and her good judgment in all matters relating to our marriage has never failed her — or us. She had already said to me before that Saturday afternoon that a successful marriage depended in part on the two persons' developing and maintaining a certain number of separate interests in life. She was all for my keeping up my golf, my hunting, my fishing. And, unlike my own family, she saw no reason that I shouldn't keep up my peculiar interest in Latin, though she had to confess that she thought it almost the funniest thing she had ever heard of a man of my sort going in for.

Caroline liked any sort of individualism in men. But I already knew her ways sufficiently well to understand that there was no use trying to persuade her to come along with me to the college. I wished she would come with me, or maybe I wished even more she would try to persuade me to come over to her house and help her with something in preparation for the wedding. After I had put down the telephone, it even occurred to me that I might simply drive over to her house and present myself at her front door. But I knew what the expression on her face would be, and I could even imagine the sort of thing she would say: "No man is going to set foot in my house this afternoon, Nat Ramsey! *I'm* getting married next Saturday, in case the fact has slipped your mind. Besides, you're coming here for dinner tonight, aren't you? And there are parties every night next week!"

This Caroline Braxley of mine was a very tall girl. (Actually

taller than she is nowadays. We have recently measured ourselves and found that each of us is an inch shorter than we used
to be.) One often had the feeling that one was looking up at her,
though of course she wasn't really so tall as that. Caroline's
height and the splendid way she carried herself was one of her
first attractions for me. It seems to me now that I was ever
attracted to tall girls — that is, when there was the possibility of
falling in love. And I think this was due in part to the fact that
even as a boy I was half in love with my father's two spinster
sisters, who were nearly six feet in height and were always more
attentive to me than to the other children in the family.

Anyhow, only moments after I had put down the telephone
that Saturday, when I still sat with my hand on the instrument
and was thinking vaguely of rushing over to Caroline's house,
the telephone underneath my hand began ringing. Perhaps, I
thought, it was Caroline calling back to say that she had changed
her mind. Instead, it was Lee Ann Deehart. As soon as she
heard my voice, she began telling me that she was bored to
death. Couldn't I think of something fun she and I could do on
this dreary winter afternoon? I laughed aloud at her. "What a
shameless wench you are, Lee Ann!" I said.

"Shameless? How so?" she said with pretended innocence.

"As if you weren't fully aware," I lectured her, "that I'm getting married a week from today!"

"What's that got to do with the price of eggs in Arkansas?"
She laughed. "Do you think, old Nat, *I* want to marry you?"

"Well," I explained, "I happen to be going out to the college
to cram for a Latin test on Monday."

I could hear her laughter at the other end. "Is your daddy
going to let you off work long enough to take your Latin test?"
she asked with heavy irony in her voice. It was the usual way
those girls had of making fun of our dependence on our fathers.

"Ah, yes," I said tolerantly.

"And is he going to let you off next Saturday, too," she went
on, "long enough to get married?"

"Listen," I said, "I've just had an idea. Why don't you ride out
to the college with me, and fool around some while I do my
Latin?" I suppose I didn't really imagine she would go, but

suddenly I had thought again of the lonely isolation of Dr.
Bartlett's classroom on a Saturday afternoon. I honestly wanted
to go ahead out there. It was something I somehow felt I had to
do. My preoccupation with the study of Latin poetry, ineffectual
student though I was, may have represented a perverse wish to
experience the isolation I was at the same time dreading or may
have represented a taste for morbidity left over from my ado-
lescence. I can allow myself to speculate on all that now, though
it would not have occurred to me to do so at the time.

"Well," said Lee Ann Deehart presently, to my surprise and
delight, "it couldn't be more boring out there than sitting here
in my room is."

"I'll pick you up in fifteen minutes," I said quickly. And I
hung up the telephone before she could possibly change her
mind.

Thirty minutes later, we were driving through Overton Park
on our way to the college. We had passed the art gallery and
were headed down the hill toward the low ground where the
park pond is. Ahead of us, on the left, were the gates to the zoo.
And on beyond was the point where the road crossed the street-
car tracks and entered a densely wooded area that is actually
the last surviving bit of the primeval forest that once grew right
up to the bluffs above the Mississippi River. Here are giant oak
and yellow-poplar trees older than the memory of the earliest
white settler. Some of them surely may have been mature trees
when Hernando de Soto passed this way, and were very old
trees indeed when General Jackson, General Winchester, and
Judge John Overton purchased this land and laid out the city
of Memphis. Between the art gallery and the pond there used
to be, in my day, a little spinney of woods that ran nearly all the
way back to what was left of the old forest. It was just when I
reached this spinney, with Lee Ann beside me, that I saw a truck
approaching us on the wrong side of the icy road. There was a
moderately deep snow on the ground, and the park roads had,
to say the least, been imperfectly cleared. On the ice and the
packed snow, the driver of the truck had clearly lost control of
his vehicle. When he was within about seventy-five feet of us,
Lee Ann said, "Pull off the road, Nat!"

Lee Ann Deehart's beauty was of the most feminine sort. She

was a tiny, delicate-looking girl, and I had noticed, when I went to fetch her that day, in her fur-collared coat and knitted cap and gutta-percha boots she somehow seemed smaller than usual. And I was now struck by the tone of authority coming from this small person whose diminutive size and whose role in my life were such that it wouldn't have occurred to me to heed her advice about driving a car — or about anything else, I suppose. I remember feeling something like: This is an ordeal that I must and that I want to face in my own way. It was as though Professor Bartlett himself were in the approaching truck. It seemed my duty not to admit any weakness in my own position. At least I *thought* that was what I felt.

"Pull off the road, Nat!" Lee Ann urged again. And my incredible reply to her was "He's on *my* side of the road! Besides, trucks are not allowed in the park!" And in reply to this Lee Ann gave only a loud snicker.

I believe I did, in the last seconds, try to swing the car off onto the shoulder of the road. But the next thing I really remember is the fierce impact of the two vehicles' meeting.

It was a relatively minor sort of collision, or seemed so at the moment. Since the driver of the truck, which was actually a converted Oldsmobile sedan — and a rather ancient one at that — had the good sense not to put on his brakes and to turn off his motor, the crash was less severe than it might have been. Moreover, since I *had* pulled a little to the right it was not a head-on meeting. It is worth mentioning, though, that it was sufficiently bad to put permanently out of commission the car I was driving, which was not my own car (my car was in the shop, being refurbished for the honeymoon trip) but an aging Packard limousine of my mother's, which I knew she would actually be happy to see retired. I don't remember getting out of the car at all and I don't remember Lee Ann's getting out. The police were told by the driver of the truck, however, that within a second after the impact, Lee Ann had thrown open her door, leaped out onto the snow-covered shoulder, jumped the ditch beyond, and run up the incline and into the spinney. The truck driver's account was corroborated by two ice skaters on the pond, who also saw her run through the leafless trees of the spinney and on across a narrow stretch of the public golf course that divides the spinney from the old forest. They agreed that, considering there was a deep snow on the ground and that she was wearing those gutta-percha boots, she traveled at a remarkable speed.

I didn't even know she was out of the car until I got around on the other side and saw the door there standing open and saw her tracks in the snow, going down the bank. I suppose I was too dazed even to follow the tracks with my eyes down the bank and up the other side of the ditch. I must have stood there for several seconds, looking down blankly at the tracks she had left just outside the car door. Presently I looked up at the truck driver, who was standing before me. I know now his eyes must have been following Lee Ann's progress. Finally he turned his eyes to me, and I could tell from his expression that I wasn't a pleasant sight. "Is your head hurt bad?" he asked. I put my hand up to my forehead and when I brought it down it was covered with blood. That was when I passed out. When I came to, they wouldn't let me get up. Besides the truck driver, there were two policemen and the two ice skaters standing over me. They told me that an ambulance was on the way.

At the hospital, the doctor took four stitches in my forehead; and that was it. I went home and lay down for a couple of hours, as I had been told to do. My parents and my two brothers and my little sister and even the servants were very much concerned about me. They hovered around in a way I had never before seen them do — not even when somebody was desperately sick. I suppose it was because a piece of violence like this accident was a very extraordinary thing in our quiet Memphis life in those years. They were disturbed, too, I soon realized, by my silence as I lay there on the daybed in the upstairs sitting room and particularly by my being reticent to talk about the collision. I had other things on my mind. Every so often I would remember Lee Ann's boot tracks in the snow. And I would begin to wonder where she was now. Since I had not found an opportunity to telephone her, I could only surmise that she had somehow managed to get back to the roominghouse where she lived. I had not told anyone about her presence in the car with me. And as I lay there on the daybed, with the family and servants coming and going and making inquiries about how I felt, I would find myself wondering sometimes how and whether or not I could tell Caroline Braxley about Lee Ann's being with me that afternoon. It turned out the next day — or, rather, on Monday morning — that the truck driver had told the two policemen and then, later, repeated to someone who called from one of the newspapers that there had been a girl with me in the car. As a matter of fact, I learned that this was the case on the night of the accident, but as I lay there in the upstairs sitting room during the afternoon I didn't yet know it.

Shortly before five o'clock Caroline Braxley arrived at our house, making a proper sick call but also with the intention of taking me back to dinner with her parents and her two younger sisters. Immediately after she entered the upstairs sitting room, and almost before she and I had greeted each other, my mother's houseboy and sometime chauffeur came in, bringing my volume of Horace. Because Mother had thought it might raise my spirits, she had sent him down to the service garage where the wrecked car had been taken to fetch it for me. Smiling sympathetically, he placed it on a table near the daybed and left the room. Looking at the book, Caroline said to me with a smile that expressed a mixture of sympathy and reproach, "I hope you see now what folly your pursuit of Latin poetry is." And suddenly, then, the book on the table appeared to me as an alien object. In retrospect it seems to me that I really knew then that I would never open it again.

I went to dinner that night at Caroline's house, my head still in bandages. The Braxley family treated me with a tenderness equal to that I had received at home. At table, the serving man offered to help my plate for me, as though I were a sick child. I could have enjoyed all this immensely, I think, since I have always been one to relish loving, domestic care, if only I had not been worrying and speculating all the while about Lee Ann. As I talked genially with Caroline's family during the meal and immediately afterward before the briskly burning fire at the end of the Braxleys' long living room, I kept seeing Lee Ann's boot tracks in the snow. And then I would see my own bloody hand as I took it down from my face before I fainted. I remember still having the distinct feeling, as I sat there in the bosom of the Braxley family, that it had not been merely my bloody hand that had made me faint but my bloody hand plus the tracks in the deep snow. In a way, it is strange that I remember all these impressions so vividly after forty years, because it is not as though I have lived an uneventful life during the years since. My Second World War experiences are what I perhaps ought to remember best — those, along with the deaths of my two younger brothers in the Korean War. Even worse, really, were the deaths of my two parents in a terrible fire that destroyed our house on Central Avenue when they had got to be quite old, my mother leaping from a second-story window, my father asphyxiated inside the house. And I can hardly mention without being overcome with emotion the accidental deaths that took two of my and Caroline's children when they were in their early teens. It would seem that with all these disasters to remember, along with the various business and professional crises I have had, I might hardly be able to recall that earlier episode. But I think that, besides its coming at that impressionable period of my life and the fact that one just does remember things better from one's youth, there is the undeniable fact that life *was* different in those times. What I mean to say is that all these later, terrible events took place in a world where acts of terror are, so to speak, all around us — everyday occurrences — and are brought home to us audibly and pictorially on radio and television almost every hour. I am not saying that some of these ugly acts of terror did not need to take place or were not brought on by what our world was like in those days. But I am saying that the context was different. Our tranquil, upper-middle-class world of 1937 did not have the rest of the world crowding in on it so much. And thus when something only a little ugly did crowd in or when we, often unconsciously, reached out for it the contrasts seemed sharper. It was not just in the Braxleys' household or in my own family's that everything seemed quiet and well ordered and unchanging. The households were in a context like themselves. Suffice it to say that though the Braxleys' house in Memphis was situated on East Parkway and our house on Central Avenue, at least two miles across town from each other, I could in those days feel perfectly safe, and *was* relatively safe, in walking home many a night from Caroline's house to our house at two in the morning. It was when we young

men in Memphis ventured out with the more adventurous girls
of the demimonde that we touched on the unsafe zones of Memphis. And there were girls still more adventurous, of course,
with whom some of my contemporaries found their way into
the very most dangerous zones. But we did think of it that way,
you see, thought of it in terms of the girls' being the adventurous ones, whom we followed or didn't follow.

Anyhow, while we were sitting there before the fire, with the
portrait of Caroline's paternal grandfather peering down at us
from above the mantel and with her father in his broad-lapeled,
double-breasted suit standing on the marble hearth, occasionally poking at the logs with the brass poker or sometimes kicking
a log with the toe of his wing-tipped shoes, suddenly I was called
to the telephone by the Negro serving man who had wanted to
help my plate for me. As he preceded me the length of the living
room and then gently guided me across the hall to the telephone
in the library, I believe he would have put his hand under my
elbow to help me — as if a real invalid — if I had allowed him
to. As we passed through the hall, I glanced through one of the
broad, etched sidelights beside the front door and caught a
glimpse of the snow on the ground outside. The weather had
turned even colder. There had been no additional snowfall, but
even at a glance you could tell how crisply frozen the old snow
was on its surface. The serving man at my elbow was saying,
"It's your daddy on the phone. I'd suppose he just wants to
know how you'd be feeling by now."

But I knew in my heart it wasn't that. It was as if that glimpse
of the crisp snow through the front-door sidelight had told me
what it was. When I took up the telephone and heard my father's voice pronouncing my name, I knew almost exactly what
he was going to say. He said that his friend the editor of the
morning paper had called him and reported that there had
been a girl in the car with me, and though they didn't of course
plan to use her name, probably wouldn't even run the story
until Monday, they would have to *know* her name. And would
have to assure themselves she wasn't hurt in the crash. And that
she was unharmed after leaving the scene. Without hesitation I
gave my father Lee Ann Deehart's name, as well as her address
and telephone number. But I made no further explanation to

Father, and he asked me for none. The only other thing I said
was that I'd be home in a little while. Father was silent a moment
after that. Then he said, "Are you all right?"

I said, "I'm fine."

And he said, "Good, I'll be waiting up for you."

I hung up the telephone, and my first thought was that before
I left Caroline tonight I'd have to tell her that Lee Ann had
been in the car with me. Then, without thinking almost, I dialed
Lee Ann's roominghouse number. It felt very strange to be
doing this in the Braxleys' library. The woman who ran the
roominghouse said that Lee Ann had not been in since she left
with me in the afternoon.

As I passed back across the wide hallway and caught another
glimpse of the snow outside, the question arose in my mind for
the first time: *Had* Lee Ann come to some harm in those woods?
More than the density of the underbrush, more than its prox-
imity to the zoo, where certain unsavory characters often hung
out, it was the great size and antiquity of the forest trees somehow, and the old rumors that white settlers had once been am-
bushed there by Chickasaw Indians, that made me feel that if
anything had happened to the girl it had happened there. And
on the heels of such thoughts I found myself wondering for the
first time if all this might actually lead to my beautiful, willowy
Caroline Braxley's breaking off our engagement. I returned to
the living room, and at the sight of Caroline's tall figure at the
far end of the room, placed between that of her mother and
that of her father, the conviction became firm in me that I would
have to tell her about Lee Ann before she and I parted that
night. And as I drew nearer to her, still wondering if something
ghastly had happened to Lee Ann there in the old forest, I saw
the perplexed and even suspicious expression on Caroline's face
and presently observed similar expressions on the faces of her
two parents. And from that moment began the gnawing wonder
that would be with me for several days ahead: What precisely
would Caroline consider sufficient provocation for breaking off
our engagement to be married? I had no idea, really. Would it
be sufficient that I had had one of those unnamed "female
companions" in the car with me at the time of the accident? I
knew of engagements like ours that had been broken with ap-

parently less provocation. Or would it be the suspicious-seeming circumstance of Lee Ann's leaping out of the car and running off through the snow? Or might it be the final, worst possibility — that of delicate little Lee Ann Deehart's having actually met with foul play in that infrequently entered area of underbrush and towering forest trees?

Broken engagements were a subject of common and considerable interest to girls like Caroline Braxley. Whereas a generation earlier a broken engagement had been somewhat of a scandal — an engagement that had been formally announced at a party and in the newspaper, that is — it did not necessarily represent that in our day. Even in our day, you see, it meant something quite different from what it had once meant. There was, after all, no written contract, and it was in no sense so unalterably binding as it had been in our parents' day. For us it was not considered absolutely dishonorable for either party to break off the plans merely because he or she had had a change of heart. Since the boy was no longer expected literally to ask the father for the girl's hand (though he would probably be expected to go through the form, as I had done with Mr. Braxley), it was no longer a breach of contract between families. There was certainly nothing like a dowry any longer — not in Memphis — and there was only rarely any kind of property settlement involved, except in cases where both families were extraordinarily rich. The thought pleased me — that is, the ease with which an engagement might be ended. I suppose in part I was simply preparing myself for such an eventuality. And there in the Braxleys' long living room in the very presence of Caroline and Mr. and Mrs. Braxley themselves I found myself indulging in a perverse fantasy, a fantasy in which Caroline had broken off our engagement and I was standing up pretty well, was even seeking consolation in the arms, so to speak, of a safely returned Lee Ann Deehart.

But all at once I felt so guilty for my private indiscretion that actually for the first time in the presence of my prospective in-laws, I put my arm about Caroline Braxley's waist. And I told her that I felt so fatigued by events of the afternoon that probably I ought now to go ahead home. She and her parents agreed at once. And they agreed among themselves that they each had just now been reflecting privately that I looked exhausted. Mrs. Braxley suggested that under the circumstances she ought to ask Robert to drive me home. I accepted. No other suggestion could have seemed so welcome. Robert was the same serving man who had offered to help my plate at dinner and who had so gently guided me to the telephone when my father called. Almost at once, after I got into the front seat of the car beside him — in his dark chauffeur's uniform cap — I fell asleep. He had to wake me when we pulled up to the side door of my father's house. I remember how warmly I thanked him for bringing me home, even shaking his hand, which was a rather unusual thing to do in those days. I felt greatly refreshed and restored and personally grateful to Robert for it. There was not, in those days in Memphis, any time or occasion when one felt more secure and relaxed than when one had given oneself over completely to the care and protection of the black servants who surrounded us and who created and sustained for the most part the luxury that distinguished the lives we lived then from the lives we live now. They did so for us, whatever their motives and however degrading our demands and our acceptance of their attentions may have been to them.

At any rate, after my slumber in the front seat beside Robert I felt sufficiently restored to face my father (and his awareness of Lee Ann's having been in the car) with some degree of equanimity. And before leaving the Braxleys' house I had found a moment in the hallway to break the news to Caroline that I had not been alone in the car that afternoon. To my considerable surprise, she revealed, after a moment's hesitation, that she already knew that that had been the case. Her father, like my father, had learned it from one of the newspaper editors — only he had learned it several hours earlier than my father had. I was obliged to realize as we were saying good night to each other that she, along with her two parents, had known all evening that Lee Ann had been with me and had fled into the woods of Overton Park — that she, Caroline, had as a matter of fact known the full story when she came to my house to fetch me back to her house to dinner. "Where is Lee Ann now?" she asked me presently, holding my two hands in her own and

looking me directly in the eye. "I don't know," I said. Knowing
how much she knew, I decided I must tell her the rest of it,
holding nothing back. I felt that I was seeing a new side to my
fiancée and that unless I told her the whole truth there might
be something of this other side of her that wouldn't be revealed
to me. "I tried to telephone her after I answered my father's
call tonight. But she was not in her room and had not been in
since I picked her up at two o'clock." And I told Caroline about
Lee Ann's telephoning me (after Caroline and I had talked in
the early afternoon) and about my inviting her to go out to the
college with me. Then I gave her my uncensored version of
the accident, including the sight of Lee Ann's footprints in the
snow.

"How did she sound on the telephone?" she asked.

"What do you mean by that?" I said impatiently. "I just told
you she wasn't home when I called."

"I mean earlier — when she called you."

"But why do you want to know that? It doesn't matter, does
it?"

"I mean, did she sound depressed? But it doesn't matter for
the moment." She still held my hands in hers. "You do know,
don't you," she went on after a moment, "that you are going to
have to *find* Lee Ann? And you probably are going to need
help."

Suddenly I had the feeling that Caroline Braxley was someone twenty years older than I; but, rather than sounding like
my parents or her parents, she sounded like one or another of
the college teachers I had had — even like Dr. Bartlett, who
once had told me that I was going to need outside help if I was
going to keep up with the class. To reassure myself, I suppose,
I put my arm about Caroline's waist again and drew her to me.
But in our good-night kiss there was a reticence on her part, or
a quality that I could only define as conditional or possibly pro-
bational. Still, I knew now that she knew everything, and I suppose that was why I was able to catch such a good nap in the car
on the way home.

Girls who had been brought up the way Caroline had, in the
Memphis of forty years ago, knew not only what was going to
be expected of them in making a marriage and bringing up a

family there in Memphis — a marriage and a family of the kind
their parents had had — they knew also from a fairly early time
that they would have to contend with girls and women of certain
sorts before and frequently after they were married: with girls,
that is, who had no conception of what it was to have a certain type of performance expected of them, or girls of another
kind (and more like themselves) who came visiting in Memphis
from Mississippi or Arkansas — pretty little plantation girls, my
mother called them — or from Nashville or from the old towns
of west Tennessee. Oftentimes these other girls were their cousins, but that made them no less dangerous. Not being on their
home ground — in their own country, so to speak — these
Nashville or Mississippi or west Tennessee or Arkansas girls did
not bother to abide by the usual rules of civilized warfare. They
carried on guerrilla warfare. They were marauders. But girls
like Lee Ann Deehart were something else again. They were the
Trojan horse, more or less, established in the very citadel. They
were the fifth column, and were perhaps the most dangerous of
all. At the end of a brilliant debutante season, sometimes the
most eligible bachelor of all those on the list would still remain
uncommitted, or even secretly committed to someone who had
never seen the inside of the Memphis Country Club. This kind
of thing, girls like Caroline Braxley understood, was not to be
tolerated — not if the power of mortal women included the
power to divine the nature of any man's commitment and the
power to test the strength and nature of another kind of woman's power. Younger people today may say that that old-fashioned behavior on the part of girls doesn't matter today, that
girls don't have those problems anymore. But I suspect that in
Memphis, if not everywhere, there must be something equivalent even nowadays in the struggle of women for power among
themselves.

Perhaps, though, to the present generation these distinctions
I am making won't seem significant, after all, or worth my bothering so much about — especially the present generation outside of Memphis and the Deep South. Even in Memphis the
great majority of people might say, Why is this little band of
spoiled rich girls who lived here forty years ago so important as
to deserve our attention? In fact, during the very period I am

writing about it is likely that the majority of people in Memphis felt that way. I think the significant point is that those girls took themselves seriously — girls like Caroline — and took seriously the forms of the life they lived. They imagined they knew quite well who they were and they imagined that that was important. They were what, at any rate, those girls like Lee Ann were not. Or they claimed to be what those girls like Lee Ann didn't claim to be and what very few people nowadays claim to be. They considered themselves the heirs to something, though most likely they could not have said what: something their forebears had brought to Memphis with them from somewhere else — from the country around Memphis and from other places, from the country towns of west Tennessee, from middle Tennessee and east Tennessee, from the Valley of Virginia, from the Piedmont, even from the Tidewater. Girls like Caroline thought they were the heirs to something, and that's what the other girls didn't think about themselves, though probably they were, and probably the present generation, in and out of Memphis — even the sad generation of the sixties and seventies — is heir to more than it thinks it is, in the matter of manners, I mean to say, and of general behavior. And it is of course because these girls like Caroline are regarded as mere old-fashioned society girls that the present generation tends to dismiss them, whereas if it were their fathers we were writing about the story would, shocking though it is to say, be taken more seriously by everyone. Everyone would recognize now that the fathers and grandfathers of these girls were the sons of the old plantation South come to town and converted or half-converted into modern Memphis businessmen, only with a certain something held over from the old order that made them both better and worse than businessmen elsewhere. They are the authors of much good and much bad in modern Memphis — and modern Nashville and modern Birmingham and modern Atlanta, too. The good they mostly brought with them from the old order; the bad they mostly adopted from life in cities elsewhere in the nation, the thing they were imitating when they constructed the new life in Memphis. And why not judge their daughters and wives in much the same way? Isn't there a need to know what they were like, too? One thing those girls did know they were heirs to was the old, country manners and the insistence upon old, country connections. The first evidence of this that comes to mind is the fact that they often spoke of girls like Lee Ann as "city girls," by which they meant that such girls didn't usually have the old family connections back in the country on the cotton farms in west Tennessee, in Mississippi, in Arkansas, or back in Nashville or in Jonesboro or in Virginia.

When Robert had let me out at our side door that night and I came into the house, my father and mother both were downstairs. It was still early of course, but I had the sense of their having waited up for me to come in. They greeted me as though I were returning from some dangerous mission. Each of them asked me how the Braxleys "seemed." Finally Mother insisted upon examining the stitches underneath the bandage on my forehead. After that, I said that I thought I would hit the hay. They responded to that with the same enthusiasm that Mr. and Mrs. Braxley had evidenced when I told them I thought I should go ahead home. Nothing would do me more good than a good night's sleep, my parents agreed. It was a day everybody was glad to have come to an end.

After I got upstairs and in my room, it occurred to me that my parents both suddenly looked very old. That seems laughable to me now almost, because my parents were then ten or fifteen years younger than I am today. I look back on them now as a youngish couple in their early middle age, whose first son was about to be married and about whose possible infidelity they were concerned. But indeed what an old-fashioned pair they seem to me in the present day, waiting up for their children to come in. Because actually they stayed downstairs a long while after I went up to bed, waiting there for my younger brothers and my little sister to come in, all of whom were out on their separate dates. In my mind's eye I can see them there, waiting as parents had waited for hundreds of years for their grown-up children to come home at night. They would seem now to be violating the rights of young individuals and even interfering with the maturing process. But in those times it seemed only natural for parents to be watchful and concerned about their children's first flight away from the nest. I am referring mainly to my parents' waiting up for my brothers and my sister, who

were in their middle teens, but also as I lay in my bed I felt,
myself, more relaxed, knowing that they were downstairs in the
front room, speculating upon what Lee Ann's disappearance
meant and alert to whatever new development there might be.
After a while, my father came up and opened the door to my
room. I don't know how much later it was. I don't think I had
been to sleep, but I could not tell for sure even at the time —
my waking and sleeping thoughts were so much alike that night.
At any rate, Father stepped inside the room and came over to
my bed.

"I have just called down to the police station," he said, "and
they say they have checked and that Lee Ann has still not come
back to her roominghouse. She seems to have gone into some
sort of hiding." He said this with just the slightest trace of irritation in his voice. "Have you any notion, Nat, why she *might*
want to go into hiding?"

The next day was Sunday, December 5th. During the night it
had turned bitterly cold. The snow had frozen into a crisp sheet
that covered most of the ground. At about nine o'clock in the
morning, another snow began falling. I had breakfast with the
family, still wearing the bandage on my forehead. I sat around
in my bathrobe all morning, pretending to read the newspaper.
I didn't see any report of my accident, and my father said it
wouldn't appear till Monday. At ten o'clock, I dialed Lee Ann's
telephone number. One of the other girls who roomed in the
house answered. She said she thought Lee Ann hadn't come in
last night and she giggled. I asked her if she would make sure
about it. She left the phone and came back presently to say in a
whisper that there was no doubt about it: Lee Ann had not slept
in her bed. I knew she was whispering so that the landlady
wouldn't hear . . . And then I had a call from Caroline, who
wanted to know how my head was this morning and whether or
not there had been any word about Lee Ann. After I told her
what I had just learned, we were both silent for a time. Finally
she said she had intended to come over and see how I was
feeling but her father had decreed that nobody should go out
in such bad weather. It would just be inviting another automobile wreck, he said. She reported that her parents were not

going to church, and I said that mine weren't either. We agreed to talk later and to see each other after lunch if the weather improved. Then I could hear her father's voice in the background, and she said that he wanted to use the telephone.

At noon the snow was still falling. My father stood at a front window in the living room, wearing his dark smoking jacket. He predicted that it might be the deepest snowfall we had ever had in Memphis. He said that people in other parts of the country didn't realize how much cold weather came all the way down the Mississippi Valley from Minneapolis to Memphis. I had never heard him pay so much attention to the weather and talk so much about it. I wondered if, like me, he was really thinking about the old forest out in Overton Park and wishing he were free to go out there and make sure there was no sign of Lee Ann Deehart's having come to grief in those ancient woods. I wonder now if there weren't others besides us who were thinking of the old forest all day that day. I knew that my father, too, had been on the telephone that morning — and he was on it again during a good part of the afternoon. In retrospect, I am certain that all day that day he was in touch with a whole circle of friends and colleagues who were concerned about Lee Ann's safety. It was not only the heavy snow that checked his freedom — and mine, too, of course — to go out and search those woods and put his mind at rest on that possibility at least. It was more than just this snow, which the radio reported as snarling up and halting all traffic. What prevented him was his own unwillingness to admit fully to himself and to others that this particular danger was really there; what prevented him and perhaps all the rest of us was the fear that the answer to the gnawing question of Lee Ann's whereabouts might really be out there within that immemorial grove of snow-laden oaks and yellow poplars and hickory trees. It is a grove, I believe, that men in Memphis have feared and wanted to destroy for a long time and whose destruction they are still working at even in this latter day. It has only recently been saved by a very narrow margin from a great highway that men wished to put through there — saved by groups of women determined to save this last bit of the old forest from the axes of modern men. Perhaps in old pioneer days, before the plantation and the neoclassic towns were made, the great forests seemed woman's last refuge from the brute she lived alone with in the wilderness. Perhaps all men in Memphis who had any sense of their past felt this, though they felt more keenly (or perhaps it amounts to the same feeling) that the forest was woman's greatest danger. Men remembered mad pioneer women, driven mad by their loneliness and isolation, who ran off into the forest, never to be seen again, or incautious women who allowed themselves to be captured by Indians and returned at last so mutilated that they were unrecognizable to their husbands or who at their own wish lived out their lives among their savage captors. I think that if I had said to my father (or to myself), "What is it that's so scary about the old forest?" he (or I) would have answered, "There's nothing at all scary about it. But we can't do anything today because of the snow. It's the worst snow in history!" I think that all day long my father — like me — was busily not letting himself believe that anything awful had happened to Lee Ann Deehart or that if it had it certainly hadn't happened in those woods. Not just my father and me, though. Caroline's father, too, and all their friends — their peers. And the newspapermen and the police. If they waited long enough, it would come out all right and there would be no need to search the woods even. And it turned out, in the most literal sense, that they — we — were right. Yet what guilty feelings must not everyone have lived with — lived with in silence — all that snowbound day.

At two o'clock, Caroline called again to say that because of the snow her aunt was canceling the dinner party she had planned that night in honor of the bride and groom. I remember as well as anything else that terrible day how my mother and father looked at each other when they received this news. Surely they were wondering, as I had to also, if this was but the first gesture of withdrawal. There was no knowing what their behavior or the behavior of any of us that day meant. The day simply dragged on until the hour when we could decently go to bed. It was December, and we were near the shortest day of the year, but that day had seemed the longest day of my life.

On Monday morning, two uniformed policemen were at our house before I had finished my breakfast. When I learned they were waiting in the living room to see me, I got up from the table at once. I wouldn't let my father go in with me to see them. Mother tried to make me finish my eggs before going in, but I only laughed at her and kissed her on the top of the head as I left the breakfast room. The two policemen were sitting in the very chairs my parents had sat in the night before. This some-how made the interview easier from the outset. I felt initially that they were there to help me, not to harass me in any way. They had already, at the break of dawn, been out to Overton Park. (The whole case — if case it was — had of course been allowed to rest on Sunday.) And along with four other police-men they had conducted a full-scale search of the old forest. There was no trace of Lee Ann Deehart there. They had also been to her roominghouse on Tutwiler Avenue and questioned Mrs. Troxler, whose house it was, about all of Lee Ann's friends and acquaintances and about the habits of her daily life. They said that they were sure the girl would turn up but that the newspapers were putting pressure on them to explain her dis-appearance and — more particularly — to explain her precipi-tate flight from the scene of the accident.

I spent that day with the police, leaving them only for an hour at lunchtime, when they dropped me off at my father's office on Front Street, where I worked. There I made a small pretense of attending to some business for the firm while I consumed a club sandwich and milkshake that my father or one of my uncles in the firm had had sent up for me. At the end of the hour, I jogged down the two flights of steep wooden stairs and found the police car waiting for me at the curb, just outside the en-trance. At some time during the morning, one of the policemen had suggested that they might have a bulldozer or some other piece of machinery brought in to crack the ice on the Overton Park Pond and then drag the pond for Lee Ann's body. But I had pointed out that the two skaters had returned to the pond after the accident and skated there until dark. There was no hole in the ice anywhere. Moreover, the skaters had reported that when the girl left the scene she did not go by way of the pond but went up the rise and into the wooded area. There was every indication that she had gone that way, and so the sugges-tion that the pond be dragged was dismissed. And we continued during the rest of the morning to make the rounds of the room-inghouses and apartments of Lee Ann's friends and acquaint-ances, as well as the houses of the parents with whom some of them lived. In the afternoon we planned to go to the shops and offices in which some of the girls worked and to interview them there concerning Lee Ann's whereabouts and where it was they last had seen her. It seemed a futile procedure to me. But while I was eating my club sandwich alone in our third-floor walkup office I received a shocking telephone call.

Our office, like most of the other cotton factors' offices, was in one of the plain-faced, three- and four-story buildings put up on Front Street during the middle years of the last century, just before the Civil War. Cotton men were very fond of those offices, and the offices did possess a certain rough beauty that anyone could see. Apparently there had been few, if any, im-provements or alterations since the time they were built. All the electrical wiring and all the plumbing, such as it was, was "ex-posed." The wooden stairsteps and the floors were rough and splintery and extremely worn down. The walls were white-washed and the ceilings were twelve or fourteen feet in height. But the chief charm of the rooms was the tall windows across the front of the building — wide sash windows with small win-dow lights, windows looking down onto Front Street and from which you could catch glimpses of the brown Mississippi River at the foot of the bluff, and even of the Arkansas shoreline on the other side. I was sitting on a cotton trough beside one of those windows, eating my club sandwich, when I heard the tele-phone ring back in the inner office. I remember that when it rang my eyes were on a little stretch of the Arkansas shoreline roughly delineated by its scrubby trees, and my thoughts were on the Arkansas roadhouses where we often went with the demi-monde girls on a Saturday night. At first I thought I wouldn't answer the phone. I let it ring for a minute or two. It went on ringing — persistently. Suddenly I realized that a normal busi-ness call would have stopped ringing before now. I jumped down from my perch by the window and ran back between the cotton troughs to the office. When I picked up the receiver, a girl's voice called my name before I spoke.

"Yes," I said. The voice had sounded familiar, but I knew it

wasn't Caroline's. And it wasn't Lee Ann's. I couldn't identify it
exactly, though I did say to myself right away that it was one of
the city girls.

"Nat," the voice said, "Lee Ann wants you to stop trying to
trail her."

"Who is this?" I said. "Where is Lee Ann?"

"Never mind," the girl on the other end of the line said.
"We're not going to let you find her, and you're making her
very uncomfortable with your going around with the police
after her and all that.

"The police aren't 'after her,'" I said. "They just want to be
sure she's all right."

"She'll be all right," the voice said, "if you'll lay off and stop
chasing her. Don't you have any decency at all? Don't you have
a brain in your head? Don't you know what this is like for Lee
Ann? We all thought you were her friend."

"I am," I said. "Just let me speak to Lee Ann."

But there was a click in the telephone, and no one was there
any longer.

I turned back into the room where the cotton troughs were.
When I saw my milkshake carton and the sandwich paper up by
the window, and remembered how the girl had called my name
as soon as I picked up the telephone, I felt sure that someone
had been watching me from down the street or from a window across the way. Without going back to my lunch, I turned
quickly and started down the stairs toward the street. But when
I looked at my watch, I realized it was time for the policemen to
pick me up again. And there they were, of course, waiting at
the entrance to our building. When I got into the police car, I
didn't tell them about my call. And we began our rounds again,
going to the addresses where some of Lee Ann's friends worked.

Lee Ann Deehart and other girls like her that we went about
with, as I have already indicated, were not literally ladies of any
Memphis demimonde. Possibly they got called that first by the
only member of our generation in Memphis who had read Mar-
cel Proust, a literary boy who later became a college professor
and who wanted to make his own life in Memphis — and ours
— seem more interesting than it was. Actually, they were girls
who had gone to the public high schools, and more often than

not to some school other than Central High, which during those depression years had a degree of acceptance in Memphis society. As anyone could have observed on that morning when I rode about town with the policemen, those girls came from a variety of backgrounds. We went to the houses of some of their parents, some of whom were day laborers who spoke in accents of the old Memphis Irish, descendants of the Irish who were imported to build the railroads to Texas. Today some of the girls would inevitably have been black. But they were the daughters also of bank clerks and salesmen and of professional men, too, because they made no distinction among themselves. The parents of some of them had moved to Memphis from cities in other sections of the country or even from southern small towns. The girls were not interested in such distinctions of origin, were not conscious of them, had not been made aware of them by their parents. They would have been highly approved of by the present generation of young people. Like the present generation in general, these girls — Lee Ann included — tended to be bookish and artistic in a middlebrow sort of way, and some of them had real intellectual aspirations. They did not care who each other's families were or where they had gone to school. They met and got to know each other in roadhouses, on double dates, and in the offices and stores where they worked. As I have said, they tended to be bookish and artistic. If they had found themselves in Proust's Paris, instead of in our Memphis of the nineteen-thirties, possibly they would have played some role in the intellectual life of the place. But of course this is only my ignorant speculation. It is always impossible to know what changes might have been wrought in people under circumstances of the greatest or slightest degree of difference from the actual.

The girls we saw that afternoon at their places of work were generally more responsive to the policemen's questions than to my own. And I became aware that the two policemen — youngish men in their late thirties, for whom this special assignment was somehow distasteful — were more interested in protecting these girls from any embarrassment than in obtaining information about Lee Ann. With all but one of the half-dozen girls we sought out, the policemen sent me in to see the girl first, to ask

her if she would rather be questioned by them in her place of
business or in the police car. In each case the girl treated my
question concerning this as an affront, but always she sent word
back to the policemen to come inside. And in each case I found
myself admiring the girl not only for her boldness in dealing
with the situation (they seemed fearless in their talk with the
police and refused absolutely to acknowledge close friendship
with Lee Ann, insisting — all of them — that they saw her only
occasionally at nightspots, sometimes with me, sometimes with
other young men, that they had no idea who her parents were
or where she came to Memphis from) but also for a personal,
feminine beauty that I had never before been fully aware of.
Perhaps I saw or sensed it now for the first time because I had
not before seen them threatened or in danger. It is true, I know,
that the effect of all this questioning seemed somehow to put
them in jeopardy. Perhaps I saw now how much more vulnerable they were than were the girls in the set my parents more or
less intended me to travel in. There was a delicacy about them,
a frailty even, that didn't seem to exist in other girls I knew and
that contrasted strangely — and disturbingly — with the rough
surroundings of the roadhouses they frequented at night and
the harsh, businesslike atmosphere of the places where they
worked. Within each of them, moreover, there seemed a contrast between the delicate beauty of their bodies, their prettily
formed arms and legs, their breasts and hips, their small feet
and hands, their soft natural hair — hair worn so becomingly,
groomed, in each case, on their pretty little heads to direct one's
eyes first of all to the fair or olive complexion and the nicely
proportioned features of the face — a contrast, that is to say,
between this physical beauty and a bookishness and a certain
toughness of mind and a boldness of spirit that were unmistakable in all of them.

The last girl we paid a call on that afternoon was one Nancy
Minnifee, who happened to be the girl who was always frankest
and crudest in making jokes about families like my own and
who had made the crack that the other girls had laughed at so
irrepressibly in the beer garden: "I haven't lost anything at the
M.C.C." Or it may not have been that she just happened to be
the last we called on. Perhaps out of dread of her jokes I guided

the police last of all to the farm-implement warehouse where
Nancy was a secretary. Or perhaps it wasn't so much because of
her personality as because I knew she was Lee Ann's closest
friend and I somehow dreaded facing her for that reason. Anyway, at the warehouse she was out on the loading platform with
a clipboard and pencil in her hands when we drove up.

"That's Nancy Minnifee up there," I said to the two policemen
in the front seat. I was sitting in the back seat alone. I saw them
shake their heads. I knew that it was with a certain sadness and
a personal admiration that they did so. Nancy was a very pretty
girl, and they hated the thought of bothering this lovely creature with the kind of questions they were going to ask. They
hated it without even knowing she was Lee Ann's closest friend.
Suddenly I began seeing all those girls through the policemen's
eyes, just as the next day, when I would make a similar expedition in the company of my father and the newspaper editor, I'd
see the girls through their eyes. The worst of it, somehow, for
the policemen, was that the investigation wasn't really an official investigation but was something the newspapers had forced
upon the police in case something had happened that they
hadn't reported. The girl hadn't been missing long enough for
anyone to declare her "officially" missing. Yet the police, along
with the mayor's office and the newspaper editor, didn't want
to risk something's having happened to a girl like Lee Ann.
They — all of them — thought of such girls, in a sense, as their
special wards. It would be hard to say why they did. At any rate,
before the police car had fully stopped I saw Nancy Minnifee
up there on the platform. She was wearing a fur-collared overcoat but no hat or gloves. Immediately she began moving along
the loading platform toward us, holding the clipboard up to
shield her eyes from the late-afternoon winter sun. She came
down the steps to the graveled area where we were stopped,
and when the policeman at the wheel of the car ran down his
window she bent forward and put her arm on his door. The
casual way she did it seemed almost familiar — indeed, almost
provocative. I found myself resenting her manner, because I
was afraid she would give the wrong impression. The way she
leaned on the door reminded me of the prostitutes down on
Pontotoc Street when we, as teenage boys, used to stop in front

of their houses and leave the motor running because we were afraid of them.

"I've been expecting you two gentlemen," Nancy said, smiling amiably at the two policemen and pointedly ignoring my presence in the back seat. The policemen broke into laughter.

"I suppose your friends have been calling ahead," the driver said. Then Nancy laughed as though he had said something very funny.

"I could draw you a map of the route you've taken this afternoon," she said. She was awfully polite in her tone, and the two policemen were awfully polite, too. But before they could really begin asking their questions she began giving them her answers. She hadn't seen Lee Ann since several days before the accident. She didn't know anything about where she might be. She didn't know anything about her family. She had always understood that Lee Ann came from Texas.

"That's a big state," the policeman who wasn't driving said.

"Well, I've never been there," she said, "but I'm told it's a mighty big state."

The three of them burst into laughter again. Then the driver said quite seriously, "But we understand you're her best friend."

"I don't know her any better than most of the girls do," she said. "I can't imagine who told you that." Now for the first time she looked at me in the back seat. "Hello, Nat," she said. I nodded to her. I couldn't imagine why she was lying to them. But I didn't tell her, as I hadn't told the other girls or the police, about the call I had had in the cotton office. I knew that she must know all about it, but I said nothing.

When we had pulled away, the policeman who was driving the car said, "This Lee Ann must be all right or these girls wouldn't be closing ranks so. They've got too much sense for that. They're smart girls."

Presently the other policeman turned his head halfway around, though not looking directly at me, and asked, "She wouldn't be pregnant by any chance, would she?"

"Uh-uh," I said. It was all the answer it seemed to me he deserved. But then I couldn't resist echoing what he had said. "They've got too much sense for that. They're smart girls." He looked all the way around at me now and gave me what I am sure he thought was a straight look.

"Damn right they are," said the driver, glancing at his colleague with a frown on his forehead and speaking with a curled lip. "Get your mind out of the gutter, Fred. After all, they're just kids, all of them."

We rode on in silence after that. For the first time in several hours, I thought of Caroline Braxley, and I wondered again whether or not she would break our engagement.

When the policemen let me off at my office at five o'clock, I went to my car and drove straight to the apartment house at Crosstown where Nancy Minnifee lived. I was waiting for Nancy in the parking lot when she got home. She invited me inside, but without a smile.

"I want to know where Lee Ann is," I said as soon as she had closed the door.

"Do you imagine I'd tell you if I knew?" she said.

I sat myself down in an upholstered chair as if I were going to stay there till she told me. "I want to know what the hell's going on," I said with what I thought was considerable force, "and why you told such lies to those policemen."

"If you don't know that now, Nat," she said, sitting down opposite me, "you probably won't ever know."

"She wouldn't be pregnant by any chance, would she?" I said, without really having known I was going to say it.

Nancy's mouth dropped open. Then she laughed aloud. Presently she said, "Well, one thing's certain, Nat. It wouldn't be any concern of yours if she were."

I pulled myself up out of the big chair and left without another word's passing between us.

Lee Ann Deehart and Nancy Minnifee and that whole band of girls that we liked to refer to as the girls of the Memphis demimonde were of course no more like the ladies of the demimonde as they appear in French literature than they were like some band of angels. And I hardly need say — though it does somehow occur to me to say — their manners and morals bore no resemblance whatsoever to those of the mercenary, filthy-mouthed whores on Pontotoc Street. I might even say that their manners were practically indistinguishable from those of the girls we knew who had attended Miss Hutchison's School and St. Mary's and Lausanne and were now members of the debutante set. The fact is that some of them — only a few perhaps — were from families who were related by blood, and rather closely related, to the families of the debutante set, but families who, for one reason or another, now found themselves economically in another class from their relatives. At any rate, they were all freed from old restraints put upon them by family and community, liberated in each case, so it seems to me, by sheer strength of character, liberated in many respects, but above all else — and I cannot say how it came about — liberated sexually. The most precise thing I can say about them is that they, in their little band, were like hordes of young girls today. It seems to me that in their attitude toward sex they were at least forty years ahead of their time. But I cannot say how it came about. Perhaps it was an individual thing with each of them — or partly so. Perhaps it was because they were the second or third generation of women in Memphis who were working in offices. They were not promiscuous — not most of them — but they slept with the men they were in love with and they did not conceal the fact. The men they were in love with were usually older than we were. Generally speaking, the girls merely amused themselves with us, just as we amused ourselves with them. There was a wonderful freedom in our relations that I have never known anything else quite like. And though I may not have had the most realistic sense of what their lives were, I came to know what I did know through my friendship with Lee Ann Deehart.

She and I first met, I think, at some of those dives where we all hung out. Or it may have been at some girl's apartment. I suspect we both would have been hard put to it to say where it was or exactly when. She was simply one of the good-looking girls we ran around with. I remember dancing with her on several occasions before I had any idea what her name was. We drifted into our special kind of friendship because, as a matter of fact, she was the good friend of Nancy Minnifee, whom my own close friend Bob Childress got very serious about for a time. Bob and Nancy may even have been living together for a while in Nancy's apartment. I think Bob, who was one of six or eight boys of approximately my background who used to go about with these girls, would have married Nancy if she'd consented to have him. Possibly it was at Nancy's apartment that I met Lee

Ann. Anyway, we did a lot of double-dating, the four of us, and had some wonderful times going to the sort of rough nightspots that we all liked and found sufficiently exciting to return to again and again. We would be dancing and drinking at one of those places until about two in the morning, when most of them closed. At that hour most of us would take our girls home, because we nearly all of us had jobs — the girls and the boys, too — that we had to report to by eight or nine in the morning.

Between Lee Ann and me, as between most of the boys and their girls, I think, there was never a serious affair. That is, we never actually — as the young people today say — "had sex." But in the car on the way home or in the car parked outside her roominghouse or even outside the nightspot, as soon as we came out, we would regularly indulge in what used to be known as "heavy necking." Our stopping at that I must attribute first of all to Lee Ann's resistance, though also, in part, to a hesitation I felt about insisting with such a girl. You see, she was in all respects like the girls we called "nice girls," by which I suppose we really meant society girls. And most of us accepted the restriction that we were not to "go to bed" with society girls. They were the girls we were going to marry. These girls were not what those society girls would have termed shopgirls. They had much better taste in their clothes and in their general demeanor. And, as I have said, in the particular group I speak of there was at least an intellectual strain. Some of them had been to college for as much as a year or two, whereas others seemed hardly to have finished high school. Nearly all of them read magazines and books that most of us had never heard of. And they found my odd addiction to Latin poetry the most interesting thing about me. Most of them belonged to a national book club, from which they received a new book each month, and they nearly all bought records and listened to classical music. You would see them sometimes in groups at the art gallery. Or whenever there was an opera or a good play at the city auditorium they were all likely to be there in a group — almost never with dates. If you hadn't known who they were, you might easily have mistaken them for some committee from the Junior League, or for an exceptionally pretty group of schoolteachers — from some fashionable girls' school probably.

But mostly, of course, one saw them with their dates at one of the roadhouses, over in Arkansas or down in Mississippi or out east on the Bristol Highway, or yet again at one of the places we called the "town joints." They preferred going to those road-houses and town joints to going to the Peabody Hotel Roof or the Claridge — as I suppose nearly everyone else did, really, including society girls like Caroline. You would, as a matter of fact, frequently see girls like Caroline at such places. At her request, I had more than once taken Caroline to a town joint down on Adams Street called The Cellar and once to a road-house called The Jungle, over in Arkansas. She had met some of the city girls there and said she found them "dead attractive." And she once recognized them at a play I took her to see and afterward expressed interest in them and asked me to tell her what they were like.

The fact may be that neither the roadhouses nor the town joints were quite as tough as they seemed. Or they weren't as tough for the demimonde girls, anyway. Because the proprie-tors clearly had protective feelings about them. At The Jungle, for instance, the middle-aged couple who operated the place, an extremely obese couple who were forever grinning in our direction and who were usually barefoot (we called them Ma and Pa), would often come and stand by our table — one or the other of them — and sing the words to whatever was playing on the jukebox. Often as not, one of them would be standing there during the entire evening. Sometimes Ma would talk to us about her two little daughters, whom she kept in a private school in Memphis, and Pa, who was a practicing taxidermist, would talk to us about the dogs whose mounted heads adorned the walls on every side of the dimly lit room. All this afforded us great privacy and safety. No drunk or roughneck would come near our table while either Ma or Pa was close by. We had similar protection at other places. At The Cellar, for instance, old Mrs. Power was the sole proprietor. She had a huge goiter on her neck and was never known to smile. Not even in our direc-tion. But it was easy to see that she watched our table like a hawk, and if any other patron lingered near us even momentar-ily she would begin moving slowly toward us. And whoever it was would catch one glimpse of her and move on. We went to these places quite regularly, though some of the girls had their favorites and dislikes among them. Lee Ann would never be taken to The Cellar. She would say only that the place depressed her. And Caroline, when I took her there, felt an instant dislike for The Jungle. She would shake her head afterward and say she would never go back and have those dogs' eyes staring down through the darkness at her.

On the day after I made the rounds with the two policemen, I found myself following almost the same routine in the company of my father and the editor of the morning paper, and, as a matter of fact, the mayor of Memphis himself. The investigation or search was, you see, still entirely unofficial. And men like my father and the mayor and the editor wanted to keep it so. That's why after that routine and off-the-record series of questionings by the police, they preferred to do a bit of investigation themselves rather than entrust the matter to someone else. As I have said, that generation of men in Memphis evidenced feelings of responsibility for such girls — for "working girls of a superior kind," as they phrased it — which I find somewhat difficult to explain. For it wasn't just the men I drove about town with that day. Or the dozen or so men who gathered for conference in our driveway before we set out — that is, Caroline's father, his laywer, the driver of the other vehicle, his lawyer, my father's lawyer, ministers from three church denominations, the editor of the afternoon newspaper, and still others. That day, when I rode about town with my father and the two other men in our car, I came as near as I ever had or ever would to receiving a satisfactory explanation of the phenomenon. They were of a generation of American men who were perhaps the last to grow up in a world where women were absolutely subjected and under the absolute protection of men. While my father wheeled his big Cadillac through the side streets on which some of the girls lived and then along the wide boulevards of Memphis, they spoke of the changes they had seen. In referring to the character of the life girls like Lee Ann led — of which they showed a far greater awareness than I would have supposed they possessed — they agreed that this was the second or third generation there of women who had lived as independently, as freely

as these girls did. I felt that what they said was in no sense as
derogatory or critical as it would have been in the presence of
their wives or daughters. They spoke almost affectionately and
with a certain sadness of such girls. They spoke as if these were
daughters of dead brothers of their own or of dead compan-
ions-in-arms during the First World War. And it seemed to me
that they thought of these girls as the daughters of men who
had abdicated their authority and responsibility as fathers, men
who were not strangers or foreign to them, though they were
perhaps of a different economic class. The family names of the
girls were familiar to them. The fathers of these girls were
Americans of the great hinterland like themselves, even south-
erners like themselves. I felt that they were actually cousins of
ours who had failed as fathers somehow, had been destined to
fail, even required to do so in a changing world. And so these
men of position and power had to act as surrogate fathers during a transitional period. It was a sort of communal fatherhood
they were acting out. Eventually, they seemed to say, fathers
might not be required. I actually heard my father saying,
"That's what the whole world is going to be like someday." He
meant like the life such girls as Lee Ann were making for themselves. I often think nowadays of Father's saying that, whenever
I see his prediction being fulfilled by the students in the university where I have been teaching for twenty years now, and I
wonder if Father did really believe his prediction would come
true.

Yet while he and the other two men talked their rather san-
guine talk that day, I was thinking of a call I had had the night
before after I came back from seeing Nancy Minnifee. One of
the servants answered the telephone downstairs in the back part
of the house, and she must have guessed it was something special. Because instead of buzzing the buzzer three times, which
was the signal when a call was for me, the maid came up the
back stairs and tapped gently on my door. "It's for you, Nat,"
she said softly. "Do you want to take it downstairs?"

There was nothing peculiar about her doing this, really. Since
I didn't have an extension phone in my room, I had a tacit
understanding with the servants that I preferred to take what I
considered my private calls down in that quarter of the house.
And so I followed the maid down the back stairway and shut

myself in the little servants' dining room that was behind the great white-tiled kitchen. I answered the call on the wall phone there.

A girl's voice, which wasn't the same voice I had heard on the office telephone at noon, said, "Lee Ann doesn't want another day like this one, Nat."

"Who is this?" I said, lowering my voice to be sure even the servants didn't hear me. "What the hell is going on?" I asked. "Where is Lee Ann?"

"She's been keeping just one apartment or one roominghouse ahead of you all day."

"But why? Why is she hiding this way?"

"All I want to say is she's had about enough. You let up on pursuing her so."

"It's not me," I protested. "There's nothing I can do to stop them."

Over the phone there came a contemptuous laugh. "No. And you can't get married till they find her, can you?" Momentarily I thought I heard Lee Ann's voice in the background. "Anyhow," the same voice continued, "Lee Ann's had about as much as she can take of all this. She was depressed as it was, when she called you in the first place. Why else do you think she would call you, Nat? She was desperate for some comic relief."

"Relief from what?"

"Relief from her depression, you idiot."

"But what's she depressed about?" I was listening carefully to the voice, thinking it was that of first one girl and then another.

"Nat, we don't always have to have something to be depressed about. But Lee Ann will be all right, if you'll let her alone."

"But what is she depressed about?" I persisted. I had begun to think maybe it was Lee Ann herself on the phone, disguising her voice.

"About life in general, you bastard! Isn't that enough?" Then I knew it wasn't Lee Ann, after all.

"Listen," I said, "let me speak to Lee Ann. I want to speak to Lee Ann."

And then I heard whoever it was I was talking with break off the connection. I quietly replaced the receiver and went upstairs again.

In those days I didn't know what it was to be depressed —

not, anyway, about "life in general." Later on, you see, I did know. Later on, after years of being married and having three children and going to grown-up Memphis dinner parties three or four times a week and working in the cotton office six days a week, I got so depressed about life in general that I sold my interest in the cotton firm to a cousin of mine (my father and uncles were dead by then) and managed to make Caroline understand that what I needed was to go back to school for a while so that we could start our life all over. I took degrees at three universities, which made it possible for me to become a college professor. That may be an awful revelation about myself — I mean to say, awful that what decided me to become a teacher was that I was so depressed about life in general. But I reasoned that being an English professor — even if I was relegated to teaching composition and simple-minded survey courses — would be something useful and would throw us in with a different kind of people. (Caroline tried to persuade me to go into the sciences, but I told her she was just lucky that I didn't take up classics again.) Anyway, teaching has made me see a lot of young people over the years, in addition to my own children, and I think it is why, in retrospect, those Memphis girls I'm writing about still seem interesting to me after all these many years.

But the fact is, I was still so uneasy about the significance of both those calls from Lee Ann's friends that I was unwilling to mention them to Caroline that night. At first I thought I would tell her, but as soon as I saw her tall and graceful figure in her white, pleated evening dress and wearing the white corsage I had sent, I began worrying again about whether or not she might still break off the engagement. Besides, we had plenty of other matters to discuss, including the rounds I had made with the two policemen that day and her various activities in preparation for the wedding. We went to a dinner that one of my aunts gave for us at the Memphis Country Club that night. We came home early and spent twenty minutes or so in her living room, telling each other how much we loved each other and how we would let nothing on earth interfere with our getting married. I felt reassured, or I tried to feel so. It seemed to me, though, that Caroline still had not really made up her mind. It worried me that she didn't have more to say about Lee Ann. After I got home, I kept waking all night and wondering what if that had not been Lee Ann's voice I had heard in the background and what if she never surfaced again. The circumstances of her disappearance would have to be made public, and that would certainly be too embarrassing for Caroline and her parents to ignore.

Next day, I didn't tell my father and his two friends, the editor and the mayor, about either of the two telephone calls. I don't know why I didn't, unless it was because I feared they might begin monitoring all my calls. I could not tolerate the thought of having them hear the things that girl said to me.

In preference to interviewing the girls whose addresses I could give them, those three middle-aged men seemed much more interested in talking to the girls' roominghouse landladies, or their apartment landlords, or their mothers. They did talk to some of the girls themselves, though, and I observed that the girls were so impressed by having these older men want to talk to them they could hardly look at them directly. What I think is that the girls were *afraid* they would tell them the truth. They would reply to their questions respectfully, if evasively, but they were apt to keep their eyes on me. This was not the case, however, with the mothers and the landlords and the landladies. There was an immediate rapport between these persons and the three men. There hardly needed to be any explanation required of the unofficial nature of the investigation or of the concern of these particular men about such a girl as Lee Ann. One woman who told them that Lee Ann had roomed with her for a time described her as being always a moody sort of girl. "But lots of these girls living on their own are moody," she said.

"Where did Miss Deehart come from?" my father asked. "Who were her people?"

"She always claimed she came from Texas," the woman said. "But she could never make it clear to me where it was in Texas."

Later the mayor asked Lee Ann's current landlady, Mrs. Troxler, where she supposed Lee Ann might have gone. "Well," Mrs. Troxler said, "a girl, a decent girl, even among these modern girls, generally goes to her mother when there's trouble. Women turn to women," she said, "when there's real trouble."

The three men found no trace of Lee Ann, got no real clue to where she might have gone. When finally we were leaving the editor at his newspaper office on Union Avenue, he hesitated a moment before opening the car door. "Well," he began, but he sat for a moment beating his leg thoughtfully with a newspaper he had rolled up in his hand. "I don't know," he said. "It's going to be a matter for the police, after all, if we can't do any better than this." I still didn't say anything about my telephone calls. But the calls were worrying me a good deal, and that night I told Caroline.

And when I had told her about the calls and told her how the police and my father and his friends had failed to get any information from the girls, Caroline, who was then sitting beside me on the couch in her living room, suddenly took my hand in hers and, putting her face close to mine and looking me directly in the eye, said, "Nat, I don't want you to go to work at all tomorrow. Don't make any explanation to your father or to anybody. Just get up early and come over here and get me. I want you to take me to meet some of those girls." Then she asked me which of the girls she might possibly have met on the rare occasions when I had taken her dancing at The Jungle or at The Cellar. And before I left that night she got me to tell her all I knew about "that whole tribe of city girls." I told her everything, including an account of my innocent friendship with Lee Ann Deehart, as well as an account of my earlier relations, which were not innocent, with a girl named Fern Morris. When, next morning, I came to fetch Caroline for our expedition, there were only three girls that she wanted to be taken to see. One of the three was of course Fern Morris.

There was something that had happened to me the day before, when I was going about Memphis with my father and his two friends, that I could not tell Caroline about. You see, I had been imagining, each place we went, how as we came in the front door Lee Ann was hurriedly, quietly going out the back. This mental picture of her in flight I found not merely appealing but strangely exciting. And it seemed to me I was discovering what my true feelings toward Lee Ann had been during the past two years. I had never dared insist upon the occasional advances I had naturally made to her, because she had always

seemed too delicate, too vulnerable, for me to think of suggesting a casual sexual relationship with her. She had seemed too
clever and too intelligent for me to deceive her about my intentions or my worth as a person. And I imagined I relished the
kind of restraint there was between us because it was so altogether personal and not one placed upon us by any element or
segment of society, or by any outside circumstances whatever. It
kept coming to my mind as we stood waiting for an answer to
the pressure on each doorbell that she was the girl I ought and
wanted to be marrying. I realized the absolute folly of such
thoughts and the utter impossibility of any such conclusion to
present events. But still such feelings and thoughts had kept
swimming in and out of my head all that day. I kept seeing Lee
Ann in my mind's eye and hearing her soft, somewhat husky
voice. I kept imagining how her figure would appear in the
doorway before us. I saw her slender ankles, her small breasts,
her head of ash-blonde hair, which had a way of seeming to fall
about her face when she talked but which with one shake of her
head she could throw back into perfect place. But of course
when the door opened there was the inevitable landlady or
mother or friend. And when the next day came and I saw Caroline rolling up her sleeves, so to speak, to pitch in and settle
this matter once and for all, then my thoughts and fantasies of
the day before seemed literally like something out of a dream
that I might have had.

The first two girls Caroline had wanted to see were the two
that she very definitely remembered having met when I had
taken her — "on a lark" — to my favorite nightspots. She caught
them both before they went to work that morning, and I was
asked to wait in the car. I felt like an idiot waiting out there in
the car, because I knew I'd been seen from some window as I
gingerly hopped out and opened the door for Caroline when
she got out — and opened it again when she returned. But
there was no way around it. I waited out there, playing the car
radio even at the risk of running down the battery.

When she came back from seeing the first girl, whose name
was Lucy Phelan, Caroline was very angry. She reported that
Lucy Phelan had pretended not to remember ever having met
her. Moreover, Lucy had pretended that she knew Lee Ann

Deehart only slightly and had no idea where she could be or
what her disappearance meant. As Caroline fumed and I
started up the car, I was picturing Lee Ann quietly tiptoeing out
the back door of Lucy's roominghouse just as Lucy was telling
Caroline she scarcely knew the girl or while she was insisting
that she didn't remember Caroline. As Caroline came back
down the walk from the big Victorian house to the car, Lucy,
who had stepped out onto the narrow porch that ran across the
front of the house and around one corner of it, squatted down
on her haunches at the top of the wooden porch steps and
waved to me from behind Caroline's back. Though I knew it
was no good, I pretended not to see her there. As I put the car
into second gear and we sped away down the block, I took a
quick glance back at the house. Lucy was still standing on the
porch and waving to me the way one waves to a little child. She
knew I had seen her stooping and waving moments before. And
knew I would be stealing a glance now.

For a short time Caroline seemed undecided about calling on
the second girl. But she decided finally to press on. Lucy Phelan
she remembered meeting at The Cellar. The next girl, Betsy
Morehouse, she had met at The Jungle and at a considerably
more recent time. Caroline was a dog fancier in those days and
she recalled a conversation with Betsy about the mounted dogs'
heads that adorned the walls of The Jungle. They both had
been outraged. When she mentioned this to me there in the car,
I realized for the first time that by trying to make these girls
acknowledge an acquaintance with her she had hoped to make
them feel she was almost one of them and they would thus be
more likely to confide in her. But she failed with Betsy Morehouse, too. Betsy lived in an apartment house — an old residence, that is, converted into apartments — and when Caroline
got inside the entrance hall door she met Betsy, who was just
then coming down the stairs. Betsy carried a purse and was
wearing a fur coat and overshoes. When Caroline got back to
the car and told me about it, I could not help feeling that Betsy
had had a call from Lucy Phelan and even perhaps that Lee
Ann was hiding in her apartment, having just arrived there
from Lucy's. Because Betsy didn't offer to take Caroline back
upstairs to her apartment for a talk. Instead, they sat down on

two straightbacked chairs in the entrance hall and exchanged their few words there. Betsy at once denied the possibility of Caroline's ever having met her before. She denied that she had, herself, ever been to The Jungle. I knew this to be a lie, of course, but I didn't insist upon it to Caroline. I said that perhaps both she and I were mistaken about Betsy's being there on the night I had taken Caroline. As soon as Caroline saw she would learn nothing from Betsy, she got up and began to make motions of leaving. Betsy followed her to the door. But upon seeing my car out at the curb — so Caroline believed — she turned back, saying that she had remembered a telephone call she had to make. Caroline suspected that the girl didn't want to have to face me with her lie. That possibly was true. But my thought was that Betsy just might, also, have a telephone call she wanted to make.

There was now no question about Caroline's wanting to proceed to the third girl's house. This was the girl I had told her about having had a real affair with — the one I had gone with before Lee Ann and I had become friends. Caroline knew that she and Fern Morris had never met, but she counted on a different psychology with Fern. Most probably she had hoped it wouldn't be necessary for her to go to see Fern. She had been sure that one of those two other girls would give her the lead she needed. But as a last resort she was fully prepared to call on Fern Morris and to take me into the house with her.

Fern was a girl who still lived at home with her mother. She was in no sense a mama's girl or even a home-loving girl, since she was unhappy unless she went out on a date every night of her life. Perhaps she was not so clever and not so intellectual as most of her friends — if reading books, that is, on psychology and on China and every new volume of André Maurois indicated intellectuality. And though she was not home-loving, I suppose you would have to say she was more domestic than the other girls were. She had never "held down" a job. Rather, she stayed at home in the daytime and kept house for her mother, who was said to "hold down" a high-powered job under Boss Crump down at City Hall. Mrs. Morris was a very sensible woman, who put no restrictions on her grown-up daughter and was glad to have her as a housekeeper. She used to tell me what a good cook and housekeeper Fern was and how well fixed she would leave her when she died. I really believe Mrs. Morris hoped our romance might end in matrimony, and, as a matter of fact, it was when I began to suspect that Fern, too, was entertaining such notions that I stopped seeing her and turned my attentions to Lee Ann Deehart.

Mrs. Morris still seemed glad to see me when I arrived at their bungalow that morning with Caroline and when I proceeded to introduce Caroline to her as my fiancée. Fern herself greeted me warmly. In fact, when I told her that Caroline and I were going to be married (though she must certainly have already read about it in the newspaper) she threw her arms about my neck and kissed me. "Oh, Natty," she said, "I'm so happy for you. Really I am. But poor Lee Ann." And in later life, especially in recent years, whenever Caroline has thought I was being silly about some other woman, usually a woman she considers her mental and social inferior, she has delighted in addressing me as "Natty." On more than one such occasion I have even had her say to me, "I am so happy for you, Natty. Really I am."

The fact is, Mrs. Morris was just leaving the house for work when we arrived. And so there was no delay in Caroline's interview with Fern. "I assume you know about Lee Ann's disappearance?" Caroline began as soon as we had seated ourselves in the little front parlor, with which I was very familiar.

"Of course I do," said Fern, looking at me and laughing gleefully.

"You think it's a laughing matter, then?" Caroline asked.

"I do indeed. It's all a big joke," Fern said at once. It was as though she had her answers all prepared. "And a very successful joke it is."

"Successful?" both Caroline and I asked. We looked at each other in dismay.

"It's only my opinion, of course. But I think she only wants to make you two suffer."

"Suffer?" I said. This time Caroline was silent.

Fern was now addressing me directly. "Everybody knows Caroline is not going to marry you until Lee Ann turns up safe."

"Everybody?" Both of us again.

"Everybody in the world practically," said Fern.

Caroline's face showed no expression. Neither, I believe, did mine.

"Fern, do you know where Lee Ann is?" Caroline asked gently.

Fern Morris, her eyes on me, shook her head, smiling.

"Do you know where her people are?" Caroline asked. "And whether she's with them or hiding with her friends?"

Fern shook her head again, but now she gazed directly at Caroline. "I'm not going to tell you anything!" she asserted. But after a moment she took a deep breath and said, still looking at Caroline, "You're a smart girl. I think you'll likely be going to Lee Ann's room in that place where she lives. If you do go there, and if you are a smart girl, you'll look in the left-hand drawer of Lee Ann's dressing table." Fern had an uneasy smile on her face after she had spoken, as if Caroline had got her to say something she hadn't really meant to say, as if she felt guilty for what she had just done.

Caroline had us out of there in only a minute or so and on our way to Lee Ann's roominghouse.

It was a red brick bungalow up in north Memphis. It looked very much like the one that Fern lived in but was used as a roominghouse. When Mrs. Troxler opened the front door to us, Caroline said, "We're friends of Lee Ann's, and she wants us to pack a suitcase and bring it to her."

"You know where she is then?" Mrs. Troxler asked. "Hello, Nat," she said, looking at me over Caroline's shoulder.

"Hello, Mrs. Troxler," I said. I was so stunned by what I had just heard Caroline say that I spoke in a whisper.

"She's with her mother — or with her family, at least," Caroline said. By now she had slipped into the hallway, and I had followed without Mrs. Troxler's really inviting us in.

"Where are her family?" Mrs. Troxler asked, giving way to Caroline's forward thrust. "She never volunteered to tell me anything about them. And I never think it's my business to ask."

Caroline nodded her head at me, indicating that I should lead the way to Lee Ann's room. I knew that her room was toward the back of the house and I headed in that direction.

"I'll have to unlock the room for you," said Mrs. Troxler.

"There have been a number of people coming here and wanting to look about her room. And so I keep it locked."

"A number of people?" asked Caroline casually.

"Yes. Nat knows. There were the police. And then there were some other gentlemen. Nat knows about it, though he didn't come in. And there were two other girls. The girls just seemed idly curious, and so I've taken to locking the door. Where do her people live?"

"I don't know," said Caroline. "She's going to meet us downtown at the bus station and take a bus."

When Mrs. Troxler had unlocked the door she asked, "Is Lee Ann all right? Do you think she will be coming back here?"

"She's fine," Caroline said, "and I'm sure she'll be coming back. She just wants a few things."

"Yes, I've wondered how she's been getting along without a change of clothes. I'll fetch her suitcase. I keep my roomers' luggage in my storage closet down the hall." We waited till she came back with a piece of plaid luggage and then we went into the room and closed the door. Caroline went to the oak dresser and began pulling things out and stuffing them in the bag. I stood by, watching, hardly able to believe what I saw Caroline doing. When she had closed the bag, she looked up at me as if to say, "What are you waiting for?" She had not gone near the little mahogany dressing table, and I had not realized that was going to be my part. I went over and opened the left-hand drawer. The only thing in the drawer was a small snapshot. I took it up and examined it carefully. I said nothing to Caroline, just handed her the picture. Finally I said, "Do you know who that is? And where the picture was taken?" She recognized the woman in the picture at once. It was the old woman with the goiter who ran The Cellar. The picture had been taken with Mrs. Power standing in one of the flower beds against the side of the house. The big cut stones of the house were unmistakable. After bringing the snapshot up close to her face and peering into it for ten seconds or so, Caroline looked at me and said, "That's her family."

By the time we had stopped the car in front of The Cellar, I had told Caroline all that I knew about Lee Ann's schooling and about how it was that, though she had a "family" in Memphis, no one had known her when she was growing up. She had been to one boarding school in Shreveport, Louisiana, to one in east Texas, and to still another in St. Charles, Missouri. I had heard her make references to all of those schools. "They kept her away from home," Caroline speculated. "And so when she had finished school she wasn't prepared for the kind of 'family' she had. That's why she moved out on them and lived in a rooming-house."

She reached that conclusion while I was parking the car at the curb, near the front entrance to the house. Meanwhile, I was preparing myself mentally to accompany Caroline to the door of the old woman's living quarters, which were on the main floor and above The Cellar. But Caroline rested her hand on the steering wheel beside mine and said, "This is something I have to do without you."

"But I'd like to see Lee Ann if she's here," I said.

"I know you would," said Caroline. "Of course you would."

"But, Caroline," I said, "I've made it clear that ours was an innocent —"

"I know," she said. "That's why I don't want you to see her again." Then she took Lee Ann's bag and went up to the front entrance of the house.

The main entrance to The Cellar was to the side of and underneath the high front stoop of the old house. Caroline had to climb a flight of ten or twelve stone steps to reach the door to the residence. From the car I saw a vague figure appear at one of the long first-floor windows. I was relatively certain that it was Lee Ann I saw. I could barely restrain myself from jumping from the car and running up that flight of steps and forcing myself past Caroline and into that house. During the hundred hours or so since she had fled into the woods of Overton Park, Lee Ann Deehart had come to represent feelings of mine that I didn't try to comprehend. The notion I had had yesterday that I was in love with her and wanted to marry her didn't really adequately express the emotions that her disappearance had stirred in me. I felt that I had never looked at her really or had any conception of what sort of person she was or what her experience in life was like. Now it seemed I would never know. I suddenly realized — at that early age — that there was experience to be had in life that I might never know anything about except through hearsay and through books. I felt that this was my last moment to reach out and understand something of the world that was other than my own narrow circumstances and my own narrow nature. When, nearly fifteen years later, I came into a comfortable amount of money — after my father's death — I made my extraordinary decision to go back to the university and prepare myself to become a teacher. But I knew then, at thirty-seven, that I was only going to try to comprehend intellectually the world about me and beyond me and that I had failed somehow at some time to reach out and grasp direct experience of a larger life that no amount of intellectualizing could compensate for. It may be that the moment of my great failure was when I continued to sit there in the car and did not force my way into the house where the old woman with the goiter lived and where it now seemed Lee Ann had been hiding for four days.

I was scarcely aware of the moment when the big front door opened and Caroline was admitted to the house. She was in there for nearly an hour. During that time I don't know what thoughts I had. It was as though I ceased to exist for the time that Lee Ann Deehart and Caroline Braxley were closeted together. When Caroline reappeared on the high stone stoop of the house, I was surprised to see she was still carrying Lee Ann's suitcase. But she would soon make it all clear. It *was* Lee Ann who received her at the door. No doubt she had seen that Caroline was carrying her own piece of luggage. And no doubt Caroline had counted on just that mystification and its efficacy, because Caroline is an extremely clever psychologist when she sets her mind to it. At any rate, in that relatively brief interview between them Caroline learned that all she had surmised about Lee Ann was true. Moreover, she learned that Lee Ann had fled the scene of the accident because she feared that the publicity would reveal to everyone who her grandmother was.

Lee Ann had crossed the little strip of snow-covered golf course and had entered the part of the woods where the old-forest trees were. And something had made her want to remain there for a while. She didn't know what it was. She had leaned against one of the trees, feeling quite content. It had seemed to her that she was not alone in the woods. And whatever the other presences were, instead of interfering with her reflections they seemed to wish to help her clear her thoughts. She stood there for a long time — perhaps for an hour or more. At any rate, she remained there until all at once she realized how cold she had grown and realized that she had no choice but to go back to the real world. Yet she wasn't going back to her room or to her pretty possessions there. That wasn't the kind of freedom she wanted any longer. She was going back to her grandmother. But still she hoped to avoid the publicity that the accident might bring. She decided to go, first of all, and stay with some of her friends, so that her grandmother would not suppose she was only turning to her because she was in trouble. And while making this important change in her life she felt she must be protected by her friends. She wanted to have an interval of time to herself and she wanted, above all, not to be bothered during that time by the silly society boy in whose car she had been riding.

During the first days she had gone from one girl's house to another. Finally she went to her grandmother. In the beginning she had, it was true, been mightily depressed. That was why she had telephoned me to start with, and had wanted someone to cheer her up. But during these four days she had much time for thinking and had overcome all her depression and had no other thought but to follow through with the decision to go and live openly with her old grandmother in her quarters above The Cellar.

Caroline also, in that single interview, learned other things about Lee Ann that had been unknown to me. She had learned that Lee Ann's own mother had abandoned her in infancy to her grandmother but had always through the years sent money back for her education. She had had — the mother — an extremely successful career as a buyer for a women's clothing store in Lincoln, Nebraska. But she had never tried to see her daughter and had never expressed a wish to see her. The only word she ever sent was that children were not her dish, but that she didn't want it on her conscience that, because of her, some little girl in Memphis, Tennessee, had got no education and was therefore the domestic slave of some man. When Caroline told

me all of this about the mother's not caring to see the daughter,
it brought from her her first emotional outburst with regard to
the whole business. But that was at a later time. The first thing
she had told me when she returned to the car was that once Lee
Ann realized that her place of hiding could no longer be concealed, she was quickly and easily persuaded to speak to the
newspaper editor on the telephone and to tell him that she was
safe and well. But she did this only after Caroline had first
spoken to the editor herself, and obtained a promise from him
that there would be no embarrassing publicity for Lee Ann's
grandmother.

The reason Caroline had returned with Lee Ann's suitcase
was that Lee Ann had emptied it there in her grandmother's
front parlor and had asked that we return to her roominghouse
and bring all of her possessions to her at her grandmother's.
We obliged her in this, making appropriate, truthless explanations to her landlady, whom Lee Ann had meanwhile telephoned and given whatever little authority Mrs. Troxler required in order to let us remove her things. It seemed to me
that that poor woman scarcely listened to the explanations we
gave. Another girl was already moving into the room before we
had well got Lee Ann's things out. When we returned to the
grandmother's house with these possessions in the car, Caroline
insisted upon making an endless number of trips into the house,
carrying everything herself. She was firm in her stipulation that
Lee Ann and I not see each other again.

The incident was closed then. I could be certain that there
would be no broken engagement — not on Caroline's initiative.
But from that point — from that afternoon — my real effort
and my real concern would be to try to understand why Caroline had not been so terribly enraged or so sorely wounded
upon first discovering that there had been another girl with me
in the car at the time of the accident, and by the realization that
I had not immediately disclosed her presence, that she had not
at least once threatened to end the engagement. What her mental processes had been during the past four days, knowing now
as I did that she was the person with whom I was going to spend
the rest of my life, became of paramount interest to me.

But at that age I was so unquestioning of human behavior in

general and so accepting of events as they came, and so without
perception or reflection regarding the binding and molding effect upon people of the circumstances in which they are born,
that I actually might not have found Caroline's thoughts of such
profound interest and so vitally important to be understood had
not Caroline, as soon as we were riding down Adams Street and
were out of sight of The Cellar and of Mrs. Power's great stone
house above it, suddenly requested that I drive her out to the
Bristol Highway, and once we were on the Bristol Highway
asked me to drive as fast and as far out of town as I could or
would, to drive and drive until she should beg me to turn
around and take her home; and had she not, as soon as we were
out of town and beyond city speed limits, where I could press
down on the accelerator and send us flying along the three-lane
strip of concrete that cut through the endless expanse of cotton
fields and swamps on either side, had she not then at last, after
talking quietly about Lee Ann's mother's sending back the
money for her education, burst into weeping that began with a
kind of wailing and grinding of teeth that one ordinarily associates more with a very old person in very great physical pain, a
wailing that became mixed almost immediately with a sort of
hollow laughter in which there was no mirth. I commenced
slowing the car at once. I was searching for a place where I
could pull off to the side of the road. But through her tears and
her harsh, dry laughter she hissed at me, "Don't stop! Don't
stop! Go on. Go on. Go as far and as fast as you can, so that I
can forget this day and put it forever behind me!" I obeyed her
and sped on, reaching out my hand to hold her two hands that
were resting in her lap and were making no effort to wipe away
her tears. I was not looking at her — only thinking thoughts of
a kind I had never before had. It was the first time I had ever
witnessed a victim of genuine hysteria. Indeed, I wasn't to hear
such noises again until six or seven years later, during the Second World War. I heard them from men during days after a
battle, men who had stood with great bravery against the enemy
— particularly, as I remember now, men who had been brought
back from the first onslaught of the Normandy invasion, physically whole but shaken in their souls. I think that during the
stress of the four previous days Caroline Braxley had shed not
a tear of self-pity or of shame and had not allowed herself a

moment of genuine grief for my possible faithlessness to her. She had been far too busy with thinking — with thinking her thoughts of how to cope with Lee Ann's unexplained disappearance, with, that is, its possible effect upon her own life. But now the time had come when her checked emotions could be checked no longer.

The Bristol Highway, along which we were speeding as she wept hysterically, was a very straight and a very wide roadway for those days. It went northeast from Memphis. As its name implied, it was the old road that shot more or less diagonally across the long hinterland that is the state of Tennessee. It was the road along which many of our ancestors had first made their way from Virginia and the Carolinas to Memphis, to settle in the forest wilderness along the bluffs above the Mississippi River. And it occurred to me now that when Caroline said go as fast and as far as you can she really meant to take us all the way back into our past and begin the journey all over again, not merely from a point of four days ago or from the days of our childhood but from a point in our identity that would require a much deeper delving and a more radical return.

When we had got scarcely beyond the outskirts of Memphis, the most obvious signs of her hysteria had abated. Instead, however, she began to speak with a rapidity and in tones I was not accustomed to in her speech. This began after I had seen her give one long look over her shoulder and out the rear window of the car. Sensing some significance in that look and sensing some connection between it and the monologue she had now launched upon, I myself gave one glance into the rearview mirror. What met my eye was the skyline of modern Memphis beyond the snow-covered suburban rooftops — the modern Memphis of 1937, with its two or three high-rise office buildings. It was not clear to me immediately what there was in that skyline to inspire all that followed. She was speaking to me openly about Lee Ann and about her own feelings of jealousy and resentment of the girl — of *that* girl and of all those other girls, too, whose names and personalities and way of life had occupied our thoughts and had seemed to threaten our future during the four-day crisis that had followed my accident in the park.

"It isn't only Lee Ann that disturbs me," she said. "It began with her, of course. It began not with what she might be to you but with her freedom to jump out of your car, her freedom *from* you, her freedom to run off into the woods — with her capacity, which her special way of living provided her, simply to vanish, to remove herself from the eyes of the world, literally to disappear from the glaring light of day while the whole world, so to speak, looked on."

"*You* would like to be able to do that?" I interrupted. It seemed so unlike her role as I understood it.

"*Any*body would, wouldn't they?" she said, not looking at me but at the endless stretch of concrete that lay straight ahead. "*Men* have always been able to do it," she said. "In my own family, for as many generations back as our family stories go, there have been men who seemed to disappear from the face of the earth just because they wanted to. They used to write 'Gone to Texas' on the front door and leave the house and the farm to be sold for taxes. They walked out on dependent old parents and on sweethearts or even on wives and little children. And though they were considered black sheep for doing so, they were something of heroes, too. It seemed romantic to the rest of us that they had gone Out West somewhere and got a new start or had begun life over. But there was never a woman in our family who did that! There was no way it could happen. Or perhaps in some rare instance it did happen and the story hasn't come down to us. Her name simply isn't recorded in our family annals or reported in stories told around the fire. The assumption of course is that she is a streetwalker in Chicago or she resides in a red-plush whorehouse in Cheyenne. But with girls like Lee Ann and Lucy and Betsy it's all different. They have made their break with the past. Each of them has had the strength and intelligence to make the break for herself. But now they have formed a sort of league for their own protection. How I do admire and envy them! And how little you understand them, Nat. How little you understand Lee Ann's loneliness and depression and bravery. She and all the others are wonderful — even Fern. They occupy the real city of Memphis as none of the rest of us do. They treat men just as they please. And not the way men are treated in *our* circles. And men like them better for it. Those girls have learned to enjoy life together and to be mutually protective, but they enjoy a protection also, I hope you have observed, a kind of communal protection, from men who admire their very independence, from a league of men, mind you, not from individual men, from the police and from men like my father and your father, from men who would never say openly how much they admire them. Naturally we fear them. Those of us who are not like them in temperament — or in intelligence, because there is no use in denying it — we must fear them and find a means to give delaying action. And of course the only way we know is the age-old way!"

She became silent for a time now. But I knew I was going to hear what I had been waiting to hear. If I had been the least bit impatient with her explanation of Lee Ann and her friends, it was due in part to my impatience to see if she would explain *herself* to me. We were now speeding along the Bristol Highway at the very top speed the car would go. Except when we were passing through some crossroad or village I consciously kept the speed above ninety. In those days there was no speed limit in Tennessee. There were merely signs placed every so often along the roadside saying "Speed Limit: Please Drive Carefully." I felt somehow that, considering Caroline's emotional state and my own tension, it would be altogether unreasonable, it would constitute careless and unsafe driving, for me to reduce our speed to anything below the maximum capability of the car. And when we did of necessity slow down for some village or small town it was precisely as though we had arrived at some at once familiar and strange point in the past. And on each occasion I think we both experienced a sense of danger and disappointment. It was as though we expected to experience a satisfaction in having gone so far. But the satisfaction was not to be had. When we had passed that point, I felt only the need to press on at an even greater speed. And so we drove on and on, at first north and east through the wintry cotton land and corn land, past the old Orgill Plantation, the mansion house in plain view, its round brick columns on which the plaster was mostly gone, and now and then another white man's antebellum house, and always at the roadside or on the horizon, atop some distant ridge, a variety of black men's shacks and cabins, each with a little streamer of smoke rising from an improvised tin stovepipe or from an ill-made brick chimney bent away from the cabin at a precarious angle.

We went through the old villages of Arlington and Mason and the town of Brownsville — down streets of houses with columned porticoes and double galleries — and then we turned south to Bolivar, whose very name told you when it was built, and headed back to Memphis through Grand Junction and La Grange. (Mississippi towns really, though north of the Tennessee line.) I had slowed our speed after Bolivar, because that was where Caroline began her second monologue. The tone and pace of her speech were very different now. Her speech was slow and deliberate, her emotions more under control than usual, as she described what she had felt and thought in the time since the accident and explained how she came to reach the decision to take the action she had — that is, action toward searching out and finding Lee Ann Deehart. Though I had said nothing on the subject of what she had done about Lee Ann and not done about our engagement, expressed no request or demand for any explanation unless it was by my silence, when she spoke now it was almost as though Caroline were making a courtroom defense of accusations hurled at her by me. "I finally saw there was only one thing for me to do and saw why I had to do it. I saw that the only power in the world I had for saving myself lay in my saving you. And I saw that I could only save you by 'saving' Lee Ann Deehart. At first, of course, I thought I would have to break our engagement, or at least postpone the wedding for a year. That's what *every*body thought, of course — everybody in the family."

"Even your father and mother?" I could not help interjecting. It had seemed to me that Caroline's parents had — of all people — been most sympathetic to me.

"Yes, even my mother and father," she went on, rather serenely now. "They could not have been more sympathetic to you personally. Mother said that, after all, you were a mere man. Father said that, after all, you were only human. But circumstances were circumstances, and if some disaster had befallen Lee Ann, if she was murdered or if she was pregnant or if she was a suicide or whatever other horror you can conjure up, and it all came out, say, on our wedding day or came out afterward, for that matter — well, what then? *They* and *I* had to think of that. On the other hand, as I kept thinking, what if the wedding *was* called off? What then for me? The only power I had to save myself was to save you, and to save you by rescuing Lee Ann Deehart. It always came to that, and comes to that still. Don't you see, it was a question of how very much I had to lose and how little power I had to save myself. Because *I* had not set *my*self free the way those other girls have. One makes that choice at a much earlier age than this, I'm afraid. And so I knew already, Nat, and I know now what the only kind of power I can ever have must be."

She hesitated then. She was capable of phrasing what she said much more precisely. But it would have been indelicate, somehow, for her to have done so. And so I said it for her in my crude way: "You mean the power of a woman in a man's world."

She nodded and continued. "I had to protect *that*. Even if it had been *I* that broke our engagement, Nat, or even if you and I had been married before some second scandal broke, still I would have been a jilted, a rejected girl. And some part of my power to protect myself would be gone forever. Power, or strength, is what everybody must have some of if he — if she — is to survive in any kind of world. I have to protect and use whatever strength I have."

Caroline went on in that voice until we were back in Memphis and at her father's house on East Parkway. She kissed me before we got out of the car there, kissed me for my silence, I believe. I had said almost nothing during the whole of the long ride. And I think she has ever since been grateful to me for the silence I kept. Perhaps she mistook it for more understanding than I was capable of at the time. At any rate, I cannot help believing that it has much to do with the support and understanding — rather silent though it was — that she gave me when I made the great break in my life in my late thirties. Though it clearly meant that we must live on a somewhat more modest scale and live among people of a sort she was not used to, and even meant leaving Memphis forever behind us, the firmness with which she supported my decision, and the look in her eyes whenever I spoke of feeling I must make the change, seemed to say to me that she would dedicate her pride of power to the power of freedom I sought.

DONALD BARTHELME

There is nothing classic about the form of "The Emerald." It
joyfully breaks every rule it encounters — and some it invents —
in the process of becoming a parable of celebrity and religion in
modern times. Discussing his predilection for stories about characters who have visions, Stanley Elkin said, " 'The Emerald' is
itself a vision." Donald Barthelme, who died in 1989, was known
for his irreverent, innovative fiction. Born in Philadelphia in
1931 and raised in Houston, he was the author of a dozen
books.

The Emerald

HEY BUDDY what's your name?
  My name is Tope. What's your name?
  My name is Sallywag. You after the emerald?
  Yeah I'm after the emerald you after the emerald too?
  I am. What are you going to do with it if you get it?
  Cut it up into little emeralds. What are you going to do with
it?
  I was thinking of solid emerald armchairs. For the rich.
  That's an idea. What's your name, you?
  Wide Boy.
  You after the emerald?
  Sure as shootin'.
  How you going to get in?
  Blast.
  That's going to make a lot of noise isn't it?
  You think it's a bad idea?
  Well . . . What's your name, you there?
  Taptoe.
  You after the emerald?

Right as rain. What's more, I got a plan.

Can we see it?

No it's my plan I can't be showing it to every —

Okay okay. What's that guy's name behind you?

My name is Sometimes.

You here about the emerald, Sometimes?

I surely am.

Have you got an approach?

Tunneling. I've took some test borings. Looks like a stone cinch.

If this is the right place.

You think this may not be the right place?

The last three places haven't been the right place.

You tryin' to bring me down?

Why would I want to do that? What's that guy's name, the one with the shades?

My name is Brother. Who are all these people?

Businessmen. What do you think of the general situation, Brother?

I think it's crowded. This is my pal, Wednesday.

What say, Wednesday. After the emerald, I presume?

Thought we'd have a go.

Two heads better than one, that the idea?

Yep.

What are you going to do with the emerald, if you get it?

Facet. Facet and facet and facet.

Moll talking to a member of the news media.

Tell me, as a member of the news media, what do you do?

Well we sort of figure out what the news is, then we go out and talk to people, the news makers, those who have made the news —

These having been identified by certain people very high up in your organization.

The editors. The editors are the ones who say this is news, this is not news, maybe this is news, damned if I know whether this is news or not —

And then you go out and talk to people and they tell you everything.

They tell you a surprising number of things, if you are a member of the news media. Even if they have something to hide, questionable behavior or one thing and another, or having killed their wife, that sort of thing, still they tell you the most amazing things. Generally.

About themselves. The newsworthy.

Yes. Then we have our experts in the various fields. They are experts in who is a smart cookie and who is a dumb cookie. They write pieces saying which kind of cookie these various cookies are, so that the reader can make informed choices. About things.

Fascinating work I should think.

Your basic glamour job.

I suppose you would have to be very well educated to get that kind of job.

Extremely well educated. Typing, everything.

Admirable.

Yes. Well, back to the pregnancy. You say it was a seven-year pregnancy.

Yes. When the agency was made clear to me —

The agency was, you contend, extraterrestrial.

It's a fact. Some people can't handle it.

The father was —

He sat in that chair you're sitting in. The red chair. Naked and wearing a morion.

That's all?

Yes he sat naked in the chair wearing only a morion, and engaged me in conversation.

The burden of which was —

Passion.

What was your reaction?

I was surprised. My reaction was surprise.

Did you declare your unworthiness?

Several times. He was unmoved.

Well I don't know, all this sounds a little unreal, like I mean unreal, if you know what I mean.

Oui, je sais.

What role were you playing?

Well obviously I was playing myself. Mad Moll.

What's a morion?

Steel helmet with a crest.

You considered his offer.

More in the nature of a command.

Then, the impregnation. He approached your white or pink as yet undistended belly with his hideously engorged member —

It was more fun than that.

I find it hard to believe, if you'll forgive me, that you, although quite beautiful in your own way, quite lush of figure and fair of face, still the beard on your chin and that black mark like a furry caterpillar crawling in the middle of your forehead —

It's only a small beard after all.

That's true.

And he seemed to like the black mark on my forehead. He caressed it.

So you did in fact enjoy the . . . event. You understand I wouldn't ask these questions, some of which I admit verge on the personal, were I not a duly credentialed member of the press. Custodian as it were of the public's right to know. Everything. Every last little slippy-dippy thing.

Well okay yes I guess that's true strictly speaking. I suppose that's true. Strictly speaking. I could I suppose tell you to buzz off but I respect the public's right to know. I think. An informed public is, I suppose, one of the basic bulwarks of —

Yes I agree but of course I would wouldn't I, being I mean in my professional capacity my professional role —

Yes I see what you mean.

But of course I exist aside from that role, as a person I mean, as a woman like you —

You're not like me.

Well no in the sense that I'm not a witch.

You must forgive me if I insist on this point. You're not like me.

Well, yes, I don't disagree, I'm not arguing, I have not after all produced after a pregnancy of seven years a gigantic emerald weighing seven thousand and thirty-five carats — can I, could I, by the way, see the emerald?

No not right now it's sleeping.

The emerald is sleeping?

Yes it's sleeping right now. It sleeps.

It sleeps?

Yes didn't you hear me it's sleeping right now it sleeps just like any other —

What do you mean the emerald is sleeping?

Just what I said. It's asleep.

Do you talk to it?

Of course, sure I talk to it, it's mine, I mean I *gave birth* to it, I cuddle it and polish it and talk to it, what's so strange about that?

Does it talk to you?

Well I mean it's only one month old. How could it talk?

Hello?

Yes?

Is this Mad Moll?

Yes this is Mad Moll who are you?

You the one who advertised for somebody to stand outside the door and knock down anybody tries to come in?

Yes that's me are you applying for the position?

Yes I think so what does it pay?

Two hundred a week and found.

Well that sounds pretty good but tell me lady who is it I have to knock down for example?

Various parties. Some of them not yet known to me. I mean I have an inkling but no more than that. Are you big?

Six eight.

How many pounds?

Two forty-nine.

IQ?

One forty-six.

What's your best move?

I got a pretty good shove. A not-bad bust in the mouth. I can trip. I can fall on 'em. I can gouge. I have a good sense of where the ears are. I know thumbs and kneecaps.

Where did you get your training?

Just around. High school mostly.

What's your name?

Soapbox.

That's not a very tough name if you'll forgive me.

You want me to change it? I've been called different things in different places.

No I don't want you to change it. It's all right. It'll do.

Okay do you want to see me or do I have the job?

You sound okay to me Soapbox. You can start tomorrow.

What time?

Dawn?

Understand, ye sons of the wise, what this exceedingly precious Stone crieth out to you! Seven years, close to tears. Slept for the first two, dreaming under four blankets, black, blue, brown, brown. Slept and pissed, when I wasn't dreaming I was pissing, I was a fountain. After the first year I knew something irregular was in progress, but not what. I thought, moonstrous! Salivated like a mad dog, four quarts or more a day, when I wasn't pissing I was spitting. Chawed moose steak, moose steak and morels, and fluttered with new men — the butcher, baker, candlestick maker, especially the butcher, one Shatterhand, he was neat. Gobbled a lot of iron, liver, and rust from the bottoms of boats, I had serial nosebleeds every day of the seventeenth trimester. Mood swings of course, heigh-de-ho, instances of false labor in years six and seven, palpating the abdominal wall I felt edges and thought, edges? Then on a cold February night the denouement, at six sixty-six in the evening, or a bit past seven, they sent a Miss Leek to do the delivery, one of us but not the famous one, she gave me scopolamine and a little swan-sweat, that helped, she turned not a hair when the emerald presented itself but placed it in my arms with a kiss or two and a pat or two and drove away, in a coach pulled by a golden pig.

Vandermaster has the Foot.

Yes.

The Foot is very threatening to you.

Indeed.

He is a mage and goes around accompanied by a black blood-hound.

Yes. Tarbut. Said to have been raised on human milk.

Could you give me a little more about the Foot. Who owns it?

Monks. Some monks in a monastery in Merano or outside of Merano. That's in Italy. It's their Foot.

How did Vandermaster get it?

Stole it.

Do you by any chance know what order that is?

Let me see if I can remember — Carthusian.

Can you spell that for me?

C-a-r-t-h-u-s-i-a-n. I think.

Thank you. How did Vandermaster get into the monastery?

They hold retreats, you know, for pious laymen or people who just want to come to the monastery and think about their sins or be edified, for a week or a few days . . .

Can you describe the Foot? Physically?

The Foot proper is encased in silver. It's about the size of a foot, maybe slightly larger. It's cut off just above the ankle. The toe part is rather flat, it's as if people in those days had very flat toes. The whole is quite graceful. The Foot proper sits on top of this rather elaborate base, three levels, gold, little claw feet . . .

And you are convinced that this, uh, reliquary contains the true Foot of Mary Magdalene.

Mary Magdalene's Foot. Yes.

He's threatening you with it.

It has a history of being used against witches, throughout history, to kill them or mar them —

He wants the emerald.

My emerald. Yes.

You won't reveal its parentage. Who the father was.

Oh well hell. Yes. It was the man in the moon. Deus Lunus.

The man in the moon ha-ha.

No I mean it, it was the man in the moon. Deus Lunus as he's called, the moon god. Deus Lunus. Him.

You mean you want me to believe —

Look woman I don't give dandelions what you believe you asked me who the father was. I told you. I don't give a zipper whether you believe me or don't believe me.

You're actually asking me to —

Sat in that chair that chair right there. The red chair.

Oh for heaven's sake all right that's it I'm going to blow this pop stand I know I'm just a dumb ignorant media person but if you think for one minute that . . . I respect your uh conviction but this has got to be a delusionary belief. The man in the moon. A delusionary belief.

Well I agree it sounds funny but there it is. Where else would I get an emerald that big, seven thousand and thirty-five carats? A poor woman like me?

Maybe it's not a real emerald?

If it's not a real emerald why is Vandermaster after me?

You goin' to the hog wrassle?

No I'm after the emerald.

What's your name?

My name is Cold Cuts. What's that machine?

That's an emerald cutter.

How's it work?

Laser beam. You after the emerald too?

Yes I am.

What's your name?

My name is Pro Tem.

That a dowsing rod you got there?

No it's a giant wishbone.

Looks like a dowsing rod.

Well it dowses like a dowsing rod but you also get the wish.

Oh. What's his name?

His name is Plug.

Can't he speak for himself?

He's deaf and dumb.

After the emerald?

Yes. He has special skills.

What are they?

He knows how to diddle certain systems.

Playing it close to the vest is that it?

That's it.

Who's that guy there?

I don't know, all I know about him is he's from Antwerp.

The Emerald Exchange?

That's what I think.

What are all those little envelopes he's holding?
Sealed bids?

Look here, Soapbox, look here.
    What's your name, man?
    My name is Dietrich von Dietersdorf.
    I don't believe it.
    You don't believe my name is my name?
    Pretty fancy name for such a pissant-looking fellow as you.
    I will not be balked. Look here.
    What you got?
    Silver thalers, my friend, thalers big as onion rings.
    That's money, right?
    Right.
    What do I have to do?
    Fall asleep.
    Fall asleep at my post here in front of the door?
    Right. Will you do it?
    I could. But should I?
    Where does this "should" come from?
    My mind. I have a mind, stewing and sizzling.
    Well deal with it, man, deal with it. Will you do it?
    Will I? Will I? Will I? *I don't know!*

Where is my daddy? asked the emerald. My da?
    Moll dropped a glass, which shattered.
    Your father.
    Yes, said the emerald, amn't I supposed to have one?
    He's not here.
    Noticed that, said the emerald.
    I'm never sure what you know and what you don't know.
    I ask in true perplexity.
    He was Deus Lunus. The moon god. Sometimes thought of
as the man in the moon.
    Bosh! said the emerald. I don't believe it.
    Do you believe I'm your mother?
    I do.
    Do you believe you're an emerald?
    I am an emerald.

Used to be, said Moll, women wouldn't drink from a glass into which the moon had shone. For fear of getting knocked up.

Surely this is superstition?

Hoo, hoo, said Moll. I like superstition.

I thought the moon was female.

Don't be culture-bound. It's been female in some cultures at some times, and in others, not.

What did it feel like? The experience.

Not a proper subject for discussion with a child.

The emerald sulking. Green looks here and there.

Well it wasn't the worst. Wasn't the worst. I had an orgasm that lasted for three hours. I judge that not the worst.

What's an orgasm?

Feeling that shoots through one's electrical system giving you little jolts, *spam spam*, many little jolts, *spam spam spam spam* . . .

Teach me something. Teach me something, mother of mine, about this gray world of yours.

What have I to teach? The odd pitiful spell. Most of them won't even put a shine on a pair of shoes.

Teach me one.

"To achieve your heart's desire, burn in water, wash in fire."

What does that do?

French fries. Anything you want French fried.

That's all?

Well.

I have buggered up your tranquillity.

No no no no no.

I'm valuable, said the emerald. I am a thing of value. Over and above my personhood, if I may use the term.

You are a thing of value. A value extrinsic to what I value.

How much?

Equivalent I would say to a third of a sea.

Is that much?

Not inconsiderable.

People want to cut me up and put little chips of me into rings and bangles.

Yes. I'm sorry to say.

Vandermaster is not of this ilk.

Vandermaster is an ilk unto himself.

The more threatening for so being.

Yes.

What are you going to do?

Make me some money. Whatever else is afoot, this delight is constant.

Now the Molljourney the Molltrip into the ferocious Out with a wire shopping cart what's that sucker there doing? tips his hat bends his middle shuffles his feet why he's doing courtly not seen courtly for many a month he does a quite decent courtly I'll smile, briefly, out of my way there citizen sirens shrieking on this swarm summer's day here an idiot there an idiot that one's eying me eyed me on the corner and eyed me round the corner as the Mad Moll song has it and that one standing with his cheek crushed against the warehouse wall and that one browsing in a trash basket and that one picking that one's pocket and that one with the gotch eye and his hands on his I'll twoad 'ee bastard I'll —

Hey there woman come and stand beside me.

Buzz off buster I'm on the King's business and have no time to trifle.

You don't even want to stop a moment and look at this thing I have here?

What sort of thing is it?

Oh it's a rare thing, a beautiful thing, a jim-dandy of a thing, a thing any woman would give her eyeteeth to look upon.

Well yes okay but what is it?

Well I can't tell you. I have to show you. Come and stand over here in the entrance to this dark alley.

Naw man I'm not gonna go into an alley with you what do you think I am a nitwit?

I think you're a beautiful woman even if you do have that bit of beard there on your chin like a piece of burnt toast or something, most becoming. And that mark like a dead insect on your forehead gives you a certain —

Cut the crap daddy and show me what you got. Standing right here. Else I'm on my way.

No it's too rich and strange for the full light of day we have to have some shadow, it's too —

If this turns out to be an ordinary —

No no no nothing like that. You mean you think I might be a what-do-you-call-'em, one of those guys who —

Your discourse sir strongly suggests it.

And your name?

Moll. Mad Moll. Sometimes Moll the Poor Girl.

Beautiful name. Your mother's name or the name of some favorite auntie?

Moll totals him with a bang in the balls.

Jesus Christ these creeps what can you do?

She stops at a store and buys a can of gem polish.

Polish my emerald so bloody bright it will bloody blind you.

Sitting on the street with a basket of dirty faces for sale. The dirty faces are all colors, white black yellow tan rosy-red.

Buy a dirty face! Slap it on your wife! Buy a dirty face! Complicate your life!

But no one buys.

A boy appears pushing a busted bicycle.

Hey lady what are those things there they look like faces.

That's what they are, faces.

Lady, Halloween is not until —

Okay kid move along you don't want to buy a face move along.

But those are actual faces lady Christ I mean they're *actual faces* —

Fourteen ninety-five kid you got any money on you?

I don't even want to *touch* one, look like they came off dead people.

Would you feel better if I said they were plastic?

Well I hope to God they're not —

Okay they're plastic. What's the matter with your bike?

Chain's shot.

Give it here.

The boy hands over the bicycle chain.

Moll puts the broken ends in her mouth and chews for a moment.

Okay here you go.

The boy takes it in his hands and yanks on it. It's fixed.

Shit how'd you do that lady?

Moll spits and wipes her mouth on her sleeve.

Run along now kid beat it I'm tired of you.

Are you magic, lady?

Not enough.

Moll at home playing her oboe.

I love the oboe. The sound of the oboe.

The noble, noble oboe!

Of course it's not to every taste. Not everyone swings with the oboe.

Whoops! Goddamn oboe let me take that again.

Not perhaps the premier instrument of the present age. What would that be? The bullhorn, no doubt.

Why did he interfere with me? Why?

Maybe has to do with the loneliness of the gods. Oh thou great one whom I adore beyond measure, oh thou bastard and fatherer of bastards —

Tucked-away gods whom nobody speaks to anymore. Once so lively.

Polish my emerald so bloody bright it will bloody blind you.

Good God what's that?

Vandermaster used the Foot!

Oh my God look at that hole!

It's awful and tremendous!

What in the name of God?

Vandermaster used the Foot!

The Foot did that? I don't believe it!

You don't believe it? What's your name?

My name is Coddle. I don't believe the Foot could have done that. I one hundred percent don't believe it.

Well it's right there in front of your eyes. Do you think Moll and the emerald are safe?

The house seems structurally sound. Smoke-blackened, but sound.

What happened to Soapbox?

You mean Soapbox who was standing in front of the house poised to bop any mother's son who —

Good Lord Soapbox is nowhere to be seen!

He's not in the hole!

Let me see there. What's your name?

My name is Mixer. No, he's not in the hole. Not a shred of him in the hole.

Good, true Soapbox!

You think Moll is still inside? How do we know this is the right place after all?

Heard it on the radio. What's your name by the way?

My name is Ho Ho. Look at the ground smoking!

The whole thing is tremendous, demonstrating the awful power of the Foot!

I am shaking with awe right now! Poor Soapbox!

Noble, noble Soapbox!

Mr. Vandermaster.

Madam.

You may be seated.

I thank you.

The red chair.

Thank you very much.

May I offer you some refreshment?

Yes I will have a splash of something thank you.

It's scotch I believe.

Yes scotch.

And I will join you I think, as the week has been a most fatiguing one.

Care and cleaning I take it.

Yes, care and cleaning and in addition there was a media person here.

How tiresome.

Yes it was tiresome in the extreme her persistence in her peculiar vocation is quite remarkable.

Wanted to know about the emerald I expect.

She was most curious about the emerald.

Disbelieving.

Yes disbelieving but perhaps that is an attribute of the profession?

So they say. Did she see it?

No it was sleeping and I did not wish to —

Of course. How did this person discover that you had as

it were made yourself an object of interest to the larger public?

Indiscretion on the part of the midwitch I suppose, some people cannot maintain even minimal discretion.

Yes that's the damned thing about some people. Their discretion is out to lunch.

Blabbing things about would be an example.

Popping off to all and sundry about matters.

Ah well.

Ah well. Could we, do you think, proceed?

If we must.

I have the Foot.

Right.

You have the emerald.

Correct.

The Foot has certain properties of special interest to witches.

So I have been told.

There is a distaste, a bad taste in the brain, when one is forced to put the boots to someone.

Must be terrible for you, terrible. Where is my man Soapbox by the way?

That thug you had in front of the door?

Yes, Soapbox.

He is probably reintegrating himself with the basic matter of the universe, right now. Fascinating experience I should think.

Good to know.

I intend only the best for the emerald, however.

What is the best?

There are as you are aware others not so scrupulous in the field. Chiselers, in every sense.

And you? What do you intend for it?

I have been thinking of emerald dust. Emerald dust with soda, emerald dust with tomato juice, emerald dust with a dash of bitters, emerald dust with Ovaltine.

I beg your pardon?

I want to live twice.

Twice?

In addition to my present life, I wish another, future life.

A second life. Incremental to the one you are presently enjoying.

As a boy, I was very poor. Poor as pine.

And you have discovered a formula.

Yes.

Plucked from the arcanum.

Yes. Requires a certain amount of emerald. Powdered emerald.

Ugh!

Carat's weight a day for seven thousand thirty-five days.

Coincidence.

Not at all. Only *this* emerald will do. A moon's emerald born of human witch.

No.

I have been thinking about bouillon. Emerald dust and bouillon with a little Tabasco.

No.

No?

No.

My mother is eighty-one, said Vandermaster. I went to my mother and said, Mother, I want to be in love.

And she replied?

She said, me too.

Lily the media person standing in the hall.

I came back to see if you were ready to confess. The hoax.

It's talking now. It talks.

It what?

Lovely complete sentences. Maxims and truisms.

I don't want to hear this. I absolutely —

Look kid this is going to cost you. Sixty dollars.

Sixty dollars for what?

For the interview.

That's checkbook journalism!

Sho' nuff.

It's against the highest traditions of the profession!

You get paid, your boss gets paid, the stockholders get their whack, why not us members of the raw material? Why shouldn't the raw material get paid?

It talks?

Most assuredly it talks.

Will you take a check?

If I must.

You're really a witch.

How many times do I have to tell you?

You do tricks or anything?

Consulting, you might say.

You have clients? People who come to see you regularly on a regular basis?

People with problems, yes.

What kind of problems, for instance?

Some of them very simple, really, things that just need a specific, bit of womandrake for example —

What's womandrake?

Black bryony. Called the herb of beaten wives. Takes away black-and-blue marks.

You get beaten wives?

Stick a little of that number into the old man's pork and beans, he retches. For seven days and seven nights. It near to kills him.

I have a problem.

What's the problem?

The editor, or editor-king, as he's called around the shop.

What about him?

He takes my stuff and throws it on the floor. When he doesn't like it.

On the floor?

I know it's nothing to you but it *hurts me.* I cry. I know I shouldn't cry but I cry. When I see my stuff on the floor. Pages and pages of it, so carefully typed, *every word spelled right* —

Don't you kids have a union?

Yes but he won't speak to it.

That's this man Lather, right?

Mr. Lather. Editor-imperator.

Okay I'll look into it that'll be another sixty you want to pay now or you want to be billed?

I'll give you another check. *Can* Vandermaster live twice?

There are two theories, the General Theory and the Special Theory. I take it he is relying on the latter. Requires ingestion of a certain amount of emerald. Powdered emerald.

Can you defend yourself?

I have a few things in mind. A few little things.

Can I see the emerald now?

You may. Come this way.

Thank you. Thank you at last. My that's impressive what's that?

That's the thumb of a thief. Enlarged thirty times. Bronze. I use it in my work.

Impressive if one believed in that sort of thing ha-ha I don't mean to —

What care I? What care I? In here. Little emerald, this is Lily. Lily, this is the emerald.

Enchanté, said the emerald. What a pretty young woman you are!

This emerald is young, said Lily. Young, but good. I do not believe what I am seeing with my very eyes!

But perhaps that is a sepsis of the profession? said the emerald.

Vandermaster wants to live twice!

Oh, most foul, most foul!

He was very poor, as a boy! Poor as pine!

Hideous presumption! Cheeky hubris!

He wants to be in love! In love! Presumably with another person!

Unthinkable insouciance!

We'll have his buttons for dinner!

We'll clean the gutters with his hair!

What's your name, buddy?

My name is Tree and I'm smokin' mad!

My name is Bump and I'm just about ready to bust!

I think we should break out the naked-bladed pikes!

I think we should lay hand to torches and tar!

To live again! From the beginning! *Ab ovo!* This concept riles the very marrow of our minds!

We'll flake the white meat from his bones!

And that goes for his damned dog, too!

Hello is this Mad Moll?

Yes who is this?

My name is Lather.

The editor?

Editor-king, actually.

Yes Mr. Lather what is the name of your publication I don't know that Lily ever —

World. I put it together. When *World* is various and beautiful, it's because I am various and beautiful. When *World* is sad and dreary, it's because I am sad and dreary. When *World* is not thy friend, it's because *I* am not thy friend. And if I am not thy friend, baby —

I get the drift.

Listen, Moll, I am not satisfied with what Lily's been giving me. She's not giving me potato chips. I have decided that I am going to handle this story personally, from now on.

She's been insufficiently insightful and comprehensive?

Gore, that's what we need, actual or psychological gore, and this twitter she's been filing — anyhow, I have sent her to Detroit.

Not Detroit!

She's going to be second night-relief paper clipper in the Detroit bureau. She's standing here right now with her bags packed and ashes in her hair and her ticket in her mouth.

Why in her mouth?

Because she needs her hands to rend her garments with.

All right Mr. Lather send her back around. There is new bad news. Bad, bad, new bad news.

That's wonderful!

Moll hangs up the phone and weeps every tear she's capable of weeping, one, two, three.

Takes up a lump of clay, beats it flat with a Bible.

Let me see what do I have here?

I have Ya Ya Oil, that might do it.

I have Anger Oil, Lost & Away Oil, Confusion Oil, Weed of Misfortune, and War Water.

I have graveyard chips, salt, and coriander — enough coriander to freight a ship. Tasty coriander. Magical, magical coriander!

I'll eye-bite the son of a bitch. Have him in worm's hall by teatime.

Understand, ye sons of the wise, what this exceedingly precious Stone crieth out to you!

I'll fold that sucker's tent for him. If my stuff works. One never knows for sure, dammit. And where is Papa?

Throw in a little dwale now, a little orris . . .

Moll shapes the clay into the figure of a man.

So mote it be!

What happened was that they backed a big van up to the back door.

Yes.

There were four of them or eight of them.

Yes.

It was two in the morning or three in the morning or four in the morning — I'm not sure.

Yes.

They were great big hairy men with cudgels and ropes and pads like movers have and a dolly and come-alongs made of barbed wire — that's a loop of barbed wire big enough to slip over somebody's head, with a handle —

Yes.

They wrapped the emerald in the pads and placed it on the dolly and tied ropes around it and got it down the stairs through the door and into the van.

Did they use the Foot?

No they didn't use the Foot they had four witches with them.

Which witches?

The witches Aldrin, Endrin, Lindane, and Dieldrin. Bad-ass witches.

You knew them.

Only by repute. And Vandermaster was standing there with clouds of 1, 1, 2, 2-tetrachloroethylene seething from his nostrils.

That's toxic.

Extremely. I was staggering around bumping into things, tried to hold on to the walls but the walls fell away from me and I fell after them trying to hold on.

These other witches, they do anything to you?

Kicked me in the ribs when I was on the floor. With their pointed shoes. I woke up emeraldless.

Right. Well I guess we'd better get the vast resources of our

organization behind this. *World.* From sea to shining sea to shining sea. I'll alert all the bureaus in every direction.

What good will that do?

It will harry them. When a free press is on the case, you can't
get away with anything really terrible.

But look at this.

What is it?

A solid silver louse. They left it.

What's it mean?

Means that the devil himself has taken an interest.

A free press, madam, is not afraid of the devil himself.

Who cares what's in a witch's head? Pretty pins for sticking
pishtoshio redthread for sewing names to shrouds gallant clank-
ers I'll twoad 'ee and the gollywobbles to give away and the
trinkumtrankums to give away with a generous hand pricksticks
for the eye damned if I do and damned if I don't what's that
upon her forehead? said my father it's a mark said my mother
black mark like a furry caterpillar I'll scrub it away with the Ajax
and what's that upon her chin? said my father it's a bit of a
beard said my mother I'll pluck it away with the tweezers and
what's that upon her mouth? said my father it must be a smirk
said my mother I'll wipe it away with the heel of my hand she's
got hair down there already said my father is that natural? I'll
shave it said my mother no one will ever know and those said
my father pointing *those?* Just what they look like said my
mother I'll make a bandeau with this nice clean dish towel she'll
be flat as a jack of diamonds in no time and where's the belly
button? said my father flipping me about I don't see one anywhere must be coming along later said my mother I'll just pencil
one in here with the Magic Marker this child is a bit of a mutt
said my father recall to me if you will the circumstances of her
conception it was a dark and stormy night said my mother . . .
But who cares what's in a witch's head caskets of cankers shelves
of twoads for twoading paxwax scalpel polish people with scares
sticking to their faces memories of God who held me up and
sustained me until I fell from His hands into the world . . .

Twice? Twice? Twice? Twice?

*

Hey Moll.
Who's that?
It's me.
Me who?
Soapbox.
Soapbox!
I got it!
Got what?
The Foot! I got it right here!
I thought you were blown up!
Naw I pretended to be bought so I was out of the way. Went with them back to their headquarters, or den. Then when they put the Foot back in the refrigerator I grabbed it and beat it back here.
They kept it in the refrigerator?
It needs a constant temperature or else it gets restless. It's hot tempered. They said.
It's elegant. Weighs a ton though.
Be careful you might —
Soapbox, I am not totally without — it's warm to the hand.
Yes it is warm I noticed that, look what else I got.
What are those?
Thalers. Thalers big as onion rings. Forty-two grand worth.
What are you going to do with them?
Conglomerate!

It is wrong to want to live twice, said the emerald. If I may venture an opinion.

I was very poor, as a boy, said Vandermaster. Nothing to eat but gruel. It was gruel, gruel, gruel. I was fifteen before I ever saw an onion.

These matters are matters upon which I hesitate to pronounce, being a new thing in the world, said the emerald. A latecomer to the welter. But it seems to me that, having weltered, the wish to *re*welter might be thought greedy.

Gruel today, gruel yesterday, gruel tomorrow. Sometimes gruel substitutes. I burn to recoup.

Something was said I believe about love.

The ghostfish of love has eluded me these forty-five years.

That Lily person is a pleasant person I think. And pretty too. Very pretty. Good-looking.

Yes she is.

I particularly like the way she is dedicated. She's extremely dedicated. Very dedicated. To her work.

Yes I do not disagree. Admirable. A free press is, I believe, an essential component of —

She is true-blue. Probably it would be great fun to talk to her and get to know her and kiss her and sleep with her and everything of that nature.

What are you suggesting?

Well, there's then, said the emerald, that is to say, your splendid second life.

Yes?

And then there's now. Now is sooner than then.

You have a wonderfully clear head, said Vandermaster, for a rock.

Okay, said Lily, I want you to tap once for yes and twice for no. Do you understand that?

Tap.

You are the true Foot of Mary Magdalene?

Tap.

Vandermaster stole you from a monastery in Italy?

Tap.

A Carthusian monastery in Merano or outside Merano?

Tap.

Are you uncomfortable in that reliquary?

Tap tap.

Have you killed any witches lately? In the last year or so?

Tap tap.

Are you morally neutral or do you have opinions?

Tap.

You have opinions?

Tap.

In the conflict we are now witnessing between Moll and Vandermaster, which of the parties seems to you to have right and justice on her side?

Tap tap tap tap.

That mean Moll? One tap for each letter?
Tap.
Is it warm in there?
Tap.
Too warm?
Tap tap.
So you have been, in a sense, an unwilling partner in Vander-master's machinations.
Tap.
And you would not be averse probably to using your consid-erable powers on Moll's behalf.
Tap.
Do you know where Vandermaster is right now?
Tap tap.
Have you any idea what his next move will be?
Tap tap.
What is your opinion of the women's movement?
Tap tap tap tap tap tap tap tap tap tap tap tap tap tap.
I'm sorry I didn't get that. Do you have a favorite color what do you think of cosmetic surgery should children be allowed to watch television after ten P.M. how do you feel about aging is nuclear energy in your opinion a viable alternative to fossil fuels how do you deal with stress are you afraid to fly and do you have a chili recipe you'd care to share with the folks?
Tap tap.
The first interview in the world with the true Foot of Mary Magdalene and no chili recipe!

Mrs. Vandermaster.
    Yes.
    Please be seated.
    Thank you.
    The red chair.
    You're most kind.
    Can I get you something, some iced tea or a little hit of Sanka?
    A Ghost Dance is what I wouldn't mind if you can do it.
    What's a Ghost Dance?
    That's one part vodka to one part tequila with half an onion. Half a regular onion.

Wow wow wow wow wow.

Well when you're eighty-one, you know, there's not so much. Couple of Ghost Dances, I begin to take an interest.

I believe I can accommodate you.

Couple of Ghost Dances, I begin to look up and take notice.

Mrs. Vandermaster, you are aware are you not that your vile son has, with the aid of various parties, abducted my child? My own true emerald?

I mighta heard about it.

Well have you or haven't you?

'Course I don't pay much attention to that boy myself. He's bent.

Bent?

Him and his dog. He goes off in a corner and talks to the dog. Looking over his shoulder to see if I'm listening. As if I'd care.

The dog doesn't —

Just listens. *Intently.*

That's Tarbut.

Now I don't mind somebody who just addresses an occasional remark to the dog, like "Attaboy, dog," or something like that, or "Get the ball, dog," or something like that, but he *confides in* the dog. Bent.

You know what Vandermaster's profession is.

Yes, he's a mage. Think that's a little bent.

Is there anything you can do, or would do, to help me get my child back? My sweet emerald?

Well I don't have that much say-so.

You don't.

I don't know too much about what-all he's up to. He comes and goes.

I see.

The thing is, he's bent.

You told me.

Wants to live twice.

I know.

I think it's a sin and a shame.

You do.

And your poor little child.

Yes.

A damned scandal.
Yes.
I'd witch his eyes out if I were you.
The thought's appealing.
His eyes like onions . . .

A black bloodhound who looks as if he might have been fed on human milk. Bloodhounding down the center of the street, nose to the ground.
You think this will work?
Soapbox, do you have a better idea?
Where did you find him?
I found him on the doorstep. Sitting there. In the moonlight.
In the moonlight?
Aureoled all around with moonglow.
You think that's significant?
Well I don't think it's happenstance.
What's his name?
Tarbut.
There's something I have to tell you.
What?
I went to the refrigerator for a beer.
Yes?
The Foot's walked.

Dead! Kicked in the heart by the Foot!
That's incredible!
Deep footprint right over the breastbone!
That's ghastly and awful!
After Lily turned him down he went after the emerald with a sledge!
Was the emerald hurt?
Chipped! The Foot got there in the nick!
And Moll?
She's gluing the chips back with grume!
What's grume?
Clotted blood!
And was the corpse claimed?
Three devils showed up! Lily's interviewing them right now!

A free press is not afraid of a thousand devils!
There are only three!
What do they look like?
Like Lather, the editor!
And the Foot?
Soapbox is taking it back to Italy! He's starting a security-guard business! Hired Sallywag, Wide Boy, Taptoe, and Sometimes!
What's your name by the way?
My name is Knucks. What's your name?
I'm Pebble. And the dog?
The dog's going to work for Soapbox too!
Curious, the dog showing up on Moll's doorstep that way!
Deus Lunus works in mysterious ways!
Deus Lunus never lets down a pal!
Well how 'bout a drink!
Don't mind if I do! What'll we drink to?
We'll drink to living once!
Hurrah for the here and now!

Tell me, said the emerald, what are diamonds like?
I know little of diamonds, said Moll.
Is a diamond better than an emerald?
Apples and oranges I would say.
Would you have *preferred* a diamond?
Nope.
Diamond-hard, said the emerald, that's an expression I've encountered.
Diamonds are a little ordinary. Decent, yes. Quiet, yes. But *gray*. Give me step-cut zircons, square-cut spodumenes, jasper, sardonyx, bloodstones, Baltic amber, cursed opals, peridots of your own hue, the padparadscha sapphire, yellow chrysoberyls, the shifty tourmaline, cabochons . . . But best of all, an emerald.
But what is the *meaning* of the emerald? asked Lily. I mean overall? If you can say.
I have some notions, said Moll. You may credit them or not.
Try me.
It means, one, that the gods are not yet done with us.
Gods not yet done with us.

The gods are still trafficking with us and making interventions of this kind and that kind and are not dormant or dead as has often been proclaimed by dummies.

Still trafficking. Not dead.

Just as in former times a demon might enter a nun on a piece of lettuce she was eating so even in these times a simple Mailgram might be the thin edge of the wedge.

Thin edge of the wedge.

Two, the world may congratulate itself that desire can still be raised in the dulled hearts of the citizens by the rumor of an emerald.

Desire or cupidity?

I do not distinguish qualitatively among the desires, we have referees for that, but he who covets not at all is a lump and I do not wish to have him to dinner.

Positive attitude toward desire.

Yes. Three, I do not know what this Stone portends, whether it portends for the better or portends for the worse or merely portends a bubbling of the in-between but you are in any case rescued from the sickliness of same and a small offering in the hat on the hall table would not be ill regarded.

And what now? said the emerald. What now, beautiful mother?

We resume the scrabble for existence, said Moll. We resume the scrabble for existence, in the sweet of the here and now.

CYNTHIA OZICK

"The Shawl" was selected for the 1981 edition of both *The Best American Short Stories* and *Prize Stories: The O. Henry Awards.* Hortense Calisher called it "a long story, profoundly short." It is a Holocaust story that dramatizes inevitability, courage, and truth in what appears as a single burst of inspiration. Cynthia Ozick, an author for whom the Holocaust is a frequent subject, has published several books of fiction in addition to essays, poetry, criticism, and translations. Born, raised, and educated in New York City, she lives in New Rochelle, New York.

The Shawl

STELLA, cold, cold, the coldness of hell. How they walked on the roads together, Rosa with Magda curled up between sore breasts, Magda wound up in the shawl. Sometimes Stella carried Magda. But she was jealous of Magda. A thin girl of fourteen, too small, with thin breasts of her own, Stella wanted to be wrapped in a shawl, hidden away, asleep, rocked by the march, a baby, a round infant in arms. Magda took Rosa's nipple, and Rosa never stopped walking, a walking cradle. There was not enough milk; sometimes Magda sucked air; then she screamed. Stella was ravenous. Her knees were tumors on sticks, her elbows chicken bones.

Rosa did not feel hunger; she felt light, not like someone walking but like someone in a faint, in trance, arrested in a fit, someone who is already a floating angel, alert and seeing everything, but in the air, not there, not touching the road. As if teetering on the tips of her fingernails. She looked into Magda's face through a gap in the shawl: a squirrel in a nest, safe, no one could reach her inside the little house of the shawl's windpings. The face, very round, a pocket mirror of a face: but it was not Rosa's bleak complexion, dark like cholera, it was another kind of face altogether, eyes blue as air, smooth feathers of hair nearly as yellow as the Star sewn into Rosa's coat. You could think she was one of *their* babies.

Rosa, floating, dreamed of giving Magda away in one of the villages. She could leave the line for a minute and push Magda into the hands of any woman on the side of the road. But if she moved out of line they might shoot. And even if she fled the line for half a second and pushed the shawl-bundle at a stranger, would the woman take it? She might be surprised, or afraid; she might drop the shawl, and Magda would fall out and strike her head and die. The little round head. Such a good child, she gave up screaming, and sucked now only for the taste of the drying nipple itself. The neat grip of the tiny gums. One mite of a tooth tip sticking up in the bottom gum, how shining, an elfin tombstone of white marble gleaming there. Without complaining, Magda relinquished Rosa's teats, first the left, then the right; both were cracked, not a sniff of milk. The duct-crevice extinct, a dead volcano, blind eye, chill hole, so Magda took the corner of the shawl and milked it instead. She sucked and sucked, flooding the threads with wetness. The shawl's good flavor, milk of linen.

It was a magic shawl, it could nourish an infant for three days and three nights. Magda did not die, she stayed alive, although very quiet. A peculiar smell, of cinnamon and almonds, lifted out of her mouth. She held her eyes open every moment, forgetting how to blink or nap, and Rosa and sometimes Stella studied their blueness. On the road they raised one burden of a leg after another and studied Magda's face. "Aryan," Stella said, in a voice grown as thin as a string; and Rose thought how Stella gazed at Magda like a young cannibal. And the time that Stella said "Aryan," it sounded to Rosa as if Stella had really said "Let us devour her."

But Magda lived to walk. She lived that long, but she did not walk very well, partly because she was only fifteen months old, and partly because the spindles of her legs could not hold up her fat belly. It was fat with air, full and round. Rosa gave almost all her food to Magda, Stella gave nothing; Stella was ravenous, a growing child herself, but not growing much. Stella did not menstruate. Rosa did not menstruate. Rosa was ravenous, but also not; she learned from Magda how to drink the taste of a finger in one's mouth. They were in a place without pity, all pity was annihilated in Rosa, she looked at Stella's bones without pity. She was sure that Stella was waiting for Magda to die so she could put her teeth into the little thighs.

Rosa knew Magda was going to die very soon; she should have been dead already, but she had been buried away deep inside the magic shawl, mistaken there for the shivering mound of Rosa's breasts; Rosa clung to the shawl as if it covered only herself. No one took it away from her. Magda was mute. She never cried. Rosa hid her in the barracks, under the shawl, but she knew that one day someone would inform; or one day someone, not even Stella, would steal Magda to eat her. When Magda began to walk, Rosa knew that Magda was going to die very soon, something would happen. She was afraid to fall asleep; she slept with the weight of her thigh on Magda's body; she was afraid she would smother Magda under her thigh. The weight of Rosa was becoming less and less; Rosa and Stella were slowly turning into air.

Magda was quiet, but her eyes were horribly alive, like blue tigers. She watched. Sometimes she laughed — it seemed a laugh, but how could it be? Magda had never seen anyone laugh. Still, Magda laughed at her shawl when the wind blew its corners, the bad wind with pieces of black in it, that made Stella's and Rosa's eyes tear. Magda's eyes were always clear and tearless. She watched like a tiger. She guarded her shawl. No one could touch it; only Rosa could touch it. Stella was not allowed. The shawl was Magda's own baby, her pet, her little sister. She tangled herself up in it and sucked on one of the corners when she wanted to be very still.

Then Stella took the shawl away and made Magda die.

Afterward Stella said: "I was cold."

And afterward she was always cold, always. The cold went into her heart: Rosa saw that Stella's heart was cold. Magda flopped onward with her little pencil legs scribbling this way and that, in search of the shawl; the pencils faltered at the barracks opening, where the light began. Rosa saw and pursued. But already Magda was in the square outside the barracks, in the jolly light. It was the roll-call arena. Every morning Rosa had to conceal Magda under the shawl against a wall of the barracks and go out and stand in the arena with Stella and hundreds of others, sometimes for hours, and Magda, deserted, was quiet under the shawl, sucking on her corner. Every day Magda was silent, and so she did not die. Rosa saw that today Magda was going to die, and at the same time a fearful joy ran in Rosa's two palms, her fingers were on fire, she was astonished, febrile: Magda, in the sunlight, swaying on her pencil legs, was howling. Ever since the drying up of Rosa's nipples, ever since Magda's last scream on the road, Magda had been devoid of any syllable; Magda was a mute. Rosa believed that something had gone wrong with her vocal cords, with her windpipe, with the cave of her larynx; Magda was defective, without a voice; perhaps she was deaf; there might be something amiss with her intelligence; Magda was dumb. Even the laugh that came when the ash-stippled wind made a clown out of Magda's shawl was only the air-blown showing of her teeth. Even when the lice, head lice and body lice, crazed her so that she became as wild as one of the big rats that plundered the barracks at daybreak looking for carrion, she rubbed and scratched and kicked and bit and rolled without a whimper. But now Magda's mouth was spilling a long viscous rope of clamor.

"Maaaa —"

It was the first noise Magda had ever sent out from her throat since the drying up of Rosa's nipples.

"Maaaa . . . aaa!"

Again! Magda was wavering in the perilous sunlight of the arena, scribbling on such pitiful little bent shins. Rosa saw. She saw that Magda was grieving for the loss of her shawl, she saw that Magda was going to die. A tide of commands hammered in Rosa's nipples: Fetch, get, bring! But she did not know which to go after first, Magda or the shawl. If she jumped out into the arena to snatch Magda up, the howling would not stop, because Magda would still not have the shawl; but if she ran back into the barracks to find the shawl, and if she found it, and if she came after Magda holding it and shaking it, then she would get Magda back, Magda would put the shawl in her mouth and turn dumb again.

Rosa entered the dark. It was easy to discover the shawl. Stella was heaped under it, asleep in her thin bones. Rosa tore the shawl free and flew — she could fly, she was only air — into the arena. The sunheat murmured of another life, of butterflies in summer. The light was placid, mellow. On the other side of the steel fence, far away, there were green meadows speckled with dandelions and deep-colored violets; beyond them, even farther, innocent tiger lilies, tall, lifting their orange bonnets. In the barracks they spoke of "flowers," of "rain": excrement, thick turd-braids, and the slow stinking maroon waterfall that slunk down from the upper bunks, the stink mixed with a bitter fatty floating smoke that greased Rosa's skin. She stood for an instant at the margin of the arena. Sometimes the electricity inside the fence would seem to hum; even Stella said it was only an imagining, but Rosa heard real sounds in the wire: grainy sad voices. The farther she was from the fence, the more clearly the voices crowded at her. The lamenting voices strummed so convincingly, so passionately, it was impossible to suspect them of being phantoms. The voices told her to hold up the shawl, high; the voices told her to shake it, to whip with it, to unfurl it like a flag. Rosa lifted, shook, whipped, unfurled. Far off, very far, Magda leaned across her air-fed belly, reaching out with the rods of her arms. She was high up, elevated, riding someone's shoulder. But the shoulder that carried Magda was not coming toward Rosa and the shawl, it was drifting away, the speck of Magda was moving more and more into the smoky distance. Above the shoulder a helmet glinted. The light tapped the helmet and sparkled it into a goblet. Below the helmet a black body like a domino and a pair of black boots hurled themselves in the direction of the electrified fence. The electric voices began to chatter wildly. "Maamaa, maaamaaa," they all hummed together. How far Magda was from Rosa now, across the whole square, past a dozen barracks, all the way on the other side! She was no bigger than a moth.

All at once Magda was swimming through the air. The whole of Magda traveled through loftiness. She looked like a butterfly touching a silver vine. And the moment Magda's feathered round head and her pencil legs and balloonish belly and zigzag arms splashed against the fence, the steel voices went mad in their growling, urging Rosa to run and run to the spot where Magda had fallen from her flight against the electrified fence; but of course Rosa did not obey them. She only stood, because if she ran they would shoot, and if she tried to pick up the sticks of Magda's body they would shoot, and if she let the wolf's screech ascending now through the ladder of her skeleton break out, they would shoot; so she took Magda's shawl and filled her own mouth with it, stuffed it in and stuffed it in, until she was swallowing up the wolf's screech and tasting the cinnamon and almond depth of Magda's saliva; and Rosa drank Magda's shawl until it dried.

ROBERT COOVER

"A Working Day" concerns a chambermaid and her employer
who embark upon a memorable relationship. Is the story, asked
Hortense Calisher, "a send-up of the sad and hilarious yet sometimes exquisite repetitiousness of porn" or of "the once nouvelle
nouvelle vague"? Both? Calisher was certain of this: "Coover has
created, inch by rigorous inch, two characters who have turned,
as if in bas-relief, into real people, in a bedroom carved by these
progressions into forever's brilliant 'still.' " Robert Coover was
born in Iowa and has lived in a number of American cities and
in Europe. He has written novels, short stories, plays, film
scripts, and essays.

A Working Day

SHE ENTERS, deliberately, gravely, without affectation, circumspect in her motions (as she's been taught), not stamping too
loud, nor dragging her legs after her, but advancing sedately,
discreetly, glancing briefly at the empty rumpled bed, the cast-
off nightclothes. She hesitates. No. Again. She enters. Deliberately and gravely, without affectation, not stamping too loud,
nor dragging her legs after her, not marching as if leading a
dance, nor keeping time with her head and hands, nor staring
or turning her head either one way or the other, but advancing
sedately and discreetly through the door, across the polished
floor, past the empty rumpled bed and cast-off nightclothes (not
glancing, that's better), to the tall curtains along the far wall. As
she's been taught. Now, with a humble yet authoritative gesture,
she draws the curtains open: Ah! the morning sunlight comes
flooding in over the gleaming tiles as though (she thinks) flung
from a bucket. She opens wide the glass doors behind the curtains (there is such a song of birds all about!) and gazes for a

moment into the garden, quite prepared to let the sweet breath of morning blow in and excite her to the most generous and efficient accomplishments, but her mind is still locked on that image, at first pleasing, now troubling, of the light as it spilled into the room: as from a bucket . . . She sighs. She enters. With a bucket. She sets the bucket down, deliberately, gravely, and walks (circumspectly) across the room, over the polished tiles, past the empty rumpled bed (she doesn't glance at it), to draw open the tall curtains at the far wall. Buckets of light come flooding in (she is not thinking about this now) and the room, as she opens wide the glass doors, is sweetened by the fresh morning air blowing in from the garden. The sun is fully risen and the pink clouds of dawn are all gone out of the sky (the time lost: this is what she is thinking about), but the dew is still on every plant in the garden, and everything looks clean and bright. As will his room when she is done with it.

He awakes from a dream (something about utility, or futility, and a teacher he once had who, when he whipped his students, called it his "civil service"), still wrapped in darkness and hugged close to the sweet breast of the night, but with the new day already hard upon him, just beyond the curtains (he knows, even without looking), waiting for him out there like a brother: to love him or to kill him. He pushes the bedcovers back and sits up groggily to meet its challenge (or promise), pushes his feet into slippers, rubs his face, stretches, wonders what new blunders the maid (where is she?) will commit today. Well. I should at least give her a chance, he admonishes himself with a gaping yawn.

Oh, she knows her business well: to scrub and wax the floors, polish the furniture, make the master's bed soft and easy, lay up his nightclothes, wash, starch, and mend the bedlinens as necessary, air the blankets and clean the bathroom, making certain of ample supplies of fresh towels and washcloths, soap, toilet paper, razor blades and toothpaste — in short, to see that nothing be wanting which he desires or requires to be done, being always diligent in endeavoring to please him, silent when he is angry except to beg his pardon, and ever faithful, honest, submissive, and of good disposition. The trivial round, the common task, she knows as she sets about her morning's duties, will furnish all she needs to ask, room to deny herself, a road (speaking loosely) to bring her daily nearer God. But on that road, on the floor of the bathroom, she finds a damp towel and some pajama bottoms, all puddled together like a cast-off mop-head. Mop-head? She turns and gazes in dismay at the empty bucket by the outer door. Why, she wants to know, tears springing to the corners of her eyes, can't it be easier than this? And so she enters, sets her bucket down with firm deliberation, leans her mop gravely against the wall. Also a broom, brushes, some old rags, counting things off on her fingers as she deposits them. The curtains have been drawn open and the room is already (as though impatiently) awash with morning sunlight. She crosses the room, past the (no glances) empty rumpled bed, and opens wide the glass doors leading out into the garden, letting in the sweet breath of morning, which she hardly notices. She has resolved this morning — as every morning — to be cheerful and good-natured, such that if any accident should happen to test that resolution, she should not suffer it to put her out of temper with everything besides, but such resolutions are more easily sworn than obeyed. Things are already in such a state! Yet: virtue is made for difficulties, she reminds herself, and grows stronger and brighter for such trials, *"Oh, teach me, my God and King, in all things thee to see, and what I do in any thing, to do it as for thee!"* she sings out to the garden and to the room, feeling her heart lift like a sponge in a bucket. *"A servant with this clause makes drudgery divine: who sweeps a room, as for thy laws, makes that and th'action fine!"* And yes, she can still recover the lost time. She has everything now, the mop and bucket, broom, rags, and brushes, her apron pockets are full of polishes, dustcloths, and cleaning powders, the cupboards are well stocked with fresh linens, all she really needs now is to keep — but ah! is there, she wonders anxiously, spinning abruptly on her heels as she hears the master relieving himself noisily in the bathroom, any *water* in the bucket — ?!

He awakes, squints at his watch in the darkness, grunts (she's late, but just as well, time for a shower), and with only a mo-

ment's hesitation, tosses the blankets back, tearing himself free:
I'm so old, he thinks, and still every morning is a bloody new
birth. Somehow it should be easier than this. He sits up painfully
(that divine government!), rubs his face, pushes his feet into
slippers, stands, stretches, then strides to the windows at the far
wall and throws open the tall curtains, letting the sun in. The
room seems almost to explode with the blast of light: he resists,
then surrenders to, finally welcomes its amicable violence. He
opens wide the glass doors that lead out into the garden and
stands there in the sunshine, sucking in deeply the fresh morning air and trying to recall the dream he's just had. Something
about a teacher who had once lectured him on humility. Severely. Only now, in the dream, he was himself the teacher
and the student was a woman he knew, or thought he knew,
and in his lecture "humility" kept getting mixed up somehow
with "humor," such that, in effect, he was trying, in all severity,
to teach her how to laugh. He's standing there in the sunlight
in his slippers and pajama bottoms, remembering the curious
strained expression on the woman's face as she tried — desperately, it seemed — to laugh, and wondering why this provoked
(in the dream) such a fury in him, when the maid comes in. She
gazes impassively a moment (yet humbly, circumspectly) at the
gaping fly of his pajamas, then turns away, sets her bucket down
against the wall. Her apron strings are loose, there's a hole in
one of her black stockings, and she's forgotten her mop again.
I'd be a happier man, he acknowledges to himself with a wry
sigh, if I could somehow fail to notice these things. "I'll start in
the bathroom," she says discreetly. "Sir," he reminds her. "Sir,"
she says.

And she enters. Deliberately and gravely, as though once and
for all, without affectation, somewhat encumbered by the vital
paraphernalia of her office, yet radiant with that clear-browed
self-assurance achieved only by long and generous devotion to
duty. She plants her bucket and brushes beside the door, leans
the mop and broom against the wall, then crosses the room to
fling open (humbly, authoritatively) the curtains and the garden
doors: the fragrant air and sunlight come flooding in, a flood
she now feels able to appreciate. The sun is already high in the
sky, but the garden is still bejeweled with morning dew and (she

remembers to notice) there is such a song of birds all about! What inspiration! She enjoys this part of her work: flushing out the stale darkness of the dead night with such grand (yet circumspect) gestures — it's almost an act of magic! Of course, she takes pleasure in *all* her appointed tasks (she reminds herself), whether it be scrubbing floors or polishing furniture or even scouring out the tub or toilet, for she knows that only in giving herself (as he has told her) can she find herself: true service (he doesn't have to tell her!) is perfect freedom. And so, excited by the song of the birds, the sweet breath of morning, and her own natural eagerness to please, she turns with a glad heart to her favorite task of all: the making of the bed. Indeed, all the rest of her work is embraced by it, for the opening up and airing of the bed is the first of her tasks, the making of it her last. Today, however, when she tosses the covers back, she finds, coiled like a dark snake near the foot, a bloodstained leather belt. She starts back. The sheets, too, are flecked with blood. Shadows seem to creep across the room and the birds fall silent. Perhaps, she thinks, her heart sinking, I'd better go out and come in again . . .

At least, he cautions himself while taking a shower, give her a chance. Her forgetfulness, her clumsiness, her endless comings and goings and stupid mistakes are a trial of course, and he feels sometimes like he's been living with them forever, but she means well and, with patience, instruction, discipline, she can still learn. Indeed, to the extent that she fails, it could be said, *he* has failed. He knows he must be firm, yet understanding, severe if need be, but caring and protective. He vows to treat her today with the civility and kindness due to an inferior, and not to lose his temper, even should she resist. Our passions (he reminds himself) are our infirmities. A sort of fever of the mind, which ever leaves us weaker than it found us. But when he turns off the taps and reaches for the towel, he finds it damp. Again! He can feel the rage rising in him, turning to ash with its uncontrollable heat his gentler intentions. Has she forgotten to change them yet again, he wonders furiously, standing there in a puddle with the cold wet towels clutched in his fists — or has she not even come yet?

*

She enters once and for all encumbered with her paraphernalia which she deposits by the wall near the door, thinking: it should be easier than this. Indeed, why bother at all when it always seems to turn out the same? Yet she cannot do otherwise. She is driven by a sense of duty and a profound appetite for hope never quite stifled by even the harshest punishments: this time, today, perhaps it will be perfect . . . So, deliberately and gravely, not staring or turning her head either one way or the other, she crosses the room to the far wall and with a determined flourish draws open the tall curtains, flooding the room with buckets of sunlight, but her mind is clouded with an old obscurity: When, she wants to know as she opens wide the glad doors to let the sweet breath of morning in (there are birds, too, such a song, she doesn't hear it), did all this really begin? When she entered? Before that? Long ago? Not yet? Or just now as, bracing herself as though for some awful trial, she turns upon the bed and flings the covers back, her morning's tasks begun. "Oh!" she cries. "I beg your pardon, sir!" He stares groggily down at the erection poking up out of the fly of his pajama pants, like (she thinks) some kind of luxuriant but dangerous dew-bejeweled blossom: a monster in the garden. "I was having a dream," he announces sleepily, yet gravely. "Something about tumidity. But it kept getting mixed up somehow with —" But she is no longer listening. Watching his knobby plant waggle puckishly in the morning breeze, then dip slowly, wilting toward the shadows like a closing morning glory, a solution of sorts has occurred to her to that riddle of genesis that has been troubling her mind: to wit, that a condition *has* no beginning. Only *change* can begin or end.

She enters, dressed crisply in her black uniform with its starched white apron and lace cap, leans her mop against the wall like a standard, and strides across the gleaming tile floor to fling open the garden doors as though (he thinks) calling forth the morning. What's left of it. Watching her from behind the bathroom door, he is moved by her transparent earnestness, her uncomplicated enthusiasm, her easy self-assurance. What more, really, does he want of her? Never mind that she's forgotten her broom again, or that her shoe's unbuckled and her cap on crooked, or that in her exuberance she nearly broke the glass doors (and sooner or later will), what is wonderful is the quickening of her spirits as she enters, the light that seems to dawn on her face as she opens the room, the way she makes a maid's oppressive routine seem like a sudden invention of love. See now how she tosses back the blankets and strips off the sheets as though, in childish excitement, unwrapping a gift! How in fluffing up the pillows she seems almost to bring them to life! She calls it: "doing the will of God from the heart!" *"Teach me, my God and King, in all things thee to see,"* she sings, *"and what I do in any thing, to do it as for thee!"* Ah well, he envies her: would that he had it so easy! All life is a service, he knows that. To live in the full sense of the word is not to exist or subsist merely, but to make oneself over, to *give* oneself: to some high purpose, to others, to some social end, to life itself beyond the shell of ego. But he, lacking superiors, must devote himself to abstractions, never knowing when he has succeeded, when he has failed, or even if he has the abstractions right, whereas she, needing no others, has him. He would like to explain this to her, to ease the pain of her routine, of her chastisement — what he calls his disciplinary interventions — but he knows that it is he, not she, who is forever in need of such explanations. Her mop fairly flies over the tiles (today she has remembered the mop), making them gleam like mirrors, her face radiant with their reflected light. He checks himself in the bathroom mirror, flicks lint off one shoulder, smooths the ends of his moustache. If only she could somehow understand how difficult it is for me, he thinks as he steps out to receive her greeting: "Good morning, sir." "Good morning," he replies crisply, glancing around the room. He means to give her some encouragement, to reward her zeal with praise or gratitude or at least a smile to match her own, but instead he finds himself flinging his dirty towels at her feet and snapping: "These towels are damp! See to it that they are replaced!" "Yes, sir!" "Moreover, your apron strings are dangling untidily and there are flyspecks on the mirror!" "Sir." "And another thing!" He strides over to the bed and tears it apart. "Isn't it about time these sheets were changed? Or am I supposed to wear them through before they are taken to be washed?" "But, sir, I just put new — !" "What? *WHAT* — ?" he

storms. "Answering back to a reproof? Have you forgotten all
I've taught you?" "I — I'm sorry, sir!" "Never answer back if
your master takes occasion to reprove you, except — ?" "Except
it be to acknowledge my fault, sir, and that I am sorry for having
committed it, promising to amend for the time to come, and
to . . . to . . ." "Am I being unfair?" he insists, unbuckling his
belt. "No, sir," she says, her eyes downcast, shoulders trembling,
her arms pressed tight to her sides.

He is strict but not unkindly. He pays her well, is grateful for
her services, treats her respectfully, she doesn't dislike him or
even fear him. Nor does she have to work very hard; he is
essentially a tidy man, picks up after himself, comes and goes
without disturbing things much. A bit of dusting and polishing
now and then, fold his pajamas, change the towels, clean the
bathroom, scrub the floor, make his bed; really there's nothing
to complain about. Yet, vaguely, even as she opens up the garden doors, letting the late morning sunshine and freshness
in, she feels unhappy. Not because of what she must do — no,
she truly serves with gladness. When she straightens a room,
polishes a floor, bleaches a sheet or scrubs a tub, always doing
the very best she can, she becomes, she knows, a part of what
is good in the world, creating a kind of beauty, revealing a
kind of truth. About herself, about life, the things she touches.
It's just that, somehow, something is missing. Some response,
some enrichment, some direction . . . it's, well, it's too repetitive.
Something like that. That's part of the problem anyway. The
other part is what she keeps finding in his bed. Things that
oughtn't to be there, like old razor blades, broken bottles, ba-
nana skins, bloody pessaries, crumbs and ants, leather thongs,
mirrors, empty books, old toys, dark stains. Once, even, a frog
jumped out at her. No matter how much sunlight and fresh air
she lets in, there's always this dark little pocket of lingering
night which she has to uncover. It can ruin everything, all her
careful preparations. This morning, however, all she finds is a
pair of flannelette drawers. Ah: she recognizes them. She glances
about guiltily, pulls them on hastily. Lucky the master's in the
bathroom, she thinks, patting down her skirt and apron, or
there'd be the devil to pay.

*

Something about scouring, or scourging, he can't remember, and a teacher he once had who called his lectures "lechers." The maid is standing over him, staring down in some astonishment at his erection. "Oh! I beg your pardon, sir!" "I was having a dream . . ." he explains, trying to bring it back. "Something about a woman . . ." But by then he is alone again. He hears her in the bathroom, running water, singing, whipping the wet towels off the racks and tossing them out the door. Ah well, it's easy for her, she can come and go. He sits up, squinting in the bright light, watching his erection dip back inside his pajamas like a sleeper pulling the blankets over his head (oh yes! to return there!), then dutifully shoves his feet into slippers, stretches, staggers to the open garden doors. The air is fragrant and there's a morning racket of birds and insects, vaguely threatening. Sometimes, as now, scratching himself idly and dragging himself still from the stupor of sleep, he wonders about his calling, how it came to be his, and when it all began: on his coming here? on *her* coming here? before that, in some ancient time beyond recall? And has he chosen it? or has he, like that woman in his dream, showing him something that for some reason enraged him, been "born with it, sir, for your very utility"?

She strives, understanding the futility of it, for perfection. To arrive properly equipped, to cross the room deliberately, circumspectly, without affectation (as he has taught her), to fling open the garden doors and let the sweet breath of morning flow in and chase the night away, to strip and air the bed and, after all her common tasks, her trivial round, to remake it smooth and tight, all the sheets and blankets tucked in neatly at the sides and bottom, the upper sheet and blankets turned down at the head just so far that their fold covers only half the pillows, all topped with the spread, laid to hang evenly at all sides. And today — perhaps at last! She straightens up, wipes her brow, looks around: yes! he'll be so surprised! Everything perfect! Her heart is pounding as the master, dressed for the day, steps out of the bathroom, marches directly over to the bed, hauls back the covers, picks up a pillow, and hits her in the face with it. Now what did he do that for? "And another thing!" he says.

*

He awakes, feeling sorry for himself (he's not sure why, something he's been dreaming perhaps, or merely the need to wake just by itself: come, day, do your damage!), tears himself painfully from the bed's embrace, sits up, pushes his feet into slippers. He grunts, squinting in the dimness at his watch: she's late. Just as well. He can shower before she gets here. He staggers into the bathroom and drops his pajamas, struggling to recall his dream. Something about a woman in the civil service, which in her ignorance or cupidity, she insisted on calling the "sybil service." He is relieving himself noisily when the maid comes in. "Oh! I beg your pardon, sir!" "Good morning," he replies crisply, and pulls his pajamas up, but she is gone. He can hear her outside the door, walking quickly back and forth, flinging open the curtains and garden doors, singing to herself as though lifted by the tasks before her. Sometimes he envies her, having him. Her footsteps carry her to the bed and he hears the rush and flutter of sheets and blankets being thrown back. Hears her scream.

He's not unkind, demands no more than is his right, pays her well, and teaches her things like, "All life is a service, a consecration to some high end," and, "If domestic service is to be tolerable, there must be an attitude of habitual deference on the one side and one of sympathetic protection on the other." "Every state and condition of life has its particular duties," he has taught her. "The duty of a servant is to be obedient, diligent, sober, just, honest, frugal, orderly in her behavior, submissive and respectful toward her master. She must be contented in her station, because it is necessary that some should be above others in this world, and it was the will of the Almighty to place you in a state of servitude." Her soul, in short, is his invention, and she is grateful to him for it. *"Whatever thy hand findeth to do,"* he has admonished her, *"do it with all thy might!"* Nevertheless, looking over her shoulder at her striped sit-me-down in the wardrobe mirror, she wishes he might be a little less literal in applying his own maxims: *he's drawn blood!*

He awakes, mumbling something about a dream, a teacher he once had, some woman, infirmities. "A sort of fever of the mind," he explains, his throat phlegmy with sleep. "Yes, sir," she says, and flings open the curtains and the garden doors, letting light and air into the stale bedroom. She takes pleasure in all her appointed tasks, but enjoys this one most of all, more so when the master is already out of bed, for he seems to resent her waking him like this. Just as he resents her arriving late, after he's risen. Either way, sooner or later, she'll have to pay for it. "It's a beautiful day," she remarks hopefully. He sits up with an ambiguous grunt, rubs his eyes, yawns, shudders. "You may speak when spoken to," he grumbles, tucking his closing morning glory back inside his pajamas (behind her, bees are humming in the garden and there's a crackly pulsing of insects, but the birds have fallen silent: she had thought today might be perfect, but already it is slipping away from her), "unless it be to deliver a message or ask a necessary question." "Yes, sir." He shoves his feet into slippers and staggers off to the bathroom, leaving her to face (she expects the worst) — shadows have invaded the room — the rumpled bed alone.

It's not just the damp towels. It's also the streaked floor, the careless banging of the garden doors, her bedraggled uniform, the wrinkled sheets, the confusion of her mind. He lectures her patiently on the proper way to make a bed, the airing of the blankets, turning of the mattress, changing of the sheets, the importance of a smooth surface. "Like a blank sheet of crisp new paper," he tells her. He shows her how to make the correct diagonal creases at the corners, how to fold the top edge of the upper sheet back over the blankets, how to carry the spread under and then over the pillows. Oh, not for his benefit and advantage — he could sleep anywhere or for that matter (in extremity) could make his own bed — but for hers. How else would she ever be able to realize what is best for herself? "A little arrangement and thought will give you method and habit," he explains (it is his "two fairies" lecture), but though she seems willing enough, is polite and deferential, even eager to please, she can never seem to get it just right. Is it a weakness on her part, he wonders as he watches her place the pillows on the bed upside down, then tug so hard on the bottom blanket that it comes out at the foot, or some perversity? Is she testing him? She refits the bottom blanket, tucks it in again, but he knows the sheet beneath is now wrinkled. He sighs, removes his belt. Perfection is elusive, but what else is there worth striving for? "Am I being unfair?" he insists.

He's standing there in the sunlight in his slippers and pajama bottoms, cracking his palm with a leather strap, when she enters (once and for all) with all her paraphernalia. She plants the bucket and brushes beside the door, leans the mop and broom against the wall, stacks the fresh linens and towels on a chair. She is late — the curtains and doors are open, her circumspect crossing of the room no longer required — but she remains hopeful. Running his maxims over in her head, she checks off her rags and brushes, her polishes, cleaning powders, razor blades, toilet paper, dustpans — oh no . . . ! Her heart sinks like soap in a bucket. The soap she has forgotten to bring. She sighs, then deliberately and gravely, without affectation, not stamping too loud, nor dragging her legs after her, not marching as if leading a dance, nor keeping time with her head and hands, nor staring or turning her head either one way or the other, she advances sedately and discreetly across the gleaming tiles to the bed, and tucking up her dress and apron, pulling down her flan-nelette drawers, bends over the foot of it, exposing her soul's ingress to the sweet breath of morning, blowing in from the garden. "I wonder if you can appreciate," he says, picking a bit of lint off his target before applying his corrective measures to it, "how difficult this is for me?"

He awakes, vaguely frightened by something he's dreamt (it was about order or odor and a changed condition — but how did it begin . . . ?), wound up in damp sheets and unable at first even to move, defenseless against the day already hard upon him. Its glare blinds him, but he can hear the maid moving about the room, sweeping the floor, changing the towels, running water, pushing furniture around. "Good morning, sir," she says. "Come here a moment," he replies gruffly, then clears his throat. "Sir?" "Look under the bed. Tell me what you see." He expects the worst: blood, a decapitated head, a bottomless hole . . . "I'm — I'm sorry, sir," she says, tucking up her skirt and apron, lowering her drawers, "I thought I *had* swept it . . ."

*

No matter how much fresh air and sunlight she lets in, there is always this little pocket of lingering night which she has to uncover. Once she found a dried bull's pizzle in there, another time a dead mouse in a trap. Even the nice things she finds in the bed are somehow horrible; the toys broken, the food moldy, the clothing torn and bloody. She knows she must always be circumspect and self-effacing, never letting her countenance betray the least dislike toward any task, however trivial or distasteful, and she resolves every morning to be cheerful and good-natured, letting nothing she finds there put her out of temper with everything besides, but sometimes she just cannot help herself. "Oh, teach me, my God and King, in all things thee to see, and what I do in any thing, to do it as for thee," she tells herself, seeking courage, and flings back the sheets and blankets. She screams. But it's only money, a little pile of gold coins, agleam with promise. Or challenge: is he testing her?

Ah well, he envies her, even as that seat chosen by Mother Nature for such interventions quivers and reddens under the whistling strokes of the birch rod in his hand. "Again!" "Be . . . be diligent in endeavoring to please your master — be faithful and . . . and . . ." Swish — *SNAP!* "Oh, sir!" "Honest!" "Yes, sir!" She, after all, is free to come and go, her correction finitely inscribed by time and the manuals, but he . . . He sighs unhappily. How did it all begin, he wonders. Was it destiny, choice, generosity? If she would only get it right for once, he reasons, bringing his stout engine of duty down with a sharp report on her brightly striped but seemingly unimpressionable hinder parts, he might at least have time for a stroll in the garden. Does she — *CRACK!* — think he enjoys this? "Well?" "Be . . . be faithful, honest, and submissive to him, sir, and —" Whish — *SLASH!* "And — *gasp!* — do not incline to be slothful! Or —" *THWOCK!* "Ow! Please, sir!" Hiss — *WHAP!* She groans, quivers, starts. The two raised hemispheres upon which the blows from the birch rod have fallen begin (predictably) to make involuntary motions both vertically and horizontally, the constrictor muscle being hard at work, the thighs also participating in the general vibrations, all in all a dismal spectacle. And for nothing? So it would seem . . . "Or?" "Or lie long in bed, but rise . . . rise early in a morning!" The weals crisscross each other on her flushed posterior like branches against the pink clouds of dawn, which for some reason saddens him. "Am I being unfair?" "No — no, s —" Whisp — *CRACK!* She shows no tears, but her face pressed against the bedding is flushed, her lips trembling, and she breathes heavily as though she's been running, confirming the quality of the rod which is his own construction. "Sir," he reminds her, turning away. "Sir," she replies faintly. "Thank you, sir."

She enters once and for all, radiant and clear-browed (a long devotion to duty), with all her paraphernalia, her mop and bucket, brooms, rags, soaps, polishes, sets them all down, counting them off on her fingers, then crosses the room deliberately and circumspectly, not glancing at the rumpled bed, and flings open the curtains and the garden doors to call forth the morning, what's left of it. There is such a song of insects all about (the preying birds are silent) — what inspiration! "Lord, keep me in my place!" The master is in the shower: she hears the water. "Let me be diligent in performing whatever my master commands me," she prays, "neat and clean in my habit, modest in my carriage, silent when he is angry, willing to please, quick and neat-handed about what I do, and always of an humble and good disposition!" Then, excited to the most generous and efficient accomplishments, she turns with a palpitating heart (she is thinking about perfect service and freedom and the unpleasant things she has found) to the opening up and airing of the bed. She braces herself, expecting the worst, but finds only a wilted flower from the garden: ah! today then! she thinks hopefully — perhaps at last! But then she hears the master turn the taps off, step out of the shower. Oh no . . . ! She lowers her drawers to her knees, lifts her dress, and bends over the unmade bed. *"These towels are damp!"* he blusters, storming out of the bathroom, wielding the fearsome rod, that stout engine of duty, still wet from the shower.

Sometimes he uses a rod, sometimes his hand, his belt, sometimes a whip, a cane, a cat-o'-nine-tails, a bull's pizzle, a hickory switch, a martinet, ruler, slipper, a leather strap, a hairbrush.

There are manuals for this. Different preparations and positions to be assumed, the number and severity of the strokes
generally prescribed to fit the offense, he has explained it all to
her, though it is not what is important to her. She knows he is
just, could not be otherwise if he tried, even if the relative seri-
ousness of the various infractions seems somewhat obscure to
her at times. No, what matters to her is the idea behind the
regulations that her daily tasks, however trivial, are perfectible.
Not absolutely perhaps, but at least in terms of the manuals.
This idea, which is almost tangible — made manifest, as it were,
in the weals on her behind — is what the punishment is for, she
assumes. She does not enjoy it certainly, nor (she believes —
and it wouldn't matter if he did) does he. Rather, it is a road
(speaking loosely), the rod, to bring her daily nearer God —
and what's more, it seems that she's succeeding at last! Today
everything has been perfect: her entry, all her vital paraphernalia, her circumspect crossing of the room and opening of the
garden doors, her scrubbing and waxing and dusting and polishing, her opening up and airing and making of the master's
bed — everything! True service, she knows (he has taught her!),
is perfect freedom, and today she feels it: almost like a breeze
— the sweet breath of success — lifting her! But then the master
emerges from the bathroom, his hair wild, fumbles through the
clothes hanging in the wardrobe, pokes through the dresser
drawers, whips back the covers of her perfectly made bed.
"What's this doing here — ?!" he demands, holding up his
comb. "I — I'm sorry, sir! It wasn't there when I —" "What?
What — ?!" He seizes her by the elbow, drags her to the foot of
the bed, forces her to bend over it. "I have been very indulgent
to you up to now, but now I am going to punish you severely,
to cure you of your insolent clumsiness once and for all! So pull
up your skirt — come! pull it up! you know well enough that
the least show of resistance means ten extra cuts of the — *what's
this — ?!*" She peers round her shoulder at her elevated sit-me-
down, so sad and pale above her stockings. "I — I don't understand, sir! I had them on when I came in — !"

Perhaps he's been pushing her too hard, he muses, soaping
himself in the shower and trying to recall the dream he was

having when she woke him up (something about ledgers and manual positions, a woman, and the merciless invention of souls which was a sort of fever of the mind), perhaps he's been expecting too much too soon, making her overanxious, for in some particulars now she is almost too efficient, clattering in with her paraphernalia like a soldier, blinding him with a sudden brutal flood of sunlight from the garden, hauling the sheets out from under him while he's still trying to stuff his feet into his slippers. Perhaps he should back off a bit, give her a chance to recover some of her ease and spontaneity, even at the expense of a few undisciplined errors. Perhaps . . . yet he knows he could never let up, even if he tried. Not that he enjoys all this punishment, any more (he assumes, but it doesn't matter) than she does. No, he would rather do just about anything else — crawl back into bed, read his manuals, even take a stroll in the garden — but he is committed to a higher end, his life a mission of sorts, a consecration, and so punish her he must, for to the extent that she fails, he fails. As he turns off the taps and steps out of the shower, reaching for the towel, the maid rushes in. "Oh, I beg your pardon, sir!" He grabs a towel and wraps it around him, but she snatches it away again: "That one's damp, sir!" She dashes out to fetch him a fresh one and he is moved by her transparent enthusiasm, her eagerness to please, her seemingly unquenchable appetite for hope: perhaps today . . . ! But he has already noticed that she has forgotten her lace cap, there's a dark stain on the bib of her apron, and her garters are dangling. He sighs, reaches for the leather strap. Somehow (is there to be no end to this? he wonders ruefully) it should be easier than this.

She does not enjoy the discipline of the rod, nor does he — or so she believes, though what would it matter if he did? Rather, they are both dedicated to the fundamental proposition (she winces at the painful but unintended pun, while peering over her shoulder at herself in the wardrobe mirror, tracing the weals with her fingertips) that her daily tasks, however trivial, are perfectible, her punishments serving her as a road, loosely speaking, to bring her daily nearer God, at least in terms of the manuals. Tenderly, she lifts her drawers up over her blistered

sit-me-down, smooths down her black alpaca dress and white
lace apron, wipes the tears from her eyes, and turns once more
to the unmade bed. Outside, the bees humming in the noonday
sun remind her of all the time she's lost. At least, she consoles
herself, the worst is past. But the master is pacing the room
impatiently and she's fearful his restlessness will confuse her
again. "Why don't you go for a stroll in the garden, sir?" she
suggests deferentially. "You may speak when spoken to!" he
reminds her, jabbing a finger at her sharply. "I — I'm sorry,
sir!" "You must be careful not only to do your work quietly, but
to keep out of sight as much as possible, and never begin to
speak to your master unless — ?" "Unless it be to deliver a message, sir, or ask a necessary question!" "And then to do it in as
few words as possible," he adds, getting down his riding whip.
"Am I being unfair?" "But, sir! you've already — !" "What?
What — ?! Answering back to a reproof — ?" "But — !"
"*Enough!*" he rages, seizing her by the arm and dragging her
over to the bed. "*Please* — !" But he pulls her down over his left
knee, pushes her head down on the stripped mattress, locking
her legs in place with his right leg, clamps her right wrist in the
small of her back, throws her skirt back and jerks her drawers
down. "*Oh, sir* — !" she pleads, what is now her highest part still
radiant and throbbing from the previous lesson. "SILENCE!"
he roars, lifting the whip high above his head, a curious strained
expression on his face. She can hear the whip sing as he brings
it down, her cheeks pinch together involuntarily, her heart leaps
— *he'll draw blood!*

Where does she come from? Where does she go? He doesn't
know. All he knows is that every day she comes here, dressed in
her uniform and carrying all her paraphernalia with her, which
she sets down by the door; then she crosses the room, opens up
the curtains and garden doors, makes his bed soft and easy, first
airing the bedding, turning the mattress, and changing the linens, scrubs and waxes the tiled floor, cleans the bathroom, polishes the furniture and all the mirrors, replenishes all supplies,
and somewhere along the way commits some fundamental blun-
der, obliging him to administer the proper correction. Every
day the same. Why does he persist? It's not so much that he

shares her appetite for hope (though sometimes, late in the day, he does), but that he could not do otherwise should he wish. To live in the full sense of the word, he knows, is not merely to exist, but to give oneself to some mission, surrender to a higher purpose, but in truth he often wonders, watching that broad part destined by Mother Nature for such solemnities quiver and redden under his hand (he thinks of it as a blank ledger on which to write), whether it is he who has given himself to a higher end, or that end which has chosen and in effect captured him?

Perhaps, she thinks, I'd better go out and come in again . . . And so she enters. As though once and for all, though she's aware she can never be sure of this. She sets down beside the door all the vital paraphernalia of her office, checking off each item on her fingers, then crosses the room (circumspectly etc.) and flings open the curtains and garden doors to the midday sun. Such a silence all about! She tries to take heart from it, but it is not so inspiring as the song of birds, and even the bees seem to have ceased their humming. Though she has resolved, as always, to be cheerful and good-natured, truly serving with gladness as she does, she nevertheless finds her will flagging, her mind clouded with old obscurities: somehow, something is missing. "Teach me, my God and King, in all things thee to see," she recites dutifully, but the words seem meaningless to her and go nowhere. And now, once again, the hard part. She holds back, trembling — but what can she do about it? For she knows her place and is contented with her station, as he has taught her. She takes a deep breath of the clean warm air blowing in from the garden and, fearing the worst, turns on the bed, hurls the covers back, and screams. But it is only the master. "Oh! I beg your pardon, sir!" "A . . . a dream," he explains huskily, as his erection withdraws into his pajamas like a worm caught out in the sun, burrowing for shade. "Something about a lecture on civil severity, what's left of it, and an inventory of soaps . . . or hopes . . ." He's often like that as he struggles (never very willingly, it seems to her) out of sleep. She leaves him there, sitting on the edge of the bed, squinting in the bright light, yawning and scratching himself and muttering something depressing about being born again, and goes to the bathroom to change the towels, check the toothpaste and toilet paper, wipe the mirror and toilet seat, and put fresh soap in the shower tray, doing the will of God and the manuals, endeavoring to please. As he shuffles groggily in, already reaching inside his fly, she slips out, careful not to speak as she's not been spoken to, and returns to the rumpled bed. She tosses back the blankets afresh (nothing new, thank you, sir), strips away the soiled linens, turns and brushes the mattress (else it might imbibe an unhealthy kind of dampness and become unpleasant), shakes the feather pillows, and sets everything out to air. While the master showers, she dusts the furniture, polishes the mirrors, and mops the floor, then remakes the bed, smooth and tight, all the sheets and blankets tucked in neatly at the sides and bottom, the top sheet turned down at the head, over the blankets, the spread carried under, then over the pillows, and hanging equally low at both sides and the foot: ah! it's almost an act of magic! But are those flyspecks on the mirror? She rubs the mirror, and seeing herself reflected there, thinks to check that her apron strings are tied and her stocking seams are straight. Peering over her shoulder at herself, her eye falls on the mirrored bed: one of the sheets is dangling at the foot, peeking out from under the spread as though exposing itself rudely. She hurries over, tucks it in, being careful to make the proper diagonal fold, but now the spread seems to be hanging lower on one side than the other. She whips it back, dragging the top sheet and blankets partway with it. The taps have been turned off, the master is drying himself. Carefully, she remakes the bed, tucking in all the sheets and blankets properly, fluffing the pillows up once more, covering it all with the spread, hung evenly. All this bedmaking has raised a lot of dust: she can see her own tracks on the floor. Hurriedly she wipes the furniture again and sweeps the tiles. Has she bumped the bed somehow? The spread is askew once again like a gift coming unwrapped. She tugs it to one side, sees ripples appear on top. She tries to smooth them down, but apparently the blankets are wrinkled underneath. She hasn't pushed the dresser back against the wall. The wardrobe door is open, reflecting the master standing in the doorway to the bathroom, slapping his palm with a bull's pizzle. She stands there, downcast, shoulders trembling, her arms pressed to her sides, unable to move. It's like some kind of failure of communication, she thinks, her diligent endeavors to please him forever thwarted by her irremediable clumsiness. "Come, come! A little arrangement and thought will give you method and habit," he reminds her gravely, "two fairies that will make the work disappear before a ready pair of hands!" In her mind she doesn't quite believe it, but her heart is ever hopeful, her hands readier than he knows. She takes the bed apart once more and remakes it from the beginning, tucking everything in correctly, fluffing the pillows, laying the spread evenly: all tight and smooth it looks. Yes! She pushes the dresser (once he horsed her there: she shudders to recall it, a flush of dread racing through her) back against the wall, collects the wet towels he has thrown on the floor, closes the wardrobe door. In the mirror, she sees the bed. The spread and blankets have been thrown back, the sheets pulled out. In the bathroom doorway, the master taps his palm with the stretched-out bull's pizzle, testing its firmness and elasticity, which she knows to be terrifying in its perfection. She remakes the bed tight and smooth, not knowing what else to do, vaguely aware as she finishes of an unpleasant odor. Under the bed? Also her apron is missing and she seems to have a sheet left over. Shadows creep across the room, silent now but for the rhythmic tapping of the pizzle in the master's hand and the pounding of her own palpitating heart.

Sometimes he stretches her across his lap. Sometimes she must bend over a chair or on the bed, or lie flat out on it, or be horsed over the pillows, the dresser or a stool, there are manuals for this. Likewise her drawers: whether they are to be drawn tight over her buttocks like a second skin or lowered, and if lowered, by which of them, how far, and so on. Her responses are assumed in the texts (the writhing, sobbing, convulsive quivering, blushing, moaning, etc.), but not specified, except insofar as they determine his own further reactions — to resistance, for example, or premature acquiescence, fainting, improper language, an unclean bottom, and the like. Thus, once again, her relative freedom: her striped buttocks tremble and dance spontaneously under the whip which his hand must bring whistling

down on them according to canon — ah well, it's not so much
that he envies her (her small freedoms cost her something, he
knows that), but that he is saddened by her inability to understand how difficult it is for him, and without that understanding
it's as though something is always missing, no matter how faith-
fully he adheres to the regulations. "And — ?" "And be neat
and clean in your —" whisp — *CRACK!* "— *OW!* habit! Oh!
and wash yourself all over once a day to avoid bad smells
and —" hiss — *SNAP!* "— and — *gasp!* — wear strong decent
underclothing!" The whip sings a final time, smacks its broad
target with a loud report, and little drops of blood appear like
punctuation, gratitude, morning dew. "That will do, then. See
that you don't forget to wear them again!" "Yes, sir." She lowers
her black alpaca skirt gingerly over the glowing crimson flesh as
though hooding a lamp, wincing at each touch. "Thank you, sir."

For a long time she struggled to perform her tasks in such a way
as to avoid the thrashings. But now, with time, she has come to
understand that the tasks, truly common, are only the periph-
eral details in some larger scheme of things which includes her
punishment — indeed, perhaps depends upon it. Of course she
still performs her duties *as though* they were perfectible and her
punishment could be avoided, ever diligent in endeavoring to
please him who guides her, but though each day the pain surprises her afresh, the singing of the descending instrument does
not. That God has ordained bodily punishment (and Mother
Nature designed the proper place of martyrdom) is beyond
doubt — every animal is governed by it, understands and fears
it, and the fear of it keeps every creature in its own sphere, forever preventing (as he has taught her) that natural confusion and
disorder that would instantly arise without it. Every state and
condition of life has its particular duties, and each is subject to
the divine government of pain, nothing could be more obvious,
and looked on this way, his chastisements are not merely necessary, they might even be beautiful. Or so she consoles herself,
trying to take heart, calm her rising panic, as she crosses the
room under his stern implacable gaze, lowers her drawers as far
as her knees, tucks her skirt up, and bends over the back of a
chair, hands on the seat, thighs taut and pressed closely to-

gether, what is now her highest part tensing involuntarily as though to reduce the area of pain, if not the severity. "It's . . . it's a beautiful day, sir," she says hopefully. "What? *WHAT* — *?!*"

Relieving himself noisily in the bathroom, the maid's daily recitals in the next room (such a blast of light out there — even in here he keeps his eyes half closed) thus drowned out, he wonders if there's any point in going on. She is late, has left half her paraphernalia behind, is improperly dressed, and he knows, even without looking, that the towels are damp. Maybe it's some kind of failure of communication. A mutual failure. Is that possible? A loss of syntax between stroke and weal? No, no, even if possible, it is unthinkable. He turns on the shower taps and lets fall his pajama pants, just as the maid comes in with a dead fetus and drops it down the toilet, flushes it. "I found it in your bed, sir," she explains gratuitously (is she testing him?), snatching up the damp towels, but failing to replace them with fresh ones. At least she's remembered her drawers today: she's wearing them around her ankles. He sighs, as she shuffles out. Maybe he should simply forget it, go for a stroll in the garden or something, crawl back into bed (a dream, he recalls now: something about lectures or ledgers — an inventory perhaps — and a bottomless hole, glass breaking, a woman doing what she called "the hard part" . . . or did she say "heart part"?), but of course he cannot, even if he truly wished to. He is not a free man, his life is consecrated, for though he is *her* master, her failures are inescapably *his*. He turns off the shower taps, pulls up his pajama pants, takes down the six-thonged martinet. "I have been very indulgent to you up to now," he announces, stepping out of the bathroom, "but now I am going to punish you severely, so pull up your skirt, come! pull it up!" But, alas, it is already up. She is bent over the foot of the bed, her pale hinder parts already exposed for his ministrations, an act of insolence not precisely covered by his manuals. Well, he reasons wryly, making the martinet sing whole chords, if improvisation is denied him, interpretation is not. "Ow, sir! Please! *You'll draw blood, sir!*"

"Neat and clean in habit, modest —" *WHACK!* "— in . . . in carriage, silent when —" Whisp — *SNAP!* "OW!!" "Be careful! If

you move, the earlier blow won't count!" "I — I'm sorry, sir!"
Her soul, she knows, is his invention and she is grateful to him
for it, but exposed like this to the whining slashes of the cane
and the sweet breath of mid-afternoon which should cool his
righteous ardor but doesn't (once a bee flew in and stung him
on the hand: what did it mean? nothing: she got it on her sit-
me-down once, too, and he took the swelling for a target), her
thighs shackled by flannelette drawers and blood rushing to her
head, she can never remember (for all the times he has explained it to her) why it is that Mother Nature has chosen that
particular part of her for such solemnities: it seems more like a
place for letting things out than putting things in. "Well? Silent
when — ?" "Silent when he is angry, willing to please, quick
and —" swish — CRACK! "— and of good disposition!" "Sir,"
he reminds her: THWOCK! "SIR!" she cries. "Very well, but you
must learn to take more pleasure in your appointed tasks, however trivial or unpleasant, and when you are ordered to do
anything, do not grumble or let your countenance betray any
dislike thereunto, but do it cheerfully and readily!" "Yes, sir!
Thank you, sir!" She is all hot behind, and peering over her
shoulder at herself in the wardrobe mirror after the master has
gone to shower, she can see through her tears that it's like on
fire, flaming crimson it is, with large blistery welts rising and
throbbing like things alive: he's drawn blood! She dabs at it with
her drawers, recalling a dream he once related to her about a
teacher he'd had who called his chastisements "scripture lessons," and she understands now what he's always meant by demanding "a clean sheet of paper." Well, certainly it has always
been clean, neat and clean as he's taught her, that's one thing
she's never got wrong, always washing it well every day in three
hot lathers, letting the last lather be made thin of the soap, then
not rinsing it or toweling it, but drying it over brimstone, keeping it as much from the air as possible, for that, she knows, will
spoil it if it comes to it. She finishes drying it by slapping it
together in her hands, then holding it before a good fire until it
be thoroughly hot, then clapping it and rubbing it between her
hands from the fire, occasionally adding to its fairness by giving
it a final wash in a liquor made of rosemary flower boiled in
white wine. Now, she reasons, lifting her drawers up gingerly

over the hot tender flesh, which is still twitching convulsively, if she could just apply those same two fairies, method and habit, to the rest of her appointed tasks, she might yet find in them that pleasure he insists she take, according to the manuals. Well, anyway, the worst is past. Or so she consoles herself as, smoothing down her black skirt and white lace apron, she turns to the bed. *"Oh, teach me, my God and King, in all things thee to . . ."* What — ? There's something under there! *And it's moving . . . !*

"Thank you, sir." "I know that perfection is elusive," he explains, putting away his stout engine of duty, while she staggers over, her knees bound by her drawers, to examine her backside in the wardrobe mirror (it is well cut, he knows, and so aglow one might cook little birds over it or roast chestnuts, as the manuals suggest), "but what else is there worth striving for?" "Yes, sir." She shows no tears, but her face is flushed, her lips are trembling, and she breathes as though she has just been running. He goes to gaze out into the garden, vaguely dissatisfied. The room is clean, the bed stripped and made, the maid whipped, why isn't that enough? Is there something missing in the manuals? No, more likely, he has failed somehow to read them rightly. Yet again. Outside in the sleepy afternoon heat of the garden, the bees are humming, insects chattering, gentler sounds to be sure than the hiss of a birch rod, the sharp report as it smacks firm resonant flesh, yet strangely alien to him, sounds of natural confusion and disorder from a world without precept or invention. He sighs. Though he was thinking "invention," what he has heard in his inner ear was "intention," and now he's not sure which it was he truly meant. Perhaps he should back off a bit — or even let her off altogether for a few days. A kind of holiday from the divine government of pain. Certainly he does not enjoy it nor (presumably) does she. If he could ever believe in her as she believes in him, he might even change places with her for a while, just to ease his own burden and let her understand how difficult it is for him. A preposterous idea of course, pernicious in fact, an unthinkable betrayal . . . yet sometimes, late in the day, something almost like a kind of fever of the mind (speaking loosely) steals over — enough! *enough!* no shrinking! "And another thing!" he shouts, turning on the bed (she is at the door, gathering up her paraphernalia) and throwing back the covers: at the foot on the clean crisp sheets there is a little pile of wriggling worms, still coated with dirt from the garden. "WHAT DOES THIS MEAN — ?!" he screams. "I — I'm sorry, sir! I'll clean it up right away, sir!" Is she testing him? taunting him? It's almost an act of madness! "Am I being unfair?" "But, sir, you've already — !" "What? *WHAT* — ?! Is there to be no *end* to this — ?!"

He holds her over his left knee, her legs locked between his, wrist clamped in the small of her back, her skirt up and her drawers down, and slaps her with his bare hand, first one buttock, reddening it smartly in contrast to the dazzling alabaster (remembering the manuals) of the other, then attacking its companion with equal alacrity. "Ow! Please, sir!" "Come, come, you know that the least show of resistance means ten extra cuts of the rod!" he admonishes her, doubling her over a chair. "When you are ordered to do anything, do not grumble or let your countenance betray any dislike thereunto, but do it cheerfully and generously!" "Yes, sir, but —" "What? *WHAT* — ?!" Whish — *CRACK!* "OW!" *SLASH!* Her crimson bottom, hugged close to the pillows, bobs and dances under the whistling cane. "When anyone finds fault with you, do not answer rudely!" Whirr — *SMACK!* "NO, SIR!" Each stroke, surprising her afresh, makes her jerk with pain and wrings a little cry from her (as anticipated by the manuals when the bull's pizzle is employed), which she attempts to stifle by burying her face in the horsehair cushion. "Be respectful — ?" "Be respectful and obedient, sir, to those —" swish — *THWOCK!* "— placed — OW! — placed OVER you — AARGH!" Whizz — *SWACK!* "With fear and trembling —" *SMASH!* "— and in singleness of your heart!" he reminds her gravely as she groans, starts, quivers under his patient instruction. "Ouch! Yes, sir!" The leather strap whistles down to land with a loud crack across the center of her glowing buttocks, seeming almost to explode, and making what lilies there are left into roses. *SMACK! Ker-WHACK!* He's working well now. "Am I being unfair?" "N-no, sir!" *WHAP! SLAP!* Horsed over the dresser her limbs launch out helplessly with each blow. *"Kneel down!"* She falls humbly to her hands and knees, her head

bowed between his slippered feet, that broad part destined by
Mother Nature for such devotions elevated but pointed away
from toward the wardrobe mirror (as though trying, flushed
and puffed up, to cry out to itself), giving him full and immediate access to that large division referred to in the texts as the
Paphian grove. "And resolve every morning — ?" "Resolve —
gasp! — resolve every morning to be cheerful and —" He raises
the whip, snaps it three times around his head, and brings it
down with a crash on her hinder parts, driving her head forward between his legs. "And — *YOW!* — and good-natured that
. . . that day, and if any . . . if any accident — *groan!* — should
happen to —" swish — *WHACK!* "— to break that resolution,
suffer it . . . suffer it not —" *SLASH!* "Oh, sir!" *SWOCK!* He's
pushing himself, too hard perhaps, but he can't — "Please, sir!
PLEASE!" She is clinging to his knee, sobbing into his pajama
pants, the two raised hemispheres upon which the strokes have
fallen making involuntary motions both vertically and horizontally as though sending a message of distress, all the skin wrinkling like the surface of a lake rippled by the wind. "What are
you doing?! *WHAT DOES THIS MEAN — ?!*" He spanks her
with a hairbrush, lashes her with a cat-o'-nine-tails, flagellates
her with nettles, not shrinking from the hard service to be done,
this divine drudgery, clear-browed in his devotion to duty. Perhaps today . . . ! "SIR!" He pauses, breathing heavily. His arm
hurts. There is a curious strained expression on her face,
flushed like her behind and wet with tears. "Sir, if you . . . if you
don't stop —" "What? *WHAT — ?!*" "You — you won't know
what to do *next!*" "Ah." He has just been smacking her with a
wet towel, and the damp rush and pop, still echoing in his inner
ear, reminds him dimly of a dream, perhaps the one she interrupted when she arrived. In it there was something about humidity, but it kept getting mixed up somehow with hymnody,
such that every time she opened her mouth (there was a woman
in the dream) damp chords flowed out and stained his ledgers,
bleached white as clean sheets. "I'm so old," he says, letting
his arm drop, "and still each day . . ." "Sir?" "Nothing. A
dream . . ." Where was he? It doesn't matter. "Why don't you
go for a stroll in the garden, sir? It's a beautiful day." Such
impudence: he ignores it. "It's all right," he says, draping the

blood-flecked towel over his shoulder, scratching himself idly.
He yawns. "The worst is past."

Has he devoted himself to a higher end, he wonders, standing
there in the afternoon sunlight in his slippers and pajama bottoms, flexing a cane, testing it, snapping it against his palm, or
has he been taken captive by it? Is choice itself an illusion? Or
an act of magic? And *is* the worst over, or has it not yet begun?
He shudders, yawns, stretches. And the manuals... He is
afraid even to ask, takes a few practice strokes with the cane
against a horsehair cushion instead. When the riddles and par-
adoxes of his calling overtake him, wrapping him in momentary
darkness, he takes refuge in the purity of technique. The
proper stretching of a bull's pizzle, for example, this can occupy
him for hours. Or the fabrication of whipping chairs, the index
of duties and offenses, the synonymy associated with corporal
discipline and with that broad part destined by Mother Nature
for such services. And a cane is not simply any cane, but preferably one made like this one of brown Malacca — the stem of
an East Indian rattan palm — about two and a half feet long
(give or take an inch and a half) and a quarter of an inch thick.
Whing-*SNAP!* listen to it! Or take the birch rod, not a mere
random handful of birchen twigs, as often supposed, but an
instrument of precise and elaborate construction. First, the
twigs must be meticulously selected for strength and elasticity,
each about two feet long, full of snap and taken from a young
tree, the tips sharp as needles. Then carefully combining the
thick with the thin and slender, they must be bound together
for half their length, tightly enough that they might enjoy long
service, yet not too tightly or else the rod will be like a stick and
the twigs have no play. The rod must fit conveniently to the
hand, have reach and swing so as to sing in the air, the larger
part of all punishments being the anticipation, not the pain of
course, and immediately raise welts and blisters, surprising the
chastised flesh afresh with each stroke. To be sure, it is easier to
construct a birch rod than to employ it correctly — that's always
the hard part, he doesn't enjoy it, nor does she surely, but the
art of the rod is incomplete without its perfect application. And
though elusive, what else is there worth striving for? Indeed, he

knows he has been too indulgent to her up till now, treating her
with the civility and kindness due to an inferior, but forgetting
the forging of her soul by way of those "vivid lessons," as a
teacher he once had used to put it, "in holy scripture, hotly
writ." So when she arrives, staggering in late with all her paraphernalia, her bucket empty and her bib hanging down, he
orders her straight to the foot of the bed. "But, sir, I haven't
even —" "Come, come, no dallying! The least show of resistance will double the punishment! Up with your skirt, up, up!
for I intend to — WHAT? IS THERE TO BE NO END TO
THIS — ?!" "I — I'm sorry! I was wearing them when I came
— I must have left them somewhere . . . !" Maybe it's some
kind of communication problem, he thinks, staring gloomily at
her soul's ingress which confronts him like blank paper, laundered tiffany, a perversely empty ledger. The warm afternoon
sun blows in through the garden doors, sapping his brave resolve. He feels himself drifting, yawning, must literally shake
himself to bring the manuals back to mind, his duties, his devotion . . . "Sir," she reminds him. "Sir," he sighs.

It never ends. Making the bed, she scatters dust and feathers
afresh or tips over the mop bucket. Cleaning up the floor, she
somehow disturbs the bed. Or something does. It's almost as if
it were alive. Blankets wrinkle, sheets peek perversely out from
under the spread, pillows seem to sag or puff up all by themselves if she turns her back, and if she doesn't, then flyspecks
break out on the mirror behind her like pimples, towels start to
drip, stains appear on her apron. If she hasn't forgotten it. She
sighs, turns once more on the perfidious bed. Though always of
an humble and good disposition (as she's been taught), diligent
in endeavoring to please him, and grateful for the opportunity
to do the will of God from the heart by serving him (true service,
perfect freedom, she knows all about that), sometimes, late in
the day like this (shadows are creeping across the room and in
the garden the birds are beginning to sing again), she finds
herself wishing she could make the bed once and for all: glue
down the sheets, sew on the pillows, stiffen the blankets as hard
as boards and nail them into place. But then what? She cannot
imagine. Something frightening. No, no, better this trivial

round, these common tasks, and a few welts on her humble sit-me-down, she reasons, tucking the top sheet and blankets in neatly at the sides and bottom, turning them down at the head just so far that their fold covers half the pillows, than be over-taken by confusion and disorder. *"Teach me, my God and King,"* she sings out hopefully, floating the spread out over the bed, allowing it to fall evenly on all sides, *"in all things thee to —"* But then, as the master steps out of the bathroom behind her, she sees the blatant handprints on the wardrobe mirror, the stream-ers of her lace cap peeking out from under the dresser, standing askew. "I'm sorry, sir," she says, bending over the foot of the bed, presenting to him that broad part destined by Mother Na-ture for the arduous invention of souls. But he ignores it. In-stead he tears open the freshly made bed, crawls into it fully dressed, kicking her in the face through the blankets with his shoes, pulls the sheets over his head, and commences to snore. Perhaps, she thinks, her heart sinking, I'd better go out and come in again . . .

Perhaps I should go for a stroll in the garden, he muses, duti-fully reddening one resonant cheek with a firm volley of slaps, then the other, according to the manuals. I'm so old, and still . . . He sighs ruefully, recalling a dream he was having when the maid arrived (when was that?), something about a woman, bloody morning glories (or perhaps in the dream they were "mourning" glories: there was also something about a Paphian grave), and a bee that flew in and stung him on his tumor, which kept getting mixed up somehow with his humor, such that, swollen, with pain, he was laughing like a dead man . . . "Sir?" "What? *WHAT — ?!"* he cries, starting up, "Ah." His hand is resting idly on her flushed behind as though he meant to leave it there. "I . . . I was just testing the heat," he explains gruffly, taking up the birch rod, testing it for strength and elasticity to wake his fingers up. "When I'm finished, you'll be able to cook little birds over it or roast chestnuts!" He raises the rod, swings it three times round his head, and brings it down with a whirr and a slash, reciting to himself from the manuals to keep his mind, clouded with old obscurities, on the task before him: "Sometimes the operation is begun a little above the garter —"

whish-*SNAP!* "— and ascending the pearly inverted cones —"
hiss-*WHACK!* "— is carried by degrees to the dimpled promon-
tories —" *THWOCK!* "— which are vulgarly called the buttocks!" *SMASH!* "Ow, sir! PLEASE!" She twists about on his
knee, biting her lip, her highest part flexing and quivering with
each blow, her knees scissoring frantically between his legs. "Oh,
teach me," she cries out, trying to stifle the sobs, "my God
and —" whizz-*CRACK!* "— King, thee — *gasp!* — to —" *WHAP!*
"— SEE!" Sometimes, especially late in the day like this, watching the weals emerge from the blank page of her soul's ingress
like secret writing, he finds himself searching it for something,
he doesn't know what exactly, a message of sorts, the revelation
of a mystery in the spreading flush, in the pout and quiver of
her cheeks, the repressed stutter of the little explosions of wind,
the — whush-*SMACK!* — dew-bejeweled hieroglyphs of cross-
hatched stripes. But no, the futility of his labors, that's all there
is to read there. Birdsong, no longer threatening, floats in on
the warm afternoon breeze while he works. There *was* a bee
once, he remembers, that part of his dream was true. Only it
stung him on his hand, as though to remind him of the painful burden of his office. For a long time after that he kept
the garden doors closed altogether, until he realized one day,
spanking the maid for failing to air the bedding properly, that
he was in some wise interfering with the manuals. And what
has she done wrong today? He wonders, tracing the bloody
welts with his fingertips. He has forgotten. It doesn't matter. He
can lecture her on those two fairies, confusion and disorder.
Method and habit, rather . . . "Sir . . . ?" "Yes, yes, in a minute . . ." He leans against the bedpost. To live in the full sense
of the word, he reminds himself, is not to exist or subsist merely,
but to . . . to . . . He yawns. He doesn't remember.

While examining the dismal spectacle of her throbbing sit-me-
down in the wardrobe mirror (at least the worst is past, she
consoles herself, only half believing it), a solution of sorts to that
problem of genesis that's been troubling her occurs to her: to
wit, that change (she is thinking about change now, and conditions) is eternal, has no beginning — only conditions can begin
or end. Who knows, perhaps he has even taught her that. He
has taught her so many things, she can't be sure of anymore.

Everything from habitual deference and the washing of tiffany to pillow fluffing, true service and perfect freedom, the two fairies that make the work (speaking loosely) disappear, proper carriage, sheet folding, and the divine government of pain. Sometimes, late in the day, or on being awakened, he even tells her about his dreams, which seem to be mostly about lechers and ordure and tumors and bottomless holes (once he said "souls"). In a way it's the worst part of her job (that and the things she finds in the bed; today it was broken glass). Once he told her of a dream about a bird with blood in its beak. She asked him, in all deference, if he was afraid of the garden, whereupon he ripped her drawers down, horsed her over a stool, and flogged her so mercilessly she couldn't stand up after, much less sit down. Now she merely says, "Yes, sir," but that doesn't always temper the vigor of his disciplinary interventions, as he likes to call them. Such a one for words and all that! Tracing the radiant weals on that broad part of her so destined with her fingertips, she wishes that just once she might hear something more like, "Well done, thou good and faithful servant, depart in peace!" But then what? When she returned, could it ever be the same? Would he even want her back? No, no, she thinks with a faint shudder, lifting her flannelette drawers up gingerly over her soul's well-ruptured ingress (she hopes more has got in than is leaking out), the sweet breath of late afternoon blowing in to remind her of the time lost, the work yet to be done: no, far better her appointed tasks, her trivial round and daily act of contrition, no matter how pitiless the master's interpretation, than consequences so utterly unimaginable. So, inspirited by her unquenchable appetite for hope and clear-browed devotion to duty, and running his maxims over in her head, she sets about doing the will of God from the heart, scouring the toilet, scrubbing the tiled floor, polishing the furniture and mirrors, checking supplies, changing the towels. All that remains finally is the making of the bed. But how can she do that, she worries, standing there in the afternoon sunlight with stacks of crisp clean sheets in her arms like empty ledgers, her virtuous resolve sapped by a gathering sense of dread as penetrating and aseptic as ammonia, if the master won't get out of it?

*

She enters, encumbered with her paraphernalia, which she deposits by the wall near the door, crosses the room (circumspectly, precipitately, etc.), and flings open the garden doors, smashing the glass, as though once and for all. "Teach me, my God and King," she remarks ruefully (such a sweet breath of amicable violence all about!), "in all things thee to — oh! I beg your pardon, sir!" "A . . . a dream," he stammers, squinting in the glare. He is bound tightly in the damp sheets, can barely move. "Something about blood and a . . . a . . ." I'm so old, and still each day — "Sir . . . ?" He clears his throat. "Would you look under the bed, please, and tell me what you see?" "I — I'm sorry, sir," she replies kneeling down to look, a curious strained expression on her face. With a scream, she disappears. He awakes, his heart pounding. The maid is staring down at his erection as though frightened of his righteous ardor: "Oh, I beg your pardon, sir!" "It's nothing . . . a dream," he explains, rising like the pink clouds of dawn. "Something about . . ." But he can no longer remember, his mind is a blank sheet. Anyway, she is no longer listening. He can hear her moving busily about the room, dusting furniture, sweeping the floor, changing the towels, taking a shower. He's standing there abandoned to the afternoon sunlight in his slippers and pajama bottoms, which seem to have imbibed an unhealthy kind of dampness, when a bird comes in and perches on his erection, what's left of it. "Ah — !" "Oh, I beg your pardon, sir!" "It's — it's nothing," he replies hoarsely, blinking up at her, gripped still by claws as fine as waxed threads. "A dream . . ." But she has left him, gone off singing to her God and King. He tries to pull the blanket back over his head (the bird, its beak opening and closing involuntarily like whipped thighs, was brown as a chestnut, he recalls, and still smoldering), but she returns and snatches it away, the sheets too. Sometimes she can be too efficient. Maybe he has been pushing her too hard, expecting too much too soon. He sits up, feeling rudely exposed (his erection dips back into his pajamas like a frog diving for cover — indeed, it has a greenish cast to it in the half-light of the curtained room: what? isn't she here yet?), and lowers his feet over the side shuffling dutifully for his slippers. But he can't find them. He can't even find the floor! He jerks back, his skin wrinkling in involuntary panic, but feels the bottom sheet slide out from under him — "What? WHAT — ?!" "Oh, I beg your pardon, sir!" "Ah . . . it's nothing," he gasps, struggling to awaken, his heart pounding still (it should be easier than this!), as, screaming, she tucks up her skirt. "A dream . . ."

She enters, as though once and for all, circumspectly deposits her vital paraphernalia beside the door, then crosses the room to fling open (humbly yet authoritatively) the curtains and the garden doors: there is such a song of birds all about! Excited by that, and by the sweet breath of late afternoon, her own eagerness to serve, and faith in the perfectibility of her tasks, she turns with a glad heart and tosses back the bedcovers: "Oh! I beg your pardon, sir!" "A . . . a dream," he mutters gruffly, his erection slipping back inside his pajamas like an abandoned moral. "Something about glory and a pizzle — or puzzle — and a fundamental position in the civil service . . ." But she is no longer listening, busy now at her common round, dusting furniture and sweeping the floor: so much to do! When (not very willingly, she observes) he leaves the bed at last, she strips the sheets and blankets off, shaking the dead bees into the garden, fluffs and airs the pillows, turns the mattress. She hears the master relieving himself noisily in the bathroom: yes, there's water in the bucket, soap too, a sponge, she's remembered everything! Today then, perhaps at last . . . ! Quickly she polishes the mirror, mops the floor, snaps open the fresh sheets and makes the bed. Before she has the spread down, however, he comes out of the bathroom, staggers across the room muttering something about a "bloody new birth," and crawls back into it. "But, sir — !" "What, what?" he yawns, and rolls over on his side, pulling the blanket over his head. She snatches it away. He sits up, blinking, a curious strained expression on his face. "I — I'm sorry, sir," she says, and pushing her drawers down to her knees, tucking her skirt up and bending over, she presents to him that broad part preferred by him and Mother Nature for the invention of souls. He retrieves the blanket and disappears under it, all but his feet, which stick out at the bottom, still slippered. She stuffs her drawers hastily behind her apron bib, knocks over the mop bucket, smears the mirror, throws the

fresh towels in the toilet, and jerks the blanket away again. "I —
I'm sorry, sir," she insists, bending over and lifting her skirt:
"I'm sure I had them on when I came in . . ." What? Is he
snoring? She peers at him past what is now her highest part,
that part invaded suddenly by a dread as chilling as his chastisements are, when true to his manuals, enflaming, and realizes
with a faint shudder (she cannot hold back the little explosions
of wind) that change and condition are coeval and everlasting:
a truth as hollow as the absence of birdsong (but they are singing!) . . .

So she stands there in the open doorway, the glass doors having
long since been flung open (when was that? she cannot remember), her thighs taut and pressed closely together, her face buried in his cast-off pajamas. She can feel against her cheeks, her
lips the soft consoling warmth of them, so recently relinquished,
can smell in them the terror — no, the painful sadness, the divine drudgery (sweet, like crushed flowers, dead birds) — of his
dreams. Mother Nature having provided, she knows all too well,
the proper place for what God has ordained. But there is another odor in them too, musty, faintly sour, like that of truth or
freedom, the fear of which governs every animal, thereby preventing natural confusion and disorder. Or so he has taught
her. Now, her face buried in this pungent warmth and her heart
sinking, the comforting whirr and smack of his rod no more
than a distant echo, disappearing now into the desolate throb of
late-afternoon birdsong, she wonders about the manuals, his
service to them and hers to him, or to that beyond him which
he has not quite named. Whence such an appetite? — she shudders, groans, chewing helplessly on the pajamas — So little relief?

Distantly blows are falling, something about freedom and government, but he is strolling in the garden with a teacher he once
had, discussing the condition of humanity, which keeps getting
mixed up somehow with homonymity, such that each time his
teacher issues a new lament it comes out like slapped laughter.
He is about to remark on the generous swish and snap of a
morning glory that has sprung up in their path as though in-

spired ("Paradox, too, has its techniques," his teacher is saying,
"and so on . . ."), when it turns out to be a woman he once knew
on the civil surface. "What? *WHAT* — *?!*" But she only wants
him to change his position, or perhaps his condition ("You see!"
remarks his teacher sagely, unbuckling his belt, "it's like a kind
of callipygomancy, speaking loosely — am I being unfair?"),
he's not sure, but anyway it doesn't matter, for what she really
wants is to get him out of the sheets he's wrapped in, turn him
over (he seems to have imbibed an unhealthy kind of dampness), and give him a lecture (she says "elixir") on method and
fairies, two dew-bejeweled habits you can roast chestnuts over.
What more, really, does he want of her? (Perhaps his teacher
asks him this, buzzing in and out of his ear like the sweet breath
of solemnity: whirr-*SMACK!*) His arm is rising and falling
through great elastic spaces as though striving for something
fundamental like a forgotten dream or lost drawers. "I — I'm
sorry, sir!" Is she testing him, perched there on his stout engine
of duty like a cooked bird with the lingering bucket of night in
her beak (see how it opens, closes, opens), or is it only a dimpled
fever of the mind? He doesn't know, is almost afraid to ask.
"Something about a higher end," he explains hoarsely, taking
rueful refuge, "or hired end perhaps, and boiled flowers, hard
parts — and another thing, what's left of it . . ." She screams.
The garden groans, quivers, starts, its groves radiant and throbbing. His teacher, no longer threatening, has withdrawn discreetly to a far corner with diagonal creases, where he is turning
what lilacs remain into roses with his rumpled bull's pizzle: it's
almost an act of magic! Still his arm rises and falls, rises and
falls, that broad part of Mother Nature destined for such inven-
tions dancing and bobbing soft and easy under the indulgent
sun: "It's a beautiful day!" "What? *WHAT* — *?!* Answering back
to a reproof?" he inquires gratefully, taunting her with that
civility and kindness due to an inferior, as — hiss — *WHAP!* —
flicking lint off one shoulder and smoothing the ends of his
moustache with involuntary vertical and horizontal motions, he
floats helplessly backwards ("Thank you, sir!"), twitching ami-
cably yet authoritatively like a damp towel, down a bottomless
hole, relieving himself noisily: *Perhaps today then . . . at last!*

RAYMOND CARVER

Raymond Carver's influence on young fiction writers in the
1980s was profound. As a writer, he concentrated almost
entirely on the short story, and, of all his stories, "Cathedral"
perhaps best exemplifies his fictional style, known now as minimalism. In Carver's hands (and in his words) minimalism
involved "realistic characters . . . the gradual accretion of mean-
ingful detail, the concrete word as opposed to the abstract or
arbitrary or slippery word." John Gardner saw "Cathedral" as
fulfilling Carver's goal of "a much more conventional and at the
same time much wilder kind of fiction." Raymond Carver was
born in 1938 in Oregon. At the time of his death in 1988, he
lived in Port Angeles, Washington.

Cathedral

THIS BLIND MAN, an old friend of my wife's, he was on his
way to spend the night. His wife had died. So he was visiting
the dead wife's relatives in Connecticut. He called my wife from
his in-laws'. Arrangements were made. He would come by train,
a five-hour trip, and my wife would meet him at the station. She
hadn't seen him since she worked for him one summer in Seattle
ten years ago. But she and the blind man had kept in touch.
They made tapes and mailed them back and forth. I wasn't
enthusiastic about his visit. He was no one I knew. And his being
blind bothered me. My idea of blindness came from the movies.
In movies, the blind moved slowly and never laughed. Sometimes they were led by seeing-eye dogs. A blind man in my
house was not something I looked forward to.

That summer in Seattle she had needed a job. She didn't have
any money. The man she was going to marry at the end of the
summer was in officer's training school. He didn't have any

money, either. But she was in love with the guy, and he was in love with her, etc. She'd seen something in the paper: Help Wanted — Reading for Blind Man, and a telephone number. She phoned and went over, was hired on the spot. She'd worked with this blind man all summer. She read stuff to him, case studies, reports, that sort of thing. She helped him organize his little office in the county social service department. They'd become good friends, my wife and the blind man. How do I know these things? She told me. And she told me something else. On her last day in the office, the blind man asked if he could touch her face. She agreed to this. She told me he ran his fingers over every part of her face, her nose — even her neck! She never forgot it. She even tried to write a poem about it. She was always writing a poem. She wrote a poem or two every year, usually after something really important had happened to her.

When we first started going out together, she showed me the poem. In the poem she recalled his fingers and the way they had moved around over her face. In the poem she talked about what she had felt at the time, about what went through her mind as he touched her nose and lips. I can recall I didn't think much of the poem. Of course I didn't tell her that. Maybe I just don't understand poetry. I admit it's not the first thing I reach for when I pick up something to read.

Anyway, this man who'd first enjoyed her favors, the officer-to-be, he'd been her childhood sweetheart. So okay. I'm saying that at the end of the summer she let the blind man run his hands over her face, said good-bye to him, married her childhood etc., who was now a commissioned officer, and she moved away from Seattle. But they'd kept in touch, she and the blind man. She made the first contact after a year or so. She called him up one night from an Air Force base in Alabama. She wanted to talk. They talked. He asked her to send him a tape and tell him about her life. She did this. She sent the tape. On the tape she told the blind man about her husband and about their life together in the military. She told the blind man she loved her husband but she didn't like it where they lived and she didn't like it that he was a part of the military-industrial complex. She told the blind man she'd written a poem and he was in it. She told him that she was writing a poem about what it was like to be an Air Force officer's wife in the Deep South. The poem wasn't finished yet. She was still writing it. The blind man made a tape. He sent her the tape. She made a tape. This went on for years. My wife's officer was posted to one base and then another. She sent tapes from Moody AFB, McGuire, McConnell, and finally Travis, near Sacramento, where one night she got to feeling lonely and cut off from people she kept losing in that moving-around life. She balked, couldn't go it another step. She went in and swallowed all the pills and capsules in the medicine cabinet and washed them down with a bottle of gin. Then she got into a hot bath and passed out.

But instead of dying she got sick. She threw up. Her officer — Why should he have a name? He was the childhood sweetheart, and what more does he want? — came home from a training mission, found her, and called the ambulance. In time, she put it on the tape and sent the tape to the blind man. Over the years she put all kinds of stuff on tapes and sent the tapes off lickety-split. Next to writing a poem every year, I think it was her chief means of recreation. On one tape she told the blind man she'd decided to live away from her officer for a time. On another tape she told him about her divorce. She and I began going out, and of course she told her blind man about this. She told him everything, so it seemed to me. Once she asked me if I'd like to hear the latest tape from the blind man. This was a year ago. I was on the tape, she said. So I said okay, I'd listen to it. I got us drinks and we settled down in the living room. We made ready to listen. First she inserted the tape into the player and adjusted a couple of dials. Then she pushed a lever. The tape squeaked and someone began to talk in this loud voice. She lowered the volume. After a few minutes of harmless chitchat, I heard my own name rasped out by this stranger, this man I didn't even know! And then this: "From all you've said about him, I can only conclude —" But we were interrupted, a knock at the door, something, and we didn't get back to the tape. Maybe it was just as well. I'd heard enough, anyway.

Now this same blind stranger was coming to sleep in my house.

"Maybe I could take him bowling," I said to my wife. She was at the draining board doing scalloped potatoes. She put down the knife she was using on the onion and turned around.

"If you love me," she said, "you can do this for me. If you don't love me, okay. But if you had a friend, any friend, and the friend came to visit, I'd make him feel comfortable." She wiped her hands with the dish towel.

"I don't have any blind friends," I said.

"You don't have *any* friends," she said. "Period. Besides," she said, "goddamnit, his wife's just died! Don't you understand that? The man's lost his wife!"

I didn't answer. She'd told me a little about the blind man's wife. The wife's name was Beulah. Beulah! That's a name for a colored woman.

"Was his wife a Negro?" I asked.

"Are you crazy?" my wife said. "Have you just flipped or something?" She picked up the onion. I saw it hit the floor, then roll under the stove. "What's wrong with you?" she said. "Are you drunk?"

"I'm just asking," I said.

Right then my wife filled me in with more detail than I cared to know. I made a drink and sat at the kitchen table to listen. Pieces of the story began to fall into place.

Beulah had gone to work for the blind man the summer after my wife had stopped working for him. Pretty soon Beulah and the blind man had themselves a church wedding. It was a little wedding — who'd be anxious to attend such a wedding in the first place? — just the two of them, and the minister and the minister's wife. But it was a church wedding just the same. What Beulah had wanted, he'd said. But even then Beulah must have been carrying cancer in her lymph glands. After they had been inseparable for eight years — my wife's word, *inseparable* — Beulah's health went into a rapid decline. She died in a Seattle hospital room, the blind man sitting beside the bed and holding on to her hand. They'd married, lived and worked together, slept together — had sex, sure — and then the blind man buried her. All this without his having ever seen what the goddamned woman looked like. It was beyond my understanding. Hearing this, I felt sorry for the blind man for a minute. And then I found myself thinking what a pitiful life this woman must have led. Imagine a woman who could never see herself reflected in the eyes of her loved one. A woman who could go on day after day and never receive the smallest compliment from her beloved. A woman whose husband would never read the expression on her face, be it misery or something better. Someone who could wear make-up or not — what difference to him? She could, if she wanted, wear green eye shadow around one eye, a straight pin in her nostril, yellow slacks and burgundy pumps, no matter. And then to slip off into death, the blind man's hand on her hand, his blind eyes streaming tears — I'm imagining now — her last thought maybe this: that her beloved never knew what she looked like, and she on an express to the grave. Robert was left with a small insurance policy and half of a twenty-peso Mexican coin. The other half of the coin went into the box with her. Pathetic.

So when the time rolled around, my wife went to the rail station. With nothing to do but wait — and sure, I blamed him for that — I was having a drink and watching TV when I heard the car pull into the drive. I got up from the sofa with my drink and went to the window to have a look.

I saw my wife laughing as she parked the car. I saw her get out of the car and shut the door. She was still wearing a smile. Just amazing. She went around to the other side of the car to where the blind man was already starting to get out. This blind man, feature this, he was wearing a full beard! A beard on a blind man! Too much, I say. The blind man reached into the back seat and dragged out a suitcase. My wife took his arm, shut the car door, and, talking all the way, moved him down the drive and then up the steps to the front porch. I turned off the TV. I finished my drink, rinsed the glass, dried my hands. Then I went to the door.

My wife said, "I want you to meet Robert. Robert, this is my husband. I've told you all about him." She closed the porch screen. She was beaming. She had this blind man by his coat sleeve.

The blind man let go of his suitcase and up came his hand.

I took it. He squeezed hard, held my hand, and then he let it go.

"I feel like we've already met," he boomed.

"Likewise," I said. I didn't know what else to say. Then I said, "Welcome. I've heard a lot about you." We began to move then, a little group, from the porch into the living room, my wife guiding him by the arm. He carried his suitcase in his other hand. My wife said things like, "To your left here, Robert. That's right. Now watch it, there's a chair. That's it. Sit down right here. This is the sofa. We just bought this sofa two weeks ago."

I started to say something about the old sofa. I'd liked that old sofa. But I didn't say anything. Then I wanted to say something else, small talk, about the scenic Hudson River. How going *to* New York, sit on the right-hand side of the train, and coming *from* New York, the left-hand side.

"Did you have a good train ride?" I said. "Which side of the train did you sit on, by the way?"

"What a question, which side!" my wife said. "What's it matter which side?" she said.

"I just asked," I said.

"Right side," the blind man said. "For the sun. Until this morning," the blind man said, "I hadn't been on a train in nearly forty years. Not since I was a kid. With my folks. That's been a long time. I'd nearly forgotten that sensation. I have winter in my beard now," he said. "So I've been told, anyway. Do I look distinguished, my dear?" he said to my wife.

"You look distinguished, Robert," she said. "Robert," she said. "Robert, it's just so good to see you." My wife finally took her eyes off the blind man and looked at me.

I had the distinct feeling she didn't like what she saw. I shrugged.

I've never met or personally known anyone who was blind. This blind man was late forties, a heavyset, balding man with stooped shoulders, as if he carried a great weight there. He wore brown slacks, brown cordovan shoes, a light brown shirt, a tie, a sports coat. Spiffy. He also had this full beard. But he didn't carry a cane and he didn't wear dark glasses. I'd always thought dark glasses were a must for the blind. Fact was, I wished he had a pair. At first glance, his eyes looked like anyone else's eyes. But if you looked close there was something different about them. Too much white in the iris, for one thing, and the pupils seemed to move around in the sockets without his knowing it or being able to control it. Creepy. As I stared at his face,

I saw the left pupil turn in toward his nose, while the other made a futile effort to keep in one place. But it was only an effort, for that eye was on the roam without his knowing it or wanting it to be.

I said, "Let me get you a drink. What's your pleasure? We have a little of everything. It's one of our pastimes."

"Bub, I'm a Scotch man myself," he said fast enough, in this big voice.

"Right," I said. Bub! "Sure you are. I knew it."

He let his fingers touch his suitcase, which was sitting alongside the sofa. He was taking his bearings. I didn't blame him for that.

"I'll move that up to your room," my wife said.

"No, that's fine," he said loudly. "It can go up when I go up."

"A little water with the Scotch?" I said.

"Very little," he said.

"I knew it," I said.

He said, "Just a tad. The Irish actor, Barry Fitzgerald? I'm like that fellow. When I drink water, Fitzgerald said, I drink water. When I drink whiskey, I drink whiskey." My wife laughed. The blind man brought his hand up under his beard. He lifted his beard slowly and let it drop.

I did the drinks, three big glasses of Scotch with a splash of water in each. Then we made ourselves comfortable and talked about Robert's travels. First the long flight from the West Coast to Connecticut, we covered that. Then from Connecticut up here by train. We had another drink concerning that leg of the trip.

I remembered having read somewhere that the blind didn't smoke because, speculation had it, they couldn't see the smoke they exhaled. I thought I knew that much and that much only about blind people. But this blind man smoked his cigarette down to the nubbin and then lit another one. This blind man filled his ashtray and my wife emptied it.

When we sat down to the table for dinner we had another drink. My wife heaped Robert's plate with cube steak, scalloped potatoes, green beans. I buttered him up two slices of bread. I said, "Here's bread and butter for you." I swallowed some of

my drink. "Now let us pray," I said, and the blind man lowered
his head. My wife looked at me, her mouth agape. "Pray the
phone won't ring and the food doesn't get cold," I said.

We dug in. We ate everything there was to eat on the table.
We ate like there was no tomorrow. We didn't talk. We ate. We
scarfed. We grazed that table. We were into serious eating. The
blind man had right away located his foods, he knew just where
everything was on his plate. I watched with admiration as he
used his knife and fork on the meat. He'd cut two pieces
of meat, fork the meat into his mouth, and then go all out for
the scalloped potatoes, the beans next, and then he'd tear
off a hunk of buttered bread and eat that. He'd follow this up
with a big drink of milk. It didn't seem to bother him to use his
fingers once in a while, either. He used his bread to scoop
beans.

We finished everything, including half of a strawberry pie.
For a few moments we sat as if stunned. Sweat beaded on our
faces. Finally, we got up from the table and left the dirty plates.
We didn't look back. We took ourselves into the living room and
sank into our places again. Robert and my wife sat on the sofa.
I took the big chair. We had us two or three more drinks while
they talked about the major things that had transpired for them
in the past ten years. For the most part, I just listened. Now and
then I joined in. I didn't want him to think I'd left the room,
and I didn't want her to think I was feeling left out. They talked
of things that had happened to them — to them! — these past
ten years. I waited in vain to hear my name on my wife's sweet
lips: "And then my dear husband came into my life" — something like that. But I heard nothing of the sort. More talk of
Robert. Robert had done a little of everything, it seemed, a
regular blind jack-of-all-trades. But most recently he and his
wife had had an Amway distributorship, from which, I gathered, they'd earned their living, such as it was. The blind man
was also a ham radio operator. He talked in his loud voice about
conversations he'd had with fellow operators in Guam, the Phil-
ippines, Alaska, even Tahiti. He said he'd have a lot of friends
there if he ever wanted to go visit those places. From time to
time he'd turn his blind face toward me, put his hand under his
beard, ask me something. How long had I been at my present

position? (Three years.) Did I like my work? (I didn't.) Was I going to stay with it? (What were the options?)

Finally, when I thought he was beginning to run down, I got up and turned on the TV.

My wife looked at me with irritation. She was heading toward a boil. Then she looked at the blind man and said, "Robert, do you have a TV?"

The blind man said, "My dear, I have two TVs. I have a color set and a black-and-white thing, an old relic. It's funny, but if I turn the TV on, and I'm always turning it on, I turn the color set on. Always. It's funny."

I didn't know what to say to that. I had absolutely nothing to say about that. No opinion. So I watched the news program and tried to listen to what the announcer was saying.

"This is a color TV," the blind man said. "Don't ask me how, but I can tell."

"We traded up a while ago," I said.

The blind man had another taste of his drink. He lifted his beard, sniffed it, and let it fall. He leaned forward on the sofa. He positioned his ashtray on the coffee table, then put the lighter to his cigarette. He leaned back on the sofa and crossed his legs at the ankles.

My wife covered her mouth, and then she yawned. She stretched. She said, "I think I'll go upstairs and put on my robe. I think I'll change into something else. Robert, you make yourself comfortable," she said.

"I'm comfortable," the blind man said.

"I want you to feel comfortable in this house," she said.

"I am comfortable," the blind man said.

After she'd left the room, he and I listened to the weather report and then to the sports roundup. My wife had been gone so long I didn't know if she was going to come back. I thought she might have gone to bed. I wished she'd come back downstairs. I didn't want to be left alone with a blind man. I asked him if he wanted another drink, and he said sure. Then I asked if he wanted to smoke dope with me. I said I'd just rolled a number. I hadn't, but I planned to do so in about two shakes.

"I'll try some with you," he said.

"Damn right," I said. "That's the stuff."

I got our drinks and sat down on the sofa with him. Then I rolled us two fat numbers. I lit one and passed it. I brought it to his fingers. He took it and inhaled.

"Hold it as long as you can," I said. I could tell he didn't know the first thing.

My wife came back downstairs wearing her robe and pink slippers. "What do I smell?" she said.

"We thought we'd have us some cannabis," I said.

My wife gave me a purely savage look. Then she looked at him and said, "Robert, I didn't know you smoked."

He said, "I do now, my dear. First time for everything," he said. "But I don't feel anything yet."

"This stuff is pretty mellow," I said. "This stuff is mild. It's dope you can reason with. It doesn't mess you up."

"Not much it doesn't, bub," he said, and laughed.

My wife sat on the sofa between the blind man and me. I passed her the number. She took it and inhaled and then passed it back to me. "Which way is this going?" she said. Then she said, "I shouldn't be smoking this. I can hardly keep my eyes open as it is. That dinner did me in. I shouldn't have eaten so much."

"It was the strawberry pie," the blind man said. "That's what did it," he said, and he laughed his big laugh. Then he shook his head.

"There's more strawberry pie," I said.

"Do you want some more, Robert?" my wife asked.

"Maybe in a little while," he said.

We gave our attention to the TV. My wife yawned again. She said, "Your bed is made up when you feel like going to bed, Robert. I know you must have had a long day. When you're ready to go to bed, say so." She pulled his arm. "Robert?"

He came to and said, "I've had a real nice time. This beats tapes, doesn't it?"

I said, "Coming at you," and I put the number between his fingers. He inhaled, held the smoke, and then let it go. It was like he'd been doing it since he was nine years old.

"Thanks, bub," he said. "But I think this is all for me. I think I'm beginning to feel it," he said. He held the burning roach out for my wife.

"Same here," she said. "Ditto. Me too." She took the roach and passed it to me. "I may just sit here for a while between you two guys with my eyes closed. But don't let me bother you, okay? Either one of you. If it bothers you, say so. Otherwise, I may just sit here with my eyes closed until you're ready to go to bed," she said. "Your bed's made up, Robert, when you're ready. It's right next to our room at the top of the stairs. We'll show you up when you're ready. You wake me now, you guys, if I fall asleep." She said that and then she closed her eyes and went to sleep.

The news program ended. I got up and turned the channel. I sat back down on the sofa. I wished my wife hadn't pooped out. Her head lay across the back of the sofa, her mouth open. She'd turned so that her robe had slipped away from her legs, exposing a juicy thigh. I reached to draw her robe over the thigh, and it was then I glanced at the blind man. What the hell! I flipped the robe open again.

"You say when you want some strawberry pie," I said.

"I will," he said.

I said, "Are you tired? Do you want me to take you up to your bed? Are you ready to hit the hay?"

"Not yet," he said. "No, I'll stay up with you, bub. If that's all right. I'll stay up until you're ready to turn in. We haven't had a chance to talk. Know what I mean? I feel like me and her monopolized the evening." He lifted his beard and he let it fall. He picked up his cigarettes and his lighter.

"That's all right," I said. Then I said, "I'm glad for the company." And I guess I was. Every night I smoked dope and stayed up as long as I could before I fell asleep. My wife and I hardly ever went to bed at the same time. When I did go to sleep, I had these dreams. Sometimes I'd wake up from one of them, the heart going crazy.

Something about the Church and the Middle Ages, narrated by an Englishman, was on the TV. Not your run-of-the-mill TV fare. I wanted to watch something else. I turned to the other channels. But there was nothing on them, either. So I turned back to the first channel and apologized.

"Bub, it's all right," he said. "It's fine with me. Whatever you want to watch is okay. I'm always learning something. Learning never ends. It won't hurt me to learn something tonight. I got ears," he said.

We didn't say anything for a time. He was leaning forward with his head turned at me, while his right ear was aimed in the direction of the set. Very disconcerting. Now and then his eyelids drooped and then they snapped open again. Now and then he put his fingers into his beard and tugged, as if thinking about something he was hearing on the television.

On the screen a group of men wearing cowls was being set upon and tormented by men dressed in skeleton costumes and men dressed as devils. The men dressed as devils wore devil masks, horns, and long tails. This pageant was part of a procession. The Englishman said it all took place in Málaga, Spain, once a year. I tried to explain to the blind man what was happening.

"Skeletons," he said. "I know about skeletons," he said, and he nodded.

The TV showed Chartres Cathedral. Then there was a long slow look at Sainte-Chapelle. Finally the picture switched to Notre-Dame, with its flying buttresses, its spires reaching toward clouds. The camera pulled away to show the whole of the cathedral rising above the skyline.

There were times when the Englishman who was telling the thing would shut up, would simply let the camera move around over the cathedrals. Or else the camera would tour the countryside, men in fields walking behind oxen. I waited as long as I could. Then I felt I had to say something. I said, "They're showing the outside of this cathedral now. Gargoyles. Little statues carved to look like monsters. Now I guess they're in Italy. Yeah, they're in Italy. There's fresco paintings on the walls of this one church."

"What's fresco painting, bub?" he asked, and he sipped from his drink.

I reached for my glass. But it was empty. I tried to remember what I could remember about frescoes. "You're asking me what are frescoes?" I said. "That's a good question. I don't know."

The camera moved to a cathedral outside Lisbon, Portugal. The differences in the Portuguese cathedral compared with the

French and Italian were not that great. But they were there.
Mostly the interior stuff. Then something occurred to me and I
said, "Something has occurred to me. Do you have an idea what
a cathedral is? What they look like, that is? Do you follow me?
If somebody says *cathedral* to you, do you have any notion what
they're talking about? Do you know the difference between that
and a Baptist church, say? Or that and a mosque, or syn-
agogue?"

He let the smoke issue from his mouth. "I know they took
hundreds of workers fifty or a hundred years to build," he said.
"I just heard the man say that, of course. I know generations of
the same families worked on a cathedral. I heard him say that,
too. The men who began their life's work on them, they never
lived to see the completion of their work. In that wise, bub,
they're no different from the rest of us, right?" He laughed.
Then his eyelids drooped again. His head nodded. He seemed
to be snoozing. Maybe he was imagining himself in Portugal.
The TV was showing another cathedral now. This one was in
Germany. The Englishman's voice droned on. "Cathedrals," the
blind man said. He sat up and rolled his head back and forth.
"If you want the truth, bub, that's about all I know. What I just
said. What I heard him say. But maybe you could describe one
to me? I wish you'd do it. I'd like that. If you want to know, I
really don't have a good idea."

I stared hard at the shot of the cathedral on the TV. It held a
minute. Then it was gone, and the view was of the inside with
rows of benches and high windows. How could I even begin to
describe it? But say my life depended on it. Say my life was
being threatened by an insane Turkish bey.

They took the camera outside again. I stared some more at
the cathedral before the picture flipped off into the countryside.
There was no use. I turned to the blind man and said, "To begin
with, they're very tall. Very, very tall." I was looking around the
room for clues. I tried again. "They reach way up. Up and up.
Toward the sky. They soar. They're like poetry, that's what
they're like. They're so big, some of them, they have to have
these supports. To help hold them up, so to speak. These supports are called buttresses. They remind me of viaducts for
some reason. But maybe you don't know viaducts, either? Some-

times the cathedrals have devils and such carved into the front. Sometimes great lords and ladies. Don't ask me why this is," I said. He was nodding. The whole upper part of his body seemed to be moving back and forth. "I'm not doing so good, am I?" I said.

He stopped nodding and leaned forward on the edge of the sofa. As he listened to me, he was running his fingers through his beard. I wasn't getting through to him though, I could see that. But he waited for me to go on just the same. He nodded, as if trying to encourage me. I tried to think what else I could say. "They're really big. They're massive. They're built of stone. Marble, too, sometimes. In those old days, when they built cathedrals, men aspired to be close to God. In those days God was an important part of everyone's life. This was reflected in their cathedral-building. I'm sorry," I said, "but it looks like that's the best I can do for you. I'm just no good at it."

"That's all right, bub," he said. "Hey, listen. I hope you don't mind my asking you. Can I ask you something? Let me ask you a simple question, yes or no. I'm just curious and there's no offense. You're my host. But let me ask if you are in any way religious? You don't mind my asking?"

I shook my head. He couldn't see that, though. A wink is the same as a nod to a blind man. "I guess I'm agnostic or something. No, the fact is, I don't believe in it. Anything. Sometimes it's hard. You know what I'm saying?"

"Sure, I do," he said.

"Right," I said.

The Englishman was still holding forth. My wife sighed in her sleep. She drew a long breath and continued with her sleep.

"You'll have to forgive me," I said. "But I can't tell you what a cathedral looks like. It just isn't in me to do it. I can't do any more than I've done." The blind man sat very still, his head down, as he listened to me. "The truth is, cathedrals don't mean anything special to me. Nothing. Cathedrals. They're something to look at on late-night TV. That's all they are."

It was then he cleared his throat. He brought something up. He took a handkerchief from his back pocket. In a minute he said, "I get it, bub. It's okay. It happens. Don't worry about it," he said. "Hey, listen to me. Will you do me a favor? I got an

idea. Why don't you find us some heavy paper? And a pen.
We'll do something. An experiment. Sure, you can do it. You
can. We'll draw one together. Get us a pen and some heavy
paper. Go on, bub, get the stuff," he said.

So I went upstairs. My legs felt like they didn't have any strength
in them. They felt like they did sometimes after I'd run a couple
miles. In my wife's room I looked around. I found some ball-
points in a little basket on her table. And then I tried to think
where to look for the kind of paper he was talking about.

Downstairs, in the kitchen, I found a shopping bag with onion
skins in the bottom of the bag. I emptied the bag and shook it.
I brought it into the living room and sat down with it near his
legs. I moved some things, smoothed the wrinkles from the bag,
spread it out on the coffee table. The blind man got down from
the sofa and sat next to me on the carpet.

He ran his fingers over the paper. He went up and down the
sides of the paper and the edges, top and bottom. He fingered
the corners. "All right," he said. "All right. Let's do her."

He found my hand, the hand with the pen. He closed his
hand over my hand. "Go ahead, bub, draw," he said. "Draw.
You'll see. I'll follow along with you. It'll be all right. Just begin
now, like I'm telling you. You'll see. Draw," he said.

So I began. First I drew a box that resembled a house. It could
have been the house I lived in. Then I put a roof on the house.
At either end of the roof I drew spires. Crazy.

"Swell," he said. "Terrific. You're doing fine," he said. "Never
thought anything like this could happen in your lifetime, did
you? Well, it's a strange life, bub, we all know that. Go on now.
Keep it up."

I put in windows with arches. I drew flying buttresses. I hung
great doors. I couldn't stop. The TV station went off the air. I
put down the pen and closed and opened my fingers. The blind
man felt around over the paper. He moved the tips of his fingers slowly over the paper, over what I'd drawn, and he nodded. "Doing fine," he said.

I took up the pen, and he found my hand once more. I kept
at it. I'm no artist. But I kept drawing just the same.

My wife opened her eyes and gazed at us. She sat up on the

sofa, her robe hanging open. She said, "What are you doing? What in the world are you doing?"

I didn't answer her. The blind man said, "We're drawing a cathedral, dear. Me and him are working on something important. Press hard now," he said to me. "That's right. That's good," he said. "Sure. You got it, bub. I can tell. You didn't think you could. But you can, can't you? You're cooking with Crisco now. You'll see. Know what I'm saying? We're going to have us something here in a minute. How's the old arm?" he said. "Put some people in there now. What's a church without people, bub?"

"What's going on?" my wife said. "Robert, what are you doing? What's going on?"

"It's all right," he said to her. "Close your eyes now, bub," he said.

I did that. I closed them just like he said.

"Are they closed?" he said. "Don't fudge."

"They're closed," I said.

"Keep them that way," he said. He said, "Don't stop now." So we kept on with it. His fingers rode my fingers as my hand went over the rough paper. It was like nothing else in my life up to now.

In a minute he said, "I think that's enough. I think you got the idea," he said. "Take a look. What do you think?"

But I had my eyes closed. I thought I'd keep them closed a little longer. I thought it was something I ought not to forget.

"Well?" he said. "Are you looking?"

My eyes were still closed. I was in my house and I knew that. But I didn't feel inside anything.

"It's really something," I said.

CHARLES JOHNSON

John Gardner described this as "an eerie story of two young blacks' obsessive self-entrapment." Narrated by a first-time robber, the story creates the enclosed world of urban life with dramatic authenticity. As contemporary as O. Henry's "Gift of the Magi" is now dated, "Exchange Value" is a prime candidate for Best Example of the Use of Irony. Charles Johnson grew up in Chicago and lives and teaches in Seattle. He has published three novels, numerous short stories, and, as a cartoonist, more than one thousand drawings. He also writes for television.

Exchange Value

ME AND MY BROTHER Loftis came in by the old lady's window. There was some kinda boobytrap — boxes of broken glass — that shoulda warned us Miss Bailey wasn't the easy mark we made her to be. She had been living alone for twenty years in 4-B down the hall from Loftis and me, long before our folks died — a hincty, half-bald West Indian woman with a craglike face, who kept her door barricaded, shutters closed, and wore the same sorrylooking outfit — black wingtip shoes, cropfingered gloves in winter, and a man's floppy hat — like maybe she dressed half-asleep or in a dark attic. Loftis, he figured Miss Bailey had some grandtheft dough stashed inside, jim, or leastways a shoebox full of money, cause she never spent a nickel on herself, not even for food, and only left her place at night.

Anyway, we figured Miss Bailey was gone. Her mailbox be full, and Pookie White, who run the Thirty-ninth Street Creole restaurant, he say she ain't dropped by in days to collect the handouts he give her so she can get by. So here's me and Loftis, tipping around Miss Bailey's blackdark kitchen. The floor be littered with fruitrinds, roaches, old food furred with blue mold. Her dirty dishes be stacked in a sink spidered with cracks, and it looks like the old lady been living, lately, on Ritz crackers and Department of Agriculture (Welfare Office) peanut butter. Her toilet be stopped up, too, and, on the bathroom floor, there's five Maxwell House coffee cans full of shit. Me, I was closing her bathroom door when I whiffed this evil smell so bad, so thick, I could hardly breathe, and what breath I drew was horrible, like a solid thing in my throatpipes, like soup. "Cooter," Loftis whisper, low, across the room, "you smell that?" He went right on sniffing it, like people do for some reason when something be smelling stanky, then took out his headrag and held it over his mouth. "That's the awfulest stink I *ever* smelled!" Then, head low, he slipped his long self into the livingroom. Me, I stayed by the window, gulping air, and do you know why?

You oughta know, up front, that I ain't too good at this gangster stuff, and I had a real bad feeling about Miss Bailey from the get-go. Mama used to say it was Loftis, not me, who'd go places — I see her standing at the sideboard by the sink now, big as a Frigidaire, white with flour to her elbows, a washtowel over her shoulder, while we ate a breakfast of cornbread and syrup. He graduated fifth at DuSable High School, had two gigs, and, like Papa, he be always wanting the things white people had out in Hyde Park, where Mama did daywork. Loftis, he the kinda brother who buys *Esquire*, sews Hart, Schaffner and Marx labels in Robert Hall suits, talks properlike, packs his hair with Murrays, and took classes in politics and stuff at the Black People's Topographical Library in the late 1960s; who, at thirty, makes his bed military style, reads *Black Scholar* on the bus he takes to the plant, and, come hell or high water, plans to make a Big Score. Loftis, he say I'm bout as useful on a hustle — or when it comes to getting ahead — as a headcold, and he say he has to count my legs sometimes to be sure I ain't a mule, seeing how, for all my eighteen years, I can't keep no job and sorta stay close to home, watching TV or reading *World's Finest* comic books, or maybe just laying dead, listening to music, imagining I see faces or foreign places in water stains on the wallpaper, cause somedays when I remember Papa, then Mama killing theyselves for chump change — a pitiful li'l bowl of porridge —

I get to thinking that even if I ain't had all I wanted, maybe I've had, you know, all I'm ever gonna get.

"Cooter," Loftis say from the livingroom. "You best get in here quick."

Loftis, he'd switched on Miss Bailey's sulfurcolored living-room lights, so for a second I couldn't see and started coughing — the smell be so powerful it hit my nostrils like coke — and when my eyes cleared, shapes evolved from the light, and I thought for an instant like I'd slipped in space. I seen why Loftis called me, and went back two steps. See, 4-B is so small, if you ring Miss Bailey's doorbell the toilet'd flush. But her living-room, webbed in dust, be filled to the max with dollars of all denominations, stacks of stock in General Motors, Gulf Oil, and 3M Corporation in old White Owl cigar boxes, battered purses, or bound in pink rubber bands. It be like the kind of cubby-hole kids play in, but filled with . . . *things* — everything — like a world within the world, you take it from me, so like picturebook scenes of plentifulness you could seal yourself off in here and settle forever. Loftis and me both drew breath suddenly. There be unopened cases of Jack Daniel's, three safes cemented to the floor, hundreds of matchbooks, unworn clothes, a zinc laundry tub, dozens of wedding rings, rubbish, World War II magazines, a carton of one hundred canned sardines, mink stoles, old rags, a birdcage, a bucket of silver dollars, thousands of books, paintings, quarters in tobacco cans, two pianos, glass jars of pennies, a set of bagpipes, an almost complete Model A Ford dappled with rust, and, I swear, three sections of a dead tree.

"Godamighty damn!" My head be light; I sat on an upended peachcrate and picked me up a bottle of Jack Daniel's.

"Don't you touch *any*thing!" Loftis, he panting a little; he slap both hands on a table. "Not until we inventory this stuff."

"Inventory? Aw Lord, Loftis," I say, "something ain't *right* about this stash. There could be a curse on it . . ."

"Boy, sometimes you act weakminded."

"For real, Loftis, I got a feeling . . ."

Loftis, he shucked off his shoes and sat down heavily on the lumpy arm of a stuffed chair. "Don't say *any*thing." He chewed his knuckles, and for the first time Loftis looked like he didn't know his next move. "Let me think, okay?" He squeezed his nose in a way he has when thinking hard, sighed, then stood up, and say, "There's something you better see in that bedroom yonder. Cover up your mouth."

"Loftis, I ain't going in there."

He look at me right funny then. "She's a miser, that's all. She saves things."

"But a tree?" I say. "Loftis, a *tree* ain't normal!"

"Cooter, I ain't gonna tell you twice."

Like always, I followed Loftis, who swung his flashlight from the plant — he a nightwatchman — into Miss Bailey's bedroom, but me, I'm thinking how trippy this thing is getting, remembering how, last year, when I had a paper route, the old lady, with her queer crablike walk, pulled my coat for some change in the hallway, and when I give her a handful of dimes, she say in her old Inner Sanctum voice, "Thank you, Co-o-oter," then gulped the coins down like aspirin, no lie, and scurried off like a hunchback. Me, I wanted no parts of this squirrelly old broad, but Loftis, he holding my wrist now, beaming his light onto a low bed. The room had a funny, museumlike smell. Real sour. It was full of dirty laundry. And I be sure the old lady's stuff had a terrible string attached when Loftis, looking away, lifted her bedsheets and a knot of black flies rose. I stepped back and held my breath. Miss Bailey be in her long-sleeved flannel nightgown, bloated, like she'd been inflated by a tire pump, her crazy putty face bald with rot, flyblown, her fingers big as bananas. Her wristwatch be ticking softly beside a stump of half-eaten bread. Above the bed, her wall had roaches squashed in little circles of bloodstain. Maggots clustered in her eyes, her ears, and one fistsized rat rattled in her flesh. My eyes snapped shut. My knees failed, then I did a Hollywood faint. When I surfaced, Loftis, he be sitting beside me in the livingroom, where he'd drug me, reading a wrinkled, yellow article from the Chicago *Daily Defender.*

"Listen to this," Loftis say. " 'Elnora Bailey, forty-five, a Negro housemaid in the Highland Park home of Henry Conners, is the beneficiary of her employer's will. An old American family, the Connerses arrived in this country on the *Providence,* shortly after the voyage of the *Mayflower.* The family flourished in the early days of the 1900s'! . . ." He went on, getting breath. " 'A distinguished and wealthy industrialist, without heirs or a wife, Conners willed his entire estate to Miss Bailey of 3347 N. Clark Street for her twenty years of service to his family' . . ." Loftis, he give that Geoffrey Holder laugh of his, low and deep, then it eased up his throat until it hit a high note and tipped his head back onto his shoulders. "Cooter, that was before we was born! Miss Bailey kept this in the Bible next to her bed."

Standing, I braced myself with one hand against the wall. "She didn't earn it?"

"Naw." Loftis, he folded the paper — "Not one penny" — and stuffed it in his shirt pocket. His jaw looked tight as a horseshoe. "Way *I* see it," he say, "this was her one shot in a lifetime to be rich, but, being country, she had backward ways and blew it." Rubbing his hands, he stood up to survey the livingroom. "Somebody's gonna find Miss Bailey soon, but if we stay on the case — Cooter, don't you square up on me now — we can tote everything to our place before daybreak. Best we start with the big stuff."

"But why didn't she *use* it, huh? Tell me that?"

Loftis, he don't pay me no mind. When he gets an idea in his head, you can't dig it out with a chisel. How long it took me and Loftis to inventory, then haul Miss Bailey's queer old stuff to our crib, I can't say, but that decrepit old ninnyhammer's hoard come to $879,543 in cash money, thirty-two bank books (some deposits be only $5), and me, I wasn't sure I was dreaming or what, but I suddenly flashed on this feeling, once we left her flat, that all the fears Loftis and me had about the future be gone, cause Miss Bailey's property was the past — the power of that fellah Henry Conners trapped like a bottle spirit, which we could live off, so it was the future, too, pure potential: can *do*. Loftis got to talking on about how that piano we pushed home be equal to a thousand bills, jim, which equals, say, a bad TEAC A-3340 tape deck, or a down payment on a deuce-and-a-quarter. Its value be (Loftis say) that of a universal standard of measure, relational, unreal as number, so that tape deck could turn, magically, into two gold lamé suits, a trip to Tijuana, or twenty-five rimjobs from a ho — we had $879,543 worth of wishes, if you can deal with that. Be like Miss Bailey's stuff is raw energy, and Loftis and me, like wizards, can transform her stuff into anything else at will. All we had to do, it seemed to me, was decide exactly what to exchange it for.

While Loftis studied this over (he looked funny, like a potato trying to say something, after the inventory, and sat, real quiet, in the kitchen), I filled my pockets with fifties, grabbed me a cab downtown to grease, yum, at one of them high-hat restaurants in the Loop . . . But then I thought better of it, you know, like I'd be out of place — just another jig putting on airs — and scarfed instead at a ribjoint till both my eyes bubbled. This fat lady making fishburgers in the back favored an old hardleg babysitter I once had, a Mrs. Paine who made me eat ochre, and I wanted so bad to say, "Loftis and me Got Ovuh," but I couldn't put that in the wind, could I, so I hatted up. Then I copped a boss silk necktie, cashmere socks, and a whistle-slick maxie leather jacket on State Street, took cabs *every*where, but when I got home that evening a funny, Pandoralike feeling hit me. I took off the jacket, boxed it — it looked so trifling in the hallway's weak light — and, tired, turned my key in the door. I couldn't get in. Loftis, he'd changed the lock and, when he finally let me in, looking vaguer, crabby, like something out of the Book of Revelations, I seen this elaborate boobytrapped tunnel of cardboard and razor blades behind him, with a two-foot space just big enough for him or me to crawl through. That wasn't all. Two bags of trash from the furnace room be sitting inside the door. Loftis, he give my leather jacket this evil look, hauled me inside, and hit me upside the head.

"How much this thing set us back?"

"Two fifty." My jaws be tight; I toss him my receipt. "You want me to take it back? Maybe I can get something else . . ."

Loftis, he say, not to me, but to the receipt, "Remember the time Mama give me that ring we had in the family for fifty years? And I took it to Merchandise Mart and sold it for a few pieces of candy?" He hitched his chair forward, and sat with his elbows on his knees. "That's what you did, Cooter. You crawled into a Clark bar." He commence to rip up my receipt, then picked up his flashlight and keys. "The instant you buy something you *lose* the power to buy something." He button up his coat with holes in the elbows, showing his blue shirt, then turned round at the tunnel to say: "Don't touch Miss Bailey's money, or drink her splo, or do *any*thing until I get back."

"Where you going?"

"To work. It's Wednesday, ain't it?"

"You going to work?"

"Yeah."

"You got to go *really?* Loftis," I say, "what you brang them bags of trash in here for?"

"It ain't trash!" He cut his eyes at me. "There's good clothes in there. Mr. Peterson tossed them out, he don't care, but I saw some use in them, that's all."

"Loftis . . ."

"Yeah?"

"What we gonna do with all this money?"

Loftis pressed his fingers to his eyelids, and for a second he look caged, or like somebody'd kicked him in his stomach. Then he cut me some slack: "Let me think on it tonight — it don't pay to rush — then we can TCB, okay?"

Five hours after Loftis leave for work, that old blister Mr. Peterson, our landlord, he come collecting rent, find Miss Bailey's body in apartment 4-B, and phoned the Fire Department. Me, I be folding my new jacket in tissue paper to keep it fresh, adding the box to Miss Bailey's unsunned treasures, when two paramedics squeezed her on a long stretcher through a crowd in the hallway. See, I had to pin her from the stairhead, looking down one last time at this dizzy old lady, and I seen something in her face, like maybe she'd been poor as Job's turkey for thirty years, suffering that special Negro fear of using up what little we get in this life — Loftis, he call that entropy — believing in her belly, and for all her faith, jim, there just ain't no more coming tomorrow from grace, or the Lord, or from her own labor, like she can't kill nothing, and won't nothing die . . . so when Conners will her his wealth, it put her through changes, she be spellbound, possessed by the promise of life, panicky about depletion, and locked now in the past cause *every* purchase, you know, has to be a poor buy: a loss of life. Me, I wasn't worried none. Loftis, he got a brain trained by years of talking trash with people in Frog Hudson's Barber Shop on Thirty-fifth Street. By morning, I knew, he'd have some kinda wheeze worked out.

But Loftis, he don't come home. Me, I got plenty worried. I listen to the hi-fi all day Thursday, only pawing outside to peep down the stairs, like that'd make Loftis come sooner. So Thursday go by; and come Friday the head's out of kilter — first there's an ogrelike belch from the toiletbowl, then water bursts from the bathroom into the kitchen — and me, I can't call the super (How do I explain the tunnel?), so I gave up and quit bailing. But on Sat'day, I could smell greens cooking next door. Twice I almost opened Miss Bailey's sardines, even though starving be less an evil than eating up our stash, but I waited till it was dark and, lightheaded with hunger, I stepped outside to Pookie White's, lay a hardluck story on him, and Pookie, he give me some jambalaya and gumbo. Back home in the livingroom, fingerfeeding myself, barricaded in by all that hope made material, the Kid felt like a king in his countingroom, or God in February, the month before He made the world (Mama's saying), and I copped some z's in an armchair till I heard the door move on its hinges, then bumping in the tunnel, and a heavy-footed walk thumped into the bedroom.

"Loftis?" I rubbed my eyes. "You back?" It be Sunday morning. Six-thirty sharp. Darkness dissolved slowly into the strangeness of twilight, with the rays of sunlight flaring at exactly the same angle they fall each night, as if the hour be an island, a moment, outside time. Me, I'm afraid Loftis gonna fuss bout my not straightening up, letting things go. I went into the bathroom, poured water in the one-spigot washstand — brown rust come bursting out in flakes — and rinsed my face. "Loftis, you supposed to be home four days ago. Hey," I say, toweling my face, "you okay, brah?" How come he don't answer me? Wiping my hands on the seat of my trousers, I tipped into Loftis's room. He sleeping with his mouth open. His legs be drawn up, both fists clenched between his knees. He'd kicked his blanket on the floor. In his sleep, Loftis laughed, or moaned, it be hard to tell. His eyelids, not quite shut, show slits of white. I decided to wait till Loftis wake up for his decision, but turning, I seen his watch, keys, and what looked in the first stain of sunlight to be a carefully wrapped piece of newspaper on his nightstand. The sun surged up in a bright shimmer, focusing the bedroom slowly like solution do a photographic image in the developer. And then something so freakish went down I ain't sure it took place.

Fumblefingered, I unfolded the paper and inside be a blemished penny. It be like somebody hit me hard between the shoulderblades. Taped on the penny be a slip of paper, and on the paper be the note, "Found while walking down Devon Avenue." I hear Loftis mumble like he trapped in a nightmare. "Hold tight," I whisper, "it's all right." Me, I wanted to tell Loftis how Miss Bailey looked four days ago, that maybe it didn't have to be like that for us — did it? — because we could change. Couldn't we? Me, I pull his packed sheets over him, wrap up the penny, and, when I locate Miss Bailey's glass jar in the livingroom, put it away carefully, for now, with the rest of our things.

JOHN UPDIKE

Anne Tyler defined the characteristic quality of John Updike's
fiction by saying that it reminds her of "those tiny paintings that,
when you examine certain details under a magnifying glass,
appear to swell and take over the room." "Deaths of Distant
Friends" involves, as so many of Updike's recent stories do, the
graying of suburban expectation and etiquette. As is usual in all
his work, the story is written with unparalleled grace and precision ("Miss Amy Merrymount, ninety-one, had at last passed
away, as a dry leaf passes into leaf mold"). John Updike, born in
Shillington, Pennsylvania, lives and writes in Massachusetts. He
has published more than thirty books.

Deaths of Distant Friends

THOUGH I WAS between marriages for several years, in a dis-
array that preoccupied me completely, other people continued
to live and die. Len, an old golf partner, overnight in the hospital for what they said was a routine examination, dropped
dead in the lavatory, having just placed a telephone call to his
hardware store saying he would be back behind the counter in
the morning. He owned the store and could take sunny afternoons off on short notice. His swing was too quick, and he kept
his weight back on his right foot, and the ball often squirted off
to the left without getting into the air at all, but he sank some
gorgeous putts in his day, and he always dressed with a nattiness
that seemed to betoken high hopes for his game. In buttercup-
yellow slacks, sky-blue turtleneck, and tangerine cashmere car-
digan he would wave from the practice green as, having driven
out from Boston through clouds of grief and sleeplessness and
moral confusion, I would drag my cart across the asphalt parking lot, my cleats scraping, like a monster's claws, at every step.

Though Len had known and liked Julia, the wife I had left, he never spoke of my personal condition or of the fact that I drove an hour out from Boston to meet him instead of, as formerly, ten minutes down the road. Golf in that interim was a great haven; as soon as I stepped off the first tee in pursuit of my drive, I felt enclosed in a luminous wide bubble, safe from women, stricken children, solemn lawyers, disapproving old acquaintances — the entire offended social order. Golf had its own order, and its own love, as the three or four of us staggered and shouted our way toward each hole, laughing at misfortune and applauding the rare strokes of relative brilliance. Sometimes the summer sky would darken and a storm arise, and we would cluster in an abandoned equipment shed or beneath a tree that seemed less tall than its brothers. Our natural nervousness and our impatience at having the excitements of golf interrupted would in this space of shelter focus into an almost amorous heat — the breaths and sweats of middle-aged men packed together in the pattering rain like cattle in a boxcar. Len's face bore a number of spots of actinic keratosis; he was going to have them surgically removed before they turned into skin cancer. Who would have thought that the lightning bolt of a coronary would fall across his plans and clean remove him from my tangled life? Never again (no two snowflakes or fingerprints, no two heartbeats traced on the oscilloscope, and no two golf swings are exactly alike) would I exultantly see his so hopefully addressed drive ("Hello dere, ball," he would joke, going into his waggle and squat) squirt off low to the left in that unique way of his, and hear him exclaim in angry frustration (he was a born-again Baptist, and had developed a personal language of avoided curses), "Ya dirty ricka-fric!"

I drove out to Len's funeral and tried to tell his son, "Your father was a great guy," but the words fell flat in that cold bare Baptist church. Len's gaudy colors, his Christian effervescence, his game and futile swing, our crowing back and forth, our fellowship within the artificial universe composed of variously resistant lengths and types of grass, were tints of life too delicate to capture, and had flown.

A time later, I read in the paper that Miss Amy Merrymount, ninety-one, had at last passed away, as a dry leaf passes into leaf

JOHN UPDIKE   153

mold. She had always seemed ancient; she was one of those New
Englanders, one of the last, who spoke of Henry James as if he
had just left the room. She possessed letters, folded and unfolded almost into pieces, from James to her parents, in which
she was mentioned, not only as a little girl but as a young lady
"coming into her 'own,' into a liveliness fully rounded." She
lived in a few rooms, crowded with antiques, of a great inherited
country house of which she was constrained to rent out the
larger portion. Why she had never married was a mystery that
sat upon her lightly in old age; the slender smooth beauty that
sepia photographs remembered, the breeding and intelligence
and, in a spiritual sense, ardor she still possessed must have
intimidated as many suitors as they attracted and given her, in
her own eyes, in an age when the word *inviolate* still had force
and renunciation, a certain prestige, a value whose winged moment of squandering never quite arose. Also, she had a sardonic
dryness to her voice and something restless and dismissive in
her manner. She was a keen self-educator; she kept up with new
developments in art and science, took up organic foods and
political outrage when they became fashionable, and liked to
have young people about her. When Julia and I moved to town
with our babies and fresh faces, we became part of her tea circle,
and in an atmosphere of tepid but mutual enchantment maintained acquaintance for twenty years.

Perhaps not so tepid: now I think Miss Merrymount loved us,
or at least loved Julia, who always took on a courteous bright-
ness, a soft daughterly shine, in those chill window-lit rooms
crowded with spindly, feathery heirlooms once spread through
the four floors of a Back Bay town house. In memory the glow
of my former wife's firm chin and exposed throat and shoulders
merges with the ghostly smoothness of those old framed studio
photos of the Merrymount sisters — three, of whom two died
sadly young, as if bequeathing their allotment of years to the
third, the survivor sitting with us in her gold-brocaded wing
chair. Her face had become unforeseeably brown with age, and
totally wrinkled, like an Indian's, with something in her dark
eyes of glittering Indian cruelty. "I found her rather disappointing," she might say of an absent mutual acquaintance, or, of one
who had been quite dropped from her circle, "She wasn't absolutely first-rate."

The search for the first-rate had been a pastime of her generation. I cannot think, now, of whom she utterly approved, except
Father Daniel Berrigan and Sir Kenneth Clark. She saw them
both on television. Her eyes with their opaque glitter were failing, and for her cherished afternoons of reading while the light
died outside her windows and a little fire of birch logs in the
brass-skirted fireplace warmed her ankles were substituted
scheduled hours tuned in to educational radio and television.
In those last years, Julia would go and read to her — Austen,
Middlemarch, Joan Didion, some Proust and Mauriac in French,
when Miss Merrymount decided that Julia's accent passed mus-
ter. Julia would practice a little on me, and, watching her lips
push forward and go small and tense around the French sounds
like the lips of an African mask of ivory, I almost fell in love
with her again. Affection between women is a touching, painful,
exciting thing for a man, and in my vision of it — tea yielding
to sherry in those cluttered rooms where twilight thickened until
the pages being slowly turned and the patient melody of Julia's
voice were the sole signs of life — love was what was happening
between this gradually dying old lady and my wife, who had
gradually become middle-aged, our children grown into absent
adults, her voice nowhere else harkened to as it was here. No
doubt there were confidences, too, between the pages. Julia always returned from Miss Merrymount's, to make my late dinner, looking younger and even blithe, somehow emboldened.

In that awkward postmarital phase when old friends still feel
obliged to extend invitations and one doesn't yet have the wit or
courage to decline, I found myself at a large gathering at which
Miss Merrymount was present. She was not quite blind and
invariably accompanied by a young person, a round-faced girl
hired as companion and guide. The fragile old lady, displayed
like peacock feathers under a glass bell, had been established
in a chair in a corner of the room beyond the punch bowl. At
my approach, she sensed a body coming near and held out
her withered hand, but when she heard my voice her hand
dropped. "You have done a dreadful thing," she said, all on one
long intake of breath, like a draft rippling a piece of crinkly
cellophane. Her face turned away, showing her hawk-nosed
profile, as though I had offended her sight. The face of her

young companion, round as a radar dish, registered slight shock; but I smiled, in truth not displeased. There is a relief at judgment, even adverse. It is good to know that somewhere a seismograph records our quakes and slippages. I imagine Miss Merrymount's death, not too many months after this, as a final serenely flat line on the hospital monitor attached to her. Something sardonic in that flat line, too — of unviolated rectitude, of magnificent patience with a world that for over ninety years failed to prove itself other than disappointing. By this time, Julia and I were at last divorced.

Everything of the abandoned home is lost, of course — the paintings on the walls, the way shadows and light contended in this or that corner, the gracious warmth from the radiators. The pets. Canute was a male golden retriever we had acquired as a puppy when the children were still a tumbling, pre-teen pack. Endlessly amiable, as his breed tends to be, he suffered all, including castration, as if life were a steady hail of blessings. Curiously, not long before he died, my youngest child, who sings in a female punk group that has just started up, brought Canute to the house where now I live with Jenny as my wife. He sniffed around politely and expressed with only a worried angle of his ears the wonder of his old master reconstituted in this strange-smelling home; then he collapsed with a heavy sigh onto the kitchen floor. He looked fat and seemed lethargic. My daughter, whose hair is cut short and dyed mauve in patches, said that the dog roamed at night and got into the neighbors' garbage, and even into one neighbor's horse feed. This sounded like mismanagement to me; Julia's new boyfriend is a middle-aged former Dartmouth quarterback, a golf and tennis and backpack freak, and she is hardly ever home, so busy is she keeping up with him and trying to learn new games. The house and lawn are neglected; the children drift in and out with their friends and once in a while clean out the rotten food in the refrigerator. Jenny, sensing my suppressed emotions, said something tactful and bent down to scratch Canute behind one ear. Since the ear was infected and sensitive, he feebly snapped at her, then thumped the kitchen floor with his tail in apology.

Like me when snubbed by Miss Merrymount, my wife seemed

more pleased than not, encountering a touch of resistance, her position in the world as it were confirmed. She discussed dog antibiotics with my daughter, and at a glance one could not have been sure who was the older, though it was clear who had the odder hair. It is true, as the cliché runs, that Jenny is young enough to be my daughter. But now that I am fifty everybody under thirty-five is young enough to be my daughter. Most of the people in the world are young enough to be my daughter.

A few days after his visit, Canute disappeared, and a few days later he was found far out on the marshes near my old house, his body bloated. The dog officer's diagnosis was a heart attack. Can that happen, I wondered, to four-footed creatures? The thunderbolt had hit my former pet by moonlight, his heart full of marshy joy and his stomach fat with garbage, and he had lain for days with ruffling fur while the tides went in and out. The image makes me happy, like the sight of a sail popping full of wind and tugging its boat swiftly out from shore. In truth — how terrible to acknowledge — all three of these deaths make me happy, in a way. Witnesses to my disgrace are being removed. The world is growing lighter. Eventually there will be none to remember me as I was in those embarrassing, disarrayed years while I scuttled without a shell, between houses and wives, a snake between skins, a monster of selfishness, my grotesque needs naked and pink, my social presence beggarly and vulnerable. The deaths of others carry us off bit by bit, until there will be nothing left; and this too will be, in a way, a mercy.

URSULA K. LE GUIN

Science fiction is an American specialty and a consuming national passion. Ursula K. Le Guin's particular style of the genre embodies the most demanding requirements of scientific thought and literary inquiry. She dares to make her own rules, one of which — that science fiction can look back as well as forward — is the impetus of this remarkable story. "Sur," in Anne Tyler's words, "uses plot to make its statement in the deftest way imaginable." Ursula K. Le Guin was born in California and lives in Oregon. She has published poetry, essays, short stories, novels, and film and radio scripts.

Sur

A Summary Report of the Yelcho Expedition to the Antarctic, 1909–10

ALTHOUGH I HAVE no intention of publishing this report, I think it would be nice if a grandchild of mine, or somebody's grandchild, happened to find it some day; so I shall keep it in the leather trunk in the attic, along with Rosita's christening dress and Juanito's silver rattle and my wedding shoes and finneskos.

The first requisite for mounting an expedition — money — is normally the hardest to come by. I grieve that even in a report destined for a trunk in the attic of a house in a very quiet suburb of Lima I dare not write the name of the generous benefactor, the great soul without whose unstinting liberality the Yelcho Expedition would never have been more than the idlest excursion into daydream. That our equipment was the best and most modern — that our provisions were plentiful and fine — that a ship of the Chilean government, with her brave officers and gallant crew, was twice sent halfway round the world for our convenience: all this is due to that benefactor whose name, alas!, I must not say, but whose happiest debtor I shall be till death.

When I was little more than a child, my imagination was caught by a newspaper account of the voyage of the *Belgica*, which, sailing south from Tierra del Fuego, was beset by ice in the Bellingshausen Sea and drifted a whole year with the floe, the men aboard her suffering a great deal from want of food and from the terror of the unending winter darkness. I read and reread that account, and later followed with excitement the reports of the rescue of Dr. Nordenskjöld from the South Shetland Islands by the dashing Captain Irizar of the *Uruguay*, and the adventures of the *Scotia* in the Weddell Sea. But all these exploits were to me but forerunners of the British National Antarctic Expedition of 1901–04, in the *Discovery*, and the wonderful account of that expedition by Captain Scott. This book, which I ordered from London and reread a thousand times, filled me with longing to see with my own eyes that strange continent, last Thule of the South, which lies on our maps and globes like a white cloud, a void, fringed here and there with scraps of coastline, dubious capes, supposititious islands, headlands that may or may not be there: Antarctica. And the desire was as pure as the polar snows: to go, to see — no more, no less. I deeply respect the scientific accomplishments of Captain Scott's expedition, and have read with passionate interest the findings of physicists, meteorologists, biologists, etc.; but having had no training in any science, nor any opportunity for such training, my ignorance obliged me to forgo any thought of adding to the body of scientific knowledge concerning Antarctica, and the same is true for all the members of my expedition. It seems a pity; but there was nothing we could do about it. Our goal was limited to observation and exploration. We hoped to go a little farther, perhaps, and see a little more; if not, simply to go and to see. A simple ambition, I think, and essentially a modest one.

Yet it would have remained less than an ambition, no more than a longing, but for the support and encouragement of my dear cousin and friend Juana ———. (I use no surnames, lest this report fall into strangers' hands at last, and embarrassment or unpleasant notoriety thus be brought upon unsuspecting husbands, sons, etc.) I had lent Juana my copy of *The Voyage of the "Discovery,"* and it was she who, as we strolled beneath our parasols across the Plaza de Armas after Mass one Sunday in 1908, said, "Well, if Captain Scott can do it, why can't we?"

It was Juana who proposed that we write Carlota ——— in Valparaíso. Through Carlota we met our benefactor, and so obtained our money, our ship, and even the plausible pretext of going on retreat in a Bolivian convent, which some of us were forced to employ (while the rest of us said we were going to Paris for the winter season). And it was my Juana who in the darkest moments remained resolute, unshaken in her determination to achieve our goal.

And there were dark moments, especially in the spring of 1909 — times when I did not see how the Expedition would ever become more than a quarter ton of pemmican gone to waste and a lifelong regret. It was so very hard to gather our expeditionary force together! So few of those we asked even knew what we were talking about — so many thought we were mad, or wicked, or both! And of those few who shared our folly, still fewer were able, when it came to the point, to leave their daily duties and commit themselves to a voyage of at least six months, attended with not inconsiderable uncertainty and danger. An ailing parent; an anxious husband beset by business cares; a child at home with only ignorant or incompetent servants to look after it: these are not responsibilities lightly to be set aside. And those who wished to evade such claims were not the companions we wanted in hard work, risk, and privation.

But since success crowned our efforts, why dwell on the setbacks and delays, or the wretched contrivances and downright lies that we all had to employ? I look back with regret only to those friends who wished to come with us but could not, by any contrivance, get free — those we had to leave behind to a life without danger, without uncertainty, without hope.

On the seventeenth of August, 1909, in Punta Arenas, Chile, all the members of the Expedition met for the first time: Juana and I, the two Peruvians; from Argentina, Zoe, Berta, and Teresa; and our Chileans, Carlota and her friends Eva, Pepita, and Dolores. At the last moment I had received word that María's husband, in Quito, was ill and she must stay to nurse him, so we were nine, not ten. Indeed, we had resigned ourselves to being but eight when, just as night fell, the indomitable Zoe arrived in a tiny pirogue manned by Indians, her yacht having sprung a leak just as it entered the Straits of Magellan.

That night before we sailed we began to get to know one another, and we agreed, as we enjoyed our abominable supper in the abominable seaport inn of Punta Arenas, that if a situation arose of such urgent danger that one voice must be obeyed without present question, the unenviable honor of speaking with that voice should fall first upon myself; if I were incapacitated, upon Carlota; if she, then upon Berta. We three were then toasted as "Supreme Inca," "La Araucana," and "The Third Mate," amid a lot of laughter and cheering. As it came out, to my very great pleasure and relief, my qualities as a "leader" were never tested; the nine of us worked things out amongst us from beginning to end without any orders being given by anybody, and only two or three times with recourse to a vote by voice or show of hands. To be sure, we argued a good deal. But then, we had time to argue. And one way or another the arguments always ended up in a decision, upon which action could be taken. Usually at least one person grumbled about the decision, sometimes bitterly. But what is life without grumbling and the occasional opportunity to say "I told you so"? How could one bear housework, or looking after babies, let alone the rigors of sledge-hauling in Antarctica, without grumbling? Officers — as we came to understand aboard the *Yelcho* — are forbidden to grumble; but we nine were, and are, by birth and upbringing, unequivocally and irrevocably, all crew.

Though our shortest course to the southern continent, and that originally urged upon us by the captain of our good ship, was to the South Shetlands and the Bellingshausen Sea, or else by the South Orkneys into the Weddell Sea, we planned to sail west to the Ross Sea, which Captain Scott had explored and described, and from which the brave Ernest Shackleton had returned only the previous autumn. More was known about this region than any other portion of the coast of Antarctica, and though that more was not much, yet it served as some insurance of the safety of the ship, which we felt we had no right to imperil. Captain Pardo had fully agreed with us after studying the charts and our planned itinerary; and so it was westward that we took our course out of the Straits next morning.

Our journey half round the globe was attended by fortune. The little *Yelcho* steamed cheerily along through gale and gleam, climbing up and down those seas of the Southern Ocean that run unbroken round the world. Juana, who had fought bulls and the far more dangerous cows on her family's *estancia*, called the ship *la vaca valiente*, because she always returned to the charge. Once we got over being seasick, we all enjoyed the sea voyage, though oppressed at times by the kindly but officious protectiveness of the captain and his officers, who felt that we were only "safe" when huddled up in the three tiny cabins that they had chivalrously vacated for our use.

We saw our first iceberg much farther south than we had looked for it, and saluted it with Veuve Clicquot at dinner. The next day we entered the ice pack, the belt of floes and bergs broken loose from the land ice and winter-frozen seas of Antarctica which drifts northward in the spring. Fortune still smiled on us: our little steamer, incapable, with her unreinforced metal hull, of forcing a way into the ice, picked her way from lane to lane without hesitation, and on the third day we were through the pack, in which ships have sometimes struggled for weeks and been obliged to turn back at last. Ahead of us now lay the dark-gray waters of the Ross Sea, and beyond that, on the horizon, the remote glimmer, the cloud-reflected whiteness of the Great Ice Barrier.

Entering the Ross Sea a little east of Longitude West 160°, we came in sight of the Barrier at the place where Captain Scott's party, finding a bight in the vast wall of ice, had gone ashore and sent up their hydrogen-gas balloon for reconnaissance and photography. The towering face of the Barrier, its sheer cliffs and azure and violet waterworn caves, all were as described, but the location had changed: instead of a narrow bight, there was a considerable bay, full of the beautiful and terrific orca whales playing and spouting in the sunshine of that brilliant southern spring.

Evidently masses of ice many acres in extent had broken away from the Barrier (which — at least for most of its vast extent —

does not rest on land but floats on water) since the *Discovery*'s passage in 1902. This put our plan to set up camp on the Barrier itself in a new light; and while we were discussing alternatives, we asked Captain Pardo to take the ship west along the Barrier face toward Ross Island and McMurdo Sound. As the sea was clear of ice and quite calm, he was happy to do so and, when we sighted the smoke plume of Mt. Erebus, to share in our celebration — another half case of Veuve Clicquot.

The *Yelcho* anchored in Arrival Bay, and we went ashore in the ship's boat. I cannot describe my emotions when I set foot on the earth, on that earth, the barren, cold gravel at the foot of the long volcanic slope. I felt elation, impatience, gratitude, awe, familiarity. I felt that I was home at last. Eight Adélie penguins immediately came to greet us with many exclamations of interest not unmixed with disapproval. "Where on earth have you been? What took you so long? The Hut is around this way. Please come this way. Mind the rocks!" They insisted on our going to visit Hut Point, where the large structure built by Captain Scott's party stood, looking just as in the photographs and drawings that illustrate his book. The area about it, however, was disgusting — a kind of graveyard of seal skins, seal bones, penguin bones, and rubbish, presided over by the mad, screaming skua gulls. Our escorts waddled past the slaughterhouse in all tranquillity, and one showed me personally to the door, though it would not go in.

The interior of the hut was less offensive but very dreary. Boxes of supplies had been stacked up into a kind of room within the room; it did not look as I had imagined it when the *Discovery* party put on their melodramas and minstrel shows in the long winter night. (Much later, we learned that Sir Ernest had rearranged it a good deal when he was there just a year before us.) It was dirty, and had about it a mean disorder. A pound tin of tea was standing open. Empty meat tins lay about; biscuits were spilled on the floor; a lot of dog turds were underfoot — frozen, of course, but not a great deal improved by that. No doubt the last occupants had had to leave in a hurry, perhaps even in a blizzard. All the same, they could have closed the tea tin. But housekeeping, the art of the infinite, is no game for amateurs.

Teresa proposed that we use the hut as our camp. Zoe counterproposed that we set fire to it. We finally shut the door and left it as we had found it. The penguins appeared to approve, and cheered us all the way to the boat.

McMurdo Sound was free of ice, and Captain Pardo now proposed to take us off Ross Island and across to Victoria Land, where we might camp at the foot of the Western Mountains, on dry and solid earth. But those mountains, with their storm-darkened peaks and hanging cirques and glaciers, looked as awful as Captain Scott had found them on his western journey, and none of us felt much inclined to seek shelter among them.

Aboard the ship that night we decided to go back and set up our base as we had originally planned, on the Barrier itself. For all available reports indicated that the clear way south was across the level Barrier surface until one could ascend one of the confluent glaciers to the high plateau that appears to form the whole interior of the continent. Captain Pardo argued strongly against this plan, asking what would become of us if the Barrier "calved" — if our particular acre of ice broke away and started to drift northward. "Well," said Zoe, "then you won't have to come so far to meet us." But he was so persuasive on this theme that he persuaded himself into leaving one of the *Yelcho*'s boats with us when we camped, as a means of escape. We found it useful for fishing, later on.

My first steps on Antarctic soil, my only visit to Ross Island, had not been pleasure unalloyed. I thought of the words of the English poet,

> Though every prospect pleases,
> And only Man is vile.

But then, the backside of heroism is often rather sad; women and servants know that. They know also that the heroism may be no less real for that. But achievement is smaller than men think. What is large is the sky, the earth, the sea, the soul. I looked back as the ship sailed east again that evening. We were well into September now, with eight hours or more of daylight. The spring sunset lingered on the twelve-thousand-foot peak of Erebus and shone rosy-gold on her long plume of steam. The

steam from our own small funnel faded blue on the twilit water
as we crept along under the towering pale wall of ice.

On our return to "Orca Bay" — Sir Ernest, we learned years
later, had named it the Bay of Whales — we found a sheltered
nook where the Barrier edge was low enough to provide fairly
easy access from the ship. The *Yelcho* put out her ice anchor,
and the next long, hard days were spent in unloading our supplies and setting up our camp on the ice, a half kilometre in
from the edge: a task in which the *Yelcho*'s crew lent us invaluable aid and interminable advice. We took all the aid gratefully,
and most of the advice with salt.

The weather so far had been extraordinarily mild for spring
in this latitude; the temperature had not yet gone below $-20°F$,
and there was only one blizzard while we were setting up camp.
But Captain Scott had spoken feelingly of the bitter south winds
on the Barrier, and we had planned accordingly. Exposed as
our camp was to every wind, we built no rigid structures above-
ground. We set up tents to shelter in while we dug out a series
of cubicles in the ice itself, lined them with hay insulation and
pine boarding, and roofed them with canvas over bamboo poles,
covered with snow for weight and insulation. The big central
room was instantly named Buenos Aires by our Argentineans,
to whom the center, wherever one is, is always Buenos Aires.
The heating and cooking stove was in Buenos Aires. The storage tunnels and the privy (called Punta Arenas) got some back
heat from the stove. The sleeping cubicles opened off Buenos
Aires, and were very small, mere tubes into which one crawled
feet first; they were lined deeply with hay and soon warmed by
one's body warmth. The sailors called them coffins and worm-
holes, and looked with horror on our burrows in the ice. But
our little warren or prairie-dog village served us well, permit-
ting us as much warmth and privacy as one could reasonably
expect under the circumstances. If the *Yelcho* was unable to get
through the ice in February and we had to spend the winter in
Antarctica, we certainly could do so, though on very limited
rations. For this coming summer, our base — Sudamérica del
Sur, South South America, but we generally called it the Base
— was intended merely as a place to sleep, to store our provisions, and to give shelter from blizzards.

To Berta and Eva, however, it was more than that. They were its chief architect-designers, its most ingenious builder-excavators, and its most diligent and contented occupants, forever inventing an improvement in ventilation, or learning how to make skylights, or revealing to us a new addition to our suite of rooms, dug in the living ice. It was thanks to them that our stores were stowed so handily, that our stove drew and heated so efficiently, and that Buenos Aires, where nine people cooked, ate, worked, conversed, argued, grumbled, painted, played the guitar and banjo, and kept the Expedition's library of books and maps, was a marvel of comfort and convenience. We lived there in real amity; and if you simply had to be alone for a while, you crawled into your sleeping hole head first.

Berta went a little farther. When she had done all she could to make South South America livable, she dug out one more cell just under the ice surface, leaving a nearly transparent sheet of ice like a greenhouse roof; and there, alone, she worked at sculptures. They were beautiful forms, some like a blending of the reclining human figure with the subtle curves and volumes of the Weddell seal, others like the fantastic shapes of ice cornices and ice caves. Perhaps they are there still, under the snow, in the bubble in the Great Barrier. There where she made them, they might last as long as stone. But she could not bring them north. That is the penalty for carving in water.

Captain Pardo was reluctant to leave us, but his orders did not permit him to hang about the Ross Sea indefinitely, and so at last, with many earnest injunctions to us to stay put — make no journeys — take no risks — beware of frostbite — don't use edge tools — look out for cracks in the ice — and a heartfelt promise to return to Orca Bay on February 20th, or as near that date as wind and ice would permit, the good man bade us farewell, and his crew shouted us a great goodbye cheer as they weighed anchor. That evening, in the long orange twilight of October, we saw the topmast of the *Yelcho* go down the north horizon, over the edge of the world, leaving us to ice, and silence, and the Pole.

That night we began to plan the Southern Journey.

The ensuing month passed in short practice trips and depot-laying. The life we had led at home, though in its own way strenuous, had not fitted any of us for the kind of strain met with in sledge-hauling at ten or twenty degrees below freezing. We all needed as much working out as possible before we dared undertake a long haul.

My longest exploratory trip, made with Dolores and Carlota, was southwest toward Mt. Markham, and it was a nightmare — blizzards and pressure ice all the way out, crevasses and no view of the mountains when we got there, and white weather and sastrugi all the way back. The trip was useful, however, in that we could begin to estimate our capacities; and also in that we had started out with a very heavy load of provisions, which we depoted at a hundred and a hundred and thirty miles south-southwest of Base. Thereafter other parties pushed on farther, till we had a line of snow cairns and depots right down to Latitude 80° 43′, where Juana and Zoe, on an exploring trip, had found a kind of stone gateway opening on a great glacier leading south. We established these depots to avoid, if possible, the hunger that had bedevilled Captain Scott's Southern Party, and the consequent misery and weakness. And we also established to our own satisfaction — intense satisfaction — that we were sledge-haulers at least as good as Captain Scott's husky dogs. Of course we could not have expected to pull as much or as fast as his men. That we did so was because we were favored by much better weather than Captain Scott's party ever met on the Barrier; and also the quantity and quality of our food made a very considerable difference. I am sure that the fifteen percent of dried fruits in our pemmican helped prevent scurvy; and the potatoes, frozen and dried according to an ancient Andean Indian method, were very nourishing yet very light and compact — perfect sledding rations. In any case, it was with considerable confidence in our capacities that we made ready at last for the Southern Journey.

The Southern Party consisted of two sledge teams: Juana, Dolores, and myself; Carlota, Pepita, and Zoe. The support team of Berta, Eva, and Teresa set out before us with a heavy load of supplies, going right up onto the glacier to prospect routes and leave depots of supplies for our return journey. We followed five days behind them, and met them returning between Depot Ercilla and Depot Miranda. That "night" — of course, there was no real darkness — we were all nine together in the heart of the level plain of ice. It was November 15th, Dolores's birthday. We celebrated by putting eight ounces of pisco in the hot chocolate, and became very merry. We sang. It is strange now to remember how thin our voices sounded in that great silence. It was overcast, white weather, without shadows and without visible horizon or any feature to break the level; there was nothing to see at all. We had come to that white place on the map, that void, and there we flew and sang like sparrows.

After sleep and a good breakfast the Base Party continued north and the Southern Party sledged on. The sky cleared presently. High up, thin clouds passed over very rapidly from southwest to northeast, but down on the Barrier it was calm and just cold enough, five or ten degrees below freezing, to give a firm surface for hauling.

On the level ice we never pulled less than eleven miles (seventeen kilometres) a day, and generally fifteen or sixteen miles (twenty-five kilometres). (Our instruments, being British-made, were calibrated in feet, miles, degrees Fahrenheit, etc., but we often converted miles to kilometres, because the larger numbers sounded more encouraging.) At the time we left South America, we knew only that Mr. Ernest Shackleton had mounted another expedition to the Antarctic in 1907, had tried to attain the Pole but failed, and had returned to England in June of the current year, 1909. No coherent report of his explorations had yet reached South America when we left; we did not know what route he had gone, or how far he had got. But we were not altogether taken by surprise when, far across the featureless white plain, tiny beneath the mountain peaks and the strange silent flight of the rainbow-fringed cloud wisps, we saw a fluttering dot of black. We turned west from our course to visit it: a snow heap nearly buried by the winter's storms — a flag on a bamboo pole, a mere shred of threadbare cloth, an empty oilcan — and a few footprints standing some inches above the ice. In some conditions of weather the snow compressed under one's weight remains when the surrounding soft snow melts or is scoured away by the wind; and so these reversed footprints had been left standing all these months, like rows of cobbler's lasts — a queer sight.

We met no other such traces on our way. In general I believe our course was somewhat east of Mr. Shackleton's. Juana, our surveyor, had trained herself well and was faithful and methodical in her sightings and readings, but our equipment was minimal — a theodolite on tripod legs, a sextant with artificial horizon, two compasses, and chronometers. We had only the wheel meter on the sledge to give distance actually travelled.

In any case, it was the day after passing Mr. Shackleton's waymark that I first saw clearly the great glacier among the mountains to the southwest, which was to give us a pathway from the sea level of the Barrier up to the altiplano, ten thousand feet above. The approach was magnificent: a gateway formed by immense vertical domes and pillars of rock. Zoe and Juana had called the vast ice river that flowed through that gateway the Florence Nightingale Glacier, wishing to honor the British, who had been the inspiration and guide of our Expedition; that very brave and very peculiar lady seemed to represent so much that is best, and strangest, in the island race. On maps, of course, this glacier bears the name Mr. Shackleton gave it: the Beardmore.

The ascent of the Nightingale was not easy. The way was open at first, and well marked by our support party, but after some days we came among terrible crevasses, a maze of hidden cracks, from a foot to thirty feet wide and from thirty to a thousand feet deep. Step by step we went, and step by step, and the way always upward now. We were fifteen days on the glacier. At first the weather was hot — up to 20°F — and the hot nights without darkness were wretchedly uncomfortable in our small tents. And all of us suffered more or less from snow blindness just at the time when we wanted clear eyesight to pick our way among the ridges and crevasses of the tortured ice, and to see the wonders about and before us. For at every day's advance more great, nameless peaks came into view in the west and southwest, summit beyond summit, range beyond range, stark rock and snow in the unending noon.

We gave names to these peaks, not very seriously, since we did not expect our discoveries to come to the attention of geographers. Zoe had a gift for naming, and it is thanks to her that certain sketch maps in various suburban South American attics bear such curious features as "Bolívar's Big Nose," "I Am General Rosas," "The Cloudmaker," "Whose Toe?," and "Throne of Our Lady of the Southern Cross." And when at last we got up onto the altiplano, the great interior plateau, it was Zoe who called it the pampa, and maintained that we walked there among vast herds of invisible cattle, transparent cattle pastured on the spindrift snow, their gauchos the restless, merciless winds. We were by then all a little crazy with exhaustion and the great altitude — twelve thousand feet — and the cold and the wind blowing and the luminous circles and crosses surrounding the suns, for often there were three or four suns in the sky, up there.

That is not a place where people have any business to be. We should have turned back; but since we had worked so hard to get there, it seemed that we should go on, at least for a while.

A blizzard came, with very low temperatures, so we had to stay in the tents, in our sleeping bags, for thirty hours — a rest we all needed, though it was warmth we needed most, and there was no warmth on that terrible plain anywhere at all but in our veins. We huddled close together all that time. The ice we lay on is two miles thick.

It cleared suddenly and became, for the plateau, good weather: twelve below zero and the wind not very strong. We three crawled out of our tent and met the others crawling out of theirs. Carlota told us then that her group wished to turn back. Pepita had been feeling very ill; even after the rest during the blizzard, her temperature would not rise above 94°. Carlota was having trouble breathing. Zoe was perfectly fit, but much preferred staying with her friends and lending them a hand in difficulties to pushing on toward the Pole. So we put the four ounces of pisco that we had been keeping for Christmas into the breakfast cocoa, and dug out our tents, and loaded our sledges, and parted there in the white daylight on the bitter plain.

Our sledge was fairly light by now. We pulled on to the south. Juana calculated our position daily. On the twenty-second of December, 1909, we reached the South Pole. The weather was, as always, very cruel. Nothing of any kind marked the dreary whiteness. We discussed leaving some kind of mark or monument, a snow cairn, a tent pole and flag; but there seemed no particular reason to do so. Anything we could do, anything we were, was insignificant, in that awful place. We put up the tent for shelter for an hour and made a cup of tea, and then struck "90° Camp."

Dolores, standing patient as ever in her sledging harness, looked at the snow; it was so hard frozen that it showed no trace of our footprints coming, and she said, "Which way?"

"North," said Juana.

It was a joke, because at that particular place there is no other direction. But we did not laugh. Our lips were cracked with frostbite and hurt too much to let us laugh. So we started back, and the wind at our backs pushed us along, and dulled the knife edges of the waves of frozen snow.

All that week the blizzard wind pursued us like a pack of mad dogs. I cannot describe it. I wished we had not gone to the Pole. I think I wish it even now. But I was glad even then that we had left no sign there, for some man longing to be first might come some day, and find it, and know then what a fool he had been, and break his heart.

We talked, when we could talk, of catching up to Carlota's party, since they might be going slower than we. In fact they used their tent as a sail to catch the following wind and had got far ahead of us. But in many places they had built snow cairns or left some sign for us; once, Zoe had written on the lee side of a ten-foot sastruga, just as children write on the sand of the beach at Miraflores, "This Way Out!" The wind blowing over the frozen ridge had left the words perfectly distinct.

In the very hour that we began to descend the glacier, the weather turned warmer, and the mad dogs were left to howl forever tethered to the Pole. The distance that had taken us fifteen days going up we covered in only eight days going down. But the good weather that had aided us descending the Nightingale became a curse down on the Barrier ice, where we had looked forward to a kind of royal progress from depot to depot, eating our fill and taking our time for the last three hundred-odd miles. In a tight place on the glacier I lost my goggles — I was swinging from my harness at the time in a crevasse — and then Juana broke hers when we had to do some rock-climbing coming down to the Gateway. After two days in bright sunlight with only one pair of snow goggles to pass amongst us, we were all suffering badly from snow blindness. It became acutely painful to keep lookout for landmarks or depot flags, to take sightings, even to study the compass, which had to be laid down on the snow to steady the needle. At Concolorcorvo Depot, where there was a particularly good supply of food and fuel, we gave up, crawled into our sleeping bags with bandaged eyes, and slowly boiled alive like lobsters in the tent exposed to the relentless sun. The voices of Berta and Zoe were the sweetest sound I ever heard. A little concerned about us, they had skied south to meet us. They led us home to Base.

We recovered quite swiftly, but the altiplano left its mark. When she was very little, Rosita asked if a dog "had bitted Mama's toes." I told her yes — a great, white, mad dog named Blizzard! My Rosita and my Juanito heard many stories when they were little, about that fearful dog and how it howled, and the transparent cattle of the invisible gauchos, and a river of ice eight thousand feet high called Nightingale, and how Cousin Juana drank a cup of tea standing on the bottom of the world under seven suns, and other fairy tales.

We were in for one severe shock when we reached Base at last. Teresa was pregnant. I must admit that my first response to the poor girl's big belly and sheepish look was anger — rage — fury. That one of us should have concealed anything, and such a thing, from the others! But Teresa had done nothing of the sort. Only those who had concealed from her what she most needed to know were to blame. Brought up by servants, with four years' schooling in a convent, and married at sixteen, the poor girl was still so ignorant at twenty years of age that she had thought it was "the cold weather" that made her miss her periods. Even this was not entirely stupid, for all of us on the Southern Journey had seen our periods change or stop altogether as we experienced increasing cold, hunger, and fatigue. Teresa's appetite had begun to draw general attention; and then she had begun, as she said pathetically, "to get fat." The others were worried at the thought of all the sledge-hauling she had done, but she flourished, and the only problem was her positively insatiable appetite. As well as could be determined from her shy references to her last night on the hacienda with her husband, the baby was due at just about the same time as the *Yelcho*, February 20th. But we had not been back from the Southern Journey two weeks when, on February 14th, she went into labor.

Several of us had borne children and had helped with deliveries, and anyhow most of what needs to be done is fairly self-evident; but a first labor can be long and trying, and we were all anxious, while Teresa was frightened out of her wits. She kept calling for her José till she was as hoarse as a skua. Zoe lost all patience at last and said, "By God, Teresa, if you say 'José!' once more, I hope you have a penguin!" But what she had, after twenty long hours, was a pretty little red-faced girl.

Many were the suggestions for that child's name from her eight proud midwife aunts: Polita, Penguina, McMurdo, Victoria . . . But Teresa announced, after she had had a good sleep and a large serving of pemmican, "I shall name her Rosa — Rosa del Sur," Rose of the South. That night we drank the last two bottles of Veuve Clicquot (having finished the pisco at 88° 60' South) in toasts to our little Rose.

On the nineteenth of February, a day early, my Juana came down into Buenos Aires in a hurry. "The ship," she said, "the ship has come," and she burst into tears — she who had never wept in all our weeks of pain and weariness on the long haul.

Of the return voyage there is nothing to tell. We came back safe.

In 1912 all the world learned that the brave Norwegian Amundsen had reached the South Pole; and then, much later, we heard the accounts of how Captain Scott and his men had come there after him but did not come home again.

Just this year, Juana and I wrote to the captain of the *Yelcho*, for the newspapers have been full of the story of his gallant dash to rescue Sir Ernest Shackleton's men from Elephant Island, and we wished to congratulate him, and once more to thank him. Never one word has he breathed of our secret. He is a man of honor, Luis Pardo.

I add this last note in 1929. Over the years we have lost touch with one another. It is very difficult for women to meet, when they live as far apart as we do. Since Juana died, I have seen none of my old sledgemates, though sometimes we write. Our little Rosa del Sur died of the scarlet fever when she was five years old. Teresa had many other children. Carlota took the veil in Santiago ten years ago. We are old women now, with old husbands, and grown children, and grandchildren who might some day like to read about the Expedition. Even if they are rather ashamed of having such a crazy grandmother, they may enjoy sharing in the secret. But they must not let Mr. Amundsen know! He would be terribly embarrassed and disappointed. There is no need for him or anyone else outside the family to know. We left no footprints, even.

JOYCE CAROL OATES

John Updike described the central action of "Nairobi" as "an act of prostitution, performed with the not-quite-invulnerable inner distancing whereby the prostitute preserves her dignity." Its author was herself guest editor of *The Best American Short Stories* in 1979. As one of her generation's hardest-working, most broadly skilled and prolific writers, Joyce Carol Oates has generously supported America's network of literary journals not only by contributing her short fiction but by serving as consulting editor for both established and new publications. She and her husband publish and edit *The Ontario Review*. Born in Lockport, New York, Oates lives and teaches in Princeton, New Jersey.

Nairobi

EARLY SATURDAY AFTERNOON the man who had introduced himself as Oliver took Ginny to several shops on Madison Avenue above 70th Street to buy her what he called an appropriate outfit. For an hour and forty-five minutes she modeled clothes, watching with critical interest her image in the three-way mirrors, unable to decide if this was one of her really good days or only a mediocre day. Judging by Oliver's expression she looked all right, but it was difficult to tell. The salesclerks saw too many beautiful young women to be impressed, though one told Ginny she envied her her hair — not just that shade of chestnut red but the thickness too. In the changing room she told Ginny that her own hair was "coming out in handfuls" but Ginny told her it didn't show. It will begin to show one of these days, the salesgirl said.

Ginny modeled a green velvet jumpsuit with a brass zipper and oversized buckles, and an Italian knit dress with bunchy sleeves in a zigzag pattern of beige, brown, and cream, and a

ruffled organdy "tea dress" in pale orange, and a navy-blue
blazer made of Irish linen, with a pleated white linen skirt and
a pale blue silk blouse. Assuming she could only have one cos-
tume, which seemed to be the case, she would have preferred
the jumpsuit, not just because it was the most expensive outfit
(the price tag read $475) but because the green velvet reflected
in her eyes. Oliver decided on the Irish linen blazer and the
skirt and blouse, however, and told the salesclerk to remove the
tags and to pack up Ginny's own clothes, since she intended to
wear the new outfit.

Strolling uptown, he told her that with her hair down like
that, and her bangs combed low on her forehead, she looked
like a "convent schoolgirl." In theory, that was. Tangentially.

It was a balmy, windy day in early April. Everyone was out.
Ginny kept seeing people she almost knew, Oliver waved hello
to several acquaintances. There were baby buggies, dogs being
walked, sports cars with their tops down. In shop windows —
particularly in the broad windows of galleries — Ginny's reflection in the navy-blue blazer struck her as unfamiliar and quirky
but not bad: the blazer with its built-up shoulders and wide
lapels was more stylish than she'd thought at first. Oliver too
was pleased. He had slipped on steel-frame tinted glasses. He
said they had plenty of time. A pair of good shoes — really good
shoes — might be an idea.

But first they went into a jewelry boutique at 76th Street,
where Oliver bought her four narrow silver bracelets, engraved
in bird and animal heads, and a pair of conch-shaped silver
earrings from Mexico. Ginny slipped her gold studs out and
put on the new earrings as Oliver watched. Doesn't it hurt to
force those wires through your flesh? He was standing rather
close.

No, Ginny said. My earlobes are numb, I don't feel a thing.
It's easy.

When did you get your ears pierced? Oliver asked.

Ginny felt her cheeks color slightly — as if he were asking a
favor of her and her instinct wasn't clear enough, whether to
acquiesce or draw away just perceptibly. She drew away, still
adjusting the earrings, but said: I don't have any idea, maybe I
was thirteen, maybe twelve, it was a long time ago. We all went
out and had our ears pierced.

In a salon called Michel's she exchanged her chunky-heeled red shoes for a pair of kidskin sandals that might have been the most beautiful shoes she'd ever seen. Oliver laughed quizzically over them: they were hardly anything but a few straps and a price tag, he told the salesman, but they looked like the real thing, they were what he wanted. The salesman told Oliver that his taste was "unerring."

Do you want to keep your old shoes? Oliver asked Ginny.

Of course, Ginny said, slightly hurt, but as the salesman was packing them she changed her mind. No, the hell with them, she said. They're too much trouble to take along. — Which she might regret afterward: but it was the right thing to say at that particular moment.

In the cab headed west and then north along the park, Oliver gave her instructions in a low, casual voice. The main thing was that she should say very little. She shouldn't smile unless it was absolutely necessary. While he and his friends spoke — if they spoke at any length, he couldn't predict Marguerite's attitude — Ginny might even drift away, pick up a magazine and leaf through it if something appropriate was available, not nervously, just idly, for something to do, as if she were bored; better yet, she might look out the window or even step out on the terrace, since the afternoon was so warm. Don't even look at me, Oliver said. Don't give the impression that anything I say — anything the three of us say — matters very much to you.

Yes, said Ginny.

The important thing, Oliver said, squeezing her hand and releasing it, is that you're basically not concerned. I mean with the three of us. With Marguerite. With anyone. Do you understand?

Yes, said Ginny. She was studying her new shoes. Kidskin in a shade called "vanilla," eight straps on each shoe, certainly the most beautiful shoes she'd ever owned. The price had taken her breath away too. She hadn't any questions to ask Oliver.

When Ginny had been much younger — which is to say, a few years ago, when she was new to the city — she might have had some questions to ask. In fact she had had a number of questions to ask, then. But the answers had invariably disappointed. The answers had contained so much less substance than her own questions, she had learned, by degrees, not to ask.

So she told Oliver a second time, to assure *him:* Of course I understand.

The apartment building they entered at Fifth and 88th was older than Ginny might have guessed from the outside — the mosaic murals in the lobby were in a quaint ethereal style unknown to her. Perhaps they were meant to be amusing, but she didn't think so. It was impressive that the uniformed doorman knew Oliver, whom he called "Mr. Leahy," and that he was so gracious about keeping their package for them while they visited upstairs; it was impressive that the black elevator operator nodded and murmured hello in a certain tone. Smiles were measured and respectful all around, but Ginny didn't trouble to smile; she knew it wasn't expected of her.

In the elevator — which was almost uncomfortably small — Oliver looked at Ginny critically, standing back to examine her from her toes upward and finding nothing wrong except a strand of hair or two out of place. The Irish linen blazer was an excellent choice, he said. The earrings too. The bracelets. The shoes. He spoke with assurance though Ginny had the idea he was nervous, or excited. He turned to study his own reflection in the bronze-frosted mirror on the elevator wall, facing it with a queer childlike squint. This was his "mirror face," Ginny supposed, the way he had of confronting himself in the mirror so that it wasn't *really* himself but a certain habitual expression that protected him. Ginny hadn't any mirror face herself. She had gone beyond that, she knew better, those childish frowns and half-smiles and narrowed eyes and heads turned coyly or hopefully to one side — ways of protecting her from seeing "Ginny" when the truth of "Ginny" was that she required being seen head-on. But it would have been difficult to explain to another person.

Oliver adjusted his handsome blue-striped cotton tie and ran his fingers deftly through his hair. It was pale, fine, airily colorless hair, blond perhaps, shading into premature silver, rather thin, Ginny thought, for a man his age. (She estimated his age at thirty-four, which seemed "old" to her in certain respects, but she knew it was reasonably "young" in others.) Oliver's skin was slightly coarse; his nose wide at the bridge, and the nostrils disfigured by a few dark hairs that should have been snipped off; his lower jaw was somewhat heavy. But he was a handsome man. In his steel-rimmed blue-tinted glasses he was a handsome man, and Ginny saw for the first time that they made an attractive couple.

Don't trouble to answer any questions they might ask, Oliver said. In any case the questions won't be serious — just conversation.

I understand, Ginny said.

A Hispanic maid answered the door. The elevator and the corridor had been so dimly lit, Ginny wasn't prepared for the flood of sunlight in the apartment. They were on the eighteenth floor overlooking the park and the day was still cloudless.

Oliver introduced Ginny to his friends Marguerite and Herbert — the last name sounded like Crews — and Ginny shook hands with them unhesitatingly, as if it were a customary gesture with her. The first exchanges were about the weather. Marguerite was vehement in her gratitude since the past winter, January in particular, had been uncommonly long and dark and depressing. Ginny assented without actually agreeing. For the first minute or two she felt thrown off balance, she couldn't have said why, by the fact that Marguerite Crews was so tall a woman — taller even than Ginny. And she was, or had been, a very beautiful woman as well, with a pale olive-dark complexion and severely black hair parted in the center of her head and fixed in a careless knot at the nape of her neck.

Oliver was explaining apologetically that they couldn't stay. Not even for a drink, really: they were in fact already late for another engagement in the Village. Both the Crewses expressed disappointment. And Oliver's plans for the weekend had been altered as well, unavoidably. At this announcement the disappointment was keener, and Ginny looked away before Marguerite's eyes could lock with hers.

But Oliver was working too hard, Marguerite protested.

But he *must* come out to the Point as they'd planned, Herbert said, and bring his friend along.

Ginny eased discreetly away. She was aloof, indifferent, just slightly bored, but unfailingly courteous: a mark of good breeding. And the Irish linen blazer and skirt were just right.

After a brief while Herbert Crews came over to comment on the view and Ginny thought it wouldn't be an error to agree: the view of Central Park was, after all, something quite real. He told her they'd lived here for eleven years "off and on." They traveled a good deal, he was required to travel almost more than he liked, being associated with an organization Ginny might have heard of — the Zieboldt Foundation. He had just returned from Nairobi, he said. Two days ago. And still feeling the strain — the fatigue. Ginny thought that his affable talkative "social" manner showed not the least hint of fatigue but did not make this observation to Herbert Crews.

She felt a small pinprick of pity for the way Marguerite Crews's collarbones showed through her filmy muslin Indian blouse, and for the extreme thinness of her waist (cinched tight with a belt of silver coins or medallions), and for the faint scolding voice — so conspicuously a "voice" — with which she was speaking to Oliver. She saw that Oliver, though smiling nervously, and standing in a self-conscious pose with the thumb of his right hand hooked in his sports coat pocket, was enjoying the episode very much — she noted for the first time something vehement and cruel though at the same time unmistakably boyish in his face. Herbert Crews was telling her about Nairobi but she couldn't concentrate on his words. She was wondering if it might be proper to ask where Nairobi was — she assumed it was a country somewhere in Africa — but Herbert Crews continued, speaking now with zest of the wild animals, including great herds of "the most exquisitely beautiful gazelles," in the Kenya preserves. Had she ever been there, he asked. No, Ginny said. Well, said Herbert, nodding vigorously, it really *is* worth it. Next time Marguerite promised to come along.

Ginny heard Oliver explain again that they were already late for an appointment in the Village, unfortunately they couldn't stay for a drink, yes it was a pity but he hoped they might do it another time: with which Marguerite warmly agreed. Though it was clearly all right for Oliver and Ginny to leave now, Herbert Crews was telling her about the various animals he'd seen — elands, giraffes, gnus, hippopotami, crocodiles, zebras, "feathered monkeys," impalas — he had actually eaten impala and found it fairly good. But the trip was fatiguing and his business in Nairobi disagreeable. He'd discovered — as in fact the Foundation had known from certain clumsily fudged reports — that the microbiological research being subsidized there had not only come to virtually nothing, but that vast sums of money had "disappeared" into nowhere. Ginny professed to feel some sympathy though at the same time, as she said, she wasn't surprised. Well, she said, easing away from Herbert Crews's side, that seems to be human nature, doesn't it. All around the world.

Americans and Swedes this time, Herbert Crews said — equally taken in.

It couldn't be avoided that Herbert tell Oliver what he'd been saying — Oliver in fact seemed to be interested, he might have had some indirect connection with the Foundation himself — but unfortunately they were late for their engagement downtown, and within five minutes they were out of the apartment and back in the elevator going down.

Oliver withdrew a handkerchief from his breast pocket, unfolded it, and carefully wiped his forehead. Ginny was studying her reflection in the mirror and felt a pinprick of disappointment — her eyes looked shadowed and tired, and her hair wasn't really all that wonderful, falling straight to her shoulders. Though she'd shampooed it only that morning, it was already getting dirty — the wind had been so strong on their walk up Madison.

On Fifth Avenue, in the gusty sunlight, they walked together for several blocks. Ginny slid her arm through Oliver's as if they were being watched, but at an intersection they were forced to walk at different paces and her arm slipped free. It was time in any case to say good-bye: she sensed that he wasn't going to ask her, even out of courtesy, to have a drink with him: and she had made up her mind not to feel even tangentially insulted. After all, she hadn't been insulted.

He signaled a cab for her. He handed over the pink cardboard box with her denim jumper and sweater in it and shook her hand vigorously. You were lovely up there, Oliver said — just perfect. Look, I'll call you, all right?

She felt the weight, the subtle dizzying blow, of the "were." But she thanked him just the same. And got into the cab. And wasn't so stricken by a sudden fleeting sense of loss — of loss tinged with a queer cold sickish knowledge — that, as the cab pulled away into the traffic stream, she couldn't give him a final languid wave of her hand, and even shape her mouth into a puckish kiss. All she had really lost, in a sense, was her own pair of shoes.

1984

PAUL BOWLES

An American expatriate escorts his parents on a tour of Sri
Lankan sights in "In the Red Room." It is a story that, in John
Updike's words, "presents, at a level of understatement almost
beneath thermal detection, that original hotspot, the Oedipal tri-
angle." Paul Bowles was born in New York eighty years ago. In
1931 he made his first visit to Tangier, which has been his only
home since 1959, when he sold his island off Sri Lanka. Bowles's
uncompromisingly spare style has certainly influenced the work
of writers coming of age in the eighties. His recent stories have
appeared most often in *Antaeus*.

In the Red Room

WHEN I HAD A HOUSE in Sri Lanka, my parents came out one
winter to see me. Originally I had felt some qualms about encouraging their visit. Any one of several things — the constant
heat, the unaccustomed food and drinking water, even the presence of a leprosy clinic a quarter of a mile from the house —
might easily have an adverse effect on them in one way or another. But I had underestimated their resilience; they made a
greater show of adaptability than I had thought possible, and
seemed entirely content with everything. They claimed not to
mind the lack of running water in the bathrooms, and regularly
praised the curries prepared by Appuhamy, the resident cook.
Both of them being in their seventies, they were not tempted by
the more distant or inaccessible points of interest. It was enough
for them to stay around the house reading, sleeping, taking
twilight dips in the ocean, and going on short trips along the
coast by hired car. If the driver stopped unexpectedly at a
shrine to sacrifice a coconut, they were delighted, and if they
came upon a group of elephants lumbering along the road, the

car had to be parked some distance up ahead, so that they could watch them approach and file past. They had no interest in taking photographs, and this spared me what is perhaps the most taxing duty of a cicerone: the repeated waits while the ritual between man and machine is observed. They were ideal guests.

Colombo, where all the people I knew lived, was less than a hundred miles away. Several times we went up for weekends, which I arranged with friends by telephone beforehand. There we had tea on the wide verandas of certain houses in Cinnamon Gardens, and sat at dinners with professors from the university, Protestant ministers, and assorted members of the government. (Many of the Sinhalese found it strange that I should call my parents by their first names, Dodd and Hannah; several of them inquired if I were actually their son or had been adopted.) These weekends in the city were hot and exhausting, and they were always happy to get back to the house, where they could change into comfortable clothing.

One Sunday not long before they were due to return to America, we decided to take in the horse races at Gintota, where there are also some botanical gardens that Hannah wanted to see. I engaged rooms at the New Oriental in Galle and we had lunch there before setting out.

As usual, the events were late in starting. It was the spectators, in any case, who were the focus of interest. The phalanx of women in their shot-silk saris moved Hannah to cries of delight. The races themselves were something of a disappointment. As we left the grounds, Dodd said with satisfaction: It'll be good to get back to the hotel and relax.

But we were going to the botanical gardens, Hannah reminded him. I'd like to have just a peek at them.

Dodd was not eager. Those places cover a lot of territory, you know, he said.

We'll just look inside and come out again, she promised.

The hired car took us to the entrance. Dodd was tired, and as a result was having a certain amount of difficulty in walking. The last year or so I find my legs aren't always doing exactly what I want 'em to do, he explained.

You two amble along, Hannah told us. I'll run up ahead and find out if there's anything to see.

We stopped to look up at a clove tree; its powerful odor filled the air like a gas. When we turned to continue our walk, Hannah was no longer in sight. We went on under the high vegetation, around a curve in the path, looked ahead, and still there was no sign of her.

What does your mother think she's doing? The first thing we know she'll be lost.

She's up ahead somewhere.

Soon, at the end of a short lane overhung by twisted lianas, we saw her, partially hidden by the gesticulating figure of a Sinhalese standing next to her.

What's going on? Dodd hastened his steps. Run over there, he told me, and I started ahead, walking fast. Then I saw Hannah's animated smile, and slowed my pace. She and the young man stood in front of a huge bank of brown spider orchids.

Ah! I thought we'd lost you, I said.

Look at these orchids. Aren't they incredible?

Dodd came up, nodded at the young man, and examined the display of flowers. They look to me like skunk cabbage, he declared.

The young man broke into wild laughter. Dodd stared at him.

This young man has been telling me the history of the garden, Hannah began hurriedly. About the opposition to it, and how it finally came to be planted. It's interesting.

The Sinhalese beamed triumphantly. He wore white flannels and a crimson blazer, and his sleek black hair gave off a metallic blue glint in the sunlight.

Ordinarily I steer a determined course away from the anonymous person who tries to engage me in conversation. This time it was too late; encouraged by Hannah, the stranger strolled beside her, back to the main path. Dodd and I exchanged a glance, shrugged, and began to follow along behind.

Somewhere up at the end of the gardens a pavilion had been built under the high rain trees. It had a veranda where a few sarong-draped men reclined in long chairs. The young man stopped walking. Now I invite you to a cold ginger beer.

Oh, Hannah said, at a loss. Well, yes. That would be nice. I'd welcome a chance to sit down.

Dodd peered at his wristwatch. I'll pass up the beer, but I'll sit and watch you.

We sat and looked out at the lush greenness. The young man's conversation leapt from one subject to another; he seemed unable to follow any train of thought further than its inception. I put this down as a bad sign, and tried to tell from the inflections of Hannah's voice whether she found him as disconcerting as I did.

Dodd was not listening. He found the heat of low-country Ceylon oppressive, and it was easy to see that he was tired. Thinking I might cover up the young man's chatter, I turned to Dodd and began to talk about whatever came into my head: the resurgence of mask-making in Ambalangoda, devil-dancing, the high incidence of crime among the fishermen converted to Catholicism. Dodd listened, but did no more than move his head now and then in response.

Suddenly I heard the young man saying to Hannah: I have just the house for you. A godsend to fill your requirements. Very quiet and protected.

She laughed. Mercy, no! We're not looking for a house. We're only going to be here a few weeks more.

I looked hard at her, hoping she would take my glance as a warning against going on and mentioning the place where she was staying. The young man was not paying attention, in any case. Quite all right. You are not buying houses. But you should see this house and tell your friends. A superior investment, no doubt about that. Shall I introduce myself, please? Justus Gonzag, called Sonny by friends.

His smile, which was not a smile at all, gave me an unpleasant physical sensation.

Come anyway. A five-minute walk, guaranteed. He looked searchingly at Hannah. I intend to give you a book of poems. My own. Autographed for you with your name. That will make me very happy.

Oh, Hannah said, a note of dismay in her voice. Then she braced herself and smiled. That would be lovely. But you understand, we can't stay more than a minute.

There was a silence. Dodd inquired plaintively: Can't we go in the car, at least?

Impossible, sir. We are having a very narrow road. Car can't get through. I am arranging in a jiffy. He called out. A waiter came up, and he addressed him in Sinhalese at some length.

The man nodded and went inside. Your driver is now bringing your car to this gate. Very close by.

This was going a little too far. I asked him how he thought anyone was going to know which car was ours.

No problem. I was present when you were leaving the Pontiac. Your driver is called Wickramasinghe. Up-country resident, most reliable. Down here people are hopeless.

I disliked him more each time he spoke. You're not from around here? I asked him.

No, no! I'm a Colombo chap. These people are impossible scoundrels. Every one of the blighters has a knife in his belt, guaranteed.

When the waiter brought the check, he signed it with a rapid flourish and stood up. Shall we be going on to the house, then?

No one answered, but all three of us rose and reluctantly moved off with him in the direction of the exit gate. The hired car was there; Mr. Wickramasinghe saluted us from behind the wheel.

The afternoon heat had gone, leaving only a pocket here and there beneath the trees where the air was still. Originally the lane where we were walking had been wide enough to admit a bullock-cart, but the vegetation encroaching on each side had narrowed it to little more than a footpath.

At the end of the lane were two concrete gateposts with no gate between them. We passed through, and went into a large compound bordered on two sides by ruined stables. With the exception of one small ell, the house was entirely hidden by high bushes and flowering trees. As we came to a doorway the young man stopped and turned to us, holding up one finger. No noises here, isn't it? Only birds.

It was the hour when the birds begin to awaken from their daytime lethargy. An indeterminate twittering came from the trees. He lowered his finger and turned back to the door. Mornings they are singing. Now not.

Oh, it's lovely, Hannah told him.

He led us through a series of dark empty rooms. Here the *dhobi* was washing the soiled clothing. This is the kitchen, you see? Ceylon style. Only the charcoal. My father was refusing paraffin and gas both. Even in Colombo.

We huddled in a short corridor while he opened a door, reached in, and flooded the space inside with blinding light. It was a small room, made to seem still smaller by having been given glistening crimson walls and ceiling. Almost all the space was filled by a big bed with a satin coverlet of a slightly darker red. A row of straight-backed chairs stood along one wall. Sit down and be comfy, our host advised us.

We sat, staring at the bed and at the three framed pictures on the wall above its brass-spoked headboard: on the left a girl, in the middle our host, and on the right another young man. The portraits had the imprecision of passport photographs that have been enlarged to many times their original size.

Hannah coughed. She had nothing to say. The room gave off a cloying scent of ancient incense, as in a disused chapel. The feeling of absurdity I got from seeing us sitting there side by side, wedged in between the bed and the wall, was so powerful that it briefly paralyzed my mental processes. For once the young man was being silent; he sat stiffly, looking straight ahead, like someone at the theater.

Finally I had to say something. I turned to our host and asked him if he slept in this room. The question seemed to shock him. Here? he cried, as if the thing were inconceivable. No, no! This house is unoccupied. No one sleeping on the premises. Only a stout chap to watch out at night. Excuse me one moment.

He jumped up and hurried out of the room. We heard his footsteps echo in the corridor and then grow silent. From somewhere in the house there came the sonorous chiming of a grandfather's clock; its comfortable sound made the shiny blood-colored cubicle even more remote and unlikely.

Dodd stirred uncomfortably in his chair; the bed was too close for him to cross his legs. As soon as he comes back, we go, he muttered.

He's looking for the book, I imagine, said Hannah.

We waited a while. Then I said: Look. If he's not back in two minutes, I move we just get up and leave. We can find our way out all right.

Hannah objected, saying it would be unpardonable.

Again we sat in silence, Dodd now shielding his eyes from the glare. When Sonny Gonzag returned, he was carrying a glass of water which he drank standing in the doorway. His expression had altered: he now looked preoccupied, and he was breathing heavily.

We slowly got to our feet, Hannah still looking expectant.

We are going, then? Come. With the empty glass still in his hand he turned off the lights, shut the door behind us, opened another, and led us quickly through a sumptuous room furnished with large divans, coromandel screens, and bronze Buddhas. We had no time to do more than glance from side to side as we followed him. As we went out through the front door, he called one peremptory word back into the house, presumably to the caretaker.

There was a wide unkempt lawn on this side, where a few clumps of high areca palms were being slowly strangled by the sheaths of philodendron roots and leaves that encased their trunks. Creepers had spread themselves unpleasantly over the tops of shrubs like the meshes of gigantic cobwebs. I knew that Hannah was thinking of snakes. She kept her eyes on the ground, stepping carefully from flagstone to flagstone as we followed the exterior of the house around to the stables, and thence out into the lane.

The swift twilight had come down. No one seemed disposed to speak. When we reached the car Mr. Wickramasinghe stood beside it.

Cheery-bye, then, and tell your friends to look for Sonny Gonzag when they are coming to Gintota. He offered his hand to Dodd first, then me, finally to Hannah, and turned away.

They were both very quiet on the way back to Galle. The road was narrow and the blinding lights of oncoming cars made them nervous. During dinner we made no mention of the afternoon.

At breakfast, on the veranda swept by the morning breeze, we felt sufficiently removed from the experience to discuss it. Hannah said: I kept waking up in the night and seeing that awful bed.

Dodd groaned.

I said it was like watching television without the sound. You saw everything, but you didn't get what was going on.

The kid was completely non compos mentis. You could see that a mile away, Dodd declared.

Hannah was not listening. It must have been a maid's room. But why would he take us there? I don't know; there's something terribly depressing about the whole thing. It makes me feel a little sick just to think about it. And that bed!

Well, stop thinking about it, then! Dodd told her. I for one am going to put it right out of my mind. He waited. I feel better already. Isn't that the way the Buddhists do it?

The sunny holiday continued for a few weeks more, with longer trips now to the east, to Tissamaharana and the wild elephants in the Yala Preserve. We did not go to Colombo again until it was time for me to put them onto the plane.

The black weather of the monsoons was blowing in from the southwest as we drove up the coast. There was a violent downpour when we arrived in midafternoon at Mount Lavinia and checked into our rooms. The crashing of the waves outside my room was so loud that Dodd had to shut the windows in order to hear what we were saying.

I had taken advantage of the trip to Colombo to arrange a talk with my lawyer, a Telugu-speaking Indian. We were to meet in the bar at the Galleface, some miles up the coast. I'll be back at six, I told Hannah. The rain had abated somewhat when I started out.

Damp winds moved through the lobby of the Galleface, but the smoky air in the bar was stirred only by fans. As I entered, the first person I noticed was Weston of the Chartered Bank. The lawyer had not yet come in, so I stood at the bar with Weston and ordered a whiskey.

Didn't I see you in Gintota at the races last month? With an elderly couple?

I was there with my parents. I didn't notice you.

I couldn't tell. It was too far away. But I saw the same three people later with a local character. What did you think of Sonny Gonzag?

I laughed. He dragged us off to his house.

You know the story, I take it.

I shook my head.

The story, which he recounted with relish, began on the day after Gonzag's wedding, when he stepped into a servant's room and found his bride in bed with the friend who had been best man. How he happened to have a pistol with him was not explained, but he shot them both in the face, and later chopped their bodies into pieces. As Weston remarked: That sort of thing isn't too uncommon, of course. But it was the trial that caused the scandal. Gonzag spent a few weeks in a mental hospital, and was discharged.

You can imagine, said Weston. Political excitement. The poor go to jail for a handful of rice, but the rich can kill with impunity, and that sort of thing. You still see references to the case in the press now and then.

I was thinking of the crimson blazer and the botanical gardens. No. I never heard about it, I said.

He's mad as a hatter, but there he is, free to do whatever he feels like. And all he wants now is to get people into that house and show them the room where the great event took place. The more the merrier as far as he's concerned.

I saw the Indian come into the bar. It's unbelievable, but I believe it, I told Weston.

Then I turned to greet the lawyer, who immediately complained of the stale air in the bar. We sat and talked in the lounge.

I managed to get back to Mount Lavinia in time to bathe before dinner. As I lay in the tepid water, I tried to imagine the reactions of Hannah and Dodd when I told them what I had heard. I myself felt a solid satisfaction at knowing the rest of the story. But being old, they might well brood over it, working it up into an episode so unpleasant in retrospect that it stained the memory of their holiday. I still had not decided whether to tell them or not when I went to their room to take them down to dinner.

We sat as far away from the music as we could get. Hannah had dressed a little more elaborately than usual, and they both were speaking with more than their accustomed animation. I realized that they were happy to be returning to New York. Halfway through the meal they began to review what they considered the highlights of their visit. They mentioned the Temple of the Tooth, the pair of Bengal tiger cubs in Dehiwala which they had petted but regretfully declined to purchase, the Indonesian dinner on Mr. Bultjens's lawn, where the myna bird had hopped over to Hannah and said: "Eat it up," the cobra under the couch at Mrs. de Sylva's tea party.

And that peculiar young man in the *strange* house, Hannah added meditatively.

Which one was that? asked Dodd, frowning as he tried to remember. Then it came to him. Oh, God, he muttered. Your special friend. He turned to me. Your mother certainly can pick 'em.

Outside, the ocean roared. Hannah seemed lost in thought. *I* know what it was like! she exclaimed suddenly. It was like being shown around one of the temples by a *bhikku*. Isn't that what they call them?

Dodd sniffed. Some temple! he chuckled.

No, I'm serious. That room had a particular meaning for him. It was like a sort of shrine.

I looked at her. She had got to the core without needing the details. I felt that, too, I said. Of course, there's no way of knowing.

She smiled. Well, what you don't know won't hurt you.

I had heard her use the expression a hundred times without ever being able to understand what she meant by it, because it seemed so patently untrue. But for once it was apt. I nodded my head and said: That's right.

RUSSELL BANKS

"I was extremely handsome then. And . . . I must tell you that
Sarah was very homely. In fact, she was the homeliest woman I
have ever known." So begins a piercing story in which, as Gail
Godwin points out, even the title expresses the narrator's
"dogged intention not to let himself off easy, his determination
to get to the bottom of something that cannot be comfortably
classified." Specializing in unflinching and painstaking dissec-
tions of character motivation, Russell Banks has published nine
books of fiction. Born in Newton, Massachusetts, he lives in
Princeton, New Jersey.

Sarah Cole:
A Type of Love Story

TO BEGIN, THEN, here is a scene in which I am the man and
my friend Sarah Cole is the woman. I don't mind describing it
now, because I'm a decade older and don't look the same now
as I did then, and Sarah is dead. That is to say, on hearing this
story you might think me vain if I looked the same now as I did
then, because I must tell you that I was extremely handsome
then. And if Sarah were not dead, you'd think I was cruel, for I
must tell you that Sarah was very homely. In fact, she was the
homeliest woman I have ever known. Personally, I mean. I've
seen a few women who were more unattractive than Sarah, but
they were clearly freaks of nature or had been badly injured or
had been victimized by some grotesque, disfiguring disease.
Sarah, however, was quite normal, and I knew her well, because
for three and a half months we were lovers.

Here is the scene. You can put it in the present, even though
it took place ten years ago, because nothing that matters to the

story depends on when it took place, and you can put it in
Concord, New Hampshire, even though that is indeed where it
took place, because it doesn't matter where it took place, so it
might as well be Concord, New Hampshire, a place I happen to
know well and can therefore describe with sufficient detail to
make the story believable. Around six o'clock on a Wednesday
evening in late May a man enters a bar. The place, a cocktail
lounge at street level with a restaurant upstairs, is decorated
with hanging plants and unfinished wood paneling, butcher-
block tables and captain's chairs, with a half dozen darkened,
thickly upholstered booths along one wall. Three or four men
between the ages of twenty-five and thirty-five are drinking at
the bar, and they, like the man who has just entered, wear three-
piece suits and loosened neckties. They are probably lawyers,
young, unmarried lawyers gossiping with their brethren over
martinis so as to postpone arriving home alone at their white-
washed townhouse apartments, where they will fix their evening
meals in Radaranges and, afterwards, while their TVs chuckle
quietly in front of them, sit on their couches and do a little extra
work for tomorrow. They are, for the most part, honorable,
educated, hard-working, shallow, and moderately unhappy
young men. Our man, call him Ronald, Ron, in most ways is like
these men, except that he is unusually good-looking, and that
makes him a little less unhappy than they. Ron is effortlessly
attractive, a genetic wonder, tall, slender, symmetrical, and
clean. His flaws, a small mole on the left corner of his square
but not-too-prominent chin, a slight excess of blond hair on the
tops of his tanned hands, and somewhat underdeveloped buttocks, insofar as they keep him from resembling too closely a
men's store mannequin, only contribute to his beauty, for he is
beautiful, the way we usually think of a woman as being beautiful. And he is nice, too, the consequence, perhaps, of his seeming not to know how beautiful he is, to men as well as women,
to young people, even children, as well as old, to attractive people, who realize immediately that he is so much more attractive
than they as not to be competitive with them, as well as unattractive people, who see him and gain thereby a comforting
perspective on those they have heretofore envied for their good
looks.

Ron takes a seat at the bar, unfolds the evening paper in front of him, and before he can start reading, the bartender asks to help him, calling him "Sir," even though Ron has come into this bar numerous times at this time of day, especially since his divorce last fall. Ron got divorced because, after three years of marriage, his wife had chosen to pursue the career that his had interrupted, that of a fashion designer, which meant that she had to live in New York City while he had to continue to live in New Hampshire, where his career had got its start. They agreed to live apart until he could continue his career near New York City, but after a few months, between conjugal visits, he started sleeping with other women, and she started sleeping with other men, and that was that. "No big deal," he explained to friends, who liked both Ron and his wife, even though he was slightly more beautiful than she. "We really were too young when we got married, college sweethearts. But we're still best friends," he assured them. They understood. Most of Ron's friends were divorced by then too.

Ron orders a scotch and soda, with a twist, and goes back to reading his paper. When his drink comes, before he takes a sip of it, he first carefully finishes reading an article about the recent re-appearance of coyotes in northern New Hampshire and Vermont. He lights a cigarette. He goes on reading. He takes a second sip of his drink. Everyone in the room, the three or four men scattered along the bar, the tall, thin bartender, and several people in the booths at the back, watches him do these ordinary things.

He has got to the classified section, is perhaps searching for someone willing to come in once a week and clean his apartment, when the woman who will turn out to be Sarah Cole leaves a booth in the back and approaches him. She comes up from the side and sits next to him. She's wearing heavy, tan cowboy boots and a dark brown, suede cowboy hat, lumpy jeans and a yellow tee shirt that clings to her arms, breasts, and round belly like the skin of a sausage. Though he will later learn that she is thirty-eight years old, she looks older by about ten years, which makes her look about twenty years older than he actually is. (It's difficult to guess accurately how old Ron is; he looks anywhere from a mature twenty-five to a youthful forty, so his actual age doesn't seem to matter.)

"It's not bad here at the bar," she says looking around. "More light, anyhow. Whatcha readin'?" she asks brightly, planting both elbows on the bar.

Ron looks up from his paper with a slight smile on his lips, sees the face of a woman homelier than any he has ever seen or imagined before, and goes on smiling lightly. He feels himself falling into her tiny, slightly crossed, dark brown eyes, pulls himself back, and studies for a few seconds her mottled, pocked complexion, bulbous nose, loose mouth, twisted and gapped teeth, and heavy but receding chin. He casts a glance over her thatch of dun-colored hair and along her neck and throat, where acne burns against gray skin, and returns to her eyes, and again feels himself falling into her.

"What did you say?" he asks.

She knocks a mentholated cigarette from her pack, and Ron swiftly lights it. Blowing smoke from her large, wing-shaped nostrils, she speaks again. Her voice is thick and nasal, a chocolate-colored voice. "I asked you whatcha readin', but I can see now." She belts out a single, loud laugh. "The paper!"

Ron laughs, too. "The paper! *The Concord Monitor!*" He is not hallucinating, he clearly sees what is before him and admits — no, he asserts — to himself that he is speaking to the most unattractive woman he has ever seen, a fact which fascinates him, as if instead he were speaking to the most beautiful woman he has ever seen or perhaps ever will see, so he treasures the moment, attempts to hold it as if it were a golden ball, a disproportionately heavy object which — if he doesn't hold it lightly yet with precision and firmness — will slip from his hand and roll across the lawn to the lip of the well and down, down to the bottom of the well, lost to him forever. It will be merely a memory, something to speak of wistfully and with wonder as over the years the image fades and comes in the end to exist only in the telling. His mind and body waken from their sleepy self-absorption, and all his attention focuses on the woman, Sarah Cole, her ugly face, like a warthog's, her thick, rapid voice, her dumpy, off-center wreck of a body, and to keep this moment here before him, he begins to ask questions of her, he buys her a drink, he smiles, until soon it seems, even to him, that he is taking her and her life, its vicissitudes and woe, quite seriously.

He learns her name, of course, and she volunteers the information that she spoke to him on a dare from one of the two women still sitting in the booth behind her. She turns on her stool and smiles brazenly, triumphantly, at her friends, two women, also homely (though nowhere as homely as she) and dressed, like her, in cowboy boots, hats and jeans. One of the women, a blonde with an underslung jaw and wearing heavy eye makeup, flips a little wave at her, and as if embarrassed, she and the other woman at the booth turn back to their drinks and sip fiercely at straws.

Sarah returns to Ron and goes on telling him what he wants to know, about her job at the Rumford Press, about her divorced husband who was a bastard and stupid and "sick," she says, as if filling suddenly with sympathy for the man. She tells Ron about her three children, the youngest, a girl, in junior high school and boy-crazy, the other two, boys, in high school and almost never at home anymore. She speaks of her children with genuine tenderness and concern, and Ron is touched. He can see with what pleasure and pain she speaks of her children; he watches her tiny eyes light up and water over when he asks their names.

"You're a nice woman," he informs her.

She smiles, looks at her empty glass. "No. No, I'm not. But you're a nice man, to tell me that."

Ron, with a gesture, asks the bartender to refill Sarah's glass. She is drinking white Russians. Perhaps she has been drinking them for an hour or two, for she seems very relaxed, more relaxed than women usually do when they come up and without introduction or invitation speak to him.

She asks him about himself, his job, his divorce, how long he has lived in Concord, but he finds that he is not at all interested in telling her about himself. He wants to know about her, even though what she has to tell him about herself is predictable and ordinary and the way she tells it unadorned and clichéd. He wonders about her husband. What kind of man would fall in love with Sarah Cole?

II

That scene, at Osgood's Lounge in Concord, ended with Ron's departure, alone, after having bought Sarah's second drink, and

Sarah's return to her friends in the booth. I don't know what she told them, but it's not hard to imagine. The three women were not close friends, merely fellow workers at Rumford Press, where they stood at the end of a long conveyor belt day after day packing *TV Guides* into cartons. They all hated their jobs, and frequently after work, when they worked the day shift, they would put on their cowboy hats and boots, which they kept all day in their lockers, and stop for a drink or two on their way home. This had been their first visit to Osgood's, a place that, prior to this, they had avoided out of a sneering belief that no one went there but lawyers and insurance men. It had been Sarah who had asked the others why that should keep them away, and when they had no answer for her, the three had decided to stop at Osgood's. Ron was right, they had been there over an hour when he came in, and Sarah was a little drunk. "We'll hafta come in here again," she said to her friends, her voice rising slightly.

Which they did, that Friday, and once again Ron appeared with his evening newspaper. He put his briefcase down next to his stool and ordered a drink and proceeded to read the front page, slowly, deliberately, clearly a weary, unhurried, solitary man. He did not notice the three women in cowboy hats and boots in the booth in back, but they saw him, and after a few minutes Sarah was once again at his side.

"Hi."

He turned, saw her, and instantly regained the moment he had lost when, the previous night, once outside the bar, he had forgotten about the ugliest woman he had ever seen. She seemed even more grotesque to him now than before, which made the moment all the more precious to him, and so once again he held the moment as if in his hands and began to speak with her, to ask questions, to offer his opinions and solicit hers.

I said earlier that I am the man in this story and my friend Sarah Cole, now dead, is the woman. I think back to that night, the second time I had seen Sarah, and I tremble, not with fear but in shame. My concern then, when I was first becoming involved with Sarah, was merely with the moment, holding on to it, grasping it wholly as if its beginning did not grow out of some other prior moment in her life and my life separately and at the same time did not lead into future moments in our separate

lives. She talked more easily than she had the night before, and
I listened as eagerly and carefully as I had before, again, with
the same motives, to keep her in front of me, to draw her forward from the context of her life and place her, as if she were
an object, into the context of mine. I did not know how cruel
this was. When you have never done a thing before and that
thing is not simply and clearly right or wrong, you frequently
do not know if it is a cruel thing, you just go ahead and do it,
and maybe later you'll be able to determine whether you acted
cruelly. That way you'll know if it was right or wrong of you to
have done it in the first place.

While we drank, Sarah told me that she hated her ex-husband
because of the way he treated the children. "It's not so much
the money," she said, nervously wagging her booted feet from
her perch on the high barstool. "I mean, I get by, barely, but I
get them fed and clothed on my own okay. It's because he won't
even write them a letter or anything. He won't call them on the
phone, all he calls for is to bitch at me because I'm trying to get
the state to take him to court so I can get some of the money
he's s'posed to be paying for child support. And he won't even
think to talk to the kids when he calls. Won't even ask about
them."

"He sounds like a bastard," I said.

"He is, he is," she said. "I don't know why I married him. Or
stayed married. Fourteen years, for Christ's sake. He put a spell
over me or something, I don't know," she said with a note of
wistfulness in her voice. "He wasn't what you'd call good-looking."

After her second drink, she decided she had to leave. Her
children were at home, it was Friday night and she liked to make
sure she ate supper with them and knew where they were going
and who they were with when they went out on their dates. "No
dates on schoolnights," she said to me. "I mean, you gotta have
rules, you know."

I agreed, and we left together, everyone in the place following
us with his or her gaze. I was aware of that, I knew what they
were thinking, and I didn't care, because I was simply walking
her to her car.

It was a cool evening, dusk settling onto the lot like a gray blanket. Her car, a huge, dark green Buick sedan at least ten years old, was battered, scratched, and almost beyond use. She reached for the door handle on the driver's side and yanked. Nothing. The door wouldn't open. She tried again. Then I tried. Still nothing.

Then I saw it, a V-shaped dent in the left front fender creasing the fender where the door joined it, binding the metal of the door against the metal of the fender in a large crimp that held the door fast. "Someone must've backed into you while you were inside," I said to her.

She came forward and studied the crimp for a few seconds, and when she looked back at me, she was weeping. "Jesus, Jesus, Jesus!" she wailed, her large, frog-like mouth wide open and wet with spit, her red tongue flopping loosely over gapped teeth. "I can't pay for this! I *can't!*" Her face was red, and even in the dusky light I could see it puff out with weeping, her tiny eyes seeming almost to disappear behind wet cheeks. Her shoulders slumped, and her hands fell limply to her sides.

Placing my briefcase on the ground, I reached out to her and put my arms around her body and held her close to me, while she cried wetly into my shoulder. After a few seconds, she started pulling herself back together and her weeping got reduced to sniffling. Her cowboy hat had been pushed back and now clung to her head at a precarious, absurdly jaunty angle. She took a step away from me and said, "I'll get in the other side."

"Okay," I said almost in a whisper. "That's fine."

Slowly, she walked around the front of the huge, ugly vehicle and opened the door on the passenger's side and slid awkwardly across the seat until she had positioned herself behind the steering wheel. Then she started the motor, which came to life with a roar. The muffler was shot. Without saying another word to me, or even waving, she dropped the car into reverse gear and backed it loudly out of the parking space and headed out the lot to the street.

I turned and started for my car, when I happened to glance toward the door of the bar, and there, staring after me, were the bartender, the two women who had come in with Sarah, and two of the men who had been sitting at the bar. They were lawyers, and I knew them slightly. They were grinning at me. I grinned back and got into my car, and then, without looking at them again, I left the place and drove straight to my apartment.

III

One night several weeks later, Ron meets Sarah at Osgood's, and after buying her three white Russians and drinking three scotches himself, he takes her back to his apartment in his car — a Datsun fastback coupe that she says she admires — for the sole purpose of making love to her.

I'm still the man in this story, and Sarah is still the woman, but I'm telling it this way because what I have to tell you now confuses me, embarrasses me, and makes me sad, and consequently, I'm likely to tell it falsely. I'm likely to cover the truth by making Sarah a better woman than she actually was, while making myself appear worse than I actually was or am; or else I'll do the opposite, make Sarah worse than she was and me better. The truth is, I was pretty, extremely so, and she was not, extremely so, and I knew it and she knew it. She walked out the door of Osgood's determined to make love to a man much prettier than any she had seen up close before, and I walked out determined to make love to a woman much homelier than any I had made love to before. We were, in a sense, equals.

No, that's not exactly true. (You see? This is why I have to tell the story the way I'm telling it.) I'm not at all sure she feels as Ron does. That is to say, perhaps she genuinely likes the man, in spite of his being the most physically attractive man she has ever known. Perhaps she is more aware of her homeliness than of his beauty, just as he is more aware of her homeliness than of his beauty, for Ron, despite what I may have implied, does not think of himself as especially beautiful. He merely knows that other people think of him that way. As I said before, he is a nice man.

Ron unlocks the door to his apartment, walks in ahead of her, and flicks on the lamp beside the couch. It's a small, single bedroom, modern apartment, one of thirty identical apartments in a large brick building on the heights just east of downtown Concord. Sarah stands nervously at the door, peering in.

"Come in, come in," he says.

She steps timidly in and closes the door behind her. She removes her cowboy hat, then quickly puts it back on, crosses the livingroom, and plops down in a blond easychair, seeming to shrink in its hug out of sight to safety. Ron, behind her, at the entry to the kitchen, places one hand on her shoulder, and she stiffens. He removes his hand.

"Would you like a drink?"

"No . . . I guess not," she says, staring straight ahead at the wall opposite where a large framed photograph of a bicyclist advertises in French the Tour de France. Around a corner, in an alcove off the living room, a silver-gray ten-speed bicycle leans casually against the wall, glistening and poised, slender as a thoroughbred racehorse.

"I don't know," she says. Ron is in the kitchen now, making himself a drink. "I don't know . . . I don't know."

"What? Change your mind? I can make a white Russian for you. Vodka, cream, Kahlúa, and ice, right?"

Sarah tries to cross her legs, but she is sitting too low in the chair and her legs are too thick at the thigh, so she ends, after a struggle, with one leg in the air and the other twisted on its side. She looks as if she has fallen from a great height.

Ron steps out from the kitchen, peers over the back of the chair, and watches her untangle herself, then ducks back into the kitchen. After a few seconds, he returns. "Seriously. Want me to fix you a white Russian?"

"No."

Ron, again from behind, places one hand on Sarah's shoulder, and this time she does not stiffen, though she does not exactly relax, either. She sits there, a block of wood, staring straight ahead.

"Are you scared?" he asked gently. Then he adds, "*I* am."

"Well, no, I'm not scared." She remains silent for a moment. "You're scared? Of what?" She turns to face him but avoids his eyes.

"Well . . . I don't do this all the time, you know. Bring home a woman I . . . ," he trails off.

"Picked up in a bar."

"No. I mean, I like you, Sarah, I really do. And I didn't just pick you up in a bar, you know that. We've gotten to be friends, you and me."

"You want to sleep with me?" she asks, still not meeting his steady gaze.

"Yes." He seems to mean it. He does not take a gulp or even a sip from his drink. He just says, "Yes," straight out, and cleanly, not too quickly, either, and not after a hesitant delay. A simple statement of a simple fact. The man wants to make love to the woman. She asked him, and he told her. What could be simpler?

"Do you want to sleep with *me?*" he asks.

She turns around in the chair, faces the wall again, and says in a low voice, "Sure I do, but . . . it's hard to explain."

"What? But what?" Placing his glass down on the table between the chair and the sofa, he puts both hands on her shoulders and lightly kneads them. He knows he can be discouraged from pursuing this, but he is not sure how easily. Having got this far without bumping against obstacles (except the ones he has placed in his way himself), he is not sure what it will take to turn him back. He does not know, therefore, how assertive or how seductive he should be with her. He suspects that he can be stopped very easily, so he is reluctant to give her a chance to try. He goes on kneading her doughy shoulders.

"You and me . . . we're real different." She glances at the bicycle in the corner.

"A man . . . and a woman," he says.

"No, not that. I mean, different. That's all. Real different. More than you . . . you're nice, but you don't know what I mean, and that's one of the things that makes you so nice. But we're different. Listen," she says, "I gotta go. I gotta leave now."

The man removes his hands and retrieves his glass, takes a sip, and watches her over the rim of the glass, as, not without difficulty, she rises from the chair and moves swiftly toward the door. She stops at the door, squares her hat on her head, and glances back at him.

"We can be friends. Okay?"

"Okay. Friends."

"I'll see you again down at Osgood's, right?"

"Oh, yeah, sure."

"Good. See you," she says, opening the door.

The door closes. The man walks around the sofa, snaps on the television set, and sits down in front of it. He picks up a *TV Guide* from the coffee table and flips through it, stops, runs a finger down the listings, stops, puts down the magazine and changes the channel. He does not once connect the magazine in his hand to the woman who has just left his apartment, even though he knows she spends her days packing *TV Guide*s into cartons that get shipped to warehouses in distant parts of New England. He'll think of the connection some other night; but by then the connection will be merely sentimental. It'll be too late for him to understand what she meant by "different."

IV

But that's not the point of my story. Certainly it's an aspect of the story, the political aspect, if you want, but it's not the reason I'm trying to tell the story in the first place. I'm trying to tell the story so that I can understand what happened between me and Sarah Cole that summer and early autumn ten years ago. To say we were lovers says very little about what happened; to say we were friends says even less. No, if I'm to understand the whole thing, I have to say the whole thing, for, in the end, what I need to know is whether what happened between me and Sarah Cole was right or wrong. Character is fate, which suggests that if a man can know and then to some degree control his character, he can know and to that same degree control his fate.

But let me go on with my story. The next time Sarah and I were together we were at her apartment in the south end of Concord, a second-floor flat in a tenement building on Perley Street. I had stayed away from Osgood's for several weeks, deliberately trying to avoid running into Sarah there, though I never quite put it that way to myself. I found excuses and generated interests in and reasons for going elsewhere after work. Yet I was obsessed with Sarah by then, obsessed with the idea of making love to her, which, because it was not an actual *desire* to make love to her, was an unusually complex obsession. Passion without desire, if it gets expressed, may in fact be a kind of rape, and perhaps I sensed the danger that lay behind my obsession and for that reason went out of my way to avoid meeting Sarah again.

Yet I did meet her, inadvertently, of course. After picking up shirts at the cleaner's on South Main and Perley streets, I'd gone down Perley on my way to South State and the post office. It was a Saturday morning, and this trip on my bicycle was part of my regular Saturday routine. I did not remember that Sarah lived on Perley Street, although she had told me several times in a complaining way — it's a rough neighborhood, packed dirt yards, shabby apartment buildings, the carcasses of old, half-stripped cars on cinderblocks in the driveways, broken red and yellow plastic tricycles on the cracked sidewalks — but as soon as I saw her, I remembered. It was too late to avoid meeting her, I was riding my bike, wearing shorts and tee shirt, the package containing my folded and starched shirts hooked to the carrier behind me, and she was walking toward me along the sidewalk, lugging two large bags of groceries. She saw me, and I stopped. We talked, and I offered to carry her groceries for her. I took the bags while she led the bike, handling it carefully as if she were afraid she might break it.

At the stoop we came to a halt. The wooden steps were cluttered with half-opened garbage bags spilling eggshells, coffee grounds, and old food wrappers to the walkway. "I can't get the people downstairs to take care of their garbage," she explained. She leaned the bike against the banister and reached for her groceries.

"I'll carry them up for you," I said. I directed her to loop the chain lock from the bike to the banister rail and snap it shut and told her to bring my shirts up with her.

"Maybe you'd like a beer?" she said as she opened the door to the darkened hallway. Narrow stairs disappeared in front of me into heavy, damp darkness, and the air smelled like old newspapers.

"Sure," I said and followed her up.

"Sorry there's no light. I can't get them to fix it."

"No matter, I can see you and follow along," I said, and even in the dim light of the hall I could see the large, dark blue veins that cascaded thickly down the backs of her legs. She wore tight, white-duck bermuda shorts, rubber shower sandals, and a pink sleeveless sweater. I pictured her in the cashier's line at the supermarket. I would have been behind her, a stranger, and on seeing her, I would have turned away and studied the covers of the magazines, *TV Guide, People, The National Enquirer,* for there was nothing of interest in her appearance that in the hard light of day would not have slightly embarrassed me. Yet here I was inviting myself into her home, eagerly staring at the backs of her ravaged legs, her sad, tasteless clothing, her poverty. I was not detached, however, was not staring at her with scientific curiosity, and because of my passion, did not feel or believe that what I was doing was perverse. I felt warmed by her presence and was flirtatious and bold, a little pushy, even.

Picture this. The man, tanned, limber, wearing red jogging shorts, Italian leather sandals, a clinging net tee shirt of Scandinavian design and manufacture, enters the apartment behind the woman, whose dough-colored skin, thick, short body, and homely, uncomfortable face all try, but fail, to hide themselves. She waves him toward the table in the kitchen, where he sets down the bags and looks good-naturedly around the room. "What about the beer you bribed me with?" he asks. The apartment is dark and cluttered with old, oversized furniture, yard sale and second-hand stuff bought originally for a large house in the country or a spacious apartment on a boulevard forty or fifty years ago, passed down from antique dealer to used furniture store to yard sale to thrift shop, where it finally gets purchased by Sarah Cole and gets lugged over to Perley Street and shoved up the narrow stairs, she and her children grunting and sweating in the darkness of the hallway — overstuffed armchairs and couch, huge, ungainly dressers, upholstered rocking chairs, and in the kitchen, an old maple desk for a table, a half dozen heavy oak diningroom chairs, a high, glass-fronted cabinet, all peeling, stained, chipped and squatting heavily on a dark green linoleum floor.

The place is neat and arranged in a more or less orderly way, however, and the man seems comfortable there. He strolls from the kitchen to the livingroom and peeks into the three small bedrooms that branch off a hallway behind the livingroom. "Nice place!" he calls to the woman. He is studying the framed pictures of her three children arranged like an altar atop the buffet. "Nice-looking kids!" he calls out. They are. Blond, round-faced, clean, and utterly ordinary-looking, their pleasant faces glance, as instructed, slightly off camera and down to the right, as if they are trying to remember the name of the capital of Montana.

When he returns to the kitchen, the woman is putting away her groceries, her back to him. "Where's that beer you bribed me with?" he asks again. He takes a position against the door-frame, his weight on one hip, like a dancer resting. "You sure are quiet today, Sarah," he says in a low voice. "Everything okay?"

Silently, she turns away from the grocery bags, crosses the room to the man, reaches up to him, and holding him by the head, kisses his mouth, rolls her torso against his, drops her hands to his hips and yanks him tightly to her, and goes on kissing him, eyes closed, working her face furiously against his. The man places his hands on her shoulders and pulls away, and they face each other, wide-eyed, as if amazed and frightened. The man drops his hands, and the woman lets go of his hips. Then, after a few seconds, the man silently turns, goes to the door, and leaves. The last thing he sees as he closes the door behind him is the woman standing in the kitchen doorframe, her face looking down and slightly to one side, wearing the same pleasant expression on her face as her children in their photographs, trying to remember the capital of Montana.

v

Sarah appeared at my apartment door the following morning, a Sunday, cool and rainy. She had brought me the package of freshly laundered shirts I'd left in her kitchen, and when I opened the door to her, she simply held the package out to me as if it were a penitent's gift. She wore a yellow rain slicker and cap and looked more like a disconsolate schoolgirl facing an angry teacher than a grown woman dropping a package off at a friend's apartment. After all, she had nothing to be ashamed of.

I invited her inside, and she accepted my invitation. I had been reading the Sunday *New York Times* on the couch and drinking coffee, lounging through the gray morning in bathrobe and pajamas. I told her to take off her wet raincoat and hat and hang them in the closet by the door and started for the kitchen to get her a cup of coffee, when I stopped, turned, and looked at her. She closed the closet door on her yellow raincoat and hat, turned around, and faced me.

What else can I do? I must describe it. I remember that moment of ten years ago as if it occurred ten minutes ago, the package of shirts on the table behind her, the newspapers scattered over the couch and floor, the sound of windblown rain washing the sides of the building outside, and the silence of the room, as we stood across from one another and watched, while we each simultaneously removed our own clothing, my robe, her blouse and skirt, my pajama top, her slip and bra, my pajama bottom, her underpants, until we were both standing naked in the harsh, gray light, two naked members of the same species, a male and a female, the male somewhat younger and less scarred than the female, the female somewhat less delicately constructed than the male, both individuals pale-skinned with dark thatches of hair in the area of their genitals, both individuals standing slackly, as if a great, protracted tension between them had at last been released.

VI

We made love that morning in my bed for long hours that drifted easily into afternoon. And we talked, as people usually do when they spend half a day or half a night in bed together. I told her of my past, named and described the people I had loved and had loved me, my ex-wife in New York, my brother in the Air Force, my father and mother in their condominium in Florida, and I told her of my ambitions and dreams and even confessed some of my fears. She listened patiently and intelligently throughout and talked much less than I. She had already told me many of these things about herself, and perhaps whatever she had to say to me now lay on the next inner circle of intimacy or else could not be spoken of at all.

During the next few weeks we met and made love often and always at my apartment. On arriving home from work, I would phone her, or if not, she would phone me, and after a few feints and dodges, one would suggest to the other that we get together tonight, and a half hour later she'd be at my door. Our love-making was passionate, skillful, kindly, and deeply satisfying. We didn't often speak of it to one another or brag about it, the way some couples do when they are surprised by the ease with which they have become contented lovers. We did occasionally joke and tease each other, however, playfully acknowledging that the only thing we did together was make love but that we did it so frequently there was no time for anything else.

Then one hot night, a Saturday in August, we were lying in bed atop the tangled sheets, smoking cigarettes and chatting idly, and Sarah suggested that we go out for a drink.

"Now?"

"Sure. It's early. What time is it?"

I scanned the digital clock next to the bed. "Nine forty-nine."

"There. See?"

"That's not so early. You usually go home by eleven, you know. It's almost ten."

"No, it's only a little after nine. Depends on how you look at things. Besides, Ron, it's Saturday night. Don't you want to go out and dance or something? Or is this the only thing you know how to do?" she teased and poked me in the ribs. "You know how to dance? You like to dance?"

"Yeah, sure . . . sure, but not tonight. It's too hot. And I'm tired."

But she persisted, happily pointing out that an air-condi-tioned bar would be cooler than my apartment, and we didn't have to go to a dance bar, we could go to Osgood's. "As a compromise," she said.

I suggested a place called the El Rancho, a restaurant with a large, dark cocktail lounge and dance bar located several miles from town on the old Portsmouth highway. Around nine the restaurant closed and the bar became something of a roadhouse, with a small country-western houseband and a clientele drawn from the four or five villages that adjoined Concord on the north and east. I had eaten at the restaurant once but had never gone to the bar, and I didn't know anyone who had.

Sarah was silent for a moment. Then she lit a cigarette and

drew the sheet over her naked body. "You don't want anybody
to know about us, do you? Do you?"

"That's not it . . . I just don't like gossip, and I work with a lot
of people who show up sometimes at Osgood's. On a Saturday
night especially."

"No," she said firmly. "You're ashamed of being seen with
me. You'll sleep with me, but you won't go out in public with
me."

"That's not true, Sarah."

She was silent again. Relieved, I reached across her to the
bedtable and got my cigarettes and lighter.

"You owe me, Ron," she said suddenly, as I passed over her.
"You owe me."

"What?" I lay back, lit a cigarette, and covered my body with
the sheet.

"I said, 'You owe me.' "

"I don't know what you're talking about, Sarah. I just don't
like a lot of gossip going around, that's all. I like keeping my
private life private, that's all. I don't *owe* you anything."

"Friendship you owe me. And respect. Friendship and respect. A person can't do what you've done with me without
owing them friendship and respect."

"Sarah, I really don't know what you're talking about," I said.
"I am your friend, you know that. And I respect you. I really
do."

"You really think so, don't you?"

"Yes."

She said nothing for several long moments. Then she sighed
and in a low, almost inaudible voice said, "Then you'll have to
go out in public with me. I don't care about Osgood's or the
people you work with, we don't have to go there or see any of
them," she said. "But you're gonna have to go to places like the
El Rancho with me, and a few other places I know, too, where
there's people *I* work with, people *I* know, and maybe we'll even
go to a couple of parties, because *I* get invited to parties sometimes, you know. I have friends, and I have some family, too,
and you're gonna have to meet my family. My kids think I'm
just going around bar-hopping when I'm over here with you,
and I don't like that, so you're gonna have to meet them so I

can tell them where I am when I'm not at home nights. And
sometimes you're gonna come over and spend the evening
at my place!" Her voice had risen as she heard her demands
and felt their rightness, until now she was almost shouting at
me. "You *owe* that to me. Or else you're a bad man. It's that
simple."

It was.

VII

The handsome man is over-dressed. He is wearing a navy blue
blazer, taupe shirt open at the throat, white slacks, white loafers.
Everyone else, including the homely woman with the handsome
man, is dressed appropriately, dressed, that is, like everyone
else — jeans and cowboy boots, blouses or cowboy shirts or tee
shirts with catchy sayings printed across the front, and many of
the women are wearing cowboy hats pushed back and tied
under their chins. The man doesn't know anyone at the bar or,
if they're at a party, in the room, but the woman knows most of
the people there, and she gladly introduces him. The men grin
and shake his hand, slap him on his jacketed shoulder, ask him
where he works, what's his line, after which they lapse into
silence. The women flirt briefly with their faces, but they lapse
into silence even before the men do. The woman with the man
in the blazer does most of the talking for everyone. She talks for
the man in the blazer, for the men standing around the refrigerator, or if they're at a bar, for the other men at the table, and
for the other women, too. She chats and rambles aimlessly
through loud monologues, laughs uproariously at trivial jokes,
and drinks too much, until soon she is drunk, thick-tongued,
clumsy, and the man has to say her goodbyes and ease her out
the door to his car and drive her home to her apartment on
Perley Street.

This happens twice in one week, and then three times the
next — at the El Rancho, at the Ox Bow in Northwood, at Rita's
and Jimmy's apartment on Thorndike Street, out in Warner at
Betsy Beeler's new house, and, the last time, at a cottage on
Lake Sunapee rented by some kids in shipping at Rumford
Press. Ron no longer calls Sarah when he gets home from work;
he waits for her call, and sometimes, when he knows it's she, he

doesn't answer the phone. Usually, he lets it ring five or six times, and then he reaches down and picks up the receiver. He has taken his jacket and vest off and loosened his tie and is about to put supper, frozen manicotti, into the Radarange.

"Hello?"

"Hi."

"How're you doing?"

"Okay, I guess. A little tired."

"Still hung over?"

"No. Not really. Just tired. I hate Mondays."

"You have fun last night?"

"Well, yeah, sorta. It's nice out there, at the lake. Listen," she says, brightening. *"Whyn't you come over here tonight? The kids're all going out later, but if you come over before eight, you can meet them. They really want to meet you."*

"You told them about me?"

"Sure. Long time ago. I'm not supposed to tell my own kids?"

Ron is silent.

"You don't want to come over here tonight. You don't want to meet my kids. No, you don't want my kids to meet you, that's it."

"No, no, it's just . . . I've got a lot of work to do . . ."

"We should talk," she announces in a flat voice.

"Yes," he says, "we should talk."

They agree that she will meet him at his apartment, and they'll talk, and they say goodbye and hang up.

While Ron is heating his supper and then eating alone at his kitchen table and Sarah is feeding her children, perhaps I should admit, since we are nearing the end of my story, that I don't actually know that Sarah Cole is dead. A few years ago I happened to run into one of her friends from the press, a blond woman with an underslung jaw. Her name, she reminded me, was Glenda; she had seen me at Osgood's a couple of times, and we had met at the El Rancho once when I had gone there with Sarah. I was amazed that she could remember me and a little embarrassed that I did not recognize her at all, and she laughed at that and said, "You haven't changed much, mister!" I pretended to recognize her, but I think she knew she was a stranger to me. We were standing outside the Sears store on South Main Street, where I had gone to buy paint. I had recently remarried, and my wife and I were redecorating my apartment.

"Whatever happened to Sarah?" I asked Glenda. "Is she still down at the press?"

"Jeez, no! She left a long time ago. Way back. I heard she went back with her ex-husband. I can't remember his name. Something Cole."

I asked her if she was sure of that, and she said no, she had only heard it around the bars and down at the press, but she had assumed it was true. People said Sarah had moved back with her ex-husband and was living in a trailer in a park near Hooksett, and the whole family had moved down to Florida that winter because he was out of work. He was a carpenter, she said.

"I thought he was mean to her. I thought he beat her up and everything. I thought she hated him," I said.

"Oh, well, yeah, he was a bastard, all right. I met him a couple of times, and I didn't like him. Short, ugly, and mean when he got drunk. But you know what they say."

"What do they say?"

"Oh, you know, about water seeking its own level."

"Sarah wasn't mean when she was drunk."

The woman laughed. "Naw, but she sure was short and ugly!"

I said nothing.

"Hey, don't get me wrong, I liked Sarah. But you and her . . . well, you sure made a funny-looking couple. She probably didn't feel so self-conscious and all with her husband," the woman said seriously. "I mean, with you . . . all tall and blond, and poor old Sarah . . . I mean, the way them kids in the press room used to kid her about her looks, it was embarrassing just to hear it."

"Well . . . I loved her," I said.

The woman raised her plucked eyebrows in disbelief. She smiled. "Sure, you did, honey," she said, and she patted me on the arm. "Sure, you did." Then she let the smile drift off her face, turned and walked away.

When someone you have loved dies, you accept the fact of his or her death, but then the person goes on living in your memory, dreams, and reveries. You have imaginary conversations with him or her, you see something striking and remind yourself to tell your loved one about it and then get brought up short by the knowledge of the fact of his or her death, and at night, in your sleep, the dead person visits you. With Sarah, none of that happened. When she was gone from my life, she was gone absolutely, as if she had never existed in the first place. It was only later, when I could think of her as dead and could come out and say it, my friend Sarah Cole is dead, that I was able to tell this story, for that is when she began to enter my memories, my dreams, and my reveries. In that way I learned that I truly did love her, and now I have begun to grieve over her death, to wish her alive again, so that I can say to her the things I could not know or say when she was alive, when I did not know that I loved her.

VIII

The woman arrives at Ron's apartment around eight. He hears her car, because of the broken muffler, blat and rumble into the parking lot below, and he crosses quickly from the kitchen and peers out the livingroom window and, as if through a telescope, watches her shove herself across the seat to the passenger's side to get out of the car, then walk slowly in the dusky light toward the apartment building. It's a warm evening, and she's wearing her white bermuda shorts, pink sleeveless sweater, and shower sandals. Ron hates those clothes. He hates the way the shorts cut into her flesh at the crotch and thigh, hates the large, dark caves below her arms that get exposed by the sweater, hates the flapping noise made by the sandals.

Shortly, there is a soft knock at his door. He opens it, turns away and crosses to the kitchen, where he turns back, lights a cigarette, and watches her. She closes the door. He offers her a drink, which she declines, and somewhat formally, he invites her to sit down. She sits carefully on the sofa, in the middle, with her feet close together on the floor, as if she were being interviewed for a job. Then he comes around and sits in the easy chair, relaxed, one leg slung over the other at the knee, as if he were interviewing her for the job.

"Well," he says, "you wanted to talk."

"Yes. But now you're mad at me. I can see that. I didn't do anything, Ron."

"I'm not mad at you."

They are silent for a moment. Ron goes on smoking his cigarette.

Finally, she sighs and says, "You don't want to see me anymore, do you?"

He waits a few seconds and answers, "Yes. That's right." Getting up from the chair, he walks to the silver-gray bicycle and stands before it, running a fingertip along the slender cross-bar from the saddle to the chrome-plated handlebars.

"You're a son of a bitch," she says in a low voice. "You're worse than my ex-husband." Then she smiles meanly, almost sneers, and soon he realizes that she is telling him that she won't leave. He's stuck with her, she informs him with cold precision. "You think I'm just so much meat, and all you got to do is call up the butcher shop and cancel your order. Well, now you're going to find out different. You *can't* cancel your order. I'm not meat, I'm not one of your pretty little girlfriends who come running when you want them and go away when you get tired of them. I'm *different*. I got nothing to lose, Ron. Nothing. You're stuck with me, Ron."

He continues stroking his bicycle. "No, I'm not."

She sits back in the couch and crosses her legs at the ankles. "I think I *will* have that drink you offered."

"Look, Sarah, it would be better if you go now."

"No," she says flatly. "You offered me a drink when I came in. Nothing's changed since I've been here. Not for me, and not for you. I'd like that drink you offered," she says haughtily.

Ron turns away from the bicycle and takes a step toward her. His face has stiffened into a mask. "Enough is enough," he says through clenched teeth. "I've given you enough."

"Fix me a drink, will you, honey?" she says with a phony smile.

Ron orders her to leave.

She refuses.

He grabs her by the arm and yanks her to her feet.

She starts crying lightly. She stands there and looks up into his face and weeps, but she does not move toward the door, so he pushes her. She regains her balance and goes on weeping.

He stands back and places his fists on his hips and looks at her. "Go on and leave, you ugly bitch," he says to her, and as he says the words, as one by one they leave his mouth, she's transformed into the most beautiful woman he has ever seen. He says the words again, almost tenderly. "Leave, you ugly bitch." Her hair is golden, her brown eyes deep and sad, her mouth full and affectionate, her tears the tears of love and loss, and her pleading, outstretched arms, her entire body, the arms and body of a devoted woman's cruelly rejected love. A third time he says the words. "Leave me, you disgusting, ugly bitch." She is wrapped in an envelope of golden light, a warm, dense haze that she seems to have stepped into, as into a carriage. And then she is gone, and he is alone again.

He looks around the room, as if searching for her. Sitting down in the easy chair, he places his face in his hands. It's not as if she has died; it's as if he has killed her.

WRIGHT MORRIS

In "Fellow-Creatures," a retired Army colonel finds himself
marching in time with new acquaintances. Gail Godwin says she
selected the story for the 1985 volume because "I remembered
those cows, with their craggy, primitive masks of faces, congre-
gating on the deck of a house 'like guests at a cocktail party.'
And like Colonel Huggins, U.S. Army, retired, who is 'amazed
to note the range of emotion in the cluck of a chicken,' I under-
went a change." Wright Morris was born in 1910 in Central City,
Nebraska. Since the publication of his first novel in 1942, he has
written many books, including novels, collections of stories, criticism, and, most recently, autobiography.

Fellow-Creatures

NOTHING SPECIAL, just a leghorn pullet, the pet of children
who lived in a nearby trailer, its feathers soiled by too much
handling, the little bird had escaped from its pen and found
shelter in the garage of Colonel Huggins, U.S. Army, retired.
The malfunctioning garage door stood half open, offering a
dark and convenient sanctuary that had attracted the pullet at
an early hour of the morning. Huggins had been awakened by
the mournful clucking. When it persisted, he investigated. In
the dawning light, the little bird looked ghostly, but cast a huge
shadow in the beam of the flashlight. Her jeweled eye seemed
to flash; the clucking became shrill and agitated. Huggins
crouched, extending one hand, and the bird, with some reluc-
tance, took a few steps toward him. When Huggins clucked
encouragement, the pullet responded. Huggins had grown up
in a farmyard cackling with chickens without remarking that
they were so expressive. He was amazed to note the range of
emotion in the cluck of a chicken. Fear and anxiety soon gave

way to a soft, throaty warbling for reassurance. Huggins responded. Soon the little bird pecked at the button on his shirt cuff; then, with a minimum of flutter, she allowed him to slip a hand beneath her breastbone, cradle her on his arm. She liked that, being accustomed to it.

As Huggins left the garage and entered the house, the pullet's cackle was troubled and anxious. Huggins stroked her throat feathers to calm her. The bird was quiet while he dialed the neighbors' number and heard the excitement of the children, their cries of relief. The pullet's name proved to be Lucy.

In a moment, three of the children came scrambling through the brush on the slope, trampling whatever it was Huggins' wife had planted. Had he fed her, they cried. She was probably starving! The youngest of the three hugged the little pullet like a package, and off they all raced, hooting. High on the slope Huggins heard the shrill voice of their mother, a liberated young woman who had set up her trailer in her parents' back yard; she was urging them to thank the nice man.

Was Huggins a nice man? For three years, he had endured the cackling of chickens (originally a flock), the honking of geese (now down to two), the bleating of a goat, and the bloodcurdling cry of a peacock kept in a cage too small to strut in or display his plumage. All of this illegal in an exclusively residential area. Even the trailer the young woman and her brood lived in (the tires now flat) required a special permit she had not been granted. Huggins, that nice man, had said nothing. Over the years, he *had* written several letters, all unmailed, to her father, Albrecht, a prominent figure in the foreign-car business. Huggins wondered how he himself would have handled a grown daughter (a squatter on his property) who had brought a court suit against her own father for polluting the air with his diesel-engine Mercedes. Huggins had never met her. She called her cats, her chickens, her geese, and her children by clapping her hands — a racket he found distracting. The pullet had left bits of dirt and feathers on his sleeve. How light she had been! Like a feather duster. He stood as if waiting for something to happen, plucking at his sleeve.

Huggins' daily morning walk was altered to bring him past the pen where the little pullet did her scratching. With a little coaxing, Huggins persuaded her to take birdseed from his palm. Imported Irish oatmeal also caught her fancy. He inquired in the local pet shop what was recommended to brighten up a young bird's feathers. He added the vitamin mixture to her water. He was caught red-handed by Mrs. Albrecht, the young woman's mother, who appeared with vegetable hulls and cuttings. She, too, had a weakness for chickens! Just in passing, she let it drop that this little pullet was the last of the fryers but hadn't fleshed out like the others — had he noticed? There was nothing to her. For which the bird could be thankful. Mrs. Albrecht (she drove a non-diesel Mercedes) could hardly wait to tell the children that their neighbor, Colonel Huggins, had taken on the chore of feeding their chicken — that's how starved it looked!

Huggins would surely have explained what led him to feed his neighbors' chicken, but the word "fryer" had so unsettled him that he was speechless. Was it new to him that young chickens were *fryers*? Hardly. He had once even barbecued fryers in batches — a *spécialité de la maison*, as he had put it.

A few days later, Mr. Albrecht, a jovial type with a strong, booming voice, called across from his deck to say that Huggins was welcome to the whole damn zoo if he would like it, so long as he took the peacock, too. How did Huggins stand it? Albrecht thought it sounded like some female screaming "Help!"

During the war in Europe, Colonel Huggins had enjoyed the hospitality of a French family proud of their cuisine. He had been instrumental in providing them with hard-to-find gourmet necessities. At war's end, they cooked him a five-star dinner, featuring steak. Huggins had admitted to being a connoisseur of steak.

"So," the host asked him, "how you like?"

His mouth full of the steak, Huggins smiled and nodded.

"A *spécialité, mon vieux — filet de cheval Américain!*"

Huggins was calm enough to swallow what he had already chewed. Moments later, however, he was obliged to excuse himself, leaving most of the *filet de cheval* on his plate. He perspired a good deal. A damp towel was applied to his face.

"You Americans!" his host exclaimed. "You like it fine till you know what it is. What you eat is not on your plate, it is in your mind!"

Then there was the time Huggins' wife cried out from the kitchen, "Oh my God!" Fearing the worst, he went to her rescue. But at the door to the kitchen he saw nothing unusual. His wife had prepared a plump bird for roasting with a coat of olive oil that made it glisten.

"Yes?" he said.

She took a moment to slip off the bib of her apron. Then she said, almost flatly, "It looks just like a newborn baby!" and left Huggins alone with it.

A cow, somewhat on the small side — not so large that Huggins found her intimidating — was tethered to pasture in a field that Huggins passed on his long daily walk. He was in the habit, when the spirit moved him, of pulling up the grass that grew along the bank where the cow was unable to reach it. When she raised her head to crop the sweet, fragrant offering from his hand, the breath she exhaled smelled of clover. On the instant, Huggins experienced a time displacement, familiar to poets. A boy, he stood in the shadow of a freight car down the tracks from the town, peering into a great vat of sorghum as sweet and thick as Karo syrup. Bees droned in a cloud above it. A thick green scum spotted its surface. He almost swooned at the thought that he might topple into it. So rich and fragrant had been its smell that he felt no need to taste it. The whole great vat of it, swarming with bees, the scum on the top softly undulating, had put him in mind of the old movie serials where if the hero toppled into one of the pits of terror he would be preserved like a bee in a jar of honey.

On occasion, the cow shared the pasture with a swaybacked horse. In the rainy season Huggins might pull up a tuft of the new grass, earth still clinging to the roots, and toss it to where the horse could munch it. The animal showed no interest whatever. The horse's owner occasionally forked hay from the back of a pickup, but he never checked to see what the horse thought about it. He drove in, made his drop, and drove off. Some days Huggins would stand on the bridge over the creek, where he and the animals had a good view of each other; the bare spots on the horse, worn by the harness, were the shiny black of old oilcloth. In bad weather, the beast took shelter in a shed, where Huggins, attentive as he passed, might hear a snort and the

stomp of a hoof. Somehow it troubled him that it was a mare.
On cold mornings he saw her breath smoke. He thought it
especially disturbing that she was both so big and so useless. He
had read about pet food, but he tried to put it out of his mind.

Occasionally, this pasture also nourished several black-faced
sheep, adored by children. Seen close up, their faces were like
felt masks, the heads like carnival toggery on a stick. At no time
did Huggins entertain any notion that he and the sheep shared
a common doom or aspiration. He did feel the creatures' ill-
starred need to be led somewhere, anywhere — even to slaugh-
ter. Nevertheless, for no particular reason, Colonel Huggins —
a lover of roast spring lamb — passed up the seasonal special
called to his attention by Angelo, the butcher, well known for
his own hopeless love for steak tartare with three raw eggs.

"So what is new?" queried Angelo, sensing a change.

"Less fat," replied Huggins, patting his midriff. It was old
advice he was now moved to take. What did that leave him?
Perhaps a mozzarella pizza from the freezer. One day — not
today — he would ask Angelo how horses did so well on just
hay and cereal.

Escaped or missing pets — now that Huggins had been alerted
— were having one of their high seasons. Urgent requests for
their return were posted on abandoned cars, telephone poles,
and supermarket bulletin boards, citing rewards along with descriptions of their character, identifying marks, the names to
which they sometimes responded, or — in the case of parrots —
what they would say if questioned. What parrots might say often
shocked Huggins; he had always teased them to speak with a
mere "Polly want a cracker?" but lately one had told him to buzz
off.

One day, a big cottontail rabbit, with feet like snowshoes,
hopped from behind a shrub to startle Huggins. The sight of
Huggins did not give the rabbit cause for alarm; it hopped so
close that Huggins might have seized it if he had not been so
unnerved. When he mentioned this incident to his cousin, Liz
Harcourt — a woman who had hatched several batches of quail
eggs in her kitchen and raised the broods to eat from her plate
and nest in her apron pockets — she said, "You should have
grabbed him. I love chicken-fried rabbit!"

Some years back, during a rainy season with bad mud slides and considerable flooding, a herd of Holstein cows pastured somewhere behind the ridge had made their way, pursued by a pack of baying dogs, through groves of oak and laurel, through a dense tangle of brush that streaked their hides with red as if raked with barbed wire, to where they exited, mooing distractedly, at the foot of the driveway Huggins shared with the Albrechts. He saw them from his deck, where he was barbecuing spareribs. As they made their mooing way up the driveway, he worried that they would trample his azaleas. Single file, following the leader, they continued up the slope to the Albrecht house (at that time the trailer was not there) and followed the walk around the house onto the deck at the rear. The rail fence around the deck confined them; there they formed an assembly, casually informal, like guests at a cocktail party. Peering down at Huggins, one or two mooed plaintively. He could see the red streaks on their flanks and udders. The bizarre spectacle brought to Huggins' mind a fantastic, fanciful painting. Fear that the deck might collapse — his neighbors were out that afternoon — aroused him to call the fire department for some quick action. The man who owned the cows, a shaggy, bearded fellow who did not trouble to greet Huggins, finally appeared to herd them peaceably back down to the street.

At the time, the incident seemed merely bizarre. But that night, as Huggins put his mind to it, his eyes on the play of shadows on the bedroom ceiling, it came to him that the face of a cow, a craggy primitive mask, was like a piece of the landscape seen in closeup. That congress of cows assembled on a house deck, their gaze centered in judgment on Huggins, had led him to forgo the ribs smoking on his barbecue.

Another day — it had been overcast, with a bit of drizzle, obliging him to plod along with his head down — Huggins heard a raucous clamor above and behind him. A flock of grackles, their wet feathers gleaming, sat along one of the telephone wires. On an impulse, he threw up his arms and hooted hoarsely. The birds rose about him like a leaf storm, scattered for a moment, then gathered on a wire on the street below. Did Huggins detect, as he passed by, a change in the tone of their discussion? Several flew ahead to strut about on a plot of grass. As he approached them they took off, flying in crisp military formation. He wheeled to watch them, blinking his eyes at the pelting stream of their forms. After several orderly strategic flights, they congregated in a tree along the curb walk. The tree itself was not much — a dark clump of leaves without visible branches. It was Huggins' impression, however, as he walked toward it, that the gabble of the birds caused the leaves to tremble, as if stirred by a breeze. He sensed their hovering, inscrutable presence. From beneath the tree, he peered upward just as the flock noisily departed, like bees from a hive. Bits of leaves and feathers rained on him. The agitation Huggins had observed in the leaves he now felt within himself — a tingling, pleasurable excitement. Squinting skyward, he could see strips of sky as if through cracks in leaky shingles. High at the top, perched at an angle, was a single black bird. Either that bird or another just like it — among birds it seemed unimportant — fluttered along with Huggins, its hatpin eyes checking on his interests and curious habits, all the way back to the foot of his drive, where he heard, high on the slope above him, the expectant clucking of the little pullet, and he responded in kind.

CHARLES BAXTER

"Gryphon" is the story of a substitute teacher who dazzles a
fourth-grade class with her lessons on the malleability of facts
and on predicting the future. The nine-year-old narrator pins
down the point at which a Mary Poppins–like talent for fantasy
crosses the line into pathology. Baxter's story, a rare illumina-
tion of the end of innocence, achieves Raymond Carver's standard for selection: that a story relate "what it's like to be out
there" and tell us "what everybody knows but nobody is talking
about." Charles Baxter has published three collections of stories,
a novel, and a book of poems. Born in Minneapolis, he lives and
teaches in Detroit.

Gryphon

ON WEDNESDAY AFTERNOON, between the geography lesson
on ancient Egypt's hand-operated irrigation system and an art
project that involved drawing a model city next to a mountain,
our fourth-grade teacher, Mr. Hibler, developed a cough. This
cough began with a series of muffled throat clearings and pro-
gressed to propulsive noises contained within Mr. Hibler's
closed mouth. "Listen to him," Carol Peterson whispered to me.
"He's gonna blow up." Mr. Hibler's laughter — dazed and infre-
quent — sounded a bit like his cough, but as we worked on our
model cities we would look up, thinking he was enjoying a joke,
and see Mr. Hibler's face turning red, his cheeks puffed out.
This was not laughter. Twice he bent over, and his loose tie, like
a plumb line, hung down straight from his neck as he exploded
himself into a Kleenex. He would excuse himself, then go on
coughing. "I'll bet you a dime," Carol Peterson whispered, "we
get a substitute tomorrow."

Carol sat at the desk in front of mine and was a bad person

— when she thought no one was looking she would blow her nose on notebook paper, then crumble it up and throw it into the wastebasket — but at times of crisis she spoke the truth. I knew I'd lose the dime.

"No deal," I said.

When Mr. Hibler stood us up in formation at the door just prior to the final bell, he was almost incapable of speech. "I'm sorry, boys and girls," he said. "I seem to be coming down with something."

"I hope you feel better tomorrow, Mr. Hibler," Bobby Kryzanowicz, the faultless brown-noser said, and I heard Carol Peterson's evil giggle. Then Mr. Hibler opened the door and we walked out to the buses, a clique of us starting noisily to hawk and cough as soon as we thought we were a few feet beyond Mr. Hibler's earshot.

Five Oaks being a rural community, and in Michigan, the supply of substitute teachers was limited to the town's unemployed community college graduates, a pool of about four mothers. These ladies fluttered, provided easeful class days, and nervously covered material we had mastered weeks earlier. Therefore it was a surprise when a woman we had never seen came into the class the next day, carrying a purple purse, a checkerboard lunchbox, and a few books. She put the books on one side of Mr. Hibler's desk and the lunchbox on the other, next to the Voice of Music phonograph. Three of us in the back of the room were playing with Heever, the chameleon that lived in the terrarium and on one of the plastic drapes, when she walked in.

She clapped her hands at us. "Little boys," she said, "why are you bent over together like that?" She didn't wait for us to answer. "Are you tormenting an animal? Put it back. Please sit down at your desks. I want no cabals this time of the day." We just stared at her. "Boys," she repeated, "I asked you to sit down."

I put the chameleon in his terrarium and felt my way to my desk, never taking my eyes off the woman. With white and green chalk, she had started to draw a tree on the left side of the blackboard. She didn't look usual. Furthermore, her tree was outsized, disproportionate, for some reason.

"This room needs a tree," she said, with one line drawing the suggestion of a leaf. "A large, leafy, shady, deciduous . . . oak."

Her fine, light hair had been done up in what I would learn years later was called a chignon, and she wore gold-rimmed glasses whose lenses seemed to have the faintest blue tint. Harold Knardahl, who sat across from me, whispered "Mars," and I nodded slowly, savoring the imminent weirdness of the day. The substitute drew another branch with an extravagant arm gesture, then turned around and said, "Good morning. I don't believe I said good morning to all you yet."

Facing us, she was no special age — an adult is an adult — but her face had two prominent lines, descending vertically from the sides of her mouth to her chin. I knew where I had seen those lines before: *Pinocchio*. They were marionette lines. "You may stare at me," she said to us, as a few more kids from the last bus came into the room, their eyes fixed on her, "for a few more seconds, until the bell rings. Then I will permit no more staring. Looking I will permit. Staring, no. It is impolite to stare, and a sign of bad breeding. You cannot make a social effort while staring."

Harold Knardahl did not glance at me, or nudge, but I heard him whisper "Mars" again, trying to get more mileage out of his single joke with the kids who had just come in.

When everyone was seated, the substitute teacher finished her tree, put down her chalk fastidiously on the phonograph, brushed her hands, and faced us. "Good morning," she said. "I am Miss Ferenczi, your teacher for the day. I am fairly new to your community, and I don't believe any of you know me. I will therefore start by telling you a story about myself."

While we settled back, she launched into her tale. She said her grandfather had been a Hungarian prince; her mother had been born in some place called Flanders, had been a pianist, and had played concerts for people Miss Ferenczi referred to as "crowned heads." She gave us a knowing look. "Grieg," she said, "the Norwegian master, wrote a concerto for piano that was," she paused, "my mother's triumph at her debut concert in London." Her eyes searched the ceiling. Our eyes followed. Nothing up there but ceiling tile. "For reasons that I shall not go into,

my family's fortunes took us to Detroit, then north to dreadful
Saginaw, and now here I am in Five Oaks, as your substitute
teacher, for today, Thursday, October the eleventh. I believe it
will be a good day: All the forecasts coincide. We shall start with
your reading lesson. Take out your reading book. I believe it is
called *Broad Horizons,* or something along those lines."

Jeannie Vermeesch raised her hand. Miss Ferenzi nodded at
her. "Mr. Hibler always starts the day with the Pledge of Allegiance," Jeannie whined.

"Oh, does he? In that case," Miss Ferenczi said, "you must
know it *very* well by now, and we certainly need not spend our
time on it. No, no allegiance pledging on the premises today, by
my reckoning. Not with so much sunlight coming into the room.
A pledge does not suit my mood." She glanced at her watch.
"Time *is* flying. Take out *Broad Horizons.*"

She disappointed us by giving us an ordinary lesson, complete
with vocabulary word drills, comprehension questions, and rec-
itation. She didn't seem to care for the material, however. She
sighed every few minutes and rubbed her glasses with a frilly
perfumed handkerchief that she withdrew, magician style, from
her left sleeve.

After reading we moved on to arithmetic. It was my favorite
time of the morning, when the lazy autumn sunlight dazzled
its way through ribbons of clouds past the windows on the east
side of the classroom, and crept across the linoleum floor. On
the playground the first group of children, the kindergartners,
were running on the quack grass just beyond the monkey bars.
We were doing multiplication tables. Miss Ferenczi had made
John Wazny stand up at his desk in the front row. He was
supposed to go through the tables of six. From where I was
sitting, I could smell the Vitalis soaked into John's plastered
hair. He was doing fine until he came to six times eleven and six
times twelve. "Six times eleven," he said, "is sixty-eight. Six times
twelve is . . ." He put his fingers to his head, quickly and secretly
sniffed his fingertips, and said, "seventy-two." Then he sat
down.

"Fine," Miss Ferenczi said. "Well now. That was very good."

"Miss Ferenczi!" One of the Eddy twins was waving her hand
desperately in the air. "Miss Ferenczi! Miss Ferenczi!"

"Yes?"

"John said that six times eleven is sixty-eight and you said he was right!"

"*Did* I?" She gazed at the class with a jolly look breaking across her marionette's face. "Did I say that? Well, what *is* six times eleven?"

"It's sixty-six!"

She nodded. "Yes. So it is. But, and I know some people will not entirely agree with me, at some times it is sixty-eight."

"When? When is it sixty-eight?"

We were all waiting.

"In higher mathematics, which you children do not yet understand, six times eleven can be considered to be sixty-eight." She laughed through her nose. "In higher mathematics numbers are . . . more fluid. The only thing a number does is contain a certain amount of something. Think of water. A cup is not the only way to measure a certain amount of water, is it?" We were staring, shaking our heads. "You could use saucepans or thimbles. In either case, the water *would be the same*. Perhaps," she started again, "it would be better for you to think that six times eleven is sixty-eight only when I am in the room."

"Why is it sixty-eight," Mark Poole asked, "when you're in the room?"

"Because it's more interesting that way," she said, smiling very rapidly behind her blue-tinted glasses. "Besides, I'm your substitute teacher, am I not?" We all nodded. "Well, then, think of six times eleven equals sixty-eight as a substitute fact."

"A substitute fact?"

"Yes." Then she looked at us carefully. "Do you think," she asked, "that anyone is going to be hurt by a substitute fact?"

We looked back at her.

"Will the plants on the windowsill be hurt?" We glanced at them. There were sensitive plants thriving in a green plastic tray, and several wilted ferns in small clay pots. "Your dogs and cats, or your moms and dads?" She waited. "So," she concluded, "what's the problem?"

"But it's wrong," Janice Weber said, "isn't it?"

"What's your name, young lady?"

"Janice Weber."

"And you think it's wrong, Janice?"

"I was just asking."

"Well, all right. You were just asking. I think we've spent enough time on this matter by now, don't you, class? You are free to think what you like. When your teacher, Mr. Hibler, returns, six times eleven will be sixty-six again, you can rest assured. And it will be that for the rest of your lives in Five Oaks. Too bad, eh?" She raised her eyebrows and glinted herself at us. "But for now, it wasn't. So much for that. Let us go to your assigned problems for today, as painstakingly outlined, I see, in Mr. Hibler's lesson plan. Take out a sheet of paper and write your names in the upper left-hand corner."

For the next half hour we did the rest of our arithmetic problems. We handed them in and went on to spelling, my worst subject. Spelling always came before lunch. We were taking spelling dictation and looking at the clock. "Thorough," Miss Ferenczi said. "Boundary." She walked in the aisles between the desks, holding the spelling book open and looking down at our papers. "Balcony." I clutched my pencil. Somehow, the way she said those words, they seemed foreign, Hungarian, mis-voweled and mis-consonanted. I stared down at what I had spelled. *Balconie*. I turned my pencil upside down and erased my mistake. *Balconey*. That looked better, but still incorrect. I cursed the world of spelling and tried erasing it again and saw the paper beginning to wear away. *Balkony*. Suddenly I felt a hand on my shoulder.

"I don't like that word either," Miss Ferenczi whispered, bent over, her mouth near my ear. "It's ugly. My feeling is, if you don't like a word, you don't have to use it." She straightened up, leaving behind a slight odor of Clorets.

At lunchtime we went out to get our trays of sloppy joes, peaches in heavy syrup, coconut cookies, and milk, and brought them back to the classroom, where Miss Ferenczi was sitting at the desk, eating a brown sticky thing she had unwrapped from tightly rubber-banded wax paper. "Miss Ferenczi," I said, raising my hand. "You don't have to eat with us. You can eat with the other teachers. There's a teachers' lounge," I ended up, "next to the principal's office."

"No, thank you," she said. "I prefer it here."

"We've got a room monitor," I said. "Mrs. Eddy." I pointed to where Mrs. Eddy, Joyce and Judy's mother, sat silently at the back of the room, doing her knitting.

"That's fine," Miss Ferenczi said. "But I shall continue to eat here, with you children. I prefer it," she repeated.

"How come?" Wayne Razmer asked without raising his hand.

"I talked with the other teachers before class this morning," Miss Ferenczi said, biting into her brown food. "There was a great rattling of the words for the fewness of ideas. I didn't care for their brand of hilarity. I don't like ditto machine jokes."

"Oh," Wayne said.

"What's that you're eating?" Maxine Sylvester asked, twitching her nose. "Is it food?"

"It most certainly *is* food. It's a stuffed fig. I had to drive almost down to Detroit to get it. I also bought some smoked sturgeon. And this," she said, lifting some green leaves out of her lunchbox, "is raw spinach, cleaned this morning before I came out here to the Garfield-Murry school."

"Why're you eating raw spinach?" Maxine asked.

"It's good for you," Miss Ferenczi said. "More stimulating than soda pop or smelling salts." I bit into my sloppy joe and stared blankly out the window. An almost invisible moon was faintly silvered in the daytime autumn sky. "As far as food is concerned," Miss Ferenczi was saying, "you have to shuffle the pack. Mix it up. Too many people eat . . . well, never mind."

"Miss Ferenczi," Carol Peterson said, "what are we going to do this afternoon?"

"Well," she said, looking down at Mr. Hibler's lesson plan, "I see that your teacher, Mr. Hibler, has you scheduled for a unit on the Egyptians." Carol groaned. "Yessss," Miss Ferenczi continued, "that is what we will do: the Egyptians. A remarkable people. Almost as remarkable as the Americans. But not quite." She lowered her head, did her quick smile, and went back to eating her spinach.

After noon recess we came back into the classroom and saw that Miss Ferenczi had drawn a pyramid on the blackboard, close to her oak tree. Some of us who had been playing baseball were messing around in the back of the room, dropping the bats and the gloves into the playground box, and I think that Ray Schontzeler had just slugged me when I heard Miss Ferenczi's highpitched voice quavering with emotion. "Boys," she said, "come to order right this minute and take your seats. I do not wish to waste a minute of class time. Take out your geography books." We trudged to our desks and, still sweating, pulled out *Distant Lands and Their People.* "Turn to page forty-two." She waited for thirty seconds, then looked over at Kelly Munger. "Young man," she said, "why are you still fossicking in your desk?"

Kelly looked as if his foot had been stepped on. "Why am I what?"

"Why are you . . . burrowing in your desk like that?"

"I'm lookin' for the book, Miss Ferenczi."

Bobby Kryzanowicz, the faultless brown-noser who sat in the first row by choice, softly said, "His name is Kelly Munger. He can't ever find his stuff. He always does that."

"I don't care what his name is, especially after lunch," Miss Ferenczi said. *"Where is your book?"*

"I just found it." Kelly was peering into his desk and with both hands pulled at the book, shoveling along in front of it several pencils and crayons, which fell into his lap and then to the floor.

"I hate a mess," Miss Ferenczi said. "I hate a mess in a desk or a mind. It's . . . unsanitary. You wouldn't want your house at home to look like your desk at school, now, would you?" She didn't wait for an answer. "I should think not. A house at home should be as neat as human hands can make it. What were we talking about? Egypt. Page forty-two. I note from Mr. Hibler's lesson plan that you have been discussing the modes of Egyptian irrigation. Interesting, in my view, but not so interesting as what we are about to cover. The pyramids and Egyptian slave labor. A plus on one side, a minus on the other." We had our books open to page forty-two, where there was a picture of a pyramid, but Miss Ferenczi wasn't looking at the book. Instead, she was staring at some object just outside the window.

"Pyramids," Miss Ferenczi said, still looking past the window. "I want you to think about the pyramids. And what was inside.

The bodies of the pharaohs, of course, and their attendant treasures. Scrolls. Perhaps," Miss Ferenczi said, with something gleeful but unsmiling in her face, "these scrolls were novels for the pharaohs, helping them to pass the time in their long voyage through the centuries. But then, I am joking." I was looking at the lines on Miss Ferenczi's face. "Pyramids," Miss Ferenczi went on, "were the repositories of special cosmic powers. The nature of a pyramid is to guide cosmic energy forces into a concentrated point. The Egyptians knew that; we have generally forgotten it. Did you know," she asked, walking to the side of the room so that she was standing by the coat closet, "that George Washington had Egyptian blood, from his grandmother? Certain features of the Constitution of the United States are notable for their Egyptian ideas."

Without glancing down at the book, she began to talk about the movement of souls in Egyptian religion. She said that when people die, their souls return to Earth in the form of carpenter ants or walnut trees, depending on how they behaved — "well or ill" — in life. She said that the Egyptians believed that people act the way they do because of magnetism produced by tidal forces in the solar system, forces produced by the sun and by its "planetary ally," Jupiter. Jupiter, she said, was a planet, as we had been told, but had "certain properties of stars." She was speaking very fast. She said that the Egyptians were great explorers and conquerors. She said that the greatest of all the conquerors, Genghis Khan, had had forty horses and forty young women killed on the site of his grave. We listened. No one tried to stop her. "I myself have been in Egypt," she said, "and have witnessed much dust and many brutalities." She said that an old man in Egypt who worked for a circus had personally shown her an animal in a cage, a monster, half bird and half lion. She said that this monster was called a gryphon and that she had heard about them but never seen them until she traveled to the outskirts of Cairo. She said that Egyptian astronomers had discovered the planet Saturn, but had not seen its rings. She said that the Egyptians were the first to discover that dogs, when they are ill, will not drink from rivers, but wait for rain, and hold their jaws open to catch it.

*

"She lies."

We were on the school bus home. I was sitting next to Carl Whiteside, who had bad breath and a huge collection of marbles. We were arguing. Carl thought she was lying. I said she wasn't, probably.

"I didn't believe that stuff about the bird," Carl said, "and what she told us about the pyramids? I didn't believe that either. She didn't know what she was talking about."

"Oh yeah?" I had liked her. She was strange. I thought I could nail him. "If she was lying," I said, "what'd she say that was a lie?"

"Six times eleven isn't sixty-eight. It isn't ever. It's sixty-six, I know for a fact."

"She said so. She admitted it. What else did she lie about?"

"I don't know," he said. "Stuff."

"What stuff?"

"Well." He swung his legs back and forth. "You ever see an animal that was half lion and half bird?" He crossed his arms. "It sounded real fakey to me."

"It could happen," I said. I had to improvise, to outrage him. "I read in this newspaper my mom bought in the IGA about this scientist, this mad scientist in the Swiss Alps, and he's been putting genes and chromosomes and stuff together in test tubes, and he combined a human being and a hamster." I waited, for effect. "It's called a humster."

"You never." Carl was staring at me, his mouth open, his terrible bad breath making its way toward me. "What newspaper was it?"

"The *National Enquirer*," I said, "that they sell next to the cash registers." When I saw his look of recognition, I knew I had bested him. "And this mad scientist," I said, "his name was, um, Dr. Frankenbush." I realized belatedly that this name was a mistake and waited for Carl to notice its resemblance to the name of the other famous mad master of permutations, but he only sat there.

"A man and a hamster?" He was staring at me, squinting, his mouth opening in distaste. "Jeez. What'd it look like?"

When the bus reached my stop, I took off down our dirt road and ran up through the back yard, kicking the tire swing for good luck. I dropped my books on the back steps so I could hug and kiss our dog, Mr. Selby. Then I hurried inside. I could smell Brussels sprouts cooking, my unfavorite vegetable. My mother was washing other vegetables in the kitchen sink, and my baby brother was hollering in his yellow playpen on the kitchen floor.

"Hi, Mom," I said, hopping around the playpen to kiss her. "Guess what?"

"I have no idea."

"We had this substitute today, Miss Ferenczi, and I'd never seen her before, and she had all these stories and ideas and stuff."

"Well. That's good." My mother looked out the window behind the sink, her eyes on the pine woods west of our house. Her face and hairstyle always reminded other people of Betty Crocker, whose picture was framed inside a gigantic spoon on the side of the Bisquick box; to me, though, my mother's face just looked white. "Listen, Tommy," she said, "go upstairs and pick your clothes off the bathroom floor, then go outside to the shed and put the shovel and ax away that your father left outside this morning."

"She said that six times eleven was sometimes sixty-eight!" I said. "And she said she once saw a monster that was half lion and half bird." I waited. "In Egypt, she said."

"Did you hear me?" my mother asked, raising her arm to wipe her forehead with the back of her hand. "You have chores to do."

"I know," I said. "I was just telling you about the substitute."

"It's very interesting," my mother said, quickly glancing down at me, "and we can talk about it later when your father gets home. But right now you have some work to do."

"Okay, Mom." I took a cookie out of the jar on the counter and was about to go outside when I had a thought. I ran into the living room, pulled out a dictionary next to the TV stand, and opened it to the G's. *Gryphon:* "variant of griffin." *Griffin:* "a fabulous beast with the head and wings of an eagle and the body of a lion." Fabulous was right. I shouted with triumph and ran outside to put my father's tools back in their place.

Miss Ferenczi was back the next day, slightly altered. She had pulled her hair down and twisted it into pigtails, with red rubber bands holding them tight one inch from the ends. She was wearing a green blouse and pink scarf, making her difficult to look at for a full class day. This time there was no pretense of doing a reading lesson or moving on to arithmetic. As soon as the bell rang, she simply began to talk.

She talked for forty minutes straight. There seemed to be less connection between her ideas, but the ideas themselves were, as the dictionary would say, fabulous. She said she had heard of a huge jewel, in what she called the Antipodes, that was so brilliant that when the light shone into it at a certain angle it would blind whoever was looking at its center. She said that the biggest diamond in the world was cursed and had killed everyone who owned it, and that by a trick of fate it was called the Hope diamond. Diamonds are magic, she said, and this is why women wear them on their fingers, as a sign of the magic of womanhood. Men have strength, Miss Ferenczi said, but no true magic. That is why men fall in love with women but women do not fall in love with men: they just love being loved. George Washington had died because of a mistake he made about a diamond. Washington was not the first *true* President, but she did not say who was. In some places in the world, she said, men and women still live in the trees and eat monkeys for breakfast. Their doctors are magicians. At the bottom of the sea are creatures thin as pancakes which have never been studied by scientists because when you take them up to the air, the fish explode.

There was not a sound in the classroom, except for Miss Ferenczi's voice, and Donna DeShano's coughing. No one even went to the bathroom.

Beethoven, she said, had not been deaf; it was a trick to make himself famous, and it worked. As she talked, Miss Ferenczi's pigtails swung back and forth. There are trees in the world, she said, that eat meat: their leaves are sticky and close up on bugs like hands. She lifted her hands and brought them together, palm to palm. Venus, which most people think is the next closest planet to the sun, is not always closer, and, besides, it is the planet of greatest mystery because of its thick cloud cover. "I know what lies underneath those clouds," Miss Ferenczi said, and waited. After the silence, she said, "Angels. Angels live under those clouds." She said that angels were not invisible to everyone and were in fact smarter than most people. They did not dress in robes as was often claimed but instead wore formal evening clothes, as if they were about to attend a concert. Often angels *do* attend concerts and sit in the aisles where, she said, most people pay no attention to them. She said the most terrible angel had the shape of the Sphinx. "There is no running away from that one," she said. She said that unquenchable fires burn just under the surface of the earth in Ohio, and that the baby Mozart fainted dead away in his cradle when he first heard the sound of a trumpet. She said that someone named Narzim al Harrardim was the greatest writer who ever lived. She said that planets control behavior, and anyone conceived during a solar eclipse would be born with webbed feet.

"I know you children like to hear these things," she said, "these secrets, and that is why I am telling you all this." We nodded. It was better than doing comprehension questions for the readings in *Broad Horizons*.

"I will tell you one more story," she said, "and then we will have to do arithmetic." She leaned over, and her voice grew soft. "There is no death," she said. "You must never be afraid. Never. That which is, cannot die. It will change into different earthly and unearthly elements, but I know this as sure as I stand here in front of you, and I swear it: you must not be afraid. I have seen this truth with these eyes. I know it because in a dream God kissed me. Here." And she pointed with her right index finger to the side of her head, below the mouth, where the vertical lines were carved into her skin.

Absent-mindedly we all did our arithmetic problems. At recess the class was out on the playground, but no one was playing. We were all standing in small groups, talking about Miss Ferenczi. We didn't know if she was crazy, or what. I looked out beyond the playground, at the rusted cars piled in a small heap behind a clump of sumac, and I wanted to see shapes there, approaching me.

On the way home, Carl sat next to me again. He didn't say much, and I didn't either. At last he turned to me. "You know what she said about the leaves that close up on bugs?"

"Huh?"

"The leaves," Carl insisted. "The meat-eating plants. I know it's true. I saw it on television. The leaves have this icky glue that the plants have got smeared all over them and the insects can't get off 'cause they're stuck. I saw it." He seemed demoralized. "She's tellin' the truth."

"Yeah."

"You think she's seen all those angels?"

I shrugged.

"I don't think she has," Carl informed me. "I think she made that part up."

"There's a tree," I suddenly said. I was looking out the window at the farms along County Road H. I knew every barn, every broken windmill, every fence, every anhydrous ammonia tank, by heart. "There's a tree that's . . . that I've seen . . ."

"Don't you try to do it," Carl said. "You'll just sound like a jerk."

I kissed my mother. She was standing in front of the stove. "How was your day?" she asked.

"Fine."

"Did you have Miss Ferenczi again?"

"Yeah."

"Well?"

"She was fine. Mom," I asked, "can I go to my room?"

"No," she said, "not until you've gone out to the vegetable garden and picked me a few tomatoes." She glanced at the sky. "I think it's going to rain. Skedaddle and do it now. Then you come back inside and watch your brother for a few minutes while I go upstairs. I need to clean up before dinner." She looked down at me. "You're looking a little pale, Tommy." She touched the back of her hand to my forehead and I felt her diamond ring against my skin. "Do you feel all right?"

"I'm fine," I said, and went out to pick the tomatoes.

Coughing mutedly, Mr. Hibler was back the next day, slipping lozenges into his mouth when his back was turned at forty-five-minute intervals and asking us how much of the prepared lesson plan Miss Ferenczi had followed. Edith Atwater took the responsibility for the class of explaining to Mr. Hibler that the substitute hadn't always done exactly what he would have done, but we had worked hard even though she talked a lot. About what? he asked. All kinds of things, Edith said. I sort of forgot. To our relief, Mr. Hibler seemed not at all interested in what Miss Ferenczi had said to fill the day. He probably thought it was woman's talk; unserious and not suited for school. It was enough that he had a pile of arithmetic problems from us to correct.

For the next month, the sumac turned a distracting red in the field, and the sun traveled toward the southern sky, so that its rays reached Mr. Hibler's Halloween display on the bulletin board in the back of the room, fading the scarecrow with a pumpkin head from orange to tan. Every three days I measured how much farther the sun had moved toward the southern horizon by making small marks with my black Crayola on the north wall, ant-sized marks only I knew were there, inching west.

And then in early December, four days after the first permanent snowfall, she appeared again in our classroom. The minute she came in the door, I felt my heart begin to pound. Once again, she was different: this time, her hair hung straight down and seemed hardly to have been combed. She hadn't brought her lunchbox with her, but she was carrying what seemed to be a small box. She greeted all of us and talked about the weather. Donna DeShano had to remind her to take her overcoat off.

When the bell to start the day finally rang, Miss Ferenczi looked out at all of us and said, "Children, I have enjoyed your company in the past, and today I am going to reward you." She held up the small box. "Do you know what this is?" She waited. "Of course you don't. It is a tarot pack."

Edith Atwater raised her hand. "What's a tarot pack, Miss Ferenczi?"

"It is used to tell fortunes," she said. "And that is what I shall do this morning. I shall tell your fortunes, as I have been taught to do."

"What's fortune?" Bobby Kryzanowicz asked.

"The future, young man. I shall tell you what your future will be. I can't do your whole future, of course. I shall have to limit

myself to the five-card system, the wands, cups, swords, penta-
cles, and the higher arcanes. Now who wants to be first?"

There was a long silence. Then Carol Peterson raised her
hand.

"All right," Miss Ferenczi said. She divided the pack into five
smaller packs and walked back to Carol's desk, in front of mine.
"Pick one card from each of these packs," she said. I saw that
Carol had a four of cups, a six of swords, but I couldn't see the
other cards. Miss Ferenczi studied the cards on Carol's desk for
a minute. "Not bad," she said. "I do not see much higher education. Probably an early marriage. Many children. There's
something bleak and dreary here, but I can't tell what. Perhaps
just the tasks of a housewife life. I think you'll do very well, for
the most part." She smiled at Carol, a smile with a certain lack
of interest. "Who wants to be next?"

Carl Whiteside raised his hand slowly.

"Yes," Miss Ferenczi said, "let's do a boy." She walked over to
where Carl sat. After he picked his five cards, she gazed at them
for a long time. "Travel," she said. "Much distant travel. You
might go into the Army. Not too much romantic interest here.
A late marriage, if at all. Squabbles. But the Sun is in your major
arcana, here, yes, that's a very good card." She giggled. "Maybe
a good life."

Next I raised my hand, and she told me my future. She did
the same with Bobby Kryzanowicz. Kelly Munger, Edith Atwater, and Kim Foor. Then she came to Wayne Razmer. He picked
his five cards, and I could see that the Death card was one of
them.

"What's your name?" Miss Ferenczi asked.

"Wayne."

"Well, Wayne," she said, you will undergo a *great* metamorphosis, the greatest, before you become an adult. Your earthly
element will leap away, into thin air, you sweet boy. This card,
this nine of swords here, tells of suffering and desolation. And
this ten of wands, well, that's certainly a heavy load."

"What about this one?" Wayne pointed to the Death card.

"That one? That one means you will die soon, my dear." She
gathered up the cards. We were all looking at Wayne. "But do
not fear," she said. "It's not really death, so much as change."

She put the cards on Mr. Hibler's desk. "And now, let's do some arithmetic."

At lunchtime Wayne went to Mr. Faegre, the principal, and told him what Miss Ferenczi had done. During the noon recess, we saw Miss Ferenczi drive out of the parking lot in her green Rambler. I stood under the slide, listening to the other kids coasting down and landing in the little depressive bowl at the bottom. I was kicking stones and tugging at my hair right up to the moment when I saw Wayne come out to the playground. He smiled, the dead fool, and with the fingers of his right hand he was showing everyone how he had told on Miss Ferenczi.

I made my way toward Wayne, pushing myself past two girls from another class. He was watching me with his little pinhead eyes.

"You told," I shouted at him. "She was just kidding."

"She shouldn't have," he shouted back. "We were supposed to be doing arithmetic."

"She just scared you," I said. "You're a chicken. You're a chicken, Wayne. You are. Scared of a little card," I singsonged.

Wayne fell at me, his two fists hammering down on my nose. I gave him a good one in the stomach and then I tried for his head. Aiming my fist, I saw that he was crying. I slugged him.

"She was right," I yelled. "She was always right! She told the truth!" Other kids were whooping. "You were just scared, that's all!"

And then large hands pulled at us, and it was my turn to speak to Mr. Faegre.

In the afternoon Miss Ferenczi was gone, and my nose was stuffed with cotton clotted with blood, and my lip had swelled, and our class had been combined with Mrs. Mantei's sixth-grade class for a crowded afternoon science unit on insect life in ditches and swamps. I knew where Mrs. Mantei lived: she had a new house trailer just down the road from us, at the Clearwater Park. She was no mystery. Somehow she and Mr. Bodine, the other fourth-grade teacher, had managed to fit forty-five desks into the room. Kelly Munger asked if Miss Ferenczi had been arrested, and Mrs. Mantei said no, of course not. All that afternoon, until the buses came to pick us up, we learned about field crickets and two-striped grasshoppers, water bugs, cicadas, mosquitoes, flies, and moths. We learned about insects' hard outer shell, the exoskeleton, and the usual parts of the mouth, including the labrum, mandible, maxilla, and glossa. We learned about compound eyes and the four-stage metamorphosis from egg to larva to pupa to adult. We learned something, but not much, about mating. Mrs. Mantei drew, very skillfully, the internal anatomy of the grasshopper on the blackboard. We learned about the dance of the honeybee, directing other bees in the hive to pollen. We found out about which insects were pests to man, and which were not. On lined white pieces of paper we made lists of insects we might actually see, then a list of insects too small to be clearly visible, such as fleas; Mrs. Mantei said that our assignment would be to memorize these lists for the next day, when Mr. Hibler would certainly return and test us on our knowledge.

JOY WILLIAMS

Raymond Carver wrote that he liked "the traditional (some would call them old-fashioned) methods of storytelling: one layer of reality unfolding and giving way to another . . . richer reality." Joy Williams will never be accused of being an old-fashioned writer, but her fictional hallmark is the detail that takes on layered meaning. In "Health" an "advantaged" little girl's body has been invaded by tuberculosis, and her unconsciousness by adult cynicism. Even so, lying on a tanning couch, she can imagine herself as Sleeping Beauty, safe in her glass coffin. The author of this story about the tenacity of innocence grew up in Massachusetts and lives in Connecticut and Florida.

Health

PAMMY IS IN AN unpleasant Texas city, the city where she was born, in the month of her twelfth birthday. It is cold and cloudy. Soon it will rain. The rain will wash the film of ash off the car she is traveling in, volcanic ash that has drifted across the Gulf of Mexico, all the way from the Yucatán. Pammy is a stocky, gray-eyed blonde, a daughter, traveling in her father's car, being taken to her tanning lesson.

This is her father's joke. She is being taken to a tanning session, twenty-five minutes long. She had requested this for her birthday, ten tanning sessons in a health spa. She had also asked for and received new wheels for her skates. They are purple Rannallis. She had dyed her stoppers to match although the match was not perfect. The stoppers were a duller, cruder purple. Pammy wants to be a speed skater but she worries that she doesn't have the personality for it. "You've gotta have gravel in your gut to be in speed," her coach said. Pammy has mastered the duck walk but still doesn't have a good, smooth crossover, and sometimes she fears that she never will.

Pammy and her father, Morris, are following a truck that is carrying a jumble of televison sets. There is a twenty-four-inch console facing them on the open tailgate, restrained by rope, with a bullet hole in the exact center of the screen.

Morris drinks coffee from a plastic-lidded cup that fits into a bracket mounted just beneath the car's radio. Pammy has a friend, Wanda, whose stepfather has the same kind of plastic cup in his car, but he drinks bourbon and water from his. Wanda had been adopted when she was two months old. Pammy is relieved that neither her father nor Marge, her mother, drinks. Sometimes they have wine. On her birthday, even Pammy had wine with dinner. Marge and Morris seldom quarrel and she is grateful for this. This morning, however, she had seen them quarrel. Once again, her mother had borrowed her father's hairbrush and left long, brown hairs in it. Her father had taken the brush and cleaned it with a comb over the clean kitchen sink. Her father had left a nest of brown hair in the white sink.

In the car, the radio is playing a song called "Tainted Love," a song Morris likes to refer to as "Rancid Love." The radio plays constantly when Pammy and her father drive anywhere. Morris is a good driver. He is fast and doesn't bear grudges. He enjoys driving still, after years and years of it. Pammy looks forward to learning how to drive now, but after a few years, who knows? She can't imagine it being that enjoyable after a while. Her father is skillful here, on the freeways and streets, and on the terrifying, wide two-lane highways and narrow mountain roads in Mexico, and even on the rutted, soiled beaches of the Gulf Coast. One weekend, earlier that spring, Morris had rented a Jeep in Corpus Christi and he and Pammy and Marge had driven the length of Padre Island. They sped across the sand, the only people for miles and miles. There was plastic everywhere.

"You will see a lot of plastic," the man who rented them the Jeep said, "but it is plastic from all over the world."

Morris had given Pammy a lesson in driving the Jeep. He taught her how to shift smoothly, how to synchronize acceleration with the depression and release of the clutch. "There's a way to do things right," Morris told her and when he said this she was filled with a sort of fear. They were just words, she knew, words that anybody could use, but behind words were always things, sometimes things you could never tell anyone, certainly no one you loved, frightening things that weren't even true.

"I'm sick of being behind this truck," Morris says. The screen of the injured television looks like dirty water. Morris pulls to the curb beside an Oriental market. Pammy stares into the market, where shoppers wait in line at a cash register. Many of the women wear scarves on their heads. Pammy is deeply disturbed by Orientals who kill penguins to make gloves and murder whales to make nail polish. In school, in social studies class, she is reading eyewitness accounts of the aftermath of the atomic bombing of Hiroshima. She reads about young girls running from their melting city, their hair burnt off, their burnt skin in loose folds, crying, "Stupid Americans." Morris sips his coffee, then turns the car back onto the street, a street now free from fatally wounded television sets.

Pammy gazes at the backs of her hands, which are tan but, she feels, not tan enough. They are a dusky peach color. This will be her fifth tanning lesson. In the health spa, there are ten colored photographs on the wall showing a woman in a bikini, a pale woman being transformed into a tanned woman. In the last photograph she has plucked the bikini slightly away from her hip bone to expose a sliver of white skin and she is smiling down at the sliver.

Pammy tans well. Without a tan, her face seems grainy and uneven, for she has freckles and rather large pores. Tanning draws her together, completes her. She has had all kinds of tans — golden tans, pool tans, even a Florida tan, which seemed yellow back in Texas. She had brought all her friends the same present from Florida — small plywood crates filled with tiny oranges that were actually chewing gum. The finest tan Pammy has ever had, however, was in Mexico six months ago. She had gone there with her parents for two weeks, and she had gotten a truly remarkable tan and she had gotten tuberculosis. This has caused some tension between Morris and Marge, as it had been Morris's idea to swim at the spas in the mountains rather than in the pools at the more established hotels. It was believed that Pammy had become infected at one particular public spa just outside the small, dusty town where they had gone to buy tiles, tiles of a dusky orange with blue rays flowing from the center, tiles that are now in the kitchen of their home, where each morning Pammy drinks her juice and takes three hundred milligrams of isoniazid.

"Here we are," Morris says. The health spa is in a small, concrete block building with white columns, salvaged from the wrecking of a mansion, adorning the front. There are gift shops, palmists, and all-night restaurants along the street, as well as an exterminating company that has a huge fiber glass bug with X's for eyes on the roof. This was not the company that had tented Wanda's house for termites. That had been another company. When Pammy was in Mexico getting tuberculosis, Wanda and her parents had gone to San Antonio for a week while their house was being tented. When they returned, they'd found a dead robber in the living room, the things he was stealing piled neatly nearby. He had died from inhaling the deadly gas used by the exterminators.

"Mommy will pick you up," Morris says. "She has a class this afternoon so she might be a little late. Just stay inside until she comes."

Morris kisses her on the cheek. He treats her like a child. He treats Marge like a mother, her mother.

Marge is thirty-five but she is still a student. She takes courses in art history and film at one of the city's universities, the same university where Morris teaches petroleum science. Years ago when Marge had first been a student, before she had met Morris and Pammy had been born, she had been in Spain in a museum studying a Goya and a piece of the painting had fallen at her feet. She had quickly placed it in her pocket and now has it on her bureau in a small glass box. It is a wedge of greenish-violet paint, as large as a thumbnail. It is from one of Goya's nudes.

Pammy gets out of the car and goes into the health spa. There is no equipment here except for the tanning beds, twelve tanning beds in eight small rooms. Pammy has never had to share a room with anyone. If asked to, she would probably say no, hoping that she would not hurt the other person's feelings. The receptionist is an old, vigorous woman behind a scratched metal desk, wearing a black jumpsuit and feather earrings. Behind her are shelves of powders and pills in squat brown bottles with names like Dynamic Stamina Builder and Dynamic Super Stress-End and Liver Concentrate Energizer.

The receptionist's name is Aurora. Pammy thinks that the name is magnificent and is surprised that it belongs to such an old woman. Aurora leads her to one of the rooms at the rear of the building. The room has a mirror, a sink, a small stool, a white rotating fan, and the bed, a long, bronze, coffin-like apparatus with a lid. Pammy is always startled when she sees the bed with its frosted ultraviolet tubes, its black vinyl headrest. In the next room someone coughs. Pammy imagines people lying in all the rooms, wrapped in white light, lying quietly as though they were being rested for a long, long journey. Aurora takes a spray bottle of disinfectant and a scrap of toweling from the counter above the sink and cleans the surface of the bed. She twists the timer and the light leaps out, like an animal in a dream, like a murderer in a movie.

"There you are, honey," Aurora says. She pats Pammy on the shoulder and leaves.

Pammy pushes off her sandals and undresses quickly. She leaves her clothes in a heap, her sweatshirt on top of the pile. Her sweatshirt is white with a transfer of a skater on the back. The skater is a man wearing a helmet and knee pads, side surfing goofy-footed. She lies down and with her left hand pulls the lid to within a foot of the bed's cool surface. She can see the closed door and the heap of clothing and her feet. Pammy considers her feet to be her ugliest feature. They are skinny and the toes are too far apart. She and Wanda had painted their toes the same color, but Wanda's feet were pretty and hers were not. Pammy thought her feet looked like they belonged to a dead person and there wasn't anything she could do about them. She closes her eyes.

Wanda, who read a lot, told Pammy that tuberculosis was a very romantic disease, the disease of artists and poets and "highly sensitive individuals."

"Oh yeah," her stepfather had said. "Tuberculosis has mucho cachet."

Wanda's stepfather speaks loudly and his eyes glitter. He is always joking, Pammy thinks. Pammy feels that Wanda's parents are pleasant but she is always a little uncomfortable around them. They had a puppy for a while, a purebred Doberman, which they gave to the SPCA after they disovered it had a slightly overshot jaw. Wanda's stepfather always called the puppy a sissy. "You sissy," he'd say to the puppy. "Hanging around with girls all the time." He was referring to his wife and to Wanda and Pammy. "Oh, you sissy, you sissy," he'd say to the puppy.

There was also the circumstance of Wanda's adoption. There had been another baby adopted, but it was learned that the baby's background had been misrepresented. Or perhaps it had been a boring baby. In any case the baby had been returned and they got Wanda.

Pammy doesn't think Wanda's parents are very steadfast. She is surprised that they don't make Wanda nervous, for Wanda is certainly not perfect. She's a shoplifter and gets C's in Computer Language.

The tanning bed is warm but not uncomfortably so. Pammy lies with her arms straight by her sides, palms down. She hears voices in the hall and footsteps. When she first began coming to the health spa, she was afraid that someone would open the door to the room she was in by mistake. She imagined exactly what it would be like. She would see the door open abruptly out of the corner of her eye, then someone would say, "Sorry," and the door would close again. But this had not happened. The voices pass by.

Pammy thinks of Snow White lying in her glass coffin. The Queen had deceived her how many times? Three? She had been in disguise, but still. And then Snow White had choked on an apple. In the restaurants she sometimes goes to with her parents there are posters on the walls that show a person choking and another person trying to save him. The posters take away Pammy's appetite.

Snow White lay in a glass coffin, not naked of course but in a gown, watched over by the dwarfs. But surely they had not been real dwarfs. That had just been a word that had been given to them.

When Pammy had told Morris that tuberculosis was a romantic disease, he had said, "There's nothing romantic about it. Besides, you don't have it."

It seems to be a fact that she both has and doesn't have tuberculosis. Pammy had been given the tuberculin skin test along with her classmates when she began school in the fall and within forty-eight hours had a large swelling on her arm.

"Now that you've come in contact with it, you don't have to worry about getting it," the pediatrician had said in his office, smiling.

"You mean the infection constitutes immunity," Marge said.

"Not exactly," the pediatrician said, shaking his head, still smiling.

Her lungs are clear. She is not ill but has an illness. The germs are in her body, but in a resting state, still alive but rendered powerless, successfully overcome by her healthy body's strong defenses. Outwardly she is the same, but within a great drama had taken place and Pammy feels herself in possession of a bright, secret, and unspeakable knowledge.

She knows other things too, things that would break her parents' hearts, common, ugly, easy things. She knows a girl in school who stole her mother's green stamps and bought a personal massager with the books. She knows another girl whose brother likes to wear her clothes. She knows a boy who threw a can of motor oil at his father and knocked him unconscious.

Pammy stretches. Her head tingles. Her body is about a foot and a half off the floor and appears almost gray in the glare from the tubes. She has heard of pills one could take to acquire a tan. One just took two pills a day and after twenty days one had a wonderful tan, which could be maintained just by taking two pills a day thereafter. You ordered them from Canada. It was some kind of food-coloring substance. How gross, Pammy thinks. When she had been little she had bought a quarter of an acre of land in Canada by mail for fifty cents. That had been two years ago.

Pammy hears voices from the room next to hers, coming through the thin wall. A woman talking rapidly says, "Pete went up to Detroit two days ago to visit his brother who's dying up there in the hospital. Cancer. The brother's always been a nasty type, I mean very unpleasant. Younger than Pete and always mean. Tried to commit suicide twice. Then he learns he has cancer and decides he doesn't want to die. Carries on and on. Is miserable to everyone. Puts the whole family through hell, but nothing can be done about it, he's dying of cancer. So Pete goes up to see him his last days in the hospital and you know what happens? Pete's wallet gets stolen. Right out of a dying man's room. Five hundred dollars in cash and all our credit cards. That was yesterday. What a day."

Another woman says, "If it's not one thing, it's something else."

Pammy coughs. She doesn't want to hear other people's voices. It is as though they are throwing away junk the way some people use words, as though one word were as good as another.

"Things happen so abruptly anymore," the woman says. "You know what I mean?"

Pammy does not listen and she does not open her eyes for if she did she would see this odd, bright room with her clothes in a heap and herself lying motionless and naked. She does not open her eyes because she prefers imagining that she is a magician's accomplice, levitating on a stage in a coil of pure energy. If one thought purely enough, one could create one's own truth. That's how people accomplished astral travel, walked over burning coals, cured warts. There was a girl in Pammy's class at school, Bonnie Black, a small, owlish-looking girl who was a Christian Scientist. She raised rabbits and showed them at fairs, and was always wearing the ribbons they had won at school, pinned to her blouse. She had warts all over her hands, but one day Pammy noticed that the warts were gone and Bonnie Black had told her that the warts disappeared after she had clearly realized that in her true being as God's reflection, she couldn't have warts.

It seemed that people were better off when they could concentrate on something, hold something in their mind for a long time and really believe it. Pammy had once seen a radical skater putting on a show at the opening of a shopping mall. He leapt over cars and jumped up the sides of buildings. He did flips and spins. A disc jockey who was set up for the day in the parking

lot interviewed him. "I'm really impressed with your performance," the disc jockey said, "and I'm impressed that you never
fall. Why don't you fall?" The skater was a thin boy in baggy
cut-off jeans. "I don't fall," the boy said, looking hard at the
microphone, "because I've got a deep respect for the concrete
surface and because when I make a miscalculation, instead of
falling, I turn it into a new trick."

Pammy thinks it is wonderful that the boy was able to say
something that would keep him from thinking he might fall.

The door to the room opened. Pammy had heard the turning of the knob. At first she lies without opening her eyes, willing the sound of the door shutting, but she hears nothing,
only the ticking of the bed's timer. She swings her head quickly
to the side and looks at the door. There is a man standing
there, staring at her. She presses her right hand into a fist,
and lays it between her legs. She puts her left arm across her
breasts.

"What?" she says to the figure, frightened. In an instant she
is almost panting with fear. She feels the repetition of something painful and known, but she has not known this, not ever.
The figure says nothing and pulls the door shut. With a flurry
of rapid ticking, the timer stops. The harsh lights of the bed go
out.

Pammy pushes the lid back and hurriedly gets up. She dresses
hastily and smoothes her hair with her fingers. She looks at
herself in the mirror, her lips parted. Her teeth are white behind her pale lips. She stares at herself. She can be looked at
and not discovered. She can speak and not be known. She opens
the door and enters the hall. There is no one there. The hall is
so narrow that by spreading her arms she can touch the walls
with her fingertips. In the reception area by Aurora's desk,
there are three people, a stoop-shouldered young woman and
two men. The woman was signing up for a month of unlimited
tanning, which meant that after the basic monthly fee she only
had to pay a dollar a visit. She takes her checkbook out of a
soiled handbag, which is made out of some silvery material, and
writes a check. The men look comfortable lounging in the
chairs, their legs stretched out. They know one another, Pammy
guesses, but they do not know the woman. One of them has

dark, spikey hair like a wet animal's. The other wears a tight red T-shirt. Neither is the man she had seen in the doorway.

"What time do you want to come back tomorrow, honey?" Aurora asks Pammy. "You certainly are coming along nicely. Isn't she coming along nicely?"

"I'd like to come back the same time tomorrow," Pammy says. She raises her hand to her mouth and coughs slightly.

"Not the same time, honey. Can't give you the same time. How about an hour later?"

"All right," Pammy says. The stoop-shouldered woman sits down in a chair. There are no more chairs in the room. Pammy opens the door to the street and steps outside. It has rained and the street is dark and shining. The air smells fresh and feels thick. She stands in it, a little stunned, looking. Her father will teach her how to drive, and she will drive around. Her mother will continue to take classes at the university. Whenever she meets someone new, she will mention the Goya. "I have a small Goya," she will say, and laugh.

Pammy walks slowly down the street. She smells barbecued meat and the rain lingering in the streets. By a store called Imagine, there's a clump of bamboo with some beer cans glittering in its ragged, grassy center. Imagine sells neon palm trees and silk clouds and stars. It sells greeting cards and chocolate in shapes children aren't allowed to see and it sells children's stickers and shoelaces. Pammy looks in the window at a huge satin pillow in the shape of a heart with a heavy zipper running down the center of it. Pammy turns and walks back to the building that houses the tanning beds. Her mother pulls up in the car. "Pammy!" she calls. She is leaning toward the window on the passenger side, which she has rolled down. She unlocks the car's door. Pammy gets in and the door locks again.

Pammy wishes she could tell her mother something, but what can she say? She never wants to see that figure looking at her again, so coldly staring and silent, but she knows she will, for already its features are becoming more indistinct, more general. It could be anything. She coughs, but it is not the cough of a sick person because Pammy is a healthy girl. It is the kind of cough a person might make if they were at a party and there was no one there but strangers.

Marge, driving, says, "You look very nice. That's a very pretty tan, but what will happen when you stop going there? It won't last. You'll lose it right away, won't you?"

She will. And she will grow older, but the world will remain as young as she was once, infinite in its possibilities and uncaring.

SUSAN SONTAG

In "The Way We Live Now" the reader has an oblique
encounter with a grave illness as it robs its victim not only of
health but also of communion. This is a story in which the hero
never speaks, in which his name is never spoken and his disease
never specified. What we know about him — that he is a bright,
young, professional urbanite with a circle of equally sophisticated friends — we learn from a distance, through the
recounted remarks of those who knew him. Here the story's
form is truly wed to its content. And its subject is truly emblem-
atic of the decade. Susan Sontag lives in New York City. She has
written two novels, a collection of short stories, and five volumes
of essays.

The Way We Live Now

AT FIRST HE WAS just losing weight, he felt only a little ill, Max
said to Ellen, and he didn't call for an appointment with his
doctor, according to Greg, because he was managing to keep on
working at more or less the same rhythm, but he did stop smoking, Tanya pointed out, which suggests he was frightened, but
also that he wanted, even more than he knew, to be healthy, or
healthier, or maybe just to gain back a few pounds, said Orson,
for he told her, Tanya went on, that he expected to be climbing
the walls (isn't that what people say?) and found, to his surprise,
that he didn't miss cigarettes at all and reveled in the sensation
of his lungs' being ache-free for the first time in years. But did
he have a good doctor, Stephen wanted to know, since it would
have been crazy not to go for a checkup after the pressure was
off and he was back from the conference in Helsinki, even if by
then he was feeling better. And he said, to Frank, that he would
go, even though he was indeed frightened, as he admitted to

Jan, but who wouldn't be frightened now, though, odd as that might seem, he hadn't been worrying until recently, he avowed to Quentin, it was only in the last six months that he had the metallic taste of panic in his mouth, because becoming seriously ill was something that happened to other people, a normal delusion, he observed to Paolo, if one was thirty-eight and had never had a serious illness; he wasn't, as Jan confirmed, a hypochondriac. Of course, it was hard not to worry, everyone was worried, but it wouldn't do to panic, because, as Max pointed out to Quentin, there wasn't anything one could do except wait and hope, wait and start being careful, be careful, and hope. And even if one did prove to be ill, one shouldn't give up, they had new treatments that promised an arrest of the disease's inexorable course, research was progressing. It seemed that everyone was in touch with everyone else several times a week, checking in, I've never spent so many hours at a time on the phone, Stephen said to Kate, and when I'm exhausted after the two or three calls made to me, giving me the latest, instead of switching off the phone to give myself a respite I tap out the number of another friend or acquaintance, to pass on the news. I'm not sure I can afford to think so much about it, Ellen said, and I suspect my own motives, there's something morbid I'm getting used to, getting excited by, this must be like what people felt in London during the Blitz. As far as I know, I'm not at risk, but you never know, said Aileen. This thing is totally unprecedented, said Frank. But don't you think he ought to see a doctor, Stephen insisted. Listen, said Orson, you can't force people to take care of themselves, and what makes you think the worst, he could be just run down, people still do get ordinary illnesses, awful ones, why are you assuming it has to be *that*. But all I want to be sure, said Stephen, is that he understands the options, because most people don't, that's why they won't see a doctor or have the test, they think there's nothing one can do. But is there anything one can do, he said to Tanya (according to Greg), I mean what do I gain if I go to the doctor; if I'm really ill, he's reported to have said, I'll find out soon enough.

And when he was in the hospital, his spirits seemed to lighten, according to Donny. He seemed more cheerful than he had

been in the last months, Ursula said, and the bad news seemed
to come almost as a relief, according to Ira, as a truly unexpected blow, according to Quentin, but you'd hardly expect him
to have said the same thing to all his friends, because his relation
to Ira was so different from his relation to Quentin (this according to Quentin, who was proud of their friendship), and perhaps he thought Quentin wouldn't be undone by seeing him
weep, but Ira insisted that couldn't be the reason he behaved so
differently with each, and that maybe he was feeling less
shocked, mobilizing his strength to fight for his life, at the moment he saw Ira but overcome by feelings of hopelessness when
Quentin arrived with flowers, because anyway the flowers threw
him into a bad mood, as Quentin told Kate, since the hospital
room was choked with flowers, you couldn't have crammed another flower into that room, but surely you're exaggerating,
Kate said, smiling, everybody likes flowers. Well, who wouldn't
exaggerate at a time like this, Quentin said sharply. Don't you
think *this* is an exaggeration. Of course I do, said Kate gently, I
was only teasing, I mean I didn't mean to tease. I know that,
Quentin said, with tears in his eyes, and Kate hugged him and
said well, when I go this evening I guess I won't bring flowers,
what does he want, and Quentin said, according to Max, what
he likes best is chocolate. Is there anything else, asked Kate, I
mean like chocolate but not chocolate. Licorice, said Quentin,
blowing his nose. And besides that. Aren't *you* exaggerating
now, Quentin said, smiling. Right, said Kate, so if I want to
bring him a whole raft of stuff, besides chocolate and licorice,
what else. Jelly beans, Quentin said.

He didn't want to be alone, according to Paolo, and lots of
people came in the first week, and the Jamaican nurse said there
were other patients on the floor who would be glad to have the
surplus flowers, and people weren't afraid to visit, it wasn't like
the old days, as Kate pointed out to Aileen, they're not even
segregated in the hospital anymore, as Hilda observed, there's
nothing on the door of his room warning visitors of the possibility of contagion, as there was a few years ago; in fact, he's in
a double room and, as he told Orson, the old guy on the far
side of the curtain (who's clearly on the way out, said Stephen)

doesn't even have the disease, so, as Kate went on, you really should go and see him, he'd be happy to see you, he likes having people visit, you aren't not going because you're afraid, are you. Of course not, Aileen said, but I don't know what to say, I think I'll feel awkward, which he's bound to notice, and that will make him feel worse, so I won't be doing him any good, will I. But he won't notice anything, Kate said, patting Aileen's hand, it's not like that, it's not the way you imagine, he's not judging people or wondering about their motives, he's just happy to see his friends. But I never was really a friend of his, Aileen said, you're a friend, he's always liked you, you told me he talks about Nora with you, I know he likes me, he's even attracted to me, but he respects you. But, according to Wesley, the reason Aileen was so stingy with her visits was that she could never have him to herself, there were always others there already and by the time they left still others had arrived, she'd been in love with him for years, and I can understand, said Donny, that Aileen should feel bitter that if there could have been a woman friend he did more than occasionally bed, a woman he really loved, and my God, Victor said, who had known him in those years, he was crazy about Nora, what a heart-rending couple they were, two surly angels, then it couldn't have been she.

And when some of the friends, the ones who came every day, waylaid the doctor in the corridor, Stephen was the one who asked the most informed questions, who'd been keeping up not just with the stories that appeared several times a week in the *Times* (which Greg confessed to have stopped reading, unable to stand it anymore) but with articles in the medical journals published here and in England and France, and who knew socially one of the principal doctors in Paris who was doing some much-publicized research on the disease, but his doctor said little more than that the pneumonia was not life-threatening, the fever was subsiding, of course he was still weak but he was responding well to the antibiotics, that he'd have to complete his stay in the hospital, which entailed a minimum of twenty-one days on the IV, before she could start him on the new drug, for she was optimistic about the possibility of getting him into the protocol; and when Victor said that if he had so much trouble eating (he'd

say to everyone when they coaxed him to eat some of the hospital meals, that food didn't taste right, that he had a funny
metallic taste in his mouth) it couldn't be good that friends were
bringing him all that chocolate, the doctor just smiled and said
that in these cases the patient's morale was also an important
factor, and if chocolate made him feel better she saw no harm
in it, which worried Stephen, as Stephen said later to Donny,
because they wanted to believe in the promises and taboos of
today's high-tech medicine but here this reassuringly curt and
silver-haired specialist in the disease, someone quoted frequently in the papers, was talking like some oldfangled country
GP who tells the family that tea with honey or chicken soup may
do as much for the patient as penicillin, which might mean, as
Max said, that they were just going through the motions of
treating him, that they were not sure about what to do, or
rather, as Xavier interjected, that they didn't know what the hell
they were doing, that the truth, the real truth, as Hilda said,
upping the ante, was that they didn't, the doctors, really have
any hope.

Oh, no, said Lewis, I can't stand it, wait a minute, I can't believe
it, are you sure, I mean are they sure, have they done all the
tests, it's getting so when the phone rings I'm scared to answer
because I think it will be someone telling me someone else is ill;
but did Lewis really not know until yesterday, Robert said tes-
tily, I find that hard to believe, everybody is talking about it, it
seems impossible that someone wouldn't have called Lewis; and
perhaps Lewis did know, was for some reason pretending not
to know already, because, Jan recalled, didn't Lewis say something months ago to Greg, and not only to Greg, about his not
looking well, losing weight, and being worried about him and
wishing he'd see a doctor, so it couldn't come as a total surprise.
Well, everybody is worried about everybody now, said Betsy,
that seems to be the way we live, the way we live now. And, after
all, they were once very close, doesn't Lewis still have the keys
to his apartment, you know the way you let someone keep the
keys after you've broken up, only a little because you hope the
person might just saunter in, drunk or high, late some evening,
but mainly because it's wise to have a few sets of keys strewn

around town, if you live alone, at the top of a former commercial building that, pretentious as it is, will never acquire a doorman or even a resident superintendent, someone whom you can call on for the keys late one night if you find you've lost yours or have locked yourself out. Who else has keys, Tanya inquired, I was thinking somebody might drop by tomorrow before coming to the hospital and bring some treasures, because the other day, Ira said, he was complaining about how dreary the hospital room was, and how it was like being locked up in a motel room, which got everybody started telling funny stories about motel rooms they'd known, and at Ursula's story, about the Luxury Budget Inn in Schenectady, there was an uproar of laughter around his bed, while he watched them in silence, eyes bright with fever, all the while, as Victor recalled, gobbling that damned chocolate. But, according to Jan, whom Lewis's keys enabled to tour the swank of his bachelor lair with an eye to bringing over some art consolation to brighten up the hospital room, the Byzantine icon wasn't on the wall over his bed, and that was a puzzle until Orson remembered that he'd recounted without seeming upset (this disputed by Greg) that the boy he'd recently gotten rid of had stolen it, along with four of the *maki-e* lacquer boxes, as if these were objects as easy to sell on the street as a TV or a stereo. But he's always been very generous, Kate said quietly, and though he loves beautiful things isn't really attached to them, to things, as Orson said, which is unusual in a collector, as Frank commented, and when Kate shuddered and tears sprang to her eyes and Orson inquired anxiously if he, Orson, had said something wrong, she pointed out that they'd begun talking about him in a retrospective mode, summing up what he was like, what made them fond of him, as if he were finished, completed, already a part of the past.

Perhaps he was getting tired of having so many visitors, said Robert, who was, as Ellen couldn't help mentioning, someone who had come only twice and was probably looking for a reason not to be in regular attendance, but there could be no doubt, according to Ursula, that his spirits had dipped, not that there was any discouraging news from the doctors, and he seemed now to prefer being alone a few hours of the day; and he told

Donny that he'd begun keeping a diary for the first time in his life, because he wanted to record the course of his mental reactions to this astonishing turn of events, to do something parallel to what the doctors were doing, who came every morning and conferred at his bedside about his body, and that perhaps it wasn't so important what he wrote in it, which amounted, as he said wryly to Quentin, to little more than the usual banalities about terror and amazement that this was happening to him, to him also, plus the usual remorseful assessments of his past life, his pardonable superficialities, capped by resolves to live better, more deeply, more in touch with his work and his friends, and not to care so passionately about what people thought of him, interspersed with admonitions to himself that in this situation his will to live counted more than anything else and that if he really wanted to live, and trusted life, and liked himself well enough (down, ol' debbil Thanatos!), he *would* live, he would be an exception; but perhaps all this, as Quentin ruminated, talking on the phone to Kate, wasn't the point, the point was that by the very keeping of the diary he was accumulating something to reread one day, slyly staking out his claim to a future time, in which the diary would be an object, a relic, in which he might not actually reread it, because he would want to have put this ordeal behind him, but the diary would be there in the drawer of his stupendous Majorelle desk, and he could already, he did actually say to Quentin one late sunny afternoon, propped up in the hospital bed, with the stain of chocolate framing one corner of a heartbreaking smile, see himself in the penthouse, the October sun streaming through those clear windows instead of this streaked one, and the diary, the pathetic diary, safe inside the drawer.

It doesn't matter about the treatment's side effects, Stephen said (when talking to Max), I don't know why you're so worried about that, every strong treatment has some dangerous side effects, it's inevitable, you mean otherwise the treatment wouldn't be effective, Hilda interjected, and anyway, Stephen went on doggedly, just because there *are* side effects it doesn't mean he has to get them, or all of them, each one, or even some of them. That's just a list of all the possible things that could go wrong, because the doctors have to cover themselves, so they make up a worst-case scenario, but isn't what's happening to him, and to so many other people, Tanya interrupted, a worst-case scenario, a catastrophe no one could have imagined, it's too cruel, and isn't everything a side effect, quipped Ira, even *we* are all side effects, but we're not bad side effects, Frank said, he likes having his friends around, and we're helping each other, too; because his illness sticks us all in the same glue, mused Xavier, and, whatever the jealousies and grievances from the past that have made us wary and cranky with each other, when something like this happens (the sky is falling, the sky is falling!) you understand what's really important. I agree, Chicken Little, he is reported to have said. But don't you think, Quentin observed to Max, that being as close to him as we are, making time to drop by the hospital every day, is a way of our trying to define ourselves more firmly and irrevocably as the well, those who aren't ill, who aren't going to fall ill, as if what's happened to him couldn't happen to us, when in fact the chances are that before long one of us will end up where he is, which is probably what he felt when he was one of the cohort visiting Zack in the spring (you never knew Zack, did you?), and, according to Clarice, Zack's widow, he didn't come very often, he said he hated hospitals, and didn't feel he was doing Zack any good, that Zack would see on his face how uncomfortable he was. Oh, he was one of those, Aileen said. A coward. Like me.

And after he was sent home from the hospital, and Quentin had volunteered to move in and was cooking meals and taking telephone messages and keeping the mother in Mississippi informed, well, mainly keeping her from flying to New York and heaping her grief on her son and confusing the household routine with her oppressive ministrations, he was able to work an hour or two in his study, on days he didn't insist on going out, for a meal or a movie, which tired him. He seemed optimistic, Kate thought, his appetite was good, and what he said, Orson reported, was that he agreed when Stephen advised him that the main thing was to keep in shape, he was a fighter, right, he wouldn't be who he was if he weren't, and was he ready for the big fight, Stephen asked rhetorically (as Max told it to Donny),

and he said you bet, and Stephen added it could be a lot worse,
you could have gotten the disease two years ago, but now so
many scientists are working on it, the American team and the
French team, everyone bucking for that Nobel Prize a few years
down the road, that all you have to do is stay healthy for another
year or two and then there will be good treatment, real treatment. Yes, he said, Stephen said, my timing is good. And Betsy,
who had been climbing on and rolling off macrobiotic diets for
a decade, came up with a Japanese specialist she wanted him to
see but thank God, Donny reported, he'd had the sense to refuse, but he did agree to see Victor's visualization therapist,
although what could one possibly visualize, said Hilda, when the
point of visualizing disease was to see it as an entity with contours, borders, here rather than there, something limited, something you were the host of, in the sense that you could disinvite
the disease, while this was so total; or would be, Max said. But
the main thing, said Greg, was to see that he didn't go the
macrobiotic route, which might be harmless for plump Betsy
but could only be devastating for him, lean as he'd always been,
with all the cigarettes and other appetite-suppressing chemicals
he'd been welcoming into his body for years; and now was
hardly the time, as Stephen pointed out, to be worried about
cleaning up his act, and eliminating the chemical additives and
other pollutants that we're all blithely or not so blithely feasting
on, blithely since we're healthy, healthy as we can be; so far, Ira
said. Meat and potatoes is what I'd be happy to see him eating,
Ursula said wistfully. And spaghetti and clam sauce, Greg
added. And thick cholesterol-rich omelets with smoked mozzarella, suggested Yvonne, who had flown from London for the
weekend to see him. Chocolate cake, said Frank. Maybe not
chocolate cake, Ursula said, he's already eating so much chocolate.

And when, not right away but still only three weeks later, he
was accepted into the protocol for the new drug, which took
considerable behind-the-scenes lobbying with the doctors, he
talked less about being ill, according to Donny, which seemed
like a good sign, Kate felt, a sign that he was not feeling like
a victim, feeling not that he *had* a disease but, rather, was liv-

ing *with* a disease (that was the right cliché, wasn't it?), a more hospitable arrangement, said Jan, a kind of cohabitation which implied that it was something temporary, that it could be terminated, but terminated how, said Hilda, and when you say hospitable, Jan, I hear hospital. And it was encouraging, Stephen insisted, that from the start, at least from the time he was finally persuaded to make the telephone call to his doctor, he was willing to say the name of the disease, pronounce it often and easily, as if it were just another word, like boy or gallery or cigarette or money or deal, as in no big deal, Paolo interjected, because, as Stephen continued, to utter the name is a sign of health, a sign that one has accepted being who one is, mortal, vulnerable, not exempt, not an exception after all, it's a sign that one is willing, truly willing, to fight for one's life. And we must say the name, too, and often, Tanya added, we mustn't lag behind him in honesty, or let him feel that, the effort of honesty having been made, it's something done with and he can go on to other things. One is so much better prepared to help him, Wesley replied. In a way he's fortunate, said Yvonne, who had taken care of a problem at the New York store and was flying back to London this evening, sure, fortunate, said Wesley, no one is shunning him, Yvonne went on, no one's afraid to hug him or kiss him lightly on the mouth, in London we are, as usual, a few years behind you, people I know, people who would seem to be not even remotely at risk, are just terrified, but I'm impressed by how cool and rational you all are; you find us cool, asked Quentin. But I have to say, he's reported to have said, I'm terrified, I find it very hard to read (and you know how he loves to read, said Greg; yes, reading is his television, said Paolo) or to think, but I don't feel hysterical. I feel quite hysterical, Lewis said to Yvonne. But you're able to *do* something for him, that's wonderful, how I wish I could stay longer, Yvonne answered, it's rather beautiful, I can't help thinking, this utopia of friendship you've assembled around him (this pathetic utopia, said Kate), so that the disease, Yvonne concluded, is not, anymore, out there. Yes, don't you think we're more at home here, with him, with the disease, said Tanya, because the imagined disease is so much worse than the reality of him, whom we all love, each in our fashion, having it. I know for me his getting it has quite demystified the disease, said Jan, I don't feel afraid, spooked, as I did before he became ill, when it was only news about remote acquaintances, whom I never saw again after they became ill. But you know you're not going to come down with the disease, Quentin said, to which Ellen replied, on her behalf, that's not the point, and possibly untrue, my gynecologist says that everyone is at risk, everyone who has a sexual life, because sexuality is a chain that links each of us to many others, unknown others, and now the great chain of being has become a chain of death as well. It's not the same for you, Quentin insisted, it's not the same for you as it is for me or Lewis or Frank or Paolo or Max, I'm more and more frightened, and I have every reason to be. I don't think about whether I'm at risk or not, said Hilda, I know that I was afraid to know someone with the disease, afraid of what I'd see, what I'd feel, and after the first day I came to the hospital I felt so relieved. I'll never feel that way, that fear, again; he doesn't seem different from me. He's not, Quentin said.

According to Lewis, he talked more often about those who visited more often, which is natural, said Betsy, I think he's even keeping a tally. And among those who came or checked in by phone every day, the inner circle as it were, those who were getting more points, there was still a further competition, which was what was getting on Betsy's nerves, she confessed to Jan; there's always that vulgar jockeying for position around the bedside of the gravely ill, and though we all feel suffused with virtue at our loyalty to him (speak for yourself, said Jan), to the extent that we're carving time out of every day, or almost every day, though some of us are dropping out, as Xavier pointed out, aren't we getting at least as much out of this as he is. Are we, said Jan. We're rivals for a sign from him of special pleasure over a visit, each stretching for the brass ring of his favor, wanting to feel the most wanted, the true nearest and dearest, which is inevitable with someone who doesn't have a spouse and children or an official in-house lover, hierarchies that no one would dare contest, Betsy went on, so we are the family he's founded, without meaning to, without official titles and ranks (we, we, snarled Quentin); and is it so clear, though some of us, Lewis and Quentin and Tanya and Paolo, among others, are ex-lovers and all of us more or less than friends, which one of us he prefers, Victor said (now it's us, raged Quentin), because sometimes I think he looks forward more to seeing Aileen, who has visited only three times, twice at the hospital and once since he's been home, than he does you or me; but, according to Tanya, after being very disappointed that Aileen hadn't come, now he was angry, while, according to Xavier, he was not really hurt but touchingly passive, accepting Aileen's absence as something he somehow deserved. But he's happy to have people around, said Lewis; he says when he doesn't have company he gets very sleepy, he sleeps (according to Quentin), and then perks up when someone arrives, it's important that he not feel ever alone. But, said Victor, there's one person he hasn't heard from, whom he'd probably like to hear from more than most of us; but she didn't just vanish, even right after she broke away from him, and he knows exactly where she lives now, said Kate, he told me he put in a call to her last Christmas Eve, and she said it's nice to hear from you and Merry Christmas, and he was shattered, according to Orson, and furious and disdainful, according to Ellen (what do you expect of her, said Wesley, she was burned out), but Kate wondered if maybe he hadn't phoned Nora in the middle of a sleepless night, what's the time difference, and Quentin said no, I don't think so, I think he wouldn't want her to know.

And when he was feeling even better and had regained the pounds he'd shed right away in the hospital, though the refrigerator started to fill up with organic wheat germ and grapefruit and skimmed milk (he's worried about his cholesterol count, Stephen lamented), and told Quentin he could manage by himself now, and did, he started asking everyone who visited how he looked, and everyone said he looked great, so much better than a few weeks ago, which didn't jibe with what anyone had told him at that time; but then it was getting harder and harder to know how he looked, to answer such a question honestly when among themselves they wanted to be honest, both for honesty's sake and (as Donny thought) to prepare for the worst, because he'd been looking like *this* for so long, at least it seemed so long, that it was as if he'd always been like this, how did he look before, but it was only a few months, and those words, pale and wan looking and fragile, hadn't they always applied? And one Thursday Ellen, meeting Lewis at the door of the building, said, as they rode up together in the elevator, how is he *really*? But you see how he is, Lewis said tartly, he's fine, he's perfectly healthy, and Ellen understood that of course Lewis didn't think he was perfectly healthy but that he wasn't worse, and that was true, but wasn't it, well, almost heartless to talk like that. Seems inoffensive to me, Quentin said, but I know what you mean, I remember once talking to Frank, somebody, after all, who has volunteered to do five hours a week of office work at the Crisis Center (I know, said Ellen), and Frank was going on about this guy, diagnosed almost a year ago, and so much further along, who'd been complaining to Frank on the phone about the indifference of some doctor, and had gotten quite abusive about the doctor, and Frank was saying there was no reason to be so upset, the implication being that *he*, Frank, wouldn't behave so irrationally, and I said, barely able to control my scorn, but Frank, Frank, he has every reason to be upset, he's dying, and Frank said, said according to Quentin, oh, I don't like to think about it that way.

And it was while he was still home, recuperating, getting his weekly treatment, still not able to do much work, he complained, but, according to Quentin, up and about most of the time and turning up at the office several days a week, that bad news came about two remote acquaintances, one in Houston and one in Paris, news that was intercepted by Quentin on the ground that it could only depress him, but Stephen contended that it was wrong to lie to him, it was so important for him to live in the truth; that had been one of his first victories, that he was candid, that he was even willing to crack jokes about the disease, but Ellen said it wasn't good to give him this end-of-the-world feeling, too many people were getting ill, it was becoming such a common destiny that maybe some of the will to fight for his life would be drained out of him if it seemed to be as natural as, well, death. Oh, Hilda said, who didn't know personally either the one in Houston or the one in Paris, but knew *of* the one in Paris, a pianist who specialized in twentieth-century Czech and Polish music, I have his records, he's such a valuable person, and, when Kate glared at her, continued defensively, I know every life is equally sacred, but that *is* a thought, another thought, I mean, all these valuable people who aren't going to have their normal four score as it is now, these people aren't going to be replaced, and it's such a loss to the culture. But this isn't going to go on forever, Wesley said, it can't, they're bound to come up with something (they, they, muttered Stephen), but did you ever think, Greg said, that if some people don't die, I mean even if they can keep them alive (they, they, muttered Kate), they continue to be carriers, and that means, if you have a conscience, that you can never make love, make love fully, as you'd been wont — wantonly, Ira said — to do. But it's better than dying, said Frank. And in all his talk about the future, when he allowed himself to be hopeful, according to Quentin, he never mentioned the prospect that even if he didn't die, if he were so fortunate as to be among the first generation of the disease's survivors, never mentioned, Kate confirmed, that whatever happened it was over, the way he had lived until now, but, according to Ira, he did think about it, the end of bravado, the end of folly, the end of trusting life, the end of taking life for granted, and of treating life as something that, samurai-like, he thought himself ready to throw away lightly, impudently; and Kate recalled, sighing, a brief exchange she'd insisted on having as long as two years ago, huddling on a banquette covered with steel-gray industrial carpet on an upper level of The Prophet and toking up for their next foray onto the dance floor: she'd said hesitantly, for it felt foolish asking a prince of debauchery to, well, take it easy, and she wasn't keen on playing big sister, a role, as Hilda confirmed, he inspired in many women, are you being careful, honey, you know what I mean. And he replied, Kate went on, no, I'm not, listen, I can't, I just can't, sex is too important to me, always has been (he started talking like that, according to Victor, after Nora left him), and if I get it, well, I get it. But he wouldn't talk like that now, would he, said Greg; he must feel awfully foolish now, said Betsy, like someone who went on smoking, saying I can't give up cigarettes, but when the bad X-ray is taken even the most besotted nicotine

addict can stop on a dime. But sex isn't like cigarettes, is it, said
Frank, and, besides, what good does it do to remember that he
was reckless, said Lewis angrily, the appalling thing is that you
just have to be unlucky once, and wouldn't he feel even worse
if he'd stopped three years ago and had come down with it
anyway, since one of the most terrifying features of the disease
is that you don't know when you contracted it, it could have
been ten years ago, because surely this disease has existed for
years and years, long before it was recognized; that is, named.
Who knows how long (I think a lot about that, said Max) and
who knows (I know what you're going to say, Stephen interrupted) how many are going to get it.

I'm feeling fine, he's reported to have said whenever someone
asked him how he was, which was almost always the first question anyone asked. Or: I'm feeling better, how are you? But he
said other things, too. I'm playing leapfrog with myself, he is
reported to have said, according to Victor. And: There must be
a way to get something positive out of this situation, he's reported to have said to Kate. How American of him, said Paolo.
Well, said Betsy, you know the old American adage: When
you've got a lemon, make lemonade. The one thing I'm sure I
couldn't take, Jan said he said to her, is becoming disfigured,
but Stephen hastened to point out the disease doesn't take that
form very often anymore, its profile is mutating, and, in conversation with Ellen, wheeled up words like blood-brain barrier; I
never thought there was a barrier *there,* said Jan. But he mustn't
know about Max, Ellen said, that would really depress him,
please don't tell him, he'll have to know, Quentin said grimly,
and he'll be furious not to have been told. But there's time for
that, when they take Max off the respirator, said Ellen; but isn't
it incredible, Frank said, Max was fine, not feeling ill at all, and
then to wake up with a fever of a hundred and five, unable to
breathe, but that's the way it often starts, with absolutely no
warning, Stephen said, the disease has so many forms. And
when, after another week had gone by, he asked Quentin where
Max was, he didn't question Quentin's account of a spree in the
Bahamas, but then the number of people who visited regularly
was thinning out, partly because the old feuds that had been

put aside through the first hospitalization and the return home had resurfaced, and the flickering enmity between Lewis and Frank exploded, even though Kate did her best to mediate between them, and also because he himself had done something to loosen the bonds of love that united the friends around him, by seeming to take them all for granted, as if it were perfectly normal for so many people to carve out so much time and attention for him, visit him every few days, talk about him incessantly on the phone with each other; but, according to Paolo, it wasn't that he was less grateful, it was just something he was getting used to, the visits. It had become, with time, a more ordinary kind of situation, a kind of ongoing party, first at the hospital and now since he was home, barely on his feet again, it being clear, said Robert, that I'm on the B list; but Kate said, that's absurd, there's no list; and Victor said, but there is, only it's not he, it's Quentin who's drawing it up. He wants to see us, we're helping him, we have to do it the way he wants, he fell down yesterday on the way to the bathroom, he mustn't be told about Max (but he already knew, according to Donny), it's getting worse.

When I was home, he is reported to have said, I was afraid to sleep, as I was dropping off each night it felt like just that, as if I were falling down a black hole, to sleep felt like giving in to death, I slept every night with the light on; but here, in the hospital, I'm less afraid. And to Quentin he said, one morning, the fear rips through me, it tears me open; and, to Ira, it presses me together, squeezes me toward myself. Fear gives everything its hue, its high. I feel so, I don't know how to say it, exalted, he said to Quentin. Calamity is an amazing high, too. Sometimes I feel *so* well, so powerful, it's as if I could jump out of my skin. Am I going crazy, or what? Is it all this attention and coddling I'm getting from everybody, like a child's dream of being loved? Is it the drugs? I know it sounds crazy but sometimes I think this is a *fantastic* experience, he said shyly; but there was also the bad taste in the mouth, the pressure in the head and at the back of the neck, the red, bleeding gums, the painful, if pink-lobed, breathing, and his ivory pallor, color of white chocolate. Among those who wept when told over the phone that he was back in

the hospital were Kate and Stephen (who'd been called by
Quentin), and Ellen, Victor, Aileen, and Lewis (who were called
by Kate), and Xavier and Ursula (who were called by Stephen).
Among those who didn't weep were Hilda, who said that she'd
just learned that her seventy-five-year-old aunt was dying of the
disease, which she'd contracted from a transfusion given during
her successful double bypass of five years ago, and Frank and
Donny and Betsy, but this didn't mean, according to Tanya, that
they weren't moved and appalled, and Quentin thought they
might not be coming soon to the hospital but would send presents; the room, he was in a private room this time, was filling
up with flowers, and plants, and books, and tapes. The high tide
of barely suppressed acrimony of the last weeks at home sub-
sided into the routines of hospital visiting, though more than a
few resented Quentin's having charge of the visiting book (but
it was Quentin who had the idea, Lewis pointed out); now, to
insure a steady stream of visitors, preferably no more than two
at a time (this, the rule in all hospitals, wasn't enforced here, at
least on this floor; whether out of kindness or inefficiency, no
one could decide), Quentin had to be called first, to get one's
time slot, there was no more casual dropping by. And his
mother could no longer be prevented from taking a plane and
installing herself in a hotel near the hospital; but he seemed
to mind her daily presence less than expected, Quentin said;
said Ellen it's we who mind, do you suppose she'll stay long. It
was easier to be generous with each other visiting him here in
the hospital, as Donny pointed out, than at home, where one
minded never being alone with him; coming here, in our twos
and twos, there's no doubt about what our role is, how we
should be, collective, funny, distracting, undemanding, light, it's
important to be light, for in all this dread there is gaiety, too,
as the poet said, said Kate. (His eyes, his glittering eyes, said
Lewis.) His eyes looked dull, extinguished, Wesley said to Xavier, but Betsy said his face, not just his eyes, looked soulful,
warm; whatever is there, said Kate, I've never been so aware of
his eyes; and Stephen said, I'm afraid of what my eyes show, the
way I watch him, with too much intensity, or a phony kind of
casualness, said Victor. And, unlike at home, he was clean-
shaven each morning, at whatever hour they visited him; his

curly hair was always combed; but he complained that the
nurses had changed since he was here the last time, and that he
didn't like the change, he wanted everyone to be the same. The
room was furnished now with some of his personal effects (odd
word for one's things, said Ellen), and Tanya brought drawings
and a letter from her nine-year-old dyslexic son, who was writing now, since she'd purchased a computer; and Donny brought
champagne and some helium balloons, which were anchored to
the foot of his bed; tell me about something that's going on, he
said, waking up from a nap to find Donny and Kate at the side
of his bed, beaming at him; tell me a story, he said wistfully, said
Donny, who couldn't think of anything to say; *you're* the story,
Kate said. And Xavier brought an eighteenth-century Guate-
malan wooden statue of Saint Sebastian with upcast eyes and
open mouth, and when Tanya said what's that, a tribute to eros
past, Xavier said where I come from Sebastian is venerated as a
protector against pestilence. Pestilence symbolized by arrows?
Symbolized by arrows. All people remember is the body of a
beautiful youth bound to a tree, pierced by arrows (of which he
always seems oblivious, Tanya interjected), people forget that
the story continues, Xavier continued, that when the Christian
women came to bury the martyr they found him still alive and
nursed him back to health. And he said, according to Stephen,
I didn't know Saint Sebastian didn't die. It's undeniable, isn't it,
said Kate on the phone to Stephen, the fascination of the dying.
It makes me ashamed. We're learning how to die, said Hilda,
I'm not ready to learn, said Aileen; and Lewis, who was coming
straight from the other hospital, the hospital where Max was
still being kept in ICU, met Tanya getting out of the elevator
on the tenth floor, and as they walked together down the shiny
corridor past the open doors, averting their eyes from the other
patients sunk in their beds, with tubes in their noses, irradiated
by the bluish light from the television sets, the thing I can't bear
to think about, Tanya said to Lewis, is someone dying with the
TV on.

He has that strange, unnerving detachment now, said Ellen,
that's what upsets me, even though it makes it easier to be with
him. Sometimes he was querulous. I can't stand them coming in

here taking my blood every morning, what are they doing with all that blood, he is reported to have said; but where was his anger, Jan wondered. Mostly he was lovely to be with, always saying how are *you,* how are you feeling. He's so sweet now, said Aileen. He's so nice, said Tanya. (Nice, nice, groaned Paolo.) At first he was very ill, but he was rallying, according to Stephen's best information, there was no fear of his not recovering this time, and the doctor spoke of his being discharged from the hospital in another ten days if all went well, and the mother was persuaded to fly back to Mississippi, and Quentin was readying the penthouse for his return. And he was still writing his diary, not showing it to anyone, though Tanya, first to arrive one late-winter morning, and finding him dozing, peeked, and was horrified, according to Greg, not by anything she read but by a progressive change in his handwriting: in the recent pages, it was becoming spidery, less legible, and some lines of script wandered and tilted about the page. I was thinking, Ursula said to Quentin, that the difference between a story and a painting or photograph is that in a story you can write, He's still alive. But in a painting or a photo you can't show "still." You can just show him being alive. He's still alive, Stephen said.

1987

TIM O'BRIEN

In "The Things They Carried," Tim O'Brien has taken the plainest kind of communication, the list, and turned the form itself into the theme of his powerful story. The list in question is of the objects carried by members of an infantry platoon on search and destroy missions in Vietnam. By the time we reach the end of it, the list has taken on a terrible depth of meaning. A veteran of the war in Vietnam, Tim O'Brien has published several books, both novels and story collections, that explore the experience of the war. Born in Minnesota, he lives in Massachusetts.

The Things They Carried

FIRST LIEUTENANT Jimmy Cross carried letters from a girl named Martha, a junior at Mount Sebastian College in New Jersey. They were not love letters, but Lieutenant Cross was hoping, so he kept them folded in plastic at the bottom of his rucksack. In the late afternoon, after a day's march, he would dig his foxhole, wash his hands under a canteen, unwrap the letters, hold them with the tips of his fingers, and spend the last hour of light pretending. He would imagine romantic camping trips into the White Mountains in New Hampshire. He would sometimes taste the envelope flaps, knowing her tongue had been there. More than anything, he wanted Martha to love him as he loved her, but the letters were mostly chatty, elusive on the matter of love. She was a virgin, he was almost sure. She was an English major at Mount Sebastian, and she wrote beautifully about her professors and roommates and midterm exams, about her respect for Chaucer and her great affection for Virginia Woolf. She often quoted lines of poetry; she never mentioned the war, except to say, Jimmy, take care of yourself. The letters weighed ten ounces. They were signed "Love, Martha," but

Lieutenant Cross understood that "Love" was only a way of signing and did not mean what he sometimes pretended it meant. At dusk, he would carefully return the letters to his rucksack. Slowly, a bit distracted, he would get up and move among his men, checking the perimeter, then at full dark he would return to his hole and watch the night and wonder if Martha was a virgin.

The things they carried were largely determined by necessity. Among the necessities or near necessities were P-38 can openers, pocket knives, heat tabs, wrist watches, dog tags, mosquito repellent, chewing gum, candy, cigarettes, salt tablets, packets of Kool-Aid, lighters, matches, sewing kits, Military Payment Certificates, C rations, and two or three canteens of water. Together, these items weighed between fifteen and twenty pounds, depending upon a man's habits or rate of metabolism. Henry Dobbins, who was a big man, carried extra rations; he was especially fond of canned peaches in heavy syrup over pound cake. Dave Jensen, who practiced field hygiene, carried a toothbrush, dental floss, and several hotel-size bars of soap he'd stolen on R&R in Sydney, Australia. Ted Lavender, who was scared, carried tranquilizers until he was shot in the head outside the village of Than Khe in mid-April. By necessity, and because it was SOP, they all carried steel helmets that weighed five pounds including the liner and camouflage cover. They carried the standard fatigue jackets and trousers. Very few carried underwear. On their feet they carried jungle boots — 2.1 pounds — and Dave Jensen carried three pairs of socks and a can of Dr. Scholl's foot powder as a precaution against trench foot. Until he was shot, Ted Lavender carried six or seven ounces of premium dope, which for him was a necessity. Mitchell Sanders, the RTO, carried condoms. Norman Bowker carried a diary. Rat Kiley carried comic books. Kiowa, a devout Baptist, carried an illustrated New Testament that had been presented to him by his father, who taught Sunday school in Oklahoma City, Oklahoma. As a hedge against bad times, however, Kiowa also carried his grandmother's distrust of the white man, his grandfather's old hunting hatchet. Necessity dictated. Because the land was mined and booby-trapped, it was SOP for each man to carry a steel-centered, nylon-covered flak jacket, which weighed 6.7 pounds, but which on hot days seemed much heavier. Because you could die so quickly, each man carried at least one large compress bandage, usually in the helmet band for easy access. Because the nights were cold, and because the monsoons were wet, each carried a green plastic poncho that could be used as a raincoat or ground sheet or makeshift tent. With its quilted liner, the poncho weighed almost two pounds, but it was worth every ounce. In April, for instance, when Ted Lavender was shot, they used his poncho to wrap him up, then to carry him across the paddy, then to lift him into the chopper that took him away.

They were called legs or grunts.

To carry something was to "hump" it, as when Lieutenant Jimmy Cross humped his love for Martha up the hills and through the swamps. In its intransitive form, "to hump" meant "to walk," or "to march," but it implied burdens far beyond the intransitive.

Almost everyone humped photographs. In his wallet, Lieutenant Cross carried two photographs of Martha. The first was a Kodachrome snapshot signed "Love," though he knew better. She stood against a brick wall. Her eyes were gray and neutral, her lips slightly open as she stared straight-on at the camera. At night, sometimes, Lieutenant Cross wondered who had taken the picture, because he knew she had boyfriends, because he loved her so much, and because he could see the shadow of the picture taker spreading out against the brick wall. The second photograph had been clipped from the 1968 Mount Sebastian yearbook. It was an action shot — women's volleyball — and Martha was bent horizontal to the floor, reaching, the palms of her hands in sharp focus, the tongue taut, the expression frank and competitive. There was no visible sweat. She wore white gym shorts. Her legs, he thought, were almost certainly the legs of a virgin, dry and without hair, the left knee cocked and carrying her entire weight, which was just over one hundred pounds. Lieutenant Cross remembered touching that left knee. A dark theater, he remembered, and the movie was *Bonnie and Clyde,* and Martha wore a tweed skirt, and during the final scene, when he touched her knee, she turned and looked at him in a sad, sober way that made him pull his hand back, but he would always remember the feel of the tweed skirt and the knee beneath it and the sound of the gunfire that killed Bonnie and Clyde, how embarrassing it was, how slow and oppressive. He remembered kissing her good night at the dorm door. Right then, he thought, he should've done something brave. He should've carried her up the stairs to her room and tied her to the bed and touched that left knee all night long. He should've risked it. Whenever he looked at the photographs, he thought of new things he should've done.

What they carried was partly a function of rank, partly of field specialty.

As a first lieutenant and platoon leader, Jimmy Cross carried a compass, maps, code books, binoculars, and a .45-caliber pistol that weighed 2.9 pounds fully loaded. He carried a strobe light and the responsibility for the lives of his men.

As an RTO, Mitchell Sanders carried the PRC-25 radio, a killer, twenty-six pounds with its battery.

As a medic, Rat Kiley carried a canvas satchel filled with morphine and plasma and malaria tablets and surgical tape and comic books and all the things a medic must carry, including M&M's for especially bad wounds, for a total weight of nearly twenty pounds.

As a big man, therefore a machine gunner, Henry Dobbins carried the M-60, which weighed twenty-three pounds unloaded, but which was almost always loaded. In addition, Dobbins carried between ten and fifteen pounds of ammunition draped in belts across his chest and shoulders.

As PFCs or Spec 4s, most of them were common grunts and carried the standard M-16 gas-operated assault rifle. The weapon weighed 7.5 pounds unloaded, 8.2 pounds with its full twenty-round magazine. Depending on numerous factors, such as topography and psychology, the riflemen carried anywhere from twelve to twenty magazines, usually in cloth bandoliers, adding on another 8.4 pounds at minimum, fourteen pounds at maximum. When it was available, they also carried M-16 maintenance gear — rods and steel brushes and swabs and tubes of LSA oil — all of which weighed about a pound. Among the grunts, some carried the M-79 grenade launcher, 5.9 pounds unloaded, a reasonably light weapon except for the ammunition, which was heavy. A single round weighed ten ounces. They typical load was twenty-five rounds. But Ted Lavender, who was scared, carried thirty-four rounds when he was shot and killed outside Than Khe, and he went down under an exceptional burden, more than twenty pounds of ammunition, plus the flak jacket and helmet and rations and water and toilet paper and tranquilizers and all the rest, plus the unweighed fear. He was dead weight. There was no twitching or flopping. Kiowa, who saw it happen, said it was like watching a rock fall, or a big sandbag or something — just boom, then down — not like the movies where the dead guy rolls around and does fancy spins and goes ass over teakettle — not like that, Kiowa said, the poor bastard just flat-fuck fell. Boom. Down. Nothing else. It was a bright morning in mid-April. Lieutenant Cross felt the pain. He blamed himself. They stripped off Lavender's canteens and ammo, all the heavy things, and Rat Kiley said the obvious, the guy's dead, and Mitchell Sanders used his radio to report one U.S. KIA and to request a chopper. Then they wrapped Lavender in his poncho. They carried him out to a dry paddy, established security, and sat smoking the dead man's dope until the chopper came. Lieutenant Cross kept to himself. He pictured Martha's smooth young face, thinking he loved her more than anything, more than his men, and now Ted Lavender was dead because he loved her so much and could not stop thinking about her. When the dust-off arrived, they carried Lavender aboard. Afterward they burned Than Khe. They marched until dusk, then dug their holes, and that night Kiowa kept explaining how you had to be there, how fast it was, how the poor guy just dropped like so much concrete. Boom-down, he said. Like cement.

In addition to the three standard weapons — the M-60, M-16, and M-79 — they carried whatever presented itself, or whatever seemed appropriate as a means of killing or staying alive. They carried catch-as-catch-can. At various times, in various situations, they carried M-14s and CAR-15s and Swedish Ks and grease guns and captured AK-47s and Chi-Coms and RPGs and

Simonov carbines and black-market Uzis and .38-caliber Smith
& Wesson handguns and 66 mm LAWs and shotguns and si-
lencers and blackjacks and bayonets and C-4 plastic explosives.
Lee Strunk carried a slingshot; a weapon of last resort, he called
it. Mitchell Sanders carried brass knuckles. Kiowa carried his
grandfather's feathered hatchet. Every third or fourth man
carried a Claymore antipersonnel mine — 3.5 pounds with its
firing device. They all carried fragmentation grenades —
fourteen ounces each. They all carried at least one M-18 colored
smoke grenade — twenty-four ounces. Some carried CS or tear-
gas grenades. Some carried white-phosphorus grenades. They
carried all they could bear, and then some, including a silent
awe for the terrible power of the things they carried.

In the first week of April, before Lavender died, Lieutenant
Jimmy Cross received a good-luck charm from Martha. It was a
simple pebble, an ounce at most. Smooth to the touch, it was a
milky-white color with flecks of orange and violet, oval-shaped,
like a miniature egg. In the accompanying letter, Martha wrote
that she had found the pebble on the Jersey shoreline, precisely
where the land touched water at high tide, where things came
together but also separated. It was this separate-but-together
quality, she wrote, that had inspired her to pick up the pebble
and to carry it in her breast pocket for several days, where it
seemed weightless, and then to send it through the mail, by air,
as a token of her truest feelings for him. Lieutenant Cross found
this romantic. But he wondered what her truest feelings were,
exactly, and what she meant by separate-but-together. He wondered how the tides and waves had come into play on that
afternoon along the Jersey shoreline when Martha saw the pebble and bent down to rescue it from geology. He imagined bare
feet. Martha was a poet, with the poet's sensibilities, and her feet
would be brown and bare, the toenails unpainted, the eyes chilly
and somber like the ocean in March, and though it was painful,
he wondered who had been with her that afternoon. He imagined a pair of shadows moving along the strip of sand where
things came together but also separated. It was phantom jealousy, he knew, but he couldn't help himself. He loved her so
much. On the march, through the hot days of early April, he
carried the pebble in his mouth, turning it with his tongue,

tasting sea salts and moisture. His mind wandered. He had difficulty keeping his attention on the war. On occasion he would yell at his men to spread out the column, to keep their eyes open, but then he would slip away into daydreams, just pretending, walking barefoot along the Jersey shore, with Martha, carrying nothing. He would feel himself rising. Sun and waves and gentle winds, all love and lightness.

What they carried varied by mission.

When a mission took them to the mountains, they carried mosquito netting, machetes, canvas tarps, and extra bug juice.

If a mission seemed especially hazardous, or if it involved a place they knew to be bad, they carried everything they could. In certain heavily mined AOs, where the land was dense with Toe Poppers and Bouncing Betties, they took turns humping a twenty-eight-pound mine detector. With its headphones and big sensing plate, the equipment was a stress on the lower back and shoulders, awkward to handle, often useless because of the shrapnel in the earth, but they carried it anyway, partly for safety, partly for the illusion of safety.

On ambush, or other night missions, they carried peculiar little odds and ends. Kiowa always took along his New Testament and a pair of moccasins for silence. Dave Jensen carried night-sight vitamins high in carotin. Lee Strunk carried his slingshot; ammo, he claimed, would never be a problem. Rat Kiley carried brandy and M&M's. Until he was shot, Ted Lavender carried the starlight scope, which weighed 6.3 pounds with its aluminum carrying case. Henry Dobbins carried his girlfriend's pantyhose wrapped around his neck as a comforter. They all carried ghosts. When dark came, they would move out single file across the meadows and paddies to their ambush coordinates, where they would quietly set up the Claymores and lie down and spend the night waiting.

Other missions were more complicated and required special equipment. In mid-April, it was their mission to search out and destroy the elaborate tunnel complexes in the Than Khe area south of Chu Lai. To blow the tunnels, they carried one-pound blocks of pentrite high explosives, four blocks to a man, sixty-eight pounds in all. They carried wiring, detonators, and battery-powered clackers. Dave Jensen carried earplugs. Most often, before blowing the tunnels, they were ordered by higher command to search them, which was considered bad news, but by and large they just shrugged and carried out orders. Because he was a big man, Henry Dobbins was excused from tunnel duty. The others would draw numbers. Before Lavender died there were seventeen men in the platoon, and whoever drew the number seventeen would strip off his gear and crawl in head first with a flashlight and Lieutenant Cross's .45-caliber pistol. The rest of them would fan out as security. They would sit down or kneel, not facing the hole, listening to the ground beneath them, imagining cobwebs and ghosts, whatever was down there — the tunnel walls squeezing in — how the flashlight seemed impossibly heavy in the hand and how it was tunnel vision in the very strictest sense, compression in all ways, even time, and how you had to wiggle in — ass and elbows — a swallowed-up feeling — and how you found yourself worrying about odd things — will your flashlight go dead? Do rats carry rabies? If you screamed, how far would the sound carry? Would your buddies hear it? Would they have the courage to drag you out? In some respects, though not many, the waiting was worse than the tunnel itself. Imagination was a killer.

On April 16, when Lee Strunk drew the number seventeen, he laughed and muttered something and went down quickly. The morning was hot and very still. Not good, Kiowa said. He looked at the tunnel opening, then out across a dry paddy toward the village of Than Khe. Nothing moved. No clouds or birds or people. As they waited, the men smoked and drank Kool-Aid, not talking much, feeling sympathy for Lee Strunk but also feeling the luck of the draw. You win some, you lose some, said Mitchell Sanders, and sometimes you settle for a rain check. It was a tired line and no one laughed.

Henry Dobbins ate a tropical chocolate bar. Ted Lavender popped a tranquilizer and went off to pee.

After five minutes, Lieutenant Jimmy Cross moved to the tunnel, leaned down, and examined the darkness. Trouble, he thought — a cave-in maybe. And then suddenly, without willing it, he was thinking about Martha. The stresses and fractures, the quick collapse, the two of them buried alive under all that weight. Dense, crushing love. Kneeling, watching the hole, he tried to concentrate on Lee Strunk and the war, all the dangers, but his love was too much for him, he felt paralyzed, he wanted to sleep inside her lungs and breathe her blood and be smothered. He wanted her to be a virgin and not a virgin, all at once. He wanted to know her. Intimate secrets — why poetry? Why so sad? Why that grayness in her eyes? Why so alone? Not lonely, just alone — riding her bike across campus or sitting off by herself in the cafeteria. Even dancing, she danced alone — and it was the aloneness that filled him with love. He remembered telling her that one evening. How she nodded and looked away. And how, later, when he kissed her, she received the kiss without returning it, her eyes wide open, not afraid, not a virgin's eyes, just flat and uninvolved.

Lieutenant Cross gazed at the tunnel. But he was not there. He was buried with Martha under the white sand at the Jersey shore. They were pressed together, and the pebble in his mouth was her tongue. He was smiling. Vaguely, he was aware of how quiet the day was, the sullen paddies, yet he could not bring himself to worry about matters of security. He was beyond that. He was just a kid at war, in love. He was twenty-two years old. He couldn't help it.

A few moments later Lee Strunk crawled out of the tunnel. He came up grinning, filthy but alive. Lieutenant Cross nodded and closed his eyes while the others clapped Strunk on the back and made jokes about rising from the dead.

Worms, Rat Kiley said. Right out of the grave. Fuckin' zombie.

The men laughed. They all felt great relief.

Spook City, said Mitchell Sanders.

Lee Strunk made a funny ghost sound, a kind of moaning, yet very happy, and right then, when Strunk made that high happy moaning sound, when he went *Ahhooooo*, right then Ted Lavender was shot in the head on his way back from peeing. He lay with his mouth open. The teeth were broken. There was a swollen black bruise under his left eye. The cheekbone was gone. Oh shit, Rat Kiley said, the guy's dead. The guy's dead, he kept saying, which seemed profound — the guy's dead. I mean really.

*

The things they carried were determined to some extent by superstition. Lieutenant Cross carried his good-luck pebble. Dave Jensen carried a rabbit's foot. Norman Bowker, otherwise a very gentle person, carried a thumb that had been presented to him as a gift by Mitchell Sanders. The thumb was dark brown, rubbery to the touch, and weighed four ounces at most. It had been cut from a VC corpse, a boy of fifteen or sixteen. They'd found him at the bottom of an irrigation ditch, badly burned, flies in his mouth and eyes. The boy wore black shorts and sandals. At the time of his death he had been carrying a pouch of rice, a rifle, and three magazines of ammunition.

You want my opinion, Mitchell Sanders said, there's a definite moral here.

He put his hand on the dead boy's wrist. He was quiet for a time, as if counting a pulse, then he patted the stomach, almost affectionately, and used Kiowa's hunting hatchet to remove the thumb.

Henry Dobbins asked what the moral was.

Moral?

You know. *Moral.*

Sanders wrapped the thumb in toilet paper and handed it across to Norman Bowker. There was no blood. Smiling, he kicked the boy's head, watched the flies scatter, and said, It's like with that old TV show — Paladin. Have gun, will travel.

Henry Dobbins thought about it.

Yeah, well, he finally said. I don't see no moral.

There it *is,* man.

Fuck off.

They carried USO stationery and pencils and pens. They carried Sterno, safety pins, trip flares, signal flares, spools of wire, razor blades, chewing tobacco, liberated joss sticks and statuettes of the smiling Buddha, candles, grease pencils, *The Stars and Stripes,* fingernail clippers, Psy Ops leaflets, bush hats, bolos, and much more. Twice a week, when the resupply choppers came in, they carried hot chow in green Mermite cans and large canvas bags filled with iced beer and soda pop. They carried plastic water containers, each with a two-gallon capacity. Mitchell Sanders carried a set of starched tiger fatigues for special occasions.

Henry Dobbins carried Black Flag insecticide. Dave Jensen carried empty sandbags that could be filled at night for added protection. Lee Strunk carried tanning lotion. Some things they carried in common. Taking turns, they carried the big PRC-77 scrambler radio, which weighed thirty pounds with its battery. They shared the weight of memory. They took up what others could no longer bear. Often, they carried each other, the wounded or weak. They carried infections. They carried chess sets, basketballs, Vietnamese-English dictionaries, insignia of rank, Bronze Stars and Purple Hearts, plastic cards imprinted with the Code of Conduct. They carried diseases, among them malaria and dysentery. They carried lice and ringworm and leeches and paddy algae and various rots and molds. They carried the land itself — Vietnam, the place, the soil — a powdery orange-red dust that covered their boots and fatigues and faces. They carried the sky. The whole atmosphere, they carried it, the humidity, the monsoons, the stink of fungus and decay, all of it, they carried gravity. They moved like mules. By daylight they took sniper fire, at night they were mortared, but it was not battle, it was just the endless march, village to village, without purpose, nothing won or lost. They marched for the sake of the march. They plodded along slowly, dumbly, leaning forward against the heat, unthinking, all blood and bone, simple grunts, soldiering with their legs, toiling up the hills and down into the paddies and across the rivers and up again and down, just humping, one step and then the next and then another, but no volition, no will, because it was automatic, it was anatomy, and the war was entirely a matter of posture and carriage, the hump was everything, a kind of inertia, a kind of emptiness, a dullness of desire and intellect and conscience and hope and human sensibility. Their principles were in their feet. Their calculations were biological. They had no sense of strategy or mission. They searched the villages without knowing what to look for, not caring, kicking over jars of rice, frisking children and old men, blowing tunnels, sometimes setting fires and sometimes not, then forming up and moving on to the next village, then other villages, where it would always be the same. They carried their own lives. The pressures were enormous. In the heat of early afternoon, they would remove their helmets and flak jackets, walking bare, which was dangerous but which helped ease the strain. They would often discard things along the route of march. Purely for comfort, they would throw away rations, blow their Claymores and grenades, no matter, because by nightfall the resupply choppers would arrive with more of the same, then a day or two later still more, fresh watermelons and crates of ammunition and sunglasses and woolen sweaters — the resources were stunning — sparklers for the Fourth of July, colored eggs for Easter. It was the great American war chest — the fruits of science, the smokestacks, the canneries, the arsenals at Hartford, the Minnesota forests, the machine shops, the vast fields of corn and wheat — they carried like freight trains; they carried it on their backs and shoulders — and for all the ambiguities of Vietnam, all the mysteries and unknowns, there was at least the single abiding certainty that they would never be at a loss for things to carry.

After the chopper took Lavender away, Lieutenant Jimmy Cross led his men into the village of Than Khe. They burned everything. They shot chickens and dogs, they trashed the village well, they called in artillery and watched the wreckage, then they marched for several hours through the hot afternoon, and then at dusk, while Kiowa explained how Lavender died, Lieutenant Cross found himself trembling.

He tried not to cry. With his entrenching tool, which weighed five pounds, he began digging a hole in the earth.

He felt shame. He hated himself. He had loved Martha more than his men, and as a consequence Lavender was now dead, and this was something he would have to carry like a stone in his stomach for the rest of the war.

All he could do was dig. He used his entrenching tool like an ax, slashing, feeling both love and hate, and then later, when it was full dark, he sat at the bottom of his foxhole and wept. It went on for a long while. In part, he was grieving for Ted Lavender, but mostly it was for Martha, and for himself, because she belonged to another world, which was not quite real, and because she was a junior at Mount Sebastian College in New Jersey, a poet and a virgin and uninvolved, and because he realized she did not love him and never would.

*

Like cement, Kiowa whispered in the dark. I swear to God —
boom-down. Not a word.

I've heard this, said Norman Bowker.

A pisser, you know? Still zipping himself up. Zapped while
zipping.

All right, fine. That's enough.

Yeah, but you had to see it, the guy just —

I *heard,* man. Cement. So why not shut the fuck *up?*

Kiowa shook his head sadly and glanced over at the hole
where Lieutenant Jimmy Cross sat watching the night. The air
was thick and wet. A warm, dense fog had settled over the
paddies and there was the stillness that precedes rain.

After a time Kiowa sighed.

One thing for sure, he said. The Lieutenant's in some deep
hurt. I mean that crying jag — the way he was carrying on — it
wasn't fake or anything, it was real heavy-duty hurt. The man
cares.

Sure, Norman Bowker said.

Say what you want, the man does care.

We all got problems.

Not Lavender.

No, I guess not. Bowker said. Do me a favor, though.

Shut up?

That's a smart Indian. Shut up.

Shrugging, Kiowa pulled off his boots. He wanted to say
more, just to lighten up his sleep, but instead he opened his
New Testament and arranged it beneath his head as a pillow.
The fog made things seem hollow and unattached. He tried not
to think about Ted Lavender, but then he was thinking how fast
it was, no drama, down and dead, and how it was hard to feel
anything except surprise. It seemed un-Christian. He wished he
could find some great sadness, or even anger, but the emotion
wasn't there and he couldn't make it happen. Mostly he felt
pleased to be alive. He liked the smell of the New Testament
under his cheek, the leather and ink and paper and glue, whatever the chemicals were. He liked hearing the sounds of night.
Even his fatigue, it felt fine, the stiff muscles and the prickly
awareness of his own body, a floating feeling. He enjoyed not
being dead. Lying there, Kiowa admired Lieutenant Jimmy
Cross's capacity for grief. He wanted to share the man's pain,

he wanted to care as Jimmy Cross cared. And yet when he closed his eyes, all he could think was Boom-down, and all he could feel was the pleasure of having his boots off and the fog curling in around him and the damp soil and the Bible smells and the plush comfort of night.

After a moment Norman Bowker sat up in the dark.

What the hell, he said. You want to talk, *talk*. Tell it to me.

Forget it.

No, man, go on. One thing I hate, it's a silent Indian.

For the most part they carried themselves with poise, a kind of dignity. Now and then, however, there were times of panic, when they squealed or wanted to squeal but couldn't, when they twitched and made moaning sounds and covered their heads and said Dear Jesus and flopped around on the earth and fired their weapons blindly and cringed and sobbed and begged for the noise to stop and went wild and made stupid promises to themselves and to God and to their mothers and fathers, hoping not to die. In different ways, it happened to all of them. Afterward, when the firing ended, they would blink and peek up. They would touch their bodies, feeling shame, then quickly hiding it. They would force themselves to stand. As if in slow motion, frame by frame, the world would take on the old logic — absolute silence, then the wind, then sunlight, then voices. It was the burden of being alive. Awkwardly, the men would reassemble themselves, first in private, then in groups, becoming soldiers again. They would repair the leaks in their eyes. They would check for casualties, call in dust-offs, light cigarettes, try to smile, clear their throats and spit and begin cleaning their weapons. After a time someone would shake his head and say, No lie, I almost shit my pants, and someone else would laugh, which meant it was bad, yes, but the guy had obviously not shit his pants, it wasn't that bad, and in any case nobody would ever do such a thing and then go ahead and talk about it. They would squint into the dense, oppressive sunlight. For a few moments, perhaps, they would fall silent, lighting a joint and tracking its passage from man to man, inhaling, holding in the humiliation. Scary stuff, one of them might say. But then someone else would grin or flick his eyebrows and say, Roger-dodger, almost cut me a new asshole, *almost*.

There were numerous such poses. Some carried themselves with a sort of wistful resignation, others with pride or stiff soldierly discipline or good humor or macho zeal. They were afraid of dying but they were even more afraid to show it.

They found jokes to tell.

They used a hard vocabulary to contain the terrible softness. *Greased,* they'd say. *Offed, lit up, zapped while zipping.* It wasn't cruelty, just stage presence. They were actors and the war came at them in 3-D. When someone died, it wasn't quite dying, because in a curious way it seemed scripted, and because they had their lines mostly memorized, irony mixed with tragedy, and because they called it by other names, as if to encyst and destroy the reality of death itself. They kicked corpses. They cut off thumbs. They talked grunt lingo. They told stories about Ted Lavender's supply of tranquilizers, how the poor guy didn't feel a thing, how incredibly tranquil he was.

There's a moral here, said Mitchell Sanders.

They were waiting for Lavender's chopper, smoking the dead man's dope.

The moral's pretty obvious, Sanders said, and winked. Stay away from drugs. No joke, they'll ruin your day every time.

Cute, said Henry Dobbins.

Mind-blower, get it? Talk about wiggy — nothing left, just blood and brains.

They made themselves laugh.

There it is, they'd say, over and over, as if the repetition itself were an act of poise, a balance between crazy and almost crazy, knowing without going. There it is, which meant be cool, let it ride, because oh yeah, man, you can't change what can't be changed, there it is, there it absolutely and positively and fucking well *is.*

They were tough.

They carried all the emotional baggage of men who might die. Grief, terror, love, longing — these were intangibles, but the intangibles had their own mass and specific gravity, they had tangible weight. They carried shameful memories. They carried the common secret of cowardice barely restrained, the instinct to run or freeze or hide, and in many respects this was the heaviest burden of all, for it could never be put down, it required perfect balance and perfect posture. They carried their reputations. They carried the soldier's greatest fear, which was the fear of blushing. Men killed, and died, because they were embarrassed not to. It was what had brought them to the war in the first place, nothing positive, no dreams of glory or honor, just to avoid the blush of dishonor. They died so as not to die of embarrassment. They crawled into tunnels and walked point and advanced under fire. Each morning, despite the unknowns, they made their legs move. They endured. They kept humping. They did not submit to the obvious alternative, which was simply to close the eyes and fall. So easy, really. Go limp and tumble to the ground and let the muscles unwind and not speak and not budge until your buddies picked you up and lifted you into the chopper that would roar and dip its nose and carry you off to the world. A mere matter of falling, yet no one ever fell. It was not courage, exactly; the object was not valor. Rather, they were too frightened to be cowards.

By and large they carried these things inside, maintaining the masks of composure. They sneered at sick call. They spoke bitterly about guys who had found release by shooting off their own toes or fingers. Pussies, they'd say. Candyasses. It was fierce, mocking talk, with only a trace of envy or awe, but even so, the image played itself out behind their eyes.

They imagined the muzzle against flesh. They imagined the quick, sweet pain, then the evacuation to Japan, then a hospital with warm beds and cute geisha nurses.

They dreamed of freedom birds.

At night, on guard, staring into the dark, they were carried away by jumbo jets. They felt the rush of takeoff. *Gone!* they yelled. And then velocity, wings and engines, a smiling stewardess — but it was more than a plane, it was a real bird, a big sleek silver bird with feathers and talons and high screeching. They were flying. The weights fell off, there was nothing to bear. They laughed and held on tight, feeling the cold slap of wind and altitude, soaring, thinking *It's over, I'm gone!* — they were naked, they were light and free — it was all lightness, bright and fast and buoyant, light as light, a helium buzz in the brain, a giddy bubbling in the lungs as they were taken up over the clouds and the war, beyond duty, beyond gravity and mortification and global entanglements — *Sin loi!* they yelled, *I'm sorry, motherfuckers, but I'm out of it, I'm goofed, I'm on a space cruise, I'm gone!* — and it was a restful, disencumbered sensation, just riding the light waves, sailing that big silver freedom bird over the mountains and oceans, over America, over the farms and great sleeping cities and cemeteries and highways and the golden arches of McDonald's. It was flight, a kind of fleeing, a kind of falling, falling higher and higher, spinning off the edge of the earth and beyond the sun and through the vast, silent vacuum where there were no burdens and where everything weighed exactly nothing. *Gone!* they screamed, *I'm sorry but I'm gone!* And so at night, not quite dreaming, they gave themselves over to lightness, they were carried, they were purely borne.

On the morning after Ted Lavender died, First Lieutenant Jimmy Cross crouched at the bottom of his foxhole and burned Martha's letters. Then he burned the two photographs. There was a steady rain falling, which made it difficult, but he used heat tabs and Sterno to build a small fire, screening it with his body, holding the photographs over the tight blue flame with the tips of his fingers.

He realized it was only a gesture. Stupid, he thought. Sentimental, too, but mostly just stupid.

Lavender was dead. You couldn't burn the blame.

Besides, the letters were in his head. And even now, without photographs, Lieutenant Cross could see Martha playing volleyball in her white gym shorts and yellow T-shirt. He could see her moving in the rain.

When the fire died out, Lieutenant Cross pulled his poncho over his shoulders and ate breakfast from a can.

There was no great mystery, he decided.

In those burned letters Martha had never mentioned the war, except to say, Jimmy, take care of yourself. She wasn't involved. She signed the letters "Love," but it wasn't love, and all the fine lines and technicalities did not matter.

The morning came up wet and blurry. Everything seemed part of everything else, the fog and Martha and the deepening rain.

It was a war, after all.

Half smiling, Lieutenant Jimmy Cross took out his maps. He

shook his head hard, as if to clear it, then bent forward and began planning the day's march. In ten minutes, or maybe twenty, he would rouse the men and they would pack up and head west, where the maps showed the country to be green and inviting. They would do what they had always done. The rain might add some weight, but otherwise it would be one more day layered upon all the other days.

He was realistic about it. There was that new hardness in his stomach.

No more fantasies, he told himself.

Henceforth, when he thought about Martha, it would be only to think that she belonged elsewhere. He would shut down the daydreams. This was not Mount Sebastian, it was another world, where there were no pretty poems or midterm exams, a place where men died because of carelessness and gross stupidity. Kiowa was right. Boom-down, and you were dead, never partly dead.

Briefly, in the rain, Lieutenant Cross saw Martha's gray eyes gazing back at him.

He understood.

It was very sad, he thought. The things men carried inside. The things men did or felt they had to do.

He almost nodded at her, but didn't.

Instead he went back to his maps. He was now determined to perform his duties firmly and without negligence. It wouldn't help Lavender, he knew that, but from this point on he would comport himself as a soldier. He would dispose of his good-luck pebble. Swallow it, maybe, or use Lee Strunk's slingshot, or just drop it along the trail. On the march he would impose strict field discipline. He would be careful to send out flank security, to prevent straggling or bunching up, to keep his troops moving at the proper pace and at the proper interval. He would insist on clean weapons. He would confiscate the remainder of Lavender's dope. Later in the day, perhaps, he would call the men together and speak to them plainly. He would accept the blame for what had happened to Ted Lavender. He would be a man about it. He would look them in the eyes, keeping his chin level, and he would issue the new SOPs in a calm, impersonal tone of voice, an officer's voice, leaving no room for argument or discussion. Commencing immediately, he'd tell them, they would no longer abandon equipment along the route of march. They would police up their acts. They would get their shit together, and keep it together, and maintain it neatly and in good working order.

He would not tolerate laxity. He would show strength, distancing himself.

Among the men there would be grumbling, of course, and maybe worse, because their days would seem longer and their loads heavier, but Lieutenant Cross reminded himself that his obligation was not to be loved but to lead. He would dispense with love; it was not now a factor. And if anyone quarreled or complained, he would simply tighten his lips and arrange his shoulders in the correct command posture. He might give a curt little nod. Or he might not. He might just shrug and say Carry on, then they would saddle up and form into a column and move out toward the villages west of Than Khe.

MAVIS GALLANT

Mark Helprin noted that "Dédé" is "a story about a French pyromaniac, though that hardly does it justice." Its author is a Canadian writer who has lived for many years in France. Her stories about expatriate life and about Parisians have often appeared in *Best American* volumes — seven times in just the past decade. In 1980 Stanley Elkin broke tradition by including two stories by a single author — Mavis Gallant. A master of observed detail and understated humor, Mavis Gallant unfailingly commands the reader's trust in the depth of her perception. She has published many collections of stories, essays, and reviews.

Dédé

PASCAL BROUET is fourteen now. He used to attend a lycée, but after his parents found out about the dealers in the street, outside the gates, they changed him to a private school. Here the situation is about the same, but he hasn't said so; he does not want to be removed again, this time perhaps to a boarding establishment, away from Paris, with nothing decent to eat and lights-out at ten. He would not describe himself as contriving or secretive. He tries to avoid drawing attention to the Responsibility clause in the treaty that governs peace between generations.

Like his father, the magistrate, he will offer neutrality before launching into dissent. "I'm ready to admit," he will begin, or "I don't want to take over the whole conversation . . . " Sometimes the sentence comes to nothing. Like his father, he lets his eyelids droop, tries to speak lightly and slowly. The magistrate is famous for fading out of a discussion by slow degrees. At one time he was said to be the youngest magistrate ever to fall asleep in court: he would black out when he thought he wasn't needed and snap to just as the case turned around. Apparently, he never missed a turning. He has described his own mind to Pascal: it is like a superlatively smooth car with an invisible driver in control. The driver is the magistrate's unconscious will.

To Pascal a mind is a door, ajar or shut. His grades are good, but this side of brilliant. He has a natural gift — a precise, perfectly etched memory. How will he use it? He thinks he could as easily become an actor as a lawyer. When he tells his parents so, they seem not to mind. He could turn into an actor-manager, with a private theater of his own, or the director of one of the great national theaters, commissioning new work, refurbishing the classics, settling questions at issue with a word or two.

The Brouets are tolerant parents, ready for anything. They met for the first time in May of 1968, a few yards away from a barricade of burning cars. She had a stone in her hand; when she saw him looking at her, she put it down. They walked up the Boulevard Saint-Michel together, and he told her his plan for reforming the judiciary. He was a bit older, about twenty-six. Answering his question, she said she was from Alsace. He reminded her how the poet Paul Éluard had picked up his future wife in the street, on a rainy evening. She was from Alsace, too, and starving, and in a desperate, muddled, amateurish way pretending to be a prostitute.

Well, this was not quite the same story. In 1968 the future Mme. Brouet was studying to be an analyst of handwriting, with employment to follow — so she had been promised — in the personnel section of a large department store. In the meantime, she was staying with a Protestant Reformed Church pastor and his family in Rue Fustel-de-Coulanges. She had been on her way home to dinner when she stopped to pick up the stone. She had a mother in Alsace, and a little brother, Amedée—Dédé."

"Sylvie and I have known both sides of the barricades," the magistrate likes to say, now. What he means is that they cannot be crowded into a political corner. The stone in the hand has made her a rebel, at least in his recollections. She never looks at a newspaper, because of her reputation for being against absolutely everything. So he says, but perhaps it isn't exact: she looks at the pages marked "Culture," to see what is on at the galleries. He reads three morning papers at breakfast and, if he has time,

last evening's *Le Monde*. Reading, he narrows his eyes. Sometimes he looks as though everything he thinks and believes had
been translated into a foreign language and, suddenly, back
again.

When Pascal was about nine, his father said, "What do you
suppose you will do, one day?"

They were at breakfast. Pascal's Uncle Amedée was there.
Like everyone else, Pascal called him Dédé. Pascal looked across
at him and said, "I want to be a bachelor, like Dédé."

His mother moaned, "Oh, no!" and covered her face. The
magistrate waited until she had recovered before speaking.
She looked up, smiling, a bit embarrassed. Then he explained,
slowly and carefully, that Dédé was too young to be considered
a bachelor. He was a student, a youth. "A student, a student,"
he repeated, thinking perhaps that if he kept saying it Dédé
would study hard.

Dédé had a button of a nose that looked ridiculous on someone so tall, and a mass of curly fair hair. Because of the hair,
the magistrate could not take him seriously; his private name
for Dédé was "Harpo."

That period of Pascal's life, nine rounding to ten, was also the
autumn before an important election year. The elections were
five months off, but already people argued over dinner and
Sunday lunch. One Sunday in October, the table was attacked
by wasps, drawn in from the garden by a dish of sliced melon
— the last of the season, particularly fragrant and sweet. The
French doors to the garden stood open. Sunlight entered and
struck through the wine decanters and dissolved in the waxed
tabletop in pale red and gold. From his place, Pascal could see
the enclosed garden, the apartment blocks behind it, a golden
poplar tree, and the wicker chairs where the guests, earlier, had
sat with their drinks.

There were two couples: the Turbins, older than Pascal's parents, and the Chevallier-Crochets, who had not been married
long. Mme. Chevallier-Crochet attended an art-history course
with Pascal's mother, on Thursday afternoons. They had never
been here before, and were astonished to discover a secret garden in Paris with chairs, grass, a garden rake, a tree. Just as

their expression of amazement was starting to run thin and patches of silence appeared, Abelarda, newly come from Cádiz, appeared at the door and called them to lunch. She said, "It's ready," though that was not what Mme. Brouet had asked her to say; at least, not that way. The guests got up, without haste. They were probably as hungry as Pascal but didn't want it to show. Abelarda went on standing, staring at the topmost leaves of the poplar, trying to remember what she ought to have said.

A few minutes later, just as they were starting to eat their melon, wasps came thudding against the table, like pebbles thrown. The adults froze, as though someone had drawn a gun. Pascal knew that sitting still was a good way to be stung. If you waved your napkin, shouted orders, the wasps might fly away. But he was not expected to give instructions; he was here, with adults, to discover how conversation is put together, how to sound interesting without being forward, amusing without seeming familiar. At that moment, Dédé did an unprecedented and courageous thing: he picked up the platter of melon, crawling with wasps, and took it outside, as far as the foot of the tree. And came back to applause: at least, his sister clapped, and young Mme. Chevallier-Crochet cried, "Bravo! Bravo!"

Dédé smiled, but, then, he was always smiling. His sister wished he wouldn't; the smile gave his brother-in-law another reason for calling him Harpo. Sitting down, he seemed to become entwined with his chair. He was too tall ever to be comfortable. He needed larger chairs, tables that were both higher and wider, so that he would not bump his knees, or put his feet on the shoes of the lady sitting opposite.

Pascal's father just said, "So, no more melon." It was something he particularly liked, and there might be none now until next summer. If Dédé had asked his opinion instead of jumping up so impulsively, he might have said, "Just leave it," and taken a chance on getting stung.

Well; no more for anyone. The guests sat a little straighter, waiting for the next course: beef, veal, or mutton, or the possibility of duck. Pascal's mother asked him to shut the French doors. She did not expect another wasp invasion, but there might be strays. Mme. Chevallier-Crochet remarked that Pascal was tall for his age, then asked what his age was. "He is almost ten," said Mme. Brouet, looking at her son with some wonder. "I can hardly believe it. I don't understand time."

Mme. Turbin said she did not have to consult a watch to know the exact time. It must be a quarter to two now. If it was, her daughter Brigitte had just landed in Salonika. Whenever her daughter boarded a plane, Mme. Turbin accompanied her in her mind, minute by minute.

"Thessalonika," M. Turbin explained.

The Chevallier-Crochets had spent their honeymoon in Sicily. If they had it to do over again, they said, they would change their minds and go to Greece.

Mme. Brouet said they would find it very different from Sicily. Her mind was on something else entirely: Abelarda. Probably Abelarda had expected them to linger over a second helping of melon. Perhaps she was sitting in the kitchen with nothing to do, listening to a program of Spanish music on the radio. Mme. Brouet caught a wide-awake glance from her husband, interpreted it correctly, and went out to the kitchen to see.

One of the men turned to M. Brouet, wondering if he could throw some light on the election candidates: unfortunate stories were making the rounds. Pascal's father was often asked for information. He had connections in Paris, like stout ropes attached to the upper civil service and to politics. One sister was married to a cabinet minister's chief of staff. Her children were taken to school in a car with a red-white-and-blue emblem. The driver could park wherever he liked. The magistrate's grandfather had begun as a lieutenant in the cavalry and died of a heart attack the day he was appointed head of a committee to oversee war graves. His portrait, as a child on a pony, hung in the dining room. The artist was said to have copied a photograph; that was why the pony looked so stiff and the colors were wrong. The room Pascal slept in had been that child's summer bedroom; the house had once been a suburban, almost a country dwelling. Now the road outside was like a highway; even with the doors shut they could hear Sunday traffic pouring across an intersection, on the way to Boulogne and the Saint-Cloud bridge.

The magistrate replied that he did not want to take over the whole conversation but he did feel safe in saying this: Several

men, none of whom he had any use for, were now standing face
to face. Sometimes he felt like washing his hands of the future.
(Saying this, he slid his hands together.) However, before his
guests could show shock or disappointment, he added, "But one
cannot remain indifferent. This is an old country, an ancient
civilization." Here his voice faded out. "We owe . . . One has to
. . . A certain unbreakable loyalty . . . " And he placed his hands
on the table, calmly, one on each side of his plate.

At that moment Mme. Brouet returned, her cheeks and forehead pink, as if she had got too close to a hot oven. Abelarda
came along next, to change the plates. She was pink in the face,
too.

Pascal saw the candidates lined up like rugby teams. He was
allowed to watch rugby on television. His parents did not care
for soccer: the players showed off, received absurd amounts of
money just for kicking a ball, and there was something the matter with their shorts. "With all that money, they could buy
clothes that fit," Pascal's mother had said. Rugby players were
different. They were the embodiment of action and its outcome,
in an ideal form. They got muddied for love of sport. France
had won the Five Nations tournament, beating even the
dreaded Welsh, whose fans always set up such eerie wailing in
the stands. Actually, they were trying to sing. It must have been
the way the early Celts joined in song before the Roman con-
quest, the magistrate had told Pascal.

No one at table could have made a rugby team. They were
too thin. Dédé was a broomstick. Of course, Pascal played soccer
at school, in a small cement courtyard. The smaller boys, aged
six, seven, tried to imitate Michel Platini, but they got everything
wrong. They would throw the ball high in the air and kick at
nothing, leg crossed over the chest, arms spread.

The magistrate kept an eye on the dish Abelarda was now
handing around: partridges in a nest of shredded cabbage —
an entire surprise. Pascal looked over at Dédé, who sat smiling
to himself, for no good reason. (If Pascal had continued to
follow his father's gaze he might be told gently, later, that one
does not stare at food.)

There was no more conversation to be had from M. Brouet,
for the moment. Helping themselves to partridge, the guests

told one another stories everybody knew. All the candidates were in a declining state of health and morality. One had to be given injections of ground-up Japanese seaweed; otherwise he lost consciousness, sometimes in the midst of a sentence. Others kept going on a mixture of cocaine and vitamin C. Their private means had been acquired by investing in gay bars and foreign wars, and evicting the poor. Only the Ministry of the Interior knew the nature and extent of their undercover financial dealings. And yet some of these men had to be found better than others, if democracy was not to come to a standstill. As M. Brouet had pointed out, one cannot wash one's hands of the future.

The magistrate had begun to breathe evenly and deeply. Perhaps the sunlight beating on the panes of the shut doors made him feel drowsy.

"Etienne is never quite awake or asleep," said his wife, meaning it as a compliment.

She was proud of everyone related to her, even by marriage, and took pride in her father, who had run away from home and family to live in New Caledonia. He had shown spirit and a sense of initiative, like Dédé with the wasps. (Now that Pascal is fourteen, he has heard this often.) But pride is not the same as helpless love. The person she loved best, in that particular way, was Dédé.

Dédé had come to stay with the Brouets because his mother, Pascal's grandmother, no longer knew what to do with him. He was never loud or abrupt, never forced an opinion on anyone, but he could not be left without guidance — even though he could vote, and was old enough to do some of the things he did, such as sign his mother's name to a check. (Admittedly, only once.) This was his second visit; the first, last spring, had not sharpened his character, in spite of his brother-in-law's conversation, his sister's tender anxiety, the sense of purpose to be gained by walking his little nephew to school. Sent home to Colmar (firm handshake with the magistrate at the Gare de l'Est, tears and chocolates from his sister, presentation of an original drawing from Pascal), he had accidentally set fire to his mother's kitchen, then to his own bedclothes. Accidents, the insurance people had finally agreed, but they were not too pleased. His mother was at the present time under treatment for exhaustion, with a private nurse to whom she made expensive presents. She had about as much money sense as Harpo, the magistrate said. (Without lifting his head from his homework, Pascal could take in nearly everything uttered in the hall, on the stairs, and in two adjacent rooms.)

When they were all four at breakfast Mme. Brouet repeated her brother's name in every second sentence: wondering if Dédé wanted more toast, if someone would please pass him the strawberry jam, if he had enough blankets on his bed, if he needed an extra key. (He was a great loser of keys.) The magistrate examined his three morning papers. He did not want to have to pass anything to Harpo. Mme. Brouet was really just speaking to herself.

That autumn, Dédé worked at a correspondence course, in preparation for a competitive civil-service examination. If he was among the first dozen, eliminating perhaps hundreds of clever young men and women, he would be eligible for a post in the nation's railway system. His work would be indoors, of course; no one expected him to be out in all weathers, trudging alongside the tracks, looking for something to repair. Great artists, leaders of honor and reputation, had got their start at a desk in a railway ofice. Pascal's mother, whenever she said this, had to pause, as she searched her mind for their names. The railway had always been a seedbed of outstanding careers, she would continue. She would then point out to Dédé that their father had been a supervisor of public works.

After breakfast Dédé wound a long scarf around his neck and walked Pascal to school. He had invented an apartment with movable walls. Everything one needed could be got within reach by pulling a few levers or pressing a button. You could spend your life in the middle of a room without having to stir. He and Pascal refined the invention; that was what they talked about, on the way to Pascal's school. Then Dédé came home and studied until lunchtime. In the afternoon he drew new designs of his idea. Perhaps he was lonely. The doctor looking after his mother had asked him not to call or write, for the moment.

*

Pascal's mother believed Dédé needed a woman friend, even
though he was not ready to get married. Pascal heard her say,
"Art and science, architecture, culture." These were the factors
that could change Dédé's life, and to which he would find access
through the right kind of woman. Mme. Brouet had someone
in mind — Mlle. Turbin, who held a position of some responsibility in a travel agency. She was often sent abroad to rescue
visitors or check their complaints. Today's lunch had been
planned around her, but at the last minute she had been called
to Greece, where a tourist, bitten by a dog, had received an
emergency specific for rabies, and believed the Greeks were
trying to kill him.

Her parents had come, nevertheless. It was a privilege to meet
the magistrate and to visit a rare old house, one of the last of its
kind still in private hands. Before lunch Mme. Turbin had
asked to be shown around. Mme. Brouet conducted a tour for
the women, taking care not to open the door to Dédé's room:
there had been a fire in a wastepaper basket only a few hours
before, and everything in there was charred or singed or
soaked.

At lunch, breaking out of politics, M. Turbin described the
treatment the tourist in Salonika had most probably received: it
was the same the world over, and incurred the use of a long
needle. He held out his knife, to show the approximate length.

"Stop!" cried Mme. Chevallier-Crochet. She put her napkin
over her nose and mouth; all they could see was her wild eyes.
Everyone stopped eating, forks suspended — all but the magistrate, who was pushing aside shreds of cabbage to get at the last
of the partridge.

M. Chevallier-Crochet explained that his wife was afraid of
needles. He could not account for it; he had not known her as
a child. It seemed to be a singular fear, one that set her apart.
Meantime, his wife closed her eyes; opened them, though not
as wide as before; placed her napkin neatly across her lap; and
swallowed a piece of bread.

M. Turbin said he was sorry. He had taken it for granted that
any compatriot of the great Louis Pasteur must have seen a
needle or two. Needles were only a means to an end.

Mme. Brouet glanced at her husband, pleading for help, but

he had just put a bite of food into his mouth. He was always last to be served when there were guests, and everything got to him cold. That was probably why he ate in such a hurry. He shrugged, meaning, Change the subject.

"Pascal," she said, turning to him. At last, she thought of something to say: "Do you remember Mlle. Turbin? Charlotte Turbin?"

"Brigitte?" said Pascal.

"I'm sure you remember," she said, not listening at all. "In the travel agency, on Rue Caumartin?"

"She gave me the corrida poster," said Pascal, wondering how this had slipped her mind.

"We went to see her, you and I, the time we wanted to go to Egypt? Now do you remember?"

"We never went to Egypt."

"No. Papa couldn't get away just then, so we finally went back to Deauville, where Papa has so many cousins. So you do remember Mlle. Turbin, with the pretty auburn hair?"

"Chestnut," said the two Turbins, together.

"My sister," said Dédé, all of a sudden, indicating her with his left hand, the right clutching a wine glass. "Before she got married, my mother told me . . ." The story, whatever it was, engulfed him in laughter. "A dog tried to bite her," he managed to say.

"You can tell us about it another time," said his sister.

He continued to laugh, softly, just to himself, while Abelarda changed the plates again.

The magistrate examined his clean new plate. No immediate surprises: salad, another plate, cheese, a dessert plate. His wife had given up on Mlle. Turbin. Really, it was his turn now, her silence said.

"I may have mentioned this before," said the magistrate. "And I would not wish to keep saying the same things over and over. But I wonder if you agree that the pivot of French politics today is no longer in France."

"The Middle East," said M. Turbin, nodding his head.

"Washington," said M. Chevallier-Crochet. "Washington calls Paris every morning and says, Do this, Do that."

"The Middle East and the Soviet Union," said M. Turbin.

"There," said M. Brouet. "We are all in agreement."

Many of the magistrate's relatives and friends thought he should be closer to government, to power. But his wife wanted him to stay where he was and get his pension. After he retired, when Pascal was grown, they would visit Tibet and the north of China, and winter in Kashmir.

"You know, this morning —" said Dédé, getting on with something that was on his mind.

"Another time," said his sister. "Never mind about this morning. It is all forgotten. Etienne is speaking, now."

This morning! The guests had no idea, couldn't begin to imagine what had taken place, here, in the dining room, at this very table. Dédé had announced, overjoyed, "I've got my degree." For Dédé was taking a correspondence course that could not lead to a degree of any kind. It must have been just his way of trying to stop studying so that he could go home.

"Degree?" The magistrate folded yesterday's *Le Monde* carefully before putting it down. "What do you mean, degree?"

Pascal's mother got up to make fresh coffee. "I'm glad to hear it, Dédé," she said.

"A degree in what?" said the magistrate.

Dédé shrugged, as if no one had bothered to tell him. "It came just the other day," he said. "I've got my degree, and now I can go home."

"Is there something you could show us?"

"There was just a letter, and I lost it," said Dédé. "A real diploma costs two thousand francs. I don't know where I'd find the money."

The magistrate did not seem to disbelieve; that was because of his training. But then he said, "You began your course about a month ago?"

"I had been thinking about it for a long time," said Dédé.

"And now they have awarded you a degree. You are perfectly right — it's time you went home. You can take the train tonight. I'll call your mother."

Pascal's mother returned, carrying a large white coffeepot. "I wonder where your first job will be," she said.

Why were she and her brother so remote from things as they

are? Perhaps because of their mother, the grandmother in Colmar. Once, she had taken Pascal by the chin and tried to force him to look her in the eye. She had done it to her children. Pascal knows, now, that you cannot have your chin held in a vise and undividedly meet a blue stare. Somewhere at the back of the mind is a second self with eyes tight shut. Dédé and his sister could seem to meet any glance, even the magistrate's when he was being most nearly wide awake. They seemed to be listening, but the person he thought he was talking to, trying to reach the heart of, was deaf and blind. Pascal's mother listens when she needs to know what might happen next.

All Pascal understood, for the moment, was that when Dédé had mentioned taking a degree, he was saying something he merely wished were true.

"We'll probably never see you, once you start to work," said Pascal's mother, pouring Dédé's coffee.

The magistrate looked as if such great good luck was not to be expected. Abelarda, who had gone upstairs to make the beds, screamed from the head of the staircase that Dédé's room was full of smoke.

Abelarda moved slowly around the table carrying a plum tart, purple and gold, caramelized all over its surface, and a bowl of cream. Mme. Turbin glanced at the tart and shook her head no: M. Turbin was not allowed sugar now, and she had got out of the habit of eating desserts. It seemed unfair to tempt him.

It was true, her husband said. She had even given up making sweets, on his account. He described her past achievements — her famous chocolate mousse with candied bitter orange peel, her celebrated pineapple flan.

"My semolina crown mold with apricot sauce," she said. "I must have given the recipe away a hundred times."

Mme. Chevallier-Crochet wondered if she could have a slice half the size of the wedge Abelarda had already prepared. Abelarda put down the bowl of cream and divided the wedge in half. The half piece was still too much; Abelarda said it could not be cut again without breaking into a mess of crumbs. M. Chevallier-Crochet said to his wife, "For God's sake, just take it and leave what you can't eat." Mme. Chevallier-Crochet replied that everything she said and did seemed to be wrong, she had better just sit here and say and do nothing. Abelarda, crooning encouragement, pushed onto her plate a fragment of pastry and one plum.

"No cream," she said, too late.

Mme. Brouet looked at the portrait of her husband's grandfather, then at her son, perhaps seeking a likeness. Sophie Chevallier-Crochet had seemed lively and intelligent at their history-of-art class. Mme. Brouet had never met the husband before, and was unlikely ever to lay eyes on him again. She accepted large portions of tart and cream, to set an example, in case the other two ladies had inhibited the men.

M. Turbin, after having made certain that no extra sugar had been stirred into the cream, took more cream than tart. His wife, watching him closely, sipped water over her empty plate. "It's only fruit," he said.

The magistrate helped himself to all the crumbs and fragments of burnt sugar on the dish. He rattled the spoon in the bowl of cream, scraping the sides; there was nearly none left. It was the fault of M. Chevallier-Crochet, who had gone on filling his plate, as though in a dream, until Abelarda moved the bowl away.

The guests finished drinking their coffee at half past four, and left at a quarter to five. When they had gone, Mme. Brouet lay down — not on a couch or a settee but on the living room floor. She stared at the ceiling and told Pascal to leave her alone. Abelarda, Dédé, and the magistrate were up in Dédé's room. Abelarda helped him pack. Late that night, the magistrate drove him to the Gare de l'Est.

Dédé came back to Paris about a year ago. He is said to be different now. He has a part-time job with a television polling service: every day he is given a list of telephone numbers in the Paris area and he calls them to see what people were watching the night before and which program they wish they had watched instead. His mother has bought him a one-room place overlooking Parc de Montsouris. The Brouets have never tried to get in touch with him or invited him to a meal. Dédé's Paris

— unknown, foreign almost — lies at an unmapped distance from Pascal's house.

One night, not long ago, when they all three were having dinner, Pascal said, "What if Dédé just came to the door?" He meant the front door, of course, but his parents glanced at the glass doors and the lamps reflected in the dark panes, so that night was screened from sight. Pascal imagined Dédé standing outside, watching and smiling, with that great mop of hair.

He is almost as tall as Dédé, now. Perhaps his father had not really taken notice of his height — it came about so gradually — but when Pascal got up to draw a curtain across the doors that night at dinner, his father looked at him as if he were suddenly setting a value on the kind of man he might become. It was a steady look, neither hot nor cold. For a moment Pascal said to himself, He will never fall asleep again. As for his mother, she sat smiling and dreaming, still hoping for some reason to start loving Dédé once more.

ROBERT STONE

"Helping" is one of the few short stories published by the novelist Robert Stone. Known for the intensity of his writing and the care with which he builds his characters' emotional motivation, Stone has here taken advantage of the story form's inherently limited focus. He says that "Helping" is "about the ways in which people need each other. The question at its center is whether we actually can come through for others when, in a disorderly world, it's sometimes hard for us to see clearly enough to help ourselves." Mark Helprin noted that "Helping" is a story in which "the writer's very power as a writer has lifted him beyond himself, and taken him above his story, to a striking truth." Born in Brooklyn, New York, Robert Stone lives in Connecticut.

Helping

ONE GRAY NOVEMBER DAY, Elliot went to Boston for the afternoon. The wet streets seemed cold and lonely. He sensed a broken promise in the city's elegance and verve. Old hopes tormented him like phantom limbs, but he did not drink. He had joined Alcoholics Anonymous fifteen months before.

Christmas came, childless, a festival of regret. His wife went to Mass and cooked a turkey. Sober, Elliot walked in the woods.

In January, blizzards swept down from the Arctic until the weather became too cold for snow. The Shawmut Valley grew quiet and crystalline. In the white silences, Elliot could hear the boards of his house contract and feel a shrinking in his bones. Each dusk, starveling deer came out of the wooded swamp behind the house to graze his orchard for whatever raccoons had uncovered and left behind. At night he lay beside his sleeping wife listening to the baying of dog packs running them down in the deep moon-shadowed snow.

Day in, day out, he was sober. At times it was almost stimulating. But he could not shake off the sensations he had felt in Boston. In his mind's eye he could see dead leaves rattling along brick gutters and savor that day's desperation. The brief outing had undermined him.

Sober, however, he remained, until the day a man named Blankenship came into his office at the state hospital for counseling. Blankenship had red hair, a brutal face, and a sneaking manner. He was a sponger and petty thief whom Elliot had seen a number of times before.

"I been having this dream," Blankenship announced loudly. His voice was not pleasant. His skin was unwholesome. Every time he got arrested the court sent him to the psychiatrists and the psychiatrists, who spoke little English, sent him to Elliot.

Blankenship had joined the Army after his first burglary but had never served east of the Rhine. After a few months in Wiesbaden, he had been discharged for reasons of unsuitability, but he told everyone he was a veteran of the Vietnam War. He went about in a tiger suit. Elliot had had enough of him.

"Dreams are boring," Elliot told him.

Blankenship was outraged. "Whaddaya mean?" he demanded.

During counseling sessions Elliot usually moved his chair into the middle of the room in order to seem accessible to his clients. Now he stayed securely behind his desk. He did not care to seem accessible to Blankenship. "What I said, Mr. Blankenship. Other people's dreams are boring. Didn't you ever hear that?"

"Boring?" Blankenship frowned. He seemed unable to imagine a meaning for the word.

Elliot picked up a pencil and set its point quivering on his desk-top blotter. He gazed into his client's slack-jawed face. The Blankenship family made their way through life as strolling litigants, and young Blankenship's specialty was slipping on ice cubes. Hauled off the pavement, he would hassle the doctors in Emergency for pain pills and hurry to a law clinic. The Blankenships had threatened suit against half the property owners in the southern part of the state. What they could not extort at law they stole. But even the Blankenship family had abandoned

Blankenship. His last visit to the hospital had been subsequent to an arrest for lifting a case of hot-dog rolls from Woolworth's. He lived in a Goodwill depository bin in Wyndham.

"Now I suppose you want to tell me your dream? Is that right, Mr. Blankenship?"

Blankenship looked left and right like a dog surrendering eye contact. "Don't you want to hear it?" he asked humbly.

Elliot was unmoved. "Tell me something, Blankenship. Was your dream about Vietnam?"

At the mention of the word "Vietnam," Blankenship customarily broke into a broad smile. Now he looked guilty and guarded. He shrugged. "Ya."

"How come you have dreams about that place, Blankenship? You were never there."

"Whaddaya mean?" Blankenship began to say, but Elliot cut him off.

"You were never there, my man. You never saw the goddamn place. You have no business dreaming about it! You better cut it out!"

He had raised his voice to the extent that the secretary outside his open door paused at her word processor.

"Lemme alone," Blankenship said fearfully. "Some doctor you are."

"It's all right," Elliot assured him. "I'm not a doctor."

"Everybody's on my case," Blankenship said. His moods were volatile. He began to weep.

Elliot watched the tears roll down Blankenship's chapped, pitted cheeks. He cleared his throat. "Look, fella . . ." he began. He felt at a loss. He felt like telling Blankenship that things were tough all over.

Blankenship sniffed and telescoped his neck and after a moment looked at Elliot. His look was disconcertingly trustful; he was used to being counseled.

"Really, you know, it's ridiculous for you to tell me your problems have to do with Nam. You were never over there. It was me over there, Blankenship. Not you."

Blankenship leaned forward and put his forehead on his knees.

"Your troubles have to do with here and now," Elliot told his client. "Fantasies aren't helpful."

His voice sounded overripe and hypocritical in his own ears. What a dreadful business, he thought. What an awful job this is. Anger was driving him crazy.

Blankenship straightened up and spoke through his tears. "This dream . . ." he said. "I'm scared."

Elliot felt ready to endure a great deal in order not to hear Blankenship's dream.

"I'm not the one you see about that," he said. In the end he knew his duty. He sighed. "O.K. All right. Tell me about it."

"Yeah?" Blankenship asked with leaden sarcasm. "Yeah? You think dreams are friggin' boring!"

"No, no," Elliot said. He offered Blankenship a tissue and Blankenship took one. "That was sort of off the top of my head. I didn't really mean it."

Blankenship fixed his eyes on dreaming distance. "There's a feeling that goes with it. With the dream." Then he shook his head in revulsion and looked at Elliot as though he had only just awakened. "So what do you think? You think it's boring?"

"Of course not," Elliot said. "A physical feeling?"

"Ya. It's like I'm floating in rubber."

He watched Elliot stealthily, aware of quickened attention. Elliot had caught dengue in Vietnam and during his weeks of delirium had felt vaguely as though he were floating in rubber.

"What are you seeing in this dream?"

Blankenship only shook his head. Elliot suffered a brief but intense attack of rage.

"Hey, Blankenship," he said equably, "here I am, man. You can see I'm listening."

"What I saw was black," Blankenship said. He spoke in an odd tremolo. His behavior was quite different from anything Elliot had come to expect from him.

"Black? What was it?"

"Smoke. The sky maybe."

"The sky?" Elliot asked.

"It was all black. I was scared."

In a waking dream of his own, Elliot felt the muscles on his neck distend. He was looking up at a sky that was black, filled with smoke-swollen clouds, lit with fires, damped with blood and rain.

"What were you scared of?" he asked Blankenship.

"I don't know," Blankenship said.

Elliot could not drive the black sky from his inward eye. It was as though Blankenship's dream had infected his own mind.

"You don't know? You don't know what you were scared of?"

Blankenship's posture was rigid. Elliot, who knew the aspect of true fear, recognized it there in front of him.

"The Nam," Blankenship said.

"You're not even old enough," Elliot told him.

Blankenship sat trembling with joined palms between his thighs. His face was flushed and not in the least ennobled by pain. He had trouble with alcohol and drugs. He had trouble with everything.

"So wherever your black sky is, it isn't Vietnam."

Things were so unfair, Elliot thought. It was unfair of Blankenship to appropriate the condition of a Vietnam veteran. The trauma inducing his post-traumatic stress had been nothing more serious than his own birth, a routine procedure. Now, in addition to the poverty, anxiety, and confusion that would always be his life's lot, he had been visited with irony. It was all arbitrary and some people simply got elected. Everyone knew that who had been where Blankenship had not.

"Because, I assure you, Mr. Blankenship, you were never there."

"Whaddaya mean?" Blankenship asked.

When Blankenship was gone Elliot leafed through his file and saw that the psychiatrists had passed him upstairs without recording a diagnosis. Disproportionately angry, he went out to the secretary's desk.

"Nobody wrote up that last patient," he said. "I'm not supposed to see people without a diagnosis. The shrinks are just passing the buck."

The secretary was a tall, solemn redhead with prominent front teeth and a slight speech disorder. "Dr. Sayyid will have kittens if he hears you call him a shrink, Chas. He's already complained. He hates being called a shrink."

"Then he came to the wrong country," Elliot said. "He can go back to his own."

The woman giggled. "He *is* the doctor, Chas."

"Hates being called a shrink!" He threw the file on the secretary's table and stormed back toward his office. "That fucking little zip couldn't give you a decent haircut. He's a prescription clerk."

The secretary looked about her guiltily and shook her head. She was used to him.

Elliot succeeded in calming himself down after a while, but the image of the black sky remained with him. At first he thought he would be able to simply shrug the whole thing off. After a few minutes, he picked up his phone and dialed Blankenship's probation officer.

"The Vietnam thing is all he has," the probation officer explained. "I guess he picked it up around."

"His descriptions are vivid," Elliot said.

"You mean they sound authentic?"

"I mean he had me going today. He was ringing my bells."

"Good for Blanky. Think he believes it himself?"

"Yes," Elliot said. "He believes it himself now."

Elliot told the probation officer about Blankenship's current arrest, which was for showering illegally at midnight in the Wyndham Regional High School. He asked what probation knew about Blankenship's present relationship with his family.

"You kiddin'?" the P.O. asked. "They're all locked down. The whole family's inside. The old man's in Bridgewater. Little Donny's in San Quentin or somewhere. Their dog's in the pound."

Elliot had lunch alone in the hospital staff cafeteria. On the far side of the double-glazed windows, the day was darkening as an expected snowstorm gathered. Along Route 7, ancient elms stood frozen against the gray sky. When he had finished his sandwich and coffee, he sat staring out at the winter afternoon. His anger had given way to an insistent anxiety.

On the way back to his office, he stopped at the hospital gift shop for a copy of *Sports Illustrated* and a candy bar. When he was inside again, he closed the door and put his feet up. It was Friday and he had no appointments for the remainder of the day, nothing to do but write a few letters and read the office mail.

Elliot's cubicle in the social services department was window-less and lined with bookshelves. When he found himself unable to concentrate on the magazine and without any heart for his paperwork, he ran his eye over the row of books beside his chair. There were volumes by Heinrich Muller and Carlos Cas-teneda, Jones's life of Freud, and *The Golden Bough.* The books aroused a revulsion in Elliot. Their present uselessness repelled him.

Over and over again, detail by detail, he tried to recall his conversation with Blankenship.

"You were never there," he heard himself explaining. He was trying to get the whole incident straightened out after the fact. Something was wrong. Dread crept over him like a paralysis. He ate his candy bar without tasting it. He knew that the craving for sweets was itself a bad sign.

Blankenship had misappropriated someone else's dream and made it his own. It made no difference whether you had been there, after all. The dreams had crossed the ocean. They were in the air.

He took his glasses off and put them on his desk and sat with his arms folded, looking into the well of light from his desk lamp. There seemed to be nothing but whirl inside him. Unwelcome things came and went in his mind's eye. His heart beat faster. He could not control the headlong promiscuity of his thoughts.

It was possible to imagine larval dreams traveling in sus-pended animation undetectable in a host brain. They could be divided and regenerate like flatworms, hide in seams and bed-ding, in war stories, laughter, snapshots. They could rot your socks and turn your memory into a black-and-green blister. Green for the hills, black for the sky above. At daybreak they hung themselves up in rows like bats. At dusk they went out to look for dreamers.

Elliot put his jacket on and went into the outer office, where the secretary sat frowning into the measured sound and light of her machine. She must enjoy its sleekness and order, he thought. She was divorced. Four red-headed kids between ten and seventeen lived with her in an unpainted house across from Stop & Shop. Elliot liked her and had come to find her attrac-tive. He managed a smile for her.

"Ethel, I think I'm going to pack it in," he declared. It seemed awkward to be leaving early without a reason.

"Jack wants to talk to you before you go, Chas."

Elliot looked at her blankly.

Then his colleague, Jack Sprague, having heard his voice, called from the adjoining cubicle. "Chas, what about Sunday's games? Shall I call you with the spread?"

"I don't know," Elliot said. "I'll phone you tomorrow."

"This is a big decision for him," Jack Sprague told the secretary. "He might lose twenty-five bucks."

At present, Elliot drew a slightly higher salary than Jack Sprague, although Jack had a Ph.D. and Elliot was simply an M.S.W. Different branches of the state government employed them.

"Twenty-five bucks," said the woman. "If you guys have no better use for twenty-five bucks, give it to me."

"Where are you off to, by the way?" Sprague asked.

Elliot began to answer, but for a moment no reply occurred to him. He shrugged. "I have to get back," he finally stammered. "I promised Grace."

"Was that Blankenship I saw leaving?"

Elliot nodded.

"It's February," Jack said. "How come he's not in Florida?"

"I don't know," Elliot said. He put on his coat and walked to the door. "I'll see you."

"Have a nice weekend," the secretary said. She and Sprague looked after him indulgently as he walked toward the main corridor.

"Are Chas and Grace going out on the town?" she said to Sprague. "What do you think?"

"That would be the day," Sprague said. "Tomorrow he'll come back over here and read all day. He spends every weekend holed up in this goddamn office while she does something or other at the church." He shook his head. "Every night he's at A.A. and she's home alone."

Ethel savored her overbite. "Jack," she said teasingly, "are you thinking what I think you're thinking? Shame on you."

"I'm thinking I'm glad I'm not him, that's what I'm thinking. That's as much as I'll say."

"Yeah, well, I don't care," Ethel said. "Two salaries and no kids, that's the way to go, boy."

Elliot went out through the automatic doors of the emergency bay and the cold closed over him. He walked across the hospital parking lot with his eyes on the pavement, his hands thrust deep in his overcoat pockets, skirting patches of shattered ice. There was no wind, but the motionless air stung; the metal frames of his glasses burned his skin. Curlicues of mud-brown ice coated the soiled snowbanks along the street. Although it was still afternoon, the street lights had come on.

The lock on his car door had frozen and he had to breathe on the keyhole to fit the key. When the engine turned over, Jussi Björling's recording of the Handel Largo filled the car interior. He snapped it off at once.

Halted at the first stoplight, he began to feel the want of a destination. The fear and impulse to flight that had got him out of the office faded, and he had no desire to go home. He was troubled by a peculiar impatience that might have been with time itself. It was as though he were waiting for something. The sensation made him feel anxious; it was unfamiliar but not altogether unpleasant. When the light changed he drove on, past the Gulf station and the firehouse and between the greens of Ilford Common. At the far end of the common he swung into the parking lot of the Packard Conway Library and stopped with the engine running. What he was experiencing, he thought, was the principle of possibility.

He turned off the engine and went out again into the cold. Behind the leaded library windows he could see the librarian pouring coffee in her tiny private office. The librarian was a Quaker of socialist principles named Candace Music, who was Elliot's cousin.

The Conway Library was all dark wood and etched mirrors, a Gothic saloon. Years before, out of work and booze-whipped, Elliot had gone to hide there. Because Candace was a classicist's widow and knew some Greek, she was one of the few people in the valley with whom Elliot had cared to speak in those days. Eventually, it had seemed to him that all their conversations tended toward Vietnam, so he had gone less and less often.

Elliot was the only Vietnam veteran Candace knew well enough to chat with, and he had come to suspect that he was being probed for the edification of the East Ilford Friends Meeting. At that time he had still pretended to talk easily about his war and had prepared little discourses and picaresque anecdotes to recite on demand. Earnest seekers like Candace had caused him great secret distress.

Candace came out of her office to find him at the checkout desk. He watched her brow furrow with concern as she composed a smile. "Chas, what a surprise. You haven't been in for an age."

"Sure I have, Candace. I went to all the Wednesday films last fall. I work just across the road."

"I know, dear," Candace said. "I always seem to miss you."

A cozy fire burned in the hearth, an antique brass clock ticked along on the marble mantel above it. On a couch near the fireplace an old man sat upright, his mouth open, asleep among half a dozen soiled plastic bags. Two teenage girls whispered over their homework at a table under the largest window.

"Now that I'm here," he said, laughing, "I can't remember what I came to get."

"Stay and get warm," Candace told him. "Got a minute? Have a cup of coffee."

Elliot had nothing but time, but he quickly realized that he did not want to stay and pass it with Candace. He had no clear idea of why he had come to the library. Standing at the checkout desk, he accepted coffee. She attended him with an air of benign supervision, as though he were a Chinese peasant and she a medical missionary, like her father. Candace was tall and plain, more handsome in her middle sixties than she had ever been.

"Why don't we sit down?"

He allowed her to gentle him into a chair by the fire. They made a threesome with the sleeping old man.

"Have you given up translating, Chas? I hope not."

"Not at all," he said. Together they had once rendered a few fragments of Sophocles into verse. She was good at clever rhymes.

"You come in so rarely, Chas. Ted's books go to waste."

After her husband's death, Candace had donated his books to the Conway, where they reposed in a reading room inscribed to his memory, untouched among foreign-language volumes, local genealogies, and books in large type for the elderly.

"I have a study in the barn," he told Candace. "I work there. When I have time." The lie was absurd, but he felt the need of it.

"And you're working with Vietnam veterans," Candace declared.

"Supposedly," Elliot said. He was growing impatient with her nodding solicitude.

"Actually," he said, "I came in for the new Oxford *Classical World*. I thought you'd get it for the library and I could have a look before I spent my hard-earned cash."

Candace beamed. "You've come to the right place, Chas, I'm happy to say." He thought she looked disproportionately happy. "I have it."

"Good," Elliot said, standing. "I'll just take it, then. I can't really stay."

Candace took his cup and saucer and stood as he did. When the library telephone rang, she ignored it, reluctant to let him go. "How's Grace?" she asked.

"Fine," Elliot said. "Grace is well."

At the third ring she went to the desk. When her back was turned, he hesitated for a moment and then went outside.

The gray afternoon had softened into night, and it was snowing. The falling snow whirled like a furious mist in the headlight beams on Route 7 and settled implacably on Elliot's cheeks and eyelids. His heart, for no good reason, leaped up in childlike expectation. He had run away from a dream and encountered possibility. He felt in possession of a promise. He began to walk toward the roadside lights.

Only gradually did he begin to understand what had brought him there and what the happy anticipation was that fluttered in his breast. Drinking, he had started his evening from the Conway Library. He would arrive hung over in the early afternoon to browse and read. When the old pain rolled in with dusk, he would walk down to the Midway Tavern for a remedy. Standing in the snow outside the library, he realized that he had contrived to promise himself a drink.

Ahead, through the storm, he could see the beer signs in the Midway's window warm and welcoming. Snowflakes spun around his head like an excitement.

Outside the Midway's package store, he paused with his hand on the doorknob. There was an old man behind the counter whom Elliot remembered from his drinking days. When he was inside, he realized that the old man neither knew nor cared who he was. The package store was thick with dust; it was on the counter, the shelves, the bottles themselves. The old counterman looked dusty. Elliot bought a bottle of King William Scotch and put it in the inside pocket of his overcoat.

Passing the windows of the Midway Tavern, Elliot could see the ranks of bottles aglow behind the bar. The place was crowded with men leaving the afternoon shifts at the shoe and felt factories. No one turned to note him when he passed inside. There was a single stool vacant at the bar and he took it. His heart beat faster. Bruce Springsteen was on the jukebox.

The bartender was a club fighter from Pittsfield called Jackie G., with whom Elliot had often gossiped. Jackie G. greeted him as though he had been in the previous evening. "Say, babe?"

"How do," Elliot said.

A couple of men at the bar eyed his shirt and tie. Confronted with the bartender, he felt impelled to explain his presence. "Just thought I'd stop by," he told Jackie G. "Just thought I'd have one. Saw the light. The snow . . . " He chuckled expansively.

"Good move," the bartender said. "Scotch?"

"Double," Elliot said.

When he shoved two dollars forward along the bar, Jackie G. pushed one of the bills back to him. "Happy hour, babe."

"Ah," Elliot said. He watched Jackie pour the double. "Not a moment too soon."

For five minutes or so, Elliot sat in his car in the barn with the engine running and his Handel tape on full volume. He had driven over from East Ilford in a baroque ecstasy, swinging and swaying and singing along. When the tape ended, he turned off the engine and poured some Scotch into an apple juice container to store providentially beneath the car seat. Then he took the tape and the Scotch into the house with him. He was lying on the sofa in the dark living room, listening to the Largo, when he heard his wife's car in the driveway. By the time Grace had made her way up the icy back-porch steps, he was able to hide the Scotch and rinse his glass clean in the kitchen sink. The drinking life, he thought, was lived moment by moment.

Soon she was in the tiny cloakroom struggling off with her overcoat. In the process she knocked over a cross-country ski, which stood propped against the cloakroom wall. It had been more than a year since Elliot had used the skis.

She came into the kitchen and sat down at the table to take off her boots. Her lean, freckled face was flushed with the cold, but her eyes looked weary. "I wish you'd put those skis down in the barn," she told him. "You never use them."

"I always like to think," Elliot said, "that I'll start the morning off skiing."

"Well, you never do," she said. "How long have you been home?"

"Practically just walked in," he said. Her pointing out that he no longer skied in the morning enraged him. "I stopped at the Conway Library to get the new Oxford *Classical World*. Candace ordered it."

Her look grew troubled. She had caught something in his voice. With dread and bitter satisfaction, Elliot watched his wife detect the smell of whiskey.

"Oh God," she said. "I don't believe it."

Let's get it over with, he thought. Let's have the song and dance.

She sat up straight in her chair and looked at him in fear.

"Oh, Chas," she said, "how could you?"

For a moment he was tempted to try to explain it all.

"The fact is," Elliot told his wife, "I hate people who start the day cross-country skiing."

She shook her head in denial and leaned her forehead on her palm and cried.

He looked into the kitchen window and saw his own distorted image. "The fact is I think I'll start tomorrow morning by stringing head-high razor wire across Anderson's trail."

The Andersons were the Elliots' nearest neighbors. Loyall Anderson was a full professor of government at the state uni-

versity, thirty miles away. Anderson and his wife were blond
and both of them were over six feet tall. They had two blond
children, who qualified for the gifted class in the local school
but attended regular classes in token of the Andersons' opposition to elitism.

"Sure," Elliot said. "Stringing wire's good exercise. It's life-
affirming in its own way."

The Andersons started each and every day with a brisk morning glide along a trail that they partly maintained. They skied
well and presented a pleasing, wholesome sight. If, in the course
of their adventure, they encountered a snowmobile, Darlene
Anderson would affect to choke and cough, indicating her dis-
pleasure. If the snowmobile approached them from behind and
the trail was narrow, the Andersons would decline to let it pass,
asserting their statutory right-of-way.

"I don't want to hear your violent fantasies," Grace said.

Elliot was picturing razor wire, the Army kind. He was picturing the decapitated Andersons, their blood and jaunty ski caps
bright on the white trail. He was picturing their severed heads,
their earnest blue eyes and large white teeth reflecting the vir-
ginal morning snow. Although Elliot hated snowmobiles, he
hated the Andersons far more.

He looked at his wife and saw that she had stopped crying.
Her long, elegant face was rigid and lipless.

"Know what I mean? One string at Mommy and Daddy level
for Loyall and Darlene. And a bitty wee string at kiddie level
for Skippy and Samantha, those cunning little whizzes."

"Stop it," she said to him.

"Sorry," Elliot told her.

Stiff with shame, he went and took his bottle out of the cabinet
into which he had thrust it and poured a drink. He was aware
of her eyes on him. As he drank, a fragment from old Music's
translation of *Medea* came into his mind. "Old friend, I have to
weep. The gods and I went mad together and made things as
they are." It was such a waste; eighteen months of struggle
thrown away. But there was no way to get the stuff back in the
bottle.

"I'm very sorry," he said. "You know I'm very sorry, don't
you, Grace?"

The delectable Handel arias spun on in the next room.

"You must stop," she said. "You must make yourself stop before it takes over."

"It's out of my hands," Elliot said. He showed her his empty hands. "It's beyond me."

"You'll lose your job, Chas." She stood up at the table and leaned on it, staring wide-eyed at him. Drunk as he was, the panic in her voice frightened him. "You'll end up in jail again."

"One engages," Elliot said, "and then one sees."

"How can you have done it?" she demanded. "You promised me."

"First the promises," Elliot said, "and then the rest."

"Last time was supposed to be the last time," she said.

"Yes," he said, "I remember."

"I can't stand it," she said. "You reduce me to hysterics." She wrung her hands for him to see. "See? Here I am, I'm in hysterics."

"What can I say?" Elliot asked. He went to the bottle and refilled his glass. "Maybe you shouldn't watch."

"You want me to be forbearing, Chas? I'm not going to be."

"The last thing I want," Elliot said, "is an argument."

"I'll give you a fucking argument. You didn't have to drink. All you had to do was come home."

"That must have been the problem," he said.

Then he ducked, alert at the last possible second to the missile that came for him at hairline level. Covering up, he heard the shattering of glass, and a fine rain of crystals enveloped him. She had sailed the sugar bowl at him; it had smashed against the wall above his head and there was sugar and glass in his hair.

"You bastard!" she screamed. "You are undermining me!"

"You ought not to throw things at me," Elliot said. "I don't throw things at you."

He left her frozen into her follow-through and went into the living room to turn the music off. When he returned she was leaning back against the wall, rubbing her right elbow with her left hand. Her eyes were bright. She had picked up one of her boots from the middle of the kitchen floor and stood holding it.

"What the hell do you mean, that must have been the problem?"

He set his glass on the edge of the sink with an unsteady hand

and turned to her. "What do I mean? I mean that most of the time I'm putting one foot in front of the other like a good soldier and I'm out of it from the neck up. But there are times when I don't think I will ever be dead enough — or dead long enough — to get the taste of this life off my teeth. That's what I mean!"

She looked at him dry-eyed. "Poor fella," she said.

"What you have to understand, Grace, is that this drink I'm having" — he raised the glass toward her in a gesture of salute — "is the only worthwhile thing I've done in the last year and a half. It's the only thing in my life that means jack shit, the closest thing to satisfaction I've had. Now how can you begrudge me that? It's the best I'm capable of."

"You'll go too far," she said to him. "You'll see."

"What's that, Grace? A threat to walk?" He was grinding his teeth. "Don't make me laugh. You, walk? You, the friend of the unfortunate?"

"Don't you hit me," she said when she looked at his face. "Don't you dare."

"You, the Christian Queen of Calvary, walk? Why, I don't believe that for a minute."

She ran a hand through her hair and bit her lip. "No, we stay," she said. Anger and distraction made her look young. Her cheeks blazed rosy against the general pallor of her skin. "In my family we stay until the fella dies. That's the tradition. We stay and pour it for them and they die."

He put his drink down and shook his head.

"I thought we'd come through," Grace said. "I was sure."

"No," Elliot said. "Not altogether."

They stood in silence for a minute. Elliot sat down at the oilcloth-covered table. Grace walked around it and poured herself a whiskey.

"You are undermining me, Chas. You are making things impossible for me and I just don't know." She drank and winced. "I'm not going to stay through another drunk. I'm telling you right now. I haven't got it in me. I'll die."

He did not want to look at her. He watched the flakes settle against the glass of the kitchen door. "Do what you feel the need of," he said.

"I just can't take it," she said. Her voice was not scolding but measured and reasonable. "It's February. And I went to court this morning and lost Vopotik."

Once again, he thought, my troubles are going to be obviated by those of the deserving poor. He said, "Which one was that?"

"Don't you remember them? The three-year-old with the broken fingers?"

He shrugged. Grace sipped her whiskey.

"I told you. I said I had a three-year-old with broken fingers, and you said, 'Maybe he owed somebody money.' "

"Yes," he said, "I remember now."

"You ought to see the Vopotiks, Chas. The woman is young and obese. She's so young that for a while I thought I could get to her as a juvenile. The guy is a biker. They believe the kid came from another planet to control their lives. They believe this literally, both of them."

"You shouldn't get involved that way," Elliot said. "You should leave it to the caseworkers."

"They scared their first caseworker all the way to California. They were following me to work."

"You didn't tell me."

"Are you kidding?" she asked. "Of course I didn't." To Elliot's surprise, his wife poured herself a second whiskey. "You know how they address the child? As 'dude.' She says to it, 'Hey, dude.' " Grace shuddered with loathing. "You can't imagine! The woman munching Twinkies. The kid smelling of shit. They're high morning, noon, and night, but you can't get anybody for that these days."

"People must really hate it," Elliot said, "when somebody tells them they're not treating their kids right."

"They definitely don't want to hear it," Grace said. "You're right." She sat stirring her drink, frowning into the glass. "The Vopotik child will die, I think."

"Surely not," Elliot said.

"This one I think will die," Grace said. She took a deep breath and puffed out her cheeks and looked at him forlornly. "The situation's extreme. Of course, sometimes you wonder whether it makes any difference. That's the big question, isn't it?"

"I would think," Elliot said, "that would be the one question you didn't ask."

"But you do," she said. "You wonder: Ought they to live at all? To continue the cycle?" She put a hand to her hair and shook her head as if in confusion. "Some of these folks, my God, the poor things cannot put Wednesday on top of Tuesday to save their lives."

"It's a trick," Elliot agreed, "a lot of them can't manage."

"And kids are small, they're handy and underfoot. They make noise. They can't hurt you back."

"I suppose child abuse is something people can do together," Elliot said.

"Some kids are obnoxious. No question about it."

"I wouldn't know," Elliot said.

"Maybe you should stop complaining. Maybe you're better off. Maybe your kids are better off unborn."

"Better off or not," Elliot said, "it looks like they'll stay that way."

"I mean our kids, of course," Grace said. "I'm not blaming you, understand? It's just that here we are with you drunk again and me losing Vopotik, so I thought why not get into the big unaskable questions." She got up and folded her arms and began to pace up and down the kitchen. "Oh," she said when her eye fell upon the bottle, "that's good stuff, Chas. You won't mind if I have another? I'll leave you enough to get loaded on."

Elliot watched her pour. So much pain, he thought; such anger and confusion. He was tired of pain, anger, and confusion; they were what had got him in trouble that very morning.

The liquor seemed to be giving him a perverse lucidity when all he now required was oblivion. His rage, especially, was intact in its salting of alcohol. Its contours were palpable and bleeding at the borders. Booze was good for rage. Booze could keep it burning through the darkest night.

"What happened in court?" he asked his wife.

She was leaning on one arm against the wall, her long, strong body flexed at the hip. Holding her glass, she stared angrily toward the invisible fields outside. "I lost the child," she said.

Elliot thought that a peculiar way of putting it. He said nothing.

"The court convened in an atmosphere of high hilarity. It may be Hate Month around here but it was buddy-buddy over at Ilford Courthouse. The room was full of bikers and bikers' lawyers. A colorful crowd. There was a lot of bonding." She drank and shivered. "They didn't think too well of me. They don't think too well of broads as lawyers. Neither does the judge. The judge has the common touch. He's one of the boys."

"Which judge?" Elliot asked.

"Buckley. A man of about sixty. Know him? Lots of veins on his nose?"

Elliot shrugged.

"I thought I had done my homework," Grace told him. "But suddenly I had nothing but paper. No witnesses. It was Margolis at Valley Hospital who spotted the radiator burns. He called us in the first place. Suddenly he's got to keep his reservation for a campsite in St. John. So Buckley threw his deposition out." She began to chew on a fingernail. "The caseworkers have vanished — one's in L.A., the other's in Nepal. I went in there and got run over. I lost the child."

"It happens all the time," Elliot said. "Doesn't it?"

"This one shouldn't have been lost, Chas. These people aren't simply confused. They're weird. They stink."

"You go messing into anybody's life," Elliot said, "that's what you'll find."

"If the child stays in that house," she said, "he's going to die."

"You did your best," he told his wife. "Forget it."

She pushed the bottle away. She was holding a water glass that was almost a third full of whiskey.

"That's what the commissioner said."

Elliot was thinking of how she must have looked in court to the cherry-faced judge and the bikers and their lawyers. Like the schoolteachers who had tormented their childhoods, earnest and tight-assed, humorless and self-righteous. It was not surprising that things had gone against her.

He walked over to the window and faced his reflection again. "Your optimism always surprises me."

"My optimism? Where I grew up our principal cultural expression was the funeral. Whatever keeps me going, it isn't optimism."

"No?" he asked. "What is it?"

"I forget," she said.

"Maybe it's your religious perspective. Your sense of the divine plan."

She sighed in exasperation. "Look, I don't think I want to fight anymore. I'm sorry I threw the sugar at you. I'm not your keeper. Pick on someone your own size."

"Sometimes," Elliot said, "I try to imagine what it's like to believe that the sky is full of care and concern."

"You want to take everything from me, do you?" She stood leaning against the back of her chair. "That you can't take. It's the only part of my life you can't mess up."

He was thinking that if it had not been for her he might not have survived. There could be no forgiveness for that. "Your life? You've got all this piety strung out between Monadnock and Central America. And look at yourself. Look at your life."

"Yes," she said, "look at it."

"You should have been a nun. You don't know how to live."

"I know that," she said. "That's why I stopped doing counseling. Because I'd rather talk the law than life." She turned to him. "You got everything I had, Chas. What's left I absolutely require."

"I swear I would rather be a drunk," Elliot said, "than force myself to believe such trivial horseshit."

"Well, you're going to have to do it without a straight man," she said, "because this time I'm not going to be here for you. Believe it or not."

"I don't believe it," Elliot said. "Not my Grace."

"You're really good at this," she told him. "You make me feel ashamed of my own name."

"I love your name," he said.

The telephone rang. They let it ring three times, and then Elliot went over and answered it.

"Hey, who's that?" a good-humored voice on the phone demanded.

Elliot recited their phone number.

"Hey, I want to talk to your woman, man. Put her on."

"I'll give her a message," Elliot said.

"You put your woman on, man. Run and get her."

Elliot looked at the receiver. He shook his head. "Mr. Vopotik?"

"Never you fuckin' mind, man. I don't want to talk to you. I want to talk to the skinny bitch."

Elliot hung up.

"Is it him?" she asked.

"I guess so."

They waited for the phone to ring again and it shortly did.

"I'll talk to him," Grace said. But Elliot already had the phone.

"Who are you, asshole?" the voice inquired. "What's your fuckin' name, man?"

"Elliot," Elliot said.

"Hey, don't hang up on me, Elliot. I won't put up with that. I told you go get that skinny bitch, man. You go do it."

There were sounds of festivity in the background on the other end of the line — a stereo and drunken voices.

"Hey," the voice declared. "Hey, don't keep me waiting, man."

"What do you want to say to her?" Elliot asked.

"That's none of your fucking business, fool. Do what I told you."

"My wife is resting," Elliot said. "I'm taking her calls."

He was answered by a shout of rage. He put the phone aside for a moment and finished his glass of whiskey. When he picked it up again the man on the line was screaming at him. "That bitch tried to break up my family, man! She almost got away with it. You know what kind of pain my wife went through?"

"What kind?" Elliot asked.

For a few seconds he heard only the noise of the party. "Hey, you're not drunk, are you, fella?"

"Certainly not," Elliot insisted.

"You tell that skinny bitch she's gonna pay for what she did to my family, man. You tell her she can run but she can't hide. I don't care where you go — California, anywhere — I'll get to you."

"Now that I have you on the phone," Elliot said, "I'd like to ask you a couple of questions. Promise you won't get mad?"

"Stop it!" Grace said to him. She tried to wrench the phone from his grasp, but he clutched it to his chest.

"Do you keep a journal?" Elliot asked the man on the phone. "What's your hat size?"

"Maybe you think I can't get to you," the man said. "But I can get to you, man. I don't care who you are, I'll get to you. The brothers will get to you."

"Well, there's no need to go to California. You know where we live."

"For God's sake," Grace said.

"Fuckin' right," the man on the telephone said. "Fuckin' right I know."

"Come on over," Elliot said.

"How's that?" the man on the phone asked.

"I said come on over. We'll talk about space travel. Comets and stuff. We'll talk astral projection. The moons of Jupiter."

"You're making a mistake, fucker."

"Come on over," Elliot insisted. "Bring your fat wife and your beat-up kid. Don't be embarrassed if your head's a little small."

The telephone was full of music and shouting. Elliot held it away from his ear.

"Good work," Grace said to him when he had replaced the receiver.

"I hope he comes," Elliot said. "I'll pop him."

He went carefully down the cellar stairs, switched on the overhead light, and began searching among the spiderwebbed shadows and fouled fishing line for his shotgun. It took him fifteen minutes to find it and his cleaning case. While he was still downstairs, he heard the telephone ring again and his wife answer it. He came upstairs and spread his shooting gear across the kitchen table. "Was that him?"

She nodded wearily. "He called back to play us the chain saw."

"I've heard that melody before," Elliot said.

He assembled his cleaning rod and swabbed out the shotgun barrel. Grace watched him, a hand to her forehead. "God," she said. "What have I done? I'm so drunk."

"Most of the time," Elliot said, sighting down the barrel, "I'm helpless in the face of human misery. Tonight I'm ready to reach out."

"I'm finished," Grace said. "I'm through, Chas. I mean it."

Elliot rammed three red shells into the shotgun and pumped one forward into the breech with a satisfying report. "Me, I'm

ready for some radical problem solving. I'm going to spray that
no-neck Slovak all over the yard."

"He isn't a Slovak," Grace said. She stood in the middle of the
kitchen with her eyes closed. Her face was chalk white.

"What do you mean?" Elliot demanded. "Certainly he's a Slovak."

"No he's not," Grace said.

"Fuck him anyway. I don't care what he is. I'll grease his ass."

He took a handful of deer shells from the box and stuffed
them in his jacket pockets.

"I'm not going to stay with you. Chas. Do you understand
me?"

Elliot walked to the window and peered out at his driveway.
"He won't be alone. They travel in packs."

"For God's sake!" Grace cried, and in the next instant bolted
for the downstairs bathroom. Elliot went out, turned off the
porch light and switched on a spotlight over the barn door. Back
inside, he could hear Grace in the toilet being sick. He turned
off the light in the kitchen.

He was still standing by the window when she came up behind
him. It seemed strange and fateful to be standing in the dark
near her, holding the shotgun. He felt ready for anything.

"I can't leave you alone down here drunk with a loaded shotgun," she said. "How can I?"

"Go upstairs," he said.

"If I went upstairs it would mean I didn't care what happened. Do you understand? If I go it means I don't care anymore. Understand?"

"Stop asking me if I understand," Elliot said. "I understand
fine."

"I can't think," she said in a sick voice. "Maybe I don't care.
I don't know. I'm going upstairs."

"Good," Elliot said.

When she was upstairs, Elliot took his shotgun and the whiskey
into the dark living room and sat down in an armchair beside
one of the lace-curtained windows. The powerful barn light
illuminated the length of his driveway and the whole of the back
yard. From the window at which he sat, he commanded a view

of several miles in the direction of East Ilford. The two-lane blacktop road that ran there was the only one along which an enemy could pass.

He drank and watched the snow, toying with the safety of his 12-gauge Remington. He felt neither anxious nor angry now but only impatient to be done with whatever the night would bring. Drunkenness and the silent rhythm of the falling snow combined to make him feel outside of time and syntax.

Sitting in the dark room, he found himself confronting Blankenship's dream. He saw the bunkers and wire of some long-lost perimeter. The rank smell of night came back to him, the dread evening and quick dusk, the mysteries of outer darkness: fear, combat, and death. Enervated by liquor, he began to cry. Elliot was sympathetic with other people's tears but ashamed of his own. He thought of his own tears as childish and excremental. He stifled whatever it was that had started them.

Now his whiskey tasted thin as water. Beyond the lightly frosted glass, illuminated snowflakes spun and settled sleepily on weighted pine boughs. He had found a life beyond the war after all, but in it he was still sitting in darkness, armed, enraged, waiting.

His eyes grew heavy as the snow came down. He felt as though he could be drawn up into the storm and he began to imagine that. He imagined his life with all its artifacts and appetites easing up the spout into white oblivion, everything obviated and foreclosed. He thought maybe he could go for that.

When he awakened, his left hand had gone numb against the trigger guard of his shotgun. The living room was full of pale, delicate light. He looked outside and saw that the storm was done with and the sky radiant and cloudless. The sun was still below the horizon.

Slowly Elliot got to his feet. The throbbing poison in his limbs served to remind him of the state of things. He finished the glass of whiskey on the windowsill beside his easy chair. Then he went to the hall closet to get a ski jacket, shouldered his shotgun, and went outside.

There were two cleared acres behind his house; beyond them a trail descended into a hollow of pine forest and frozen swamp. Across the hollow, white pastures stretched to the ridge line, lambent under the lightening sky. A line of skeletal elms weighted with snow marked the course of frozen Shawmut Brook.

He found a pair of ski goggles in a jacket pocket and put them on and set out toward the tree line, gripping the shotgun, step by careful step in the knee-deep snow. Two raucous crows wheeled high overhead, their cries exploding the morning's silence. When the sun came over the ridge, he stood where he was and took in a deep breath. The risen sun warmed his face and he closed his eyes. It was windless and very cold.

Only after he had stood there for a while did he realize how tired he had become. The weight of the gun taxed him. It seemed infinitely wearying to contemplate another single step in the snow. He opened his eyes and closed them again. With sunup the world had gone blazing blue and white, and even with his tinted goggles its whiteness dazzled him and made his head ache. Behind his eyes, the hypnagogic patterns formed a monsoon-heavy tropical sky. He yawned. More than anything, he wanted to lie down in the soft, pure snow. If he could do that, he was certain he could go to sleep at once.

He stood in the middle of the field and listened to the crows. Fear, anger, and sleep were the three primary conditions of life. He had learned that over there. Once he had thought fear the worst, but he had learned that the worst was anger. Nothing could fix it; neither alcohol nor medicine. It was a worm. It left him no peace. Sleep was the best.

He opened his eyes and pushed on until he came to the brow that overlooked the swamp. Just below, gliding along among the frozen cattails and bare scrub maple, was a man on skis. Elliot stopped to watch the man approach.

The skier's face was concealed by a red-and-blue ski mask. He wore snow goggles, a blue jumpsuit, and a red woolen Norwegian hat. As he came, he leaned into the turns of the trail, moving silently and gracefully along. At the foot of the slope on which Elliot stood, the man looked up, saw him, and slid to a halt. The man stood staring at him for a moment and then began to herringbone up the slope. In no time at all the skier stood no more than ten feet away, removing his goggles, and inside the woolen mask Elliot recognized the clear blue eyes of his neighbor, Professor Loyall Anderson. The shotgun Elliot was carrying seemed to grow heavier. He yawned and shook his head, trying unsuccessfully to clear it. The sight of Anderson's eyes gave him a little thrill of revulsion.

"What are you after?" the young professor asked him, nodding toward the shotgun Elliot was cradling.

"Whatever there is," Elliot said.·

Anderson took a quick look at the distant pasture behind him and then turned back to Elliot. The mouth hole of the professor's mask filled with teeth. Elliot thought that Anderson's teeth were quite as he had imagined them earlier. "Well, Polonski's cows are locked up," the professor said. "So they at least are safe."

Elliot realized that the professor had made a joke and was smiling. "Yes," he agreed.

Professor Anderson and his wife had been the moving force behind an initiative to outlaw the discharge of firearms within the boundaries of East Ilford Township. The initiative had been defeated, because East Ilford was not that kind of town.

"I think I'll go over by the river," Elliot said. He said it only to have something to say, to fill the silence before Anderson spoke again. He was afraid of what Anderson might say to him and of what might happen.

"You know," Anderson said, "that's all bird sanctuary over there now."

"Sure," Elliot agreed.

Outfitted as he was, the professor attracted Elliot's anger in an elemental manner. The mask made him appear a kind of doll, a kachina figure or a marionette. His eyes and mouth, all on their own, were disagreeable.

Elliott began to wonder if Anderson could smell the whiskey on his breath. He pushed the little red bull's-eye safety button on his gun to Off.

"Seriously," Anderson said, "I'm always having to run hunters out of there. Some people don't understand the word 'posted.'"

"I would never do that," Elliot said, "I would be afraid."

Anderson nodded his head. He seemed to be laughing. "Would you?" he asked Elliot merrily.

In imagination, Elliot rested the tip of his shotgun barrel

against Anderson's smiling teeth. If he fired a load of deer shot into them, he thought, they might make a noise like broken china. "Yes," Elliot said. "I wouldn't know who they were or where they'd been. They might resent my being alive. Telling them where they could shoot and where not."

Anderson's teeth remained in place. "That's pretty strange," he said. "I mean, to talk about resenting someone for being alive."

"It's all relative," Elliot said. "They might think, 'Why should he be alive when some brother of mine isn't?' Or they might think, 'Why should he be alive when I'm not?' "

"Oh," Anderson said.

"You see?" Elliot said. Facing Anderson, he took a long step backward. "All relative."

"Yes," Anderson said.

"That's so often true, isn't it?" Elliot asked. "Values are often relative."

"Yes," Anderson said. Elliot was relieved to see that he had stopped smiling.

"I've hardly slept, you know," Elliot told Professor Anderson. "Hardly at all. All night. I've been drinking."

"Oh," Anderson said. He licked his lips in the mouth of the mask. "You should get some rest."

"You're right," Elliot said.

"Well," Anderson said, "got to go now."

Elliot thought he sounded a little thick in the tongue. A little slow in the jaw.

"It's a nice day," Elliot said, wanting now to be agreeable.

"It's great," Anderson said, shuffling on his skis.

"Have a nice day," Elliot said.

"Yes," Anderson said, and pushed off.

Elliot rested the shotgun across his shoulders and watched Anderson withdraw through the frozen swamp. It was in fact a nice day, but Elliot took no comfort in the weather. He missed night and the falling snow.

As he walked back toward his house, he realized that now there would be whole days to get through, running before the antic energy of whiskey. The whiskey would drive him until he dropped. He shook his head in regret. "It's a revolution," he said aloud. He imagined himself talking to his wife.

Getting drunk was an insurrection, a revolution — a bad one. There would be outsize bogus emotions. There would be petty moral blackmail and cheap remorse. He had said dreadful things to his wife. He had bullied Anderson with his violence and unhappiness, and Anderson would not forgive him. There would be damn little justice and no mercy.

Nearly to the house, he was startled by the desperate feathered drumming of a pheasant's rush. He froze, and out of instinct brought the gun up in the direction of the sound. When he saw the bird break from its cover and take wing, he tracked it, took a breath, and fired once. The bird was a little flash of opulent color against the bright-blue sky. Elliot felt himself flying for a moment. The shot missed.

Lowering the gun, he remembered the deer shells he had loaded. A hit with the concentrated shot would have pulverized the bird, and he was glad he had missed. He wished no harm to any creature. Then he thought of himself wishing no harm to any creature and began to feel fond and sorry for himself. As soon as he grew aware of the emotion he was indulging, he suppressed it. Pissing and moaning, mourning and weeping, that was the nature of the drug.

The shot echoed from the distant hills. Smoke hung in the air. He turned and looked behind him and saw, far away across the pasture, the tiny blue-and-red figure of Professor Anderson motionless against the snow. Then Elliot turned again toward his house and took a few labored steps and looked up to see his wife at the bedroom window. She stood perfectly still, and the morning sun lit her nakedness. He stopped where he was. She had heard the shot and run to the window. What had she thought to see? Burnt rags and blood on the snow. How relieved was she now? How disappointed?

Elliot thought he could feel his wife trembling at the window. She was hugging herself. Her hands clasped her shoulders. Elliot took his snow goggles off and shaded his eyes with his hand. He stood in the field staring.

The length of the gun was between them, he thought. Somehow she had got out in front of it, to the wrong side of the wire. If he looked long enough he would find everything out there. He would find himself down the sight.

How beautiful she is, he thought. The effect was striking. The window was so clear because he had washed it himself, with vinegar. At the best of times he was a difficult, fussy man.

Elliot began to hope for forgiveness. He leaned the shotgun on his forearm and raised his left hand and waved to her. Show a hand, he thought. Please just show a hand.

He was cold, but it had got light. He wanted no more than the gesture. It seemed to him that he could build another day on it. Another day was all you needed. He raised his hand higher and waited.

BHARATI MUKHERJEE

Margaret Atwood described "The Management of Grief" as "a
finely tuned, acutely felt story about an Indian immigrant wife's
reactions when the plane carrying her husband and sons is
blown up over the Irish Sea by terrorists. The sleepwalking
intensity with which she gropes her way through the emotional
debris scattered by these senseless deaths and eventually makes
a mystic sense out of them for herself is sparely but unsparingly
rendered." Bharati Mukherjee, the author of seven books, has
often dealt with the various and subtle aspects of immigrant life
in the United States and Canada. Born and raised in India,
she divides her time between New York City and Berkeley,
California.

The Management of Grief

A WOMAN I don't know is boiling tea the Indian way in my
kitchen. There are a lot of women I don't know in my kitchen,
whispering and moving tactfully. They open doors, rummage
through the pantry, and try not to ask me where things are
kept. They remind me of when my sons were small, on Mother's
Day or when Vikram and I were tired, and they would make
big, sloppy omelets. I would lie in bed pretending I didn't hear
them.

Dr. Sharma, the treasurer of the Indo-Canada Society, pulls
me into the hallway. He wants to know if I am worried about
money. His wife, who has just come up from the basement with
a tray of empty cups and glasses, scolds him. "Don't bother Mrs.
Bhave with mundane details." She looks so monstrously pregnant her baby must be days overdue. I tell her she shouldn't be
carrying heavy things. "Shaila," she says, smiling, "this is the
fifth." Then she grabs a teenager by his shirttails. He slips his

Walkman off his head. He has to be one of her four children; they have the same domed and dented foreheads. "What's the official word now?" she demands. The boy slips the headphones back on. "They're acting evasive, Ma. They're saying it could be an accident or a terrorist bomb."

All morning, the boys have been muttering, Sikh bomb, Sikh bomb. The men, not using the word, bow their heads in agreement. Mrs. Sharma touches her forehead at such a word. At least they've stopped talking about space debris and Russian lasers.

Two radios are going in the dining room. They are tuned to different stations. Someone must have brought the radios down from my boys' bedrooms. I haven't gone into their rooms since Kusum came running across the front lawn in her bathrobe. She looked so funny, I was laughing when I opened the door.

The big TV in the den is being whizzed through American networks and cable channels.

"Damn!" some man swears bitterly. "How can these preachers carry on like nothing's happened?" I want to tell him we're not that important. You look at the audience, and at the preacher in his blue robe with his beautiful white hair, the potted palm trees under a blue sky, and you know they care about nothing.

The phone rings and rings. Dr. Sharma's taken charge. "We're with her," he keeps saying. "Yes, yes, the doctor has given calming pills. Yes, yes, pills are having necessary effect." I wonder if pills alone explain this calm. Not peace, just a deadening quiet. I was always controlled, but never repressed. Sound can reach me, but my body is tensed, ready to scream. I hear their voices all around me. I hear my boys and Vikram cry, "Mommy, Shaila!" and their screams insulate me, like headphones.

The woman boiling water tells her story again and again. "I got the news first. My cousin called from Halifax before six A.M., can you imagine? He'd gotten up for prayers and his son was studying for medical exams and he heard on a rock channel that something had happened to a plane. They said first it had disappeared from the radar, like a giant eraser just reached out. His father called me, so I said to him, what do you mean, 'something bad'? You mean a hijacking? And he said, *Behn*, there is no confirmation of anything yet, but check with your neighbors because a lot of them must be on that plane. So I called poor Kusum straight-away. I knew Kusum's husband and daughter were booked to go yesterday."

Kusum lives across the street from me. She and Satish had moved in less than a month ago. They said they needed a bigger place. All these people, the Sharmas and friends from the Indo-Canada Society, had been there for the housewarming. Satish and Kusum made tandoori on their big gas grill and even the white neighbors piled their plates high with that luridly red, charred, juicy chicken. Their younger daughter had danced, and even our boys had broken away from the Stanley Cup tele-cast to put in a reluctant appearance. Everyone took pictures for their albums and for the community newspapers — another of our families had made it big in Toronto — and now I wonder how many of those happy faces are gone. "Why does God give us so much if all along He intends to take it away?" Kusum asks me.

I nod. We sit on carpeted stairs, holding hands like children. "I never once told him that I loved him," I say. I was too much the well-brought-up woman. I was so well brought up I never felt comfortable calling my husband by his first name.

"It's all right," Kusum says. "He knew. My husband knew. They felt it. Modern young girls have to say it because what they feel is fake."

Kusum's daughter Pam runs in with an overnight case. Pam's in her McDonald's uniform. "Mummy! You have to get dressed!" Panic makes her cranky. "A reporter's on his way here."

"Why?"

"You want to talk to him in your bathrobe?" She starts to brush her mother's long hair. She's the daughter who's always in trouble. She dates Canadian boys and hangs out in the mall, shopping for tight sweaters. The younger one, the goody-goody one according to Pam, the one with a voice so sweet that when she sang *bhajans* for Ethiopian relief even a frugal man like my husband wrote out a hundred-dollar check, *she* was on that plane. *She* was going to spend July and August with grandparents because Pam wouldn't go. Pam said she'd rather waitress at McDonald's. "If it's a choice between Bombay and Wonderland, I'm picking Wonderland," she'd said.

"Leave me alone," Kusum yells. "You know what I want to do? If I didn't have to look after you now, I'd hang myself."

Pam's young face goes blotchy with pain. "Thanks," she says, "don't let me stop you."

"Hush," pregnant Mrs. Sharma scolds Pam. "Leave your mother alone. Mr. Sharma will tackle the reporters and fill out the forms. He'll say what has to be said."

Pam stands her ground. "You think I don't know what Mummy's thinking? *Why her?* That's what. That's sick! Mummy wishes my little sister were alive and I were dead."

Kusum's hand in mine is trembly hot. We continue to sit on the stairs.

She calls before she arrives, wondering if there's anything I need. Her name is Judith Templeton and she's an appointee of the provincial government. "Multiculturalism?" I ask, and she says "partially," but that her mandate is bigger. "I've been told you knew many of the people on the flight," she says. "Perhaps if you'd agree to help us reach the others . . . ?"

She gives me time at least to put on tea water and pick up the mess in the front room. I have a few *samosas* from Kusum's housewarming that I could fry up, but then I think, why prolong this visit?

Judith Templeton is much younger than she sounded. She wears a blue suit with a white blouse and a polka-dot tie. Her blond hair is cut short, her only jewelry is pearl-drop earrings. Her briefcase is new and expensive looking, a gleaming cordovan leather. She sits with it across her lap. When she looks out the front windows onto the street, her contact lenses seem to float in front of her light blue eyes.

"What sort of help do you want from me?" I ask. She has refused the tea, out of politeness, but I insist, along with some slightly stale biscuits.

"I have no experience," she admits. "That is, I have an M.S.W. and I've worked in liaison with accident victims, but I mean I have no experience with a tragedy of this scale —"

"Who could?" I ask.

"— and with the complications of culture, language, and customs. Someone mentioned that Mrs. Bhave is a pillar — because you've taken it more calmly."

At this, perhaps, I frown, for she reaches forward, almost to take my hand. "I hope you understand my meaning, Mrs. Bhave. There are hundreds of people in Metro directly affected, like you, and some of them speak no English. There are some widows who've never handled money or gone on a bus, and there are old parents who still haven't eaten or gone outside their bedrooms. Some houses and apartments have been looted. Some wives are still hysterical. Some husbands are in shock and profound depression. We want to help, but our hands are tied in so many ways. We have to distribute money to some people, and there are legal documents — these things can be done. We have interpreters, but we don't always have the human touch, or maybe the right human touch. We don't want to make mistakes, Mrs. Bhave, and that's why we'd like to ask you to help us."

"More mistakes, you mean," I say.

"Police matters are not in my hands," she answers.

"Nothing I can do will make any difference," I say. "We must all grieve in our own way."

"But you are coping very well. All the people said, Mrs. Bhave is the strongest person of all. Perhaps if the others could see you, talk with you, it would help them."

"By the standards of the people you call hysterical, I am behaving very oddly and very badly, Miss Templeton." I want to say to her, *I wish I could scream, starve, walk into Lake Ontario, jump from a bridge.* "They would not see me as a model. I do not see myself as a model."

I am a freak. No one who has ever known me would think of me reacting this way. This terrible calm will not go away.

She asks me if she may call again, after I get back from a long trip that we all must make. "Of course," I say. "Feel free to call, anytime."

Four days later, I find Kusum squatting on a rock overlooking a bay in Ireland. It isn't a big rock, but it juts sharply out over water. This is as close as we'll ever get to them. June breezes balloon out her sari and unpin her knee-length hair. She has the bewildered look of a sea creature whom the tides have stranded.

It's been one hundred hours since Kusum came stumbling and screaming across my lawn. Waiting around the hospital, we've heard many stories. The police, the diplomats, they tell us things thinking that we're strong, that knowledge is helpful to the grieving, and maybe it is. Some, I know, prefer ignorance, or their own versions. The plane broke into two, they say. Unconsciousness was instantaneous. No one suffered. My boys must have just finished their breakfasts. They loved eating on planes, they loved the smallness of plates, knives, and forks. Last year they saved the airline salt and pepper shakers. Half an hour more and they would have made it to Heathrow.

Kusum says that we can't escape our fate. She says that all those people — our husbands, my boys, her girl with the nightingale voice, all those Hindus, Christians, Sikhs, Muslims, Parsis, and atheists on that plane — were fated to die together off this beautiful bay. She learned this from a swami in Toronto.

I have my Valium.

Six of us "relatives" — two widows and four widowers — chose to spend the day today by the waters instead of sitting in a hospital room and scanning photographs of the dead. That's what they call us now: relatives. I've looked through twenty-seven photos in two days. They're very kind to us, the Irish are very understanding. Sometimes understanding means freeing a tourist bus for this trip to the bay, so we can pretend to spy our loved ones through the glassiness of waves or in sun-speckled cloud shapes.

I could die here, too, and be content.

"What is that, out there?" She's standing and flapping her hands, and for a moment I see a head shape bobbing in the waves. She's standing in the water, I on the boulder. The tide is low, and a round, black, head-sized rock has just risen from the waves. She returns, her sari end dripping and ruined, and her face is a twisted remnant of hope, the way mine was a hundred hours ago, still laughing but inwardly knowing that nothing but the ultimate tragedy could bring two women together at six o'clock on a Sunday morning. I watch her face sag into blankness.

"That water felt warm, Shaila," she says at length.

"You can't," I say. "We have to wait for our turn to come."

I haven't eaten in four days, haven't brushed my teeth.

"I know," she says. "I tell myself I have no right to grieve. They are in a better place than we are. My swami says depression is a sign of our selfishness."

Maybe I'm selfish. Selfishly I break away from Kusum and run, sandals slapping against stones, to the water's edge. What if my boys aren't lying pinned under the debris? What if they aren't stuck a mile below that innocent blue chop? What if, given the strong currents . . .

Now I've ruined my sari, one of my best. Kusum has joined me, knee deep in water that feels to me like a swimming pool. I could settle in the water, and my husband would take my hand and the boys would slap water in my face just to see me scream.

"Do you remember what good swimmers my boys were, Kusum?"

"I saw the medals," she says.

One of the widowers, Dr. Ranganathan from Montreal, walks out to us, carrying his shoes in one hand. He's an electrical engineer. Someone at the hotel mentioned his work is famous around the world, something about the place where physics and electricity come together. He has lost a huge family, something indescribable. "With some luck," Dr. Ranganathan suggests to me, "a good swimmer could make it safely to some island. It is quite possible that there may be many, many microscopic islets scattered around."

"You're not just saying that?" I tell Dr. Ranganathan about Vinod, my elder son. Last year he took diving as well.

"It's a parent's duty to hope," he says. "It is foolish to rule out possibilities that have not been tested. I myself have not surrendered hope."

Kusum is sobbing once again. "Dear lady," he says, laying his free hand on her arm, and she calms down.

"Vinod is how old?" he asks me. He's very careful, as we all are. *Is*, not was.

"Fourteen. Yesterday he was fourteen. His father and uncle

were going to take him down to the Taj and give him a big birthday party. I couldn't go with them because I couldn't get two weeks off from my stupid job in June." I process bills for a travel agent. June is a big travel month.

Dr. Ranganathan whips the pockets of his suit jacket inside out. Squashed roses, in darkening shades of pink, float on the water. He tore the roses off creepers in somebody's garden. He didn't ask anyone if he could pluck the roses, but now there's been an article about it in the local papers. When you see an Indian person, it says, please give them flowers.

"A strong youth of fourteen," he says, "can very likely pull to safety a younger one."

My sons, though four years apart, were very close. Vinod wouldn't let Mithun drown. *Electrical engineering*, I think, foolishly perhaps: this man knows important secrets of the universe, things closed to me. Relief spins me lightheaded. No wonder my boys' photographs haven't turned up in the gallery of photos of the recovered dead. "Such pretty roses," I say.

"My wife loved pink roses. Every Friday I had to bring a bunch home. I used to say, Why? After twenty-odd years of marriage you're still needing proof positive of my love?" He has identified his wife and three of his children. Then others from Montreal, the lucky ones, intact families with no survivors. He chuckles as he wades back to shore. Then he swings around to ask me a question. "Mrs. Bhave, you are wanting to throw in some roses for your loved ones? I have two big ones left."

But I have other things to float: Vinod's pocket calculator; a half-painted model B-52 for my Mithun. They'd want them on their island. And for my husband? For him I let fall into the calm, glassy waters a poem I wrote in the hospital yesterday. Finally he'll know my feelings for him.

"Don't tumble, the rocks are slippery," Dr. Ranganathan cautions. He holds out a hand for me to grab.

Then it's time to get back on the bus, time to rush back to our waiting posts on hospital benches.

Kusum is one of the lucky ones. The lucky ones flew here, identified in multiplicate their loved ones, then will fly to India with the bodies for proper ceremonies. Satish is one of the few males who surfaced. The photos of faces we saw on the walls in an office at Heathrow and here in the hospital are mostly of women. Women have more body fat, a nun said to me matter-of-factly. They float better.

Today I was stopped by a young sailor on the street. He had loaded bodies, he'd gone into the water when — he checks my face for signs of strength — when the sharks were first spotted. I don't blush, and he breaks down. "It's all right," I say. "Thank you." I heard about the sharks from Dr. Ranganathan. In his orderly mind, science brings understanding, it holds no terror. It is the shark's duty. For every deer there is a hunter, for every fish a fisherman.

The Irish are not shy; they rush to me and give me hugs and some are crying. I cannot imagine reactions like that on the streets of Toronto. Just strangers, and I am touched. Some carry flowers with them and give them to any Indian they see.

After lunch, a policeman I have gotten to know quite well catches hold of me. He says he thinks he has a match for Vinod. I explain what a good swimmer Vinod is.

"You want me with you when you look at photos?" Dr. Ranganathan walks ahead of me into the picture gallery. In these matters, he is a scientist, and I am grateful. It is a new perspective. "They have performed miracles," he says. "We are indebted to them."

The first day or two the policemen showed us relatives only one picture at a time; now they're in a hurry, they're eager to lay out the possibles, and even the probables.

The face on the photo is of a boy much like Vinod; the same intelligent eyes, the same thick brows dipping into a V. But this boy's features, even his cheeks, are puffier, wider, mushier.

"No." My gaze is pulled by other pictures. There are five other boys who look like Vinod.

The nun assigned to console me rubs the first picture with a fingertip. "When they've been in the water for a while, love, they look a little heavier." The bones under the skin are broken, they said on the first day — try to adjust your memories. It's important.

"It's not him. I'm his mother. I'd know."

"I know this one!" Dr. Ranganathan cries out, and suddenly,

from the back of the gallery, "And this one!" I think he senses that I don't want to find my boys. "They are the Kutty brothers. They were also from Montreal." I don't mean to be crying. On the contrary, I am ecstatic. My suitcase in the hotel is packed heavy with dry clothes for my boys.

The policeman starts to cry. "I am so sorry, I am so sorry, ma'am. I really thought we had a match."

With the nun ahead of us and the policeman behind, we, the unlucky ones without our children's bodies, file out of the make-shift gallery.

From Ireland most of us go on to India. Kusum and I take the same direct flight to Bombay, so I can help her clear customs quickly. But we have to argue with a man in uniform. He has large boils on his face. The boils swell and glow with sweat as we argue with him. He wants Kusum to wait in line and he refuses to take authority because his boss is on a tea break. But Kusum won't let her coffins out of sight, and I shan't desert her though I know that my parents, elderly and diabetic, must be waiting in a stuffy car in a scorching lot.

"You bastard!" I scream at the man with the popping boils. Other passengers press closer. "You think we're smuggling contraband in those coffins!"

Once upon a time we were well-brought-up women; we were dutiful wives who kept our heads veiled, our voices shy and sweet.

In India, I become, once again, an only child of rich, ailing parents. Old friends of the family come to pay their respects. Some are Sikh, and inwardly, involuntarily, I cringe. My parents are progressive people; they do not blame communities for a few individuals.

In Canada it is a different story now.

"Stay longer," my mother pleads. "Canada is a cold place. Why would you want to be by yourself?" I stay.

Three months pass. Then another.

"Vikram wouldn't have wanted you to give up things!" they protest. They call my husband by the name he was born with. In Toronto he'd changed to Vik so the men he worked with at his office would find his name as easy as Rod or Chris. "You know, the dead aren't cut off from us!"

My grandmother, the spoiled daughter of a rich zamindar, shaved her head with rusty razor blades when she was widowed at sixteen. My grandfather died of childhood diabetes when he was nineteen, and she saw herself as the harbinger of bad luck. My mother grew up without parents, raised indifferently by an uncle, while her true mother slept in a hut behind the main estate house and took her food with the servants. She grew up a rationalist. My parents abhor mindless mortification.

The zamindar's daughter kept stubborn faith in Vedic rituals; my parents rebelled. I am trapped between two modes of knowledge. At thirty-six, I am too old to start over and too young to give up. Like my husband's spirit, I flutter between worlds.

Courting aphasia, we travel. We travel with our phalanx of servants and poor relatives. To hill stations and to beach resorts. We play contract bridge in dusty gymkhana clubs. We ride stubby ponies up crumbly mountain trails. At tea dances, we let ourselves be twirled twice round the ballroom. We hit the holy spots we hadn't made time for before. In Varanasi, Kalighat, Rishikesh, Hardwar, astrologers and palmists seek me out and for a fee offer me cosmic consolations.

Already the widowers among us are being shown new bride candidates. They cannot resist the call of custom, the authority of their parents and older brothers. They must marry; it is the duty of a man to look after a wife. The new wives will be young widows with children, destitute but of good family. They will make loving wives, but the men will shun them. I've had calls from the men over crackling Indian telephone lines. "Save me," they say, these substantial, educated, successful men of forty. "My parents are arranging a marriage for me." In a month they will have buried one family and returned to Canada with a new bride and partial family.

I am comparatively lucky. No one here thinks of arranging a husband for an unlucky widow.

Then, on the third day of the sixth month into this odyssey, in an abandoned temple in a tiny Himalayan village, as I make my offering of flowers and sweetmeats to the god of a tribe of animists, my husband descends to me. He is squatting next to a scrawny sadhu in moth-eaten robes. Vikram wears the vanilla suit he wore the last time I hugged him. The sadhu tosses petals on a butter-fed flame, reciting Sanskrit mantras, and sweeps his face of flies. My husband takes my hands in his.

You're beautiful, he starts. Then, *What are you doing here?*

Shall I stay? I ask. He only smiles, but already the image is fading. *You must finish alone what we started together.* No seaweed wreathes his mouth. He speaks too fast, just as he used to when we were an envied family in our pink split-level. He is gone.

In the windowless altar room, smoky with joss sticks and clarified butter lamps, a sweaty hand gropes for my blouse. I do not shriek. The sadhu arranges his robe. The lamps hiss and sputter out.

When we come out of the temple, my mother says, "Did you feel something weird in there?"

My mother has no patience with ghosts, prophetic dreams, holy men, and cults.

"No," I lie. "Nothing."

But she knows that she's lost me. She knows that in days I shall be leaving.

Kusum's put up her house for sale. She wants to live in an ashram in Hardwar. Moving to Hardwar was her swami's idea. Her swami runs two ashrams, the one in Hardwar and another here in Toronto.

"Don't run away," I tell her.

"I'm not running away," she says. "I'm pursuing inner peace. You think you or that Ranganathan fellow are better off?"

Pam's left for California. She wants to do some modeling, she says. She says when she comes into her share of the insurance money she'll open a yoga-cum-aerobics studio in Hollywood. She sends me postcards so naughty I daren't leave them on the coffee table. Her mother has withdrawn from her and the world.

The rest of us don't lose touch, that's the point. Talk is all we have, says Dr. Ranganathan, who has also resisted his relatives and returned to Montreal and to his job, alone. He says, Whom better to talk with than other relatives? We've been melted down and recast as a new tribe.

He calls me twice a week from Montreal. Every Wednesday night and every Saturday afternoon. He is changing jobs, going to Ottawa. But Ottawa is over a hundred miles away, and he is forced to drive two hundred and twenty miles a day from his home in Montreal. He can't bring himself to sell his house. The house is a temple, he says; the king-sized bed in the master bedroom is a shrine. He sleeps on a folding cot. A devotee.

There are still some hysterical relatives. Judith Templeton's list of those needing help and those who've "accepted" is in nearly perfect balance. Acceptance means you speak of your family in the past tense and you make active plans for moving ahead with your life. There are courses at Seneca and Ryerson we could be taking. Her gleaming leather briefcase is full of college catalogues and lists of cultural societies that need our help. She has done impressive work, I tell her.

"In the textbooks on grief management," she replies — I am her confidante, I realize, one of the few whose grief has not sprung bizarre obsessions — "there are stages to pass through: rejection, depression, acceptance, reconstruction." She has compiled a chart and finds that six months after the tragedy, none of us still rejects reality, but only a handful are reconstructing. "Depressed acceptance" is the plateau we've reached. Remarriage is a major step in reconstruction (though she's a little surprised, even shocked, over *how* quickly some of the men have taken on new families). Selling one's house and changing jobs and cities is healthy.

How to tell Judith Templeton that my family surrounds me, and that like creatures in epics, they've changed shapes? She sees me as calm and accepting but worries that I have no job, no career. My closest friends are worse off than I. I cannot tell her my days, even my nights, are thrilling.

She asks me to help with families she can't reach at all. An elderly couple in Agincourt whose sons were killed just weeks after they had brought their parents over from a village in Punjab. From their names, I know they are Sikh. Judith Templeton and a translator have visited them twice with offers of money for airfare to Ireland, with bank forms, power-of-attorney forms, but they have refused to sign, or to leave their tiny apartment. Their sons' money is frozen in the bank. Their sons' investment apartments have been trashed by tenants, the furnishings sold off. The parents fear that anything they sign or any money they receive will end the company's or the country's obligations to them. They fear they are selling their sons for two airline tickets to a place they've never seen.

The high-rise apartment is a tower of Indians and West Indians, with a sprinkling of Orientals. The nearest bus-stop kiosk is lined with women in saris. Boys practice cricket in the parking lot. Inside the building, even I wince a bit from the ferocity of onion fumes, the distinctive and immediate Indianness of frying ghee, but Judith Templeton maintains a steady flow of information. These poor old people are in imminent danger of losing their place and all their services.

I say to her, "They are Sikh. They will not open up to a Hindu woman." And what I want to add is, as much as I try not to, I stiffen now at the sight of beards and turbans. I remember a time when we all trusted each other in this new country, it was only the new country we worried about.

The two rooms are dark and stuffy. The lights are off, and an oil lamp sputters on the coffee table. The bent old lady has let us in, and her husband is wrapping a white turban over his oiled, hip-length hair. She immediately goes to the kitchen, and I hear the most familiar sound of an Indian home, tap water hitting and filling a teapot.

They have not paid their utility bills, out of fear and inability to write a check. The telephone is gone; electricity and gas and water are soon to follow. They have told Judith their sons will provide. They are good boys, and they have always earned and looked after their parents.

We converse a bit in Hindi. They do not ask about the crash and I wonder if I should bring it up. If they think I am here merely as a translator, then they may feel insulted. There are thousands of Punjabi speakers, Sikhs, in Toronto to do a better job. And so I say to the old lady, "I too have lost my sons, and my husband, in the crash."

Her eyes immediately fill with tears. The man mutters a few words which sound like a blessing. "God provides and God takes away," he says.

I want to say, But only men destroy and give back nothing. "My boys and my husband are not coming back," I say. "We have to understand that."

Now the old woman responds. "But who is to say? Man alone does not decide these things." To this her husband adds his agreement.

Judith asks about the bank papers, the release forms. With a stroke of the pen, they will have a provincial trustee to pay their bills, invest their money, send them a monthly pension.

"Do you know this woman?" I ask them.

The man raises his hand from the table, turns it over, and seems to regard each finger separately before he answers. "This young lady is always coming here, we make tea for her, and she leaves papers for us to sign." His eyes scan a pile of papers in the corner of the room. "Soon we will be out of tea, then will she go away?"

The old lady adds, "I have asked my neighbors and no one else gets *angrezi* visitors. What have we done?"

"It's her job," I try to explain. "The government is worried. Soon you will have no place to stay, no lights, no gas, no water."

"Government will get its money. Tell her not to worry, we are honorable people."

I try to explain the government wishes to give money, not take. He raises his hand. "Let them take," he says. "We are accustomed to that. That is no problem."

"We are strong people," says the wife. "Tell her that."

"Who needs all this machinery?" demands the husband. "It is unhealthy, the bright lights, the cold air on a hot day, the cold food, the four gas rings. God will provide, not government."

"When our boys return," the mother says.

Her husband sucks his teeth. "Enough talk," he says.

Judith breaks in. "Have you convinced them?" The snaps on her cordovan briefcase go off like firecrackers in that quiet apartment. She lays the sheaf of legal papers on the coffee table.

"If they can't write their names, an X will do — I've told them that."

Now the old lady has shuffled to the kitchen and soon emerges with a pot of tea and two cups. "I think my bladder will go first on a job like this," Judith says to me, smiling. "If only there was some way of reaching them. Please thank her for the tea. Tell her she's very kind."

I nod in Judith's direction and tell them in Hindi, "She thanks you for the tea. She thinks you are being very hospitable but she doesn't have the slightest idea what it means."

I want to say, Humor her. I want to say, My boys and my husband are with me too, more than ever. I look in the old man's eyes and I can read his stubborn, peasant's message: *I have protected this woman as best I can. She is the only person I have left. Give to me or take from me what you will, but I will not sign for it. I will not pretend that I accept.*

In the car, Judith says, "You see what I'm up against? I'm sure they're lovely people, but their stubbornness and ignorance are driving me crazy. They think signing a paper is signing their sons' death warrants, don't they?"

I am looking out the window. I want to say, *In our culture, it is a parent's duty to hope.*

"Now Shaila, this next woman is a real mess. She cries day and night, and she refuses all medical help. We may have to —"

"Let me out at the subway," I say.

"I beg your pardon?" I can feel those blue eyes staring at me.

It would not be like her to disobey. She merely disapproves, and slows at a corner to let me out. Her voice is plaintive. "Is there anything I said? Anything I did?"

I could answer her suddenly in a dozen ways, but I choose not to. "Shaila? Let's talk about it," I hear, then slam the door.

A wife and mother begins her new life in a new country, and that life is cut short. Yet her husband tells her, Complete what we have started. We, who stayed out of politics and came half-way around the world to avoid religious and political feuding, have been the first in the New World to die from it. I no longer know what we started, nor how to complete it. I write letters to the editors of local papers and to members of Parliament. Now at least they admit it was a bomb. One MP answers back, with sympathy, but with a challenge. You want to make a difference? Work on a campaign. Work on mine. Politicize the Indian voter.

My husband's old lawyer helps me set up a trust. Vikram was a saver and a careful investor. He had saved the boys' boarding school and college fees. I sell the pink house at four times what we paid for it and take a small apartment downtown. I am looking for a charity to support.

We are deep in the Toronto winter, gray skies, icy pavements. I stay indoors, watching television. I have tried to assess my situation, how best to live my life, to complete what we began so many years ago. Kusum has written me from Hardwar that her life is now serene. She has seen Satish and has heard her daughter sing again. Kusum was on a pilgrimage, passing through a village, when she heard a young girl's voice, singing one of her daughter's favorite *bhajans*. She followed the music through the squalor of a Himalayan village, to a hut where a young girl, an exact replica of her daughter, was fanning coals under the kitchen fire. When she appeared, the girl cried out, "Ma!" and ran away. What did I think of that?

I think I can only envy her.

Pam didn't make it to California, but writes me from Vancouver. She works in a department store, giving makeup hints to Indian and Oriental girls. Dr. Ranganathan has given up his commute, given up his house and job, and accepted an academic position in Texas, where no one knows his story and he has vowed not to tell it. He calls me now once a week.

I wait, I listen and I pray, but Vikram has not returned to me. The voices and the shapes and the nights filled with visions ended abruptly several weeks ago.

I take it as a sign.

One rare, beautiful, sunny day last week, returning from a small errand on Yonge Street, I was walking through the park from the subway to my apartment. I live equidistant from the Ontario Houses of Parliament and the University of Toronto. The day was not cold, but something in the bare trees caught my attention. I looked up from the gravel, into the branches and the clear blue sky beyond. I thought I heard the rustling of larger forms, and I waited a moment for voices. Nothing.

"What?" I asked.

Then as I stood in the path looking north to Queen's Park and west to the university, I heard the voices of my family one last time. *Your time has come,* they said. *Go, be brave.*

I do not know where this voyage I have begun will end. I do not know which direction I will take. I dropped the package on a park bench and started walking.

ALICE MUNRO

Alice Munro, who was born in Wingham, Ontario, and lives in
Clinton, Ontario, is another Canadian writer whose stories are
often selected to appear in the *Best American* series. "Meneseteung," says Margaret Atwood, "is, for my money, one of Alice
Munro's best and, in the manner of its telling, quirkiest stories
yet. It purports to be about a minor sentimental 'poetess' . . .
living in a small, raw, cowpat-strewn, treeless nineteenth-century
town . . . Our sweet picture of bygone days is destroyed, and, in
the process, our conceptions of how a story should proceed."
Atwood ended her introduction to the 1989 *Best American*
volume by suggesting that the last seven lines of the story are
"an epigraph for the act of writing itself."

Meneseteung

I

> Columbine, bloodroot,
> And wild bergamot,
> Gathering armfuls,
> Giddily we go.

OFFERINGS, the book is called. Gold lettering on a dull-blue
cover. The author's full name underneath: Almeda Joynt Roth.
The local paper, the *Vidette*, referred to her as "our poetess."
There seems to be a mixture of respect and contempt, both for
her calling and for her sex — or for their predictable conjunc-
ture. In the front of the book is a photograph, with the photog-
rapher's name in one corner, and the date: 1865. The book was
published later, in 1873.

The poetess has a long face; a rather long nose; full, somber
dark eyes, which seem ready to roll down her cheeks like giant
tears; a lot of dark hair gathered around her face in droopy

rolls and curtains. A streak of gray hair plain to see, although she is, in this picture, only twenty-five. Not a pretty girl but the sort of woman who may age well, who probably won't get fat. She wears a tucked and braid-trimmed dark dress or jacket, with a lacy, floppy arrangement of white material — frills or a bow — filling the deep V at the neck. She also wears a hat, which might be made of velvet, in a dark color to match the dress. It's the untrimmed, shapeless hat, something like a soft beret, that makes me see artistic intentions, or at least a shy and stubborn eccentricity, in this young woman, whose long neck and forward-inclining head indicate as well that she is tall and slender and somewhat awkward. From the waist up, she looks like a young nobleman of another century. But perhaps it was the fashion.

"In 1854," she writes in the preface to her book, "my father brought us — my mother, my sister Catherine, my brother William, and me — to the wilds of Canada West (as it then was). My father was a harness-maker by trade, but a cultivated man who could quote by heart from the Bible, Shakespeare, and the writings of Edmund Burke. He prospered in this newly opened land and was able to set up a harness and leather-goods store, and after a year to build the comfortable house in which I live (alone) today. I was fourteen years old, the eldest of the children, when we came into this country from Kingston, a town whose handsome streets I have not seen again but often remember. My sister was eleven and my brother nine. The third summer that we lived here, my brother and sister were taken ill of a prevalent fever and died within a few days of each other. My dear mother did not regain her spirits after this blow to our family. Her health declined, and after another three years she died. I then became housekeeper to my father and was happy to make his home for twelve years, until he died suddenly one morning at his shop.

"From my earliest years I have delighted in verse and I have occupied myself — and sometimes allayed my griefs, which have been no more, I know, than any sojourner on earth must encounter — with many floundering efforts at its composition. My fingers, indeed, were always too clumsy for crochetwork, and those dazzling productions of embroidery which one sees often today — the overflowing fruit and flower baskets, the little Dutch boys, the bonneted maidens with their watering cans — have likewise proved to be beyond my skill. So I offer instead, as the product of my leisure hours, these rude posies, these ballads, couplets, reflections."

Titles of some of the poems: "Children at Their Games," "The Gypsy Fair," "A Visit to My Family," "Angels in the Snow," "Champlain at the Mouth of the Meneseteung," "The Passing of the Old Forest," and "A Garden Medley." There are some other, shorter poems, about birds and wildflowers and snowstorms. There is some comically intentioned doggerel about what people are thinking about as they listen to the sermon in church.

"Children at Their Games": The writer, a child, is playing with her brother and sister — one of those games in which children on different sides try to entice and catch each other. She plays on in the deepening twilight, until she realizes that she is alone, and much older. Still she hears the (ghostly) voices of her brother and sister calling. *Come over, come over, let Meda come over.* (Perhaps Almeda was called Meda in the family, or perhaps she shortened her name to fit the poem.)

"The Gypsy Fair": The Gypsies have an encampment near the town, a "fair," where they sell cloth and trinkets, and the writer as a child is afraid that she may be stolen by them, taken away from her family. Instead, her family has been taken away from her, stolen by Gypsies she can't locate or bargain with.

"A Visit to My Family": A visit to the cemetery, a one-sided conversation.

"Angels in the Snow": The writer once taught her brother and sister to make "angels" by lying down in the snow and moving their arms to create wing shapes. Her brother always jumped up carelessly, leaving an angel with a crippled wing. Will this be made perfect in Heaven, or will he be flying with his own makeshift, in circles?

"Champlain at the Mouth of the Meneseteung": This poem celebrates the popular, untrue belief that the explorer sailed down the eastern shore of Lake Huron and landed at the mouth of the major river.

"The Passing of the Old Forest": A list of all the trees — their names, appearance, and uses — that were cut down in the original forest, with a general description of the bears, wolves, eagles, deer, waterfowl.

"A Garden Medley": Perhaps planned as a companion to the forest poem. Catalogue of plants brought from European countries, with bits of history and legend attached, and final Canadianness resulting from this mixture.

The poems are written in quatrains or couplets. There are a couple of attempts at sonnets, but mostly the rhyme scheme is simple — *abab* or *abcb*. The rhyme used is what was once called "masculine" ("shore"/"before"), though once in a while it is "feminine" ("quiver"/"river"). Are those terms familiar anymore? No poem is unrhymed.

II

> White roses cold as snow
> Bloom where those "angels" lie.
> Do they but rest below
> Or, in God's wonder, fly?

In 1879, Almeda Roth was still living in the house at the corner of Pearl and Dufferin streets, the house her father had built for his family. The house is there today: the manager of the liquor store lives in it. It's covered with aluminum siding; a closed-in porch has replaced the veranda. The woodshed, the fence, the gates, the privy, the barn — all these are gone. A photograph taken in the eighteen-eighties shows them all in place. The house and fence look a little shabby, in need of paint, but perhaps that is just because of the bleached-out look of the brownish photograph. The lace-curtained windows look like white eyes. No big shade tree is in sight, and, in fact, the tall elms that overshadowed the town until the nineteen-fifties, as well as the maples that shade it now, are skinny young trees with rough fences around them to protect them from the cows. Without the shelter of those trees, there is a great exposure — back yards, clotheslines, woodpiles, patchy sheds and barns and privies — all bare, exposed, provisional looking. Few houses would have anything like a lawn, just a patch of plantains and anthills and raked dirt. Perhaps petunias growing on top of a stump, in a

round box. Only the main street is graveled; the other streets
are dirt roads, muddy or dusty according to season. Yards must
be fenced to keep animals out. Cows are tethered in vacant lots
or pastured in back yards, but sometimes they get loose. Pigs
get loose, too, and dogs roam free or nap in a lordly way on the
boardwalks. The town has taken root, it's not going to vanish,
yet it still has some of the look of an encampment. And, like an
encampment, it's busy all the time — full of people, who, within
the town, usually walk wherever they're going; full of animals,
which leave horse buns, cowpats, dog turds, that ladies have to
hitch up their skirts for; full of the noise of building and of
drivers shouting at their horses and of the trains that come in
several times a day.

I read about that life in the *Vidette*.

The population is younger than it is now, than it will ever be
again. People past fifty usually don't come to a raw, new place.
There are quite a few people in the cemetery already, but most
of them died young, in accidents or childbirth or epidemics.
It's youth that's in evidence in town. Children — boys — rove
through the streets in gangs. School is compulsory for only four
months a year, and there are lots of occasional jobs that even a
child of eight or nine can do — pulling flax, holding horses,
delivering groceries, sweeping the boardwalk in front of stores.
A good deal of time they spend looking for adventures. One
day they follow an old woman, a drunk nicknamed Queen
Aggie. They get her into a wheelbarrow and trundle her all
over town, then dump her into a ditch to sober her up. They
also spend a lot of time around the railway station. They jump
on shunting cars and dart between them and dare each other to
take chances, which once in a while result in their getting
maimed or killed. And they keep an eye out for any strangers
coming into town. They follow them, offer to carry their bags,
and direct them (for a five-cent piece) to a hotel. Strangers
who don't look so prosperous are taunted and tormented.
Speculation surrounds all of them — it's like a cloud of flies.
Are they coming to town to start up a new business, to persuade people to invest in some scheme, to sell cures or gim-
micks, to preach on the street corners? All these things are
possible any day of the week. Be on your guard, the *Vidette*

tells people. These are times of opportunity and danger.
Tramps, confidence men, hucksters, shysters, plain thieves,
are traveling the roads, and particularly the railroads. Thefts
are announced: money invested and never seen again, a pair
of trousers taken from the clothesline, wood from the woodpile, eggs from the henhouse. Such incidents increase in the hot
weather.

Hot weather brings accidents, too. More horses run wild then,
upsetting buggies. Hands caught in the wringer while doing
the washing, a man lopped in two at the sawmill, a leaping boy
killed in a fall of lumber at the lumberyard. Nobody sleeps well.
Babies wither with summer complaint, and fat people can't
catch their breath. Bodies must be buried in a hurry. One day
a man goes through the streets ringing a cowbell and calling
"Repent! Repent!" It's not a stranger this time, it's a young
man who works at the butcher shop. Take him home, wrap him
in cold wet cloths, give him some nerve medicine, keep him
in bed, pray for his wits. If he doesn't recover, he must go to the
asylum.

Almeda Roth's house faces on Dufferin Street, which is a
street of considerable respectability. On this street merchants, a
mill owner, an operator of salt wells, have their houses. But
Pearl Street, which her back windows overlook and her back
gate opens onto, is another story. Workmen's houses are adjacent to hers. Small but decent row houses — that is all right.
Things deteriorate toward the end of the block, and the next,
last one becomes dismal. Nobody but the poorest people, the
unrespectable and undeserving poor, would live there at the
edge of a boghole (drained since then), called the Pearl Street
Swamp. Bushy and luxuriant weeds grow there, makeshift
shacks have been put up, there are piles of refuse and debris
and crowds of runty children, slops are flung from doorways.
The town tries to compel these people to build privies, but they
would just as soon go in the bushes. If a gang of boys goes down
there in search of adventure, it's likely they'll get more than
they bargained for. It is said that even the town constable won't
go down Pearl Street on a Saturday night. Almeda Roth has
never walked past the row housing. In one of those houses lives
the young girl Annie, who helps her with her housecleaning.

That young girl herself, being a decent girl, has never walked down to the last block or the swamp. No decent woman ever would.

But that same swamp, lying to the east of Almeda Roth's house, presents a fine sight at dawn. Almeda sleeps at the back of the house. She keeps to the same bedroom she once shared with her sister Catherine — she would not think of moving to the larger front bedroom, where her mother used to lie in bed all day, and which was later the solitary domain of her father. From her window she can see the sun rising, the swamp mist filling with light, the bulky, nearest trees floating against that mist and the trees behind turning transparent. Swamp oaks, soft maples, tamarack, bitternut.

III

> Here where the river meets the inland sea,
> Spreading her blue skirts from the solemn wood,
> I think of birds and beasts and vanished men,
> Whose pointed dwellings on these pale sands stood.

One of the strangers who arrived at the railway station a few years ago was Jarvis Poulter, who now occupies the house next to Almeda Roth's — separated from hers by a vacant lot, which he has bought, on Dufferin Street. The house is plainer than the Roth house and has no fruit trees or flowers planted around it. It is understood that this is a natural result of Jarvis Poulter's being a widower and living alone. A man may keep his house decent, but he will never — if he is a proper man — do much to decorate it. Marriage forces him to live with more ornament as well as sentiment, and it protects him, also, from the extremities of his own nature — from a frigid parsimony or a luxuriant sloth, from squalor, and from excessive sleeping, drinking, smoking, or freethinking.

In the interests of economy, it is believed, a certain estimable gentleman of our town persists in fetching water from the public tap and supplementing his fuel supply by picking up the loose coal along the railway track. Does he think to repay the town or the railway company with a supply of free salt?

This is the *Vidette,* full of shy jokes, innuendo, plain accusation, that no newspaper would get away with today. It's Jarvis Poulter they're talking about — though in other passages he is spoken of with great respect, as a civil magistrate, an employer, a churchman. He is close, that's all. An eccentric, to a degree. All of which may be a result of his single condition, his widower's life. Even carrying his water from the town tap and filling his coal pail along the railway track. This is a decent citizen, prosperous: a tall — slightly paunchy? — man in a dark suit with polished boots. A beard? Black hair streaked with gray. A severe and self-possessed air, and a large pale wart among the bushy hairs of one eyebrow? People talk about a young, pretty, beloved wife, dead in childbirth or some horrible accident, like a house fire or a railway disaster. There is no ground for this, but it adds interest. All he has told them is that his wife is dead.

He came to this part of the country looking for oil. The first oil well in the world was sunk in Lambton County, south of here, in the eighteen-fifties. Drilling for oil, Jarvis Poulter discovered salt. He set to work to make the most of that. When he walks home from church with Almeda Roth, he tells her about his salt wells. They are twelve hundred feet deep. Heated water is pumped down into them, and that dissolves the salt. Then the brine is pumped to the surface. It is poured into great evaporator pans over slow, steady fires, so that the water is steamed off and the pure, excellent salt remains. A commodity for which the demand will never fail.

"The salt of the earth," Almeda says.

"Yes," he says, frowning. He may think this disrespectful. She did not intend it so. He speaks of competitors in other towns who are following his lead and trying to hog the market. Fortunately, their wells are not drilled so deep, or their evaporating is not done so efficiently. There is salt everywhere under this land, but it is not so easy to come by as some people think.

Does that not mean, Almeda says, that there was once a great sea?

Very likely, Jarvis Poulter says. Very likely. He goes on to tell her about other enterprises of his — a brickyard, a lime kiln. And he explains to her how this operates, and where the good clay is found. He also owns two farms, whose woodlots supply the fuel for his operations.

> Among the couples strolling home from church on a recent, sunny Sabbath morning we noted a certain salty gentleman and literary lady, not perhaps in their first youth but by no means blighted by the frosts of age. May we surmise?

This kind of thing pops up in the *Vidette* all the time.

May they surmise, and is this courting? Almeda Roth has a bit of money, which her father left her, and she has her house. She is not too old to have a couple of children. She is a good enough housekeeper, with the tendency toward fancy iced cakes and decorated tarts which is seen fairly often in old maids. (Honorable mention at the Fall Fair.) There is nothing wrong with her looks, and naturally she is in better shape than most married women of her age, not having been loaded down with work and children. But why was she passed over in her earlier, more marriageable years, in a place that needs women to be partnered and fruitful? She was a rather gloomy girl — that may have been the trouble. The deaths of her brother and sister and then of her mother, who lost her reason, in fact, a year before she died, and lay in her bed talking nonsense — those weighed on her, so she was not lively company. And all that reading and poetry — it seemed more of a drawback, a barrier, an obsession, in the young girl than in the middle-aged woman, who needed something, after all, to fill her time. Anyway, it's five years since her book was published, so perhaps she has got over that. Perhaps it was the proud, bookish father, encouraging her?

Everyone takes it for granted that Almeda Roth is thinking of Jarvis Poulter as a husband and would say yes if he asked her. And she is thinking of him. She doesn't want to get her hopes up too much, she doesn't want to make a fool of herself. She would like a signal. If he attended church on Sunday evenings, there would be a chance, during some months of the year, to walk home after dark. He would carry a lantern. (There is as yet no street lighting in town.) He would swing the lantern to light the way in front of the lady's feet and observe their narrow and delicate shape. He might catch her arm as they step off the boardwalk. But he does not go to church at night.

Nor does he call for her, and walk with her *to* church on Sunday mornings. That would be a declaration. He walks her home, past his gate as far as hers; he lifts his hat then and leaves her. She does not invite him to come in — a woman living alone could never do such a thing. As soon as a man and woman of almost any age are alone together within four walls, it is assumed that anything may happen. Spontaneous combustion, instant fornication, an attack of passion. Brute instinct, triumph of the senses. What possibilities men and women must see in each other to infer such dangers. Or, believing in the dangers, how often they must think about the possibilities.

When they walk side by side she can smell his shaving soap, the barber's oil, his pipe tobacco, the wool and linen and leather smell of his manly clothes. The correct, orderly, heavy clothes are like those she used to brush and starch and iron for her father. She misses that job — her father's appreciation, his dark, kind authority. Jarvis Poulter's garments, his smell, his movement, all cause the skin on the side of her body next to him to tingle hopefully, and a meek shiver raises the hairs on her arms. Is this to be taken as a sign of love? She thinks of him coming into her — *their* — bedroom in his long underwear and his hat. She knows this outfit is ridiculous, but in her mind he does not look so; he has the solemn effrontery of a figure in a dream. He comes into the room and lies down on the bed beside her, preparing to take her in his arms. Surely he removes his hat? She doesn't know, for at this point a fit of welcome and submission overtakes her, a buried gasp. He would be her husband.

One thing she has noticed about married women, and that is how many of them have to go about creating their husbands. They have to start ascribing preferences, opinions, dictatorial ways. Oh, yes, they say, my husband is very particular. He won't touch turnips. He won't eat fried meat. (Or he will only eat fried meat.) He likes me to wear blue (brown) all the time. He can't stand organ music. He hates to see a woman go out bareheaded. He would kill me if I took one puff of tobacco. This way, bewildered, sidelong-looking men are made over, made into husbands, head of households. Almeda Roth cannot imagine herself doing that. She wants a man who doesn't have to be made, who is firm already and determined and mysterious to her. She does not look for companionship. Men — except for her father — seem to her deprived in some way, incurious. No doubt that is necessary, so that they will do what they have to do. Would she herself, knowing that there was salt in the earth, discover how to get it out and sell it? Not likely. She would be thinking about the ancient sea. That kind of speculation is what Jarvis Poulter has, quite properly, no time for.

Instead of calling for her and walking her to church, Jarvis Poulter might make another, more venturesome declaration. He could hire a horse and take her for a drive out to the country. If he did this, she would be both glad and sorry. Glad to be beside him, driven by him, receiving this attention from him in front of the world. And sorry to have the countryside removed for her — filmed over, in a way, by his talk and preoccupations. The countryside that she has written about in her poems actually takes diligence and determination to see. Some things must be disregarded. Manure piles, of course, and boggy fields full of high, charred stumps, and great heaps of brush waiting for a good day for burning. The meandering creeks have been straightened, turned into ditches with high, muddy banks. Some of the crop fields and pasture fields are fenced with big, clumsy uprooted stumps, others are held in a crude stitchery of rail fences. The trees have all been cleared back to the woodlots. And the woodlots are all second growth. No trees along the roads or lanes or around the farmhouses, except a few that are newly planted, young and weedy looking. Clusters of log barns — the grand barns that are to dominate the countryside for the next hundred years are just beginning to be built — and mean-looking log houses, and every four or five miles a ragged little settlement with a church and school and store and a blacksmith shop. A raw countryside just wrenched from the forest, but swarming with people. Every hundred acres is a farm, every farm has a family, most families have ten or twelve children. (This is the country that will send out wave after wave of settlers — it's already starting to send them — to northern Ontario and the West.) It's true that you can gather wildflowers in spring in the woodlots, but you'd have to walk through herds of horned cows to get to them.

IV

The Gypsies have departed.
Their camping-ground is bare.
Oh, boldly would I bargain now
At the Gypsy Fair.

Almeda suffers a good deal from sleeplessness, and the doctor
has given her bromides and nerve medicine. She takes the bromides, but the drops gave her dreams that were too vivid and
disturbing, so she has put the bottle by for an emergency. She
told the doctor her eyeballs felt dry, like hot glass, and her joints
ached. Don't read so much, he said, don't study; get yourself
good and tired out with housework, take exercise. He believes
that her troubles would clear up if she got married. He believes
this in spite of the fact that most of his nerve medicine is prescribed for married women.

So Almeda cleans house and helps clean the church, she
lends a hand to friends who are wallpapering or getting ready
for a wedding, she bakes one of her famous cakes for the
Sunday-school picnic. On a hot Saturday in August she decides
to make some grape jelly. Little jars of grape jelly will make fine
Christmas presents, or offerings to the sick. But she started late
in the day and the jelly is not made by nightfall. In fact, the hot
pulp has just been dumped into the cheesecloth bag, to strain
out the juice. Almeda drinks some tea and eats a slice of cake
with butter (a childish indulgence of hers), and that's all she
wants for supper. She washes her hair at the sink and sponges
off her body, to be clean for Sunday. She doesn't light a lamp.
She lies down on the bed with the window wide open and a
sheet just up to her waist, and she does feel wonderfully tired.
She can even feel a little breeze.

When she wakes up, the night seems fiery hot and full of
threats. She lies sweating on her bed, and she has the impression
that the noises she hears are knives and saws and axes — all
angry implements chopping and jabbing and boring within her
head. But it isn't true. As she comes further awake she recognizes the sounds that she has heard sometimes before — the
fracas of a summer Saturday night on Pearl Street. Usually the
noise centers on a fight. People are drunk, there is a lot of
protest and encouragement concerning the fight, somebody will

scream "Murder!" Once, there was a murder. But it didn't happen in a fight. An old man was stabbed to death in his shack,
perhaps for a few dollars he kept in the mattress.

She gets out of bed and goes to the window. The night sky
is clear, with no moon and with bright stars. Pegasus hangs
straight ahead, over the swamp. Her father taught her that
constellation — automatically, she counts its stars. Now she can
make out distinct voices, individual contributions to the row.
Some people, like herself, have evidently been wakened from
sleep. "Shut up!" they are yelling. "Shut up that caterwauling or
I'm going to come down and tan the arse off yez!"

But nobody shuts up. It's as if there were a ball of fire rolling
up Pearl Street, shooting off sparks — only the fire is noise,
it's yells and laughter and shrieks and curses, and the sparks
are voices that shoot off alone. Two voices gradually distinguish
themselves — a rising and falling howling cry and a steady
throbbing, low-pitched stream of abuse that contains all those
words which Almeda associates with danger and depravity and
foul smells and disgusting sights. Someone — the person crying out, "Kill me! Kill me now!" — is being beaten. A woman is
being beaten. She keeps crying, "Kill me! Kill me!" and sometimes her mouth seems choked with blood. Yet there is
something taunting and triumphant about her cry. There is
something theatrical about it. And the people around are calling
out, "Stop it! Stop that!" or "Kill her! Kill her!" in a frenzy, as if
at the theater or a sporting match or a prizefight. Yes, thinks
Almeda, she has noticed that before — it is always partly a cha-
rade with these people; there is a clumsy sort of parody, an
exaggeration, a missed connection. As if anything they did —
even a murder — might be something they didn't quite believe
but were powerless to stop.

Now there is the sound of something thrown — a chair, a
plank? — and of a woodpile or part of a fence giving way. A lot
of newly surprised cries, the sound of running, people getting
out of the way, and the commotion has come much closer. Almeda can see a figure in a light dress, bent over and running.
That will be the woman. She has got hold of something like a
stick of wood or a shingle, and she turns and flings it at the
darker figure running after her.

"Ah, go get her!" the voices cry. "Go baste her one!"

Many fall back now; just the two figures come on and grapple, and break loose again, and finally fall down against Almeda's fence. The sound they make becomes very confused — gagging, vomiting, grunting, pounding. Then a long, vibrating, choking sound of pain and self-abasement, self-abandonment, which could come from either or both of them.

Almeda has backed away from the window and sat down on the bed. Is that the sound of murder she has heard? What is to be done, what is she to do? She must light a lantern, she must go downstairs and light a lantern — she must go out into the yard, she must go downstairs. Into the yard. The lantern. She falls over on her bed and pulls the pillow to her face. In a minute. The stairs, the lantern. She sees herself already down there, in the back hall, drawing the bolt of the back door. She falls asleep.

She wakes, startled, in the early light. She thinks there is a big crow sitting on her windowsill, talking in a disapproving but unsurprised way about the events of the night before. "Wake up and move the wheelbarrow!" it says to her, scolding, and she understands that it means something else by "wheelbarrow" — something foul and sorrowful. Then she is awake and sees that there is no such bird. She gets up at once and looks out the window.

Down against her fence there is a pale lump pressed — a body.

Wheelbarrow.

She puts a wrapper over her nightdress and goes downstairs. The front rooms are still shadowy, the blinds down in the kitchen. Something goes *plop, plup,* in a leisurely, censorious way, reminding her of the conversation of the crow. It's just the grape juice, straining overnight. She pulls the bolt and goes out the back door. Spiders have draped their webs over the doorway in the night, and the hollyhocks are drooping, heavy with dew. By the fence, she parts the sticky hollyhocks and looks down and she can see.

A woman's body heaped up there, turned on her side with her face squashed down into the earth. Almeda can't see her face. But there is a bare breast let loose, brown nipple pulled long like a cow's teat, and a bare haunch and leg, the haunch bearing a bruise as big as a sunflower. The unbruised skin is grayish, like a plucked, raw drumstick. Some kind of nightgown or all-purpose dress she has on. Smelling of vomit. Urine, drink, vomit.

Barefoot, in her nightgown and flimsy wrapper, Almeda runs away. She runs around the side of her house between the apple trees and the veranda; she opens the front gate and flees down Dufferin Street to Jarvis Poulter's house, which is the nearest to hers. She slaps the flat of her hand many times against the door.

"There is the body of a woman," she says when Jarvis Poulter appears at last. He is in his dark trousers, held up with braces, and his shirt is half unbuttoned, his face unshaven, his hair standing up on his head. "Mr. Poulter, excuse me. A body of a woman. At my back gate."

He looks at her fiercely. "Is she dead?"

His breath is dank, his face creased, his eyes bloodshot.

"Yes. I think murdered," says Almeda. She can see a little of his cheerless front hall. His hat on a chair. "In the night I woke up. I heard a racket down on Pearl Street," she says, struggling to keep her voice low and sensible. "I could hear this — pair. I could hear a man and a woman fighting."

He picks up his hat and puts it on his head. He closes and locks the front door, and puts the key in his pocket. They walk along the boardwalk and she sees that she is in her bare feet. She holds back what she feels a need to say next — that she is responsible, she could have run out with a lantern, she could have screamed (but who needed more screams?), she could have beat the man off. She could have run for help then, not now.

They turn down Pearl Street, instead of entering the Roth yard. Of course the body is still there. Hunched up, half bare, the same as before.

Jarvis Poulter doesn't hurry or halt. He walks straight over to the body and looks down at it, nudges the leg with the toe of his boot, just as you'd nudge a dog or a sow.

"You," he says, not too loudly but firmly, and nudges again.

Almeda tastes bile at the back of her throat.

"Alive," says Jarvis Poulter, and the woman confirms this. She stirs, she grunts weakly.

Almeda says, "I will get the doctor." If she had touched the woman, if she had forced herself to touch her, she would not have made such a mistake.

"Wait," says Jarvis Poulter. "Wait. Let's see if she can get up."

"Get up, now," he says to the woman. "Come on. Up, now. Up."

Now a startling thing happens. The body heaves itself onto all fours, the head is lifted — the hair all matted with blood and vomit — and the woman begins to bang this head, hard and rhythmically, against Almeda Roth's picket fence. As she bangs her head she finds her voice, and lets out an open-mouthed yowl, full of strength and what sounds like an anguished plea-sure.

"Far from dead," says Jarvis Poulter. "And I wouldn't bother the doctor."

"There's blood," says Almeda as the woman turns her smeared face.

"From her nose," he says. "Not fresh." He bends down and catches the horrid hair close to the scalp to stop the head bang-ing.

"You stop that now," he says. "Stop it. Gwan home now. Gwan home, where you belong." The sound coming out of the wom-an's mouth has stopped. He shakes her head slightly, warning her, before he lets go of her hair. "Gwan home!"

Released, the woman lunges forward, pulls herself to her feet. She can walk. She weaves and stumbles down the street, making intermittent, cautious noises of protest. Jarvis Poulter watches her for a moment to make sure that she's on her way. Then he finds a large burdock leaf, on which he wipes his hand. He says, "There goes your dead body!"

The back gate being locked, they walk around to the front. The front gate stands open. Almeda still feels sick. Her abdo-men is bloated; she is hot and dizzy.

"The front door is locked," she says faintly. "I came out by the kitchen." If only he would leave her, she could go straight to the privy. But he follows. He follows her as far as the back door and into the back hall. He speaks to her in a tone of harsh joviality that she has never before heard from him. "No need for alarm," he says. "It's only the consequences of drink. A lady oughtn't to be living alone so close to a bad neighborhood." He takes hold of her arm just above the elbow. She can't open her mouth to speak to him, to say thank you. If she opened her mouth she would retch.

What Jarvis Poulter feels for Almeda Roth at this moment is just what he has not felt during all those circumspect walks and all his own solitary calculations of her probable worth, undoubted respectability, adequate comeliness. He has not been able to imagine her as a wife. Now that is possible. He is sufficiently stirred by her loosened hair — prematurely gray but thick and soft — her flushed face, her light clothing, which nobody but a husband should see. And by her indiscretion, her agitation, her foolishness, her need?

"I will call on you later," he says to her. "I will walk with you to church."

> At the corner of Pearl and Dufferin streets last Sunday morning there was discovered, by a lady resident there, the body of a certain woman of Pearl Street, thought to be dead but only, as it turned out, dead drunk. She was roused from her heavenly — or otherwise — stupor by the firm persuasion of Mr. Poulter, a neighbour and a Civil Magistrate, who had been summoned by the lady resident. Incidents of this sort, unseemly, troublesome, and disgraceful to our town, have of late become all too common.

V

> I sit at the bottom of sleep,
> As on the floor of the sea.
> And fanciful Citizens of the Deep
> Are graciously greeting me.

As soon as Jarvis Poulter has gone and she has heard her front gate close, Almeda rushes to the privy. Her relief is not complete, however, and she realizes that the pain and fullness in her lower body come from an accumulation of menstrual blood that has not yet started to flow. She closes and locks the back door. Then, remembering Jarvis Poulter's words about church, she writes on a piece of paper, "I am not well, and wish to rest today." She sticks this firmly into the outside frame of the little window in the front door. She locks that door, too. She is trembling, as if from a great shock or danger. But she builds a fire, so that she can make tea. She boils water, measures the tea leaves, makes a large pot of tea, whose steam and smell sicken her further. She pours out a cup while the tea is still quite weak and adds to it several dark drops of nerve medicine. She sits to drink it without raising the kitchen blind. There, in the middle of the floor, is the cheesecloth bag hanging on its broom handle between the two chair backs. The grape pulp and juice has stained the swollen cloth a dark purple. *Plop, plup* into the basin beneath. She can't sit and look at such a thing. She takes her cup, the teapot, and the bottle of medicine into the dining room.

She is still sitting there when the horses start to go by on the way to church, stirring up clouds of dust. The roads will be getting hot as ashes. She is there when the gate is opened and a man's confident steps sound on her veranda. Her hearing is so sharp she seems to hear the paper taken out of the frame and unfolded — she can almost hear him reading it, hear the words in his mind. Then the footsteps go the other way, down the steps. The gate closes. An image comes to her of tombstones — it makes her laugh. Tombstones are marching down the street on their little booted feet, their long bodies inclined forward, their expressions preoccupied and severe. The church bells are ringing.

Then the clock in the hall strikes twelve and an hour has passed.

The house is getting hot. She drinks more tea and adds more medicine. She knows that the medicine is affecting her. It is responsible for her extraordinary languor, her perfect immobility, her unresisting surrender to her surroundings. That is all right. It seems necessary.

Her surroundings — some of her surroundings — in the dining room are these: walls covered with dark green garlanded wallpaper, lace curtains and mulberry velvet curtains on the windows, a table with a crocheted cloth and a bowl of wax fruit, a pinkish-gray carpet with nosegays of blue and pink roses, a sideboard spread with embroidered runners and holding various patterned plates and jugs and the silver tea things. A lot of things to watch. For every one of these patterns, decorations, seems charged with life, ready to move and flow and alter. Or possibly to explode. Almeda Roth's occupation throughout the day is to keep an eye on them. Not to prevent their alteration so much as to catch them at it — to understand it, to be a part of it. So much is going on in this room that there is no need to leave it. There is not even the thought of leaving it.

Of course, Almeda in her observations cannot escape words. She may think she can, but she can't. Soon this glowing and swelling begins to suggest words — not specific words but a flow of words somewhere, just about ready to make themselves known to her. Poems, even. Yes, again, poems. Or one poem. Isn't that the idea — one very great poem that will contain everything and, oh, that will make all the other poems, the poems she has written, inconsequential, mere trial and error, mere rags? Stars and flowers and birds and trees and angels in the snow and dead children at twilight — that is not the half of it. You have to get in the obscene racket on Pearl Street and the polished toe of Jarvis Poulter's boot and the plucked-chicken haunch with its blue-black flower. Almeda is a long way now from human sympathies or fears or cozy household considerations. She doesn't think about what could be done for that woman or about keeping Jarvis Poulter's dinner warm and hanging his long underwear on the line. The basin of grape juice has overflowed and is running over her kitchen floor, staining the boards of the floor, and the stain will never come out.

She has to think of so many things at once — Champlain and the naked Indians and the salt deep in the earth but as well as the salt the money, the money-making intent brewing forever in heads like Jarvis Poulter's. Also, the brutal storms of winter and the clumsy and benighted deeds on Pearl Street. The changes of climate are often violent, and if you think about it there is no peace even in the stars. All this can be borne only if it is channeled into a poem, and the word "channeled" is appropriate, because the name of the poem will be — it *is* — "The Meneseteung." The name of the poem is the name of the river. No, in fact it is the river, the Meneseteung, that is the poem — with its deep holes and rapids and blissful pools under the summer trees and its grinding blocks of ice thrown up at the end of winter and its desolating spring floods. Almeda looks deep, deep into the river of her mind and into the tablecloth, and she sees the crocheted roses floating. They look bunchy and foolish, her mother's crocheted roses — they don't look much like real flowers. But their effort, their floating independence, their pleasure in their silly selves, does seem to her so admirable. A hopeful sign. *Meneseteung*.

She doesn't leave the room until dusk, when she goes out to the privy again and discovers that she is bleeding, her flow has started. She will have to get a towel, strap it on, bandage herself up. Never before, in health, has she passed a whole day in her nightdress. She doesn't feel any particular anxiety about this. On her way through the kitchen she walks through the pool of grape juice. She knows that she will have to mop it up, but not yet, and she walks upstairs leaving purple footprints and smelling her escaping blood and the sweat of her body that has sat all day in the closed hot room.

No need for alarm.

For she hasn't thought that crocheted roses could float away or that tombstones could hurry down the street. She doesn't mistake that for reality, and neither does she mistake anything else for reality, and that is how she knows that she is sane.

VI

I dream of you by night,
I visit you by day.
Father, Mother,
Sister, Brother,
Have you no word to say?

April 22, 1903. At her residence, on Tuesday last, between three and four o'clock in the afternoon, there passed away a lady of talent and refinement whose pen, in days gone by, enriched our local literature with a volume of sensitive, eloquent verse. It is a sad misfortune that in later years the mind of this fine person had become somewhat clouded and her behaviour, in consequence, somewhat rash and unusual. Her attention to decorum and to the care and adornment of her person had suffered, to the degree that she had become, in the eyes of those unmindful of her former pride and daintiness, a familiar eccentric, or even, sadly, a figure of fun. But now all such lapses pass from memory and what is recalled is her excellent published

verse, her labours in former days in the Sunday school, her dutiful
care of her parents, her noble womanly nature, charitable concerns,
and unfailing religious faith. Her last illness was of mercifully short
duration. She caught cold, after having become thoroughly wet from
a ramble in the Pearl Street bog. (It has been said that some urchins
chased her into the water, and such is the boldness and cruelty of
some of our youth, and their observed persecution of this lady, that
the tale cannot be entirely discounted.) The cold developed into
pneumonia, and she died, attended at the last by a former neighbour,
Mrs. Bert (Annie) Friels, who witnessed her calm and faithful end.

January, 1904. One of the founders of our community, an early
maker and shaker of this town, was abruptly removed from our midst
on Monday morning last, whilst attending to his correspondence in
the office of his company. Mr. Jarvis Poulter possessed a keen and
lively commercial spirit, which was instrumental in the creation of
not one but several local enterprises, bringing the benefits of indus-
try, productivity, and employment to our town.

I looked for Almeda Roth in the graveyard. I found the family
stone. There was just one name on it — Roth. Then I noticed
two flat stones in the ground, a distance of a few feet — six feet?
— from the upright stone. One of these said "Papa," the other
"Mama." Farther out from these I found two other flat stones,
with the names William and Catherine on them. I had to clear
away some overgrowing grass and dirt to see the full name of
Catherine. No birth or death dates for anybody, nothing about
being dearly beloved. It was a private sort of memorializing, not
for the world. There were no roses, either — no sign of a rose-
bush. But perhaps it was taken out. The grounds keeper doesn't
like such things, they are a nuisance to the lawnmower, and if
there is nobody left to object he will pull them out.

I thought that Almeda must have been buried somewhere
else. When this plot was bought — at the time of the two children's deaths — she would still have been expected to marry,
and to lie finally beside her husband. They might not have left
room for her here. Then I saw that the stones in the ground
fanned out from the upright stone. First the two for the parents,
then the two for the children, but these were placed in such a
way that there was room for a third, to complete the fan. I paced
out from "Catherine" the same number of steps that it took to

get from "Catherine" to "William," and at this spot I began pulling grass and scrabbling in the dirt with my bare hands. Soon I felt the stone and knew that I was right. I worked away and got the whole stone clear and I read the name "Meda." There it was with the others, staring at the sky.

I made sure I had got to the edge of the stone. That was all the name there was — Meda. So it was true that she was called by that name in the family. Not just in the poem. Or perhaps she chose her name from the poem, to be written on her stone.

I thought that there wasn't anybody alive in the world but me who would know this, who would make the connection. And I would be the last person to do so. But perhaps this isn't so. People are curious. A few people are. They will be driven to find things out, even trivial things. They will put things together, knowing all along that they may be mistaken. You see them going around with notebooks, scraping the dirt off gravestones, reading microfilm, just in the hope of seeing this trickle in time, making a connection, rescuing one thing from the rubbish.

Contents Pages
Editorial Addresses

Contents Pages, 1980–1989

1983 · *Anne Tyler, guest editor*

1984 · *John Updike, guest editor*

1985 · *Gail Godwin, guest editor*

1986 · *Raymond Carver, guest editor*

1987 · *Ann Beattie, guest editor*

1989 · *Margaret Atwood, guest editor*

Editorial Addresses of American and Canadian Magazines Publishing Short Stories

When available, the annual subscription rate, the average number of stories published per year, and the name of the editor follow the address.

Agni Review
Creative Writing Department
Boston University
236 Bay State Road
Boston, MA 02115
$12, 15, Askold Melnyczuk

Alabama Literary Review
Troy State University, Smith 264
Troy, AL 36082
$4, Theron E. Montgomery

Alaska Quarterly Review
Department of English
University of Alaska
3221 Providence Drive
Anchorage, AK 99508
$8, 20, Ronald Spatz

Alfred Hitchcock's Mystery Magazine
Davis Publications
380 Lexington Avenue
New York, NY 10017
$19.50, 130, Cathleen Jordan

Ambergris
5521½ 12th Avenue NE
Seattle, WA 98105
$6, 4, Mark Kissling

Amelia
329 East Street
Bakersfield, CA 93304
$20, 10, Frederick A. Raborg, Jr.

American Book Review
Publications Center
English Department, Box 226
University of Colorado
Boulder, CO 80309

Analog Science Fiction/Science Fact
380 Lexington Avenue
New York, NY 10017
$19.50, 70, Stanley Schmidt

Antaeus
26 West 17th Street
New York, NY 10011
$10, 15, Daniel Halpern

Antietam Review
82 West Washington Street
Hagerstown, MD 21740
$5, 6, Ann B. Knox

Antioch Review
P.O. Box 148
Yellow Springs, OH 45387
$18, 20, Robert S. Fogarty

Apalachee Quarterly
P.O. Box 20106
Tallahassee, FL 32316
*$12, 10, Allen Woodman, Barbara
 Hanby, Monica Faeth*

Arizona Quarterly
University of Arizona
Tucson, AZ 85721
$5, 12, Albert F. Gegenheimer

Arts Journal
324 Charlotte Street
Asheville, NC 28801
$15, 5, Tom Patterson

Ascent
English Department
University of Illinois
608 South Wright Street
Urbana, IL 61801
$3, 20, Daniel Curley

Atlantic Monthly
745 Boylston Street
Boston, MA 02116
$14.95, 12, C. Michael Curtis

Aura Literary/Arts Review
P.O. Box University Center
University of Alabama
Birmingham, AL 35294
$6, 10, rotating editorship

Bellowing Ark
P.O. Box 45637
Seattle, WA 98145
$12, 5, Robert R. Ward

Beloit Fiction Journal
Beloit College, P.O. Box 11

Beloit, WI 53511
$9, 10, Clint McCown

Black Ice
P.O. Box 49
Belmont, MA 02178-0001
$6, 20, Dale Shank

Black Warrior Review
P.O. Box 2936
Tuscaloosa, AL 35487-2936
$6.50, 12, Amber Vogel

Boston Review
33 Harrison Avenue
Boston, MA 02111
$12, 6, Margaret Ann Roth

Boulevard
4 Washington Square Village, 9R
New York, NY 10012
$12, 10, David Brezovec

California Quarterly
100 Sproul Hall
University of California
Davis, CA 95616
$10, 4, Elliott L. Gilbert

Calyx
P.O. Box B
Corvallis, OR 97339
$10, 2, Margarita Donnelly

Canadian Fiction
Box 946, Station F
Toronto, Ontario
M4Y 2N9 Canada
$30, 16, Geoffrey Hancock

Capilano Review
Capilano College
2055 Purcell Way
North Vancouver
British Columbia
V7J 3H5 Canada
$12, 5, Crystal Hurdle

Carolina Quarterly
Greenlaw Hall 066A
University of North Carolina

Chapel Hill, NC 27514
$10, 20, rotating editorship

Chariton Review
Division of Language and Literature
Northeast Missouri State University
Kirksville, MO 63501
$7, 10, Jim Barnes

Chattahoochee Review
DeKalb Community College
2101 Womack Road
Dunwoody, GA 30338-4497
$15, 25, Lamar York

Chelsea
P.O. Box 5880
Grand Central Station
New York, NY 10163
$11, 6, Sonia Raiziss

Chicago Review
5801 South Kenwood
University of Chicago
Chicago, IL 60637
$18, 20, Elizabeth Arnold

Christopher Street
P.O. Box 1475
Church Street Station
New York, NY 10008
$27, 20, Tom Steele

Cimarron Review
205 Morrill Hall
Oklahoma State University
Stillwater, OK 74078-0135
$10, 15, John Kenny Crane

Clockwatch Review
737 Penbrook Way
Hartland, WI 53029
$6, 6, James Plath

Colorado Review
Department of English
360 Eddy Building
Colorado State University
Fort Collins, CO 80523
$9, 10, Bill Tremblay

Columbia
404 Dodge
Columbia University
New York, NY 10027
*$4.50, 6, Jill Bird Sall, Peter B.
Erdmann*

Commentary
165 East 56th Street
New York, NY 10022
$36, 5, Norman Podhoretz

Concho River Review
English Department
Angelo State University
San Angelo, TX 76909
$12, 7, Terrence A. Dalrymple

Confrontation
English Department
C. W. Post College of Long Island
University
Greenvale, NY 11548
$8, 25, Martin Tucker

Conjunctions
New Writing Foundation
866 Third Avenue
New York, NY 10022
$16, 6, Bradford Morrow

Cotton Boll/Atlanta Review
P.O. Box 76757, Sandy Springs
Atlanta, GA 30358-0703
$10, 12, Mary Hollingsworth

Crazyhorse
Department of English
University of Arkansas
Little Rock, AR 72204
$8, 10, David Jauss

Crescent Review
P.O. Box 15065
Winston-Salem, NC 27113
$7.50, 24, Dee Shneiderman

Crosscurrents
2200 Glastonbury Road
Westlake Village, CA 91361
$15, 36, Linda Brown Michelson

CutBank
Department of English
University of Montana
Missoula, MT 59812
$9, 10, rotating editorship

Denver Quarterly
University of Denver
Denver, CO 80208
$15, 27, David Milofsky

Descant
P.O. Box 314
Station P
Toronto, Ontario
M5S 2S8 Canada
$26, 20, Karen Mulhallen

Epoch
251 Goldwin Smith Hall
Cornell University
Ithaca, NY 14853-3201
$9.50, 36, C. S. Giscombe

Esquire
1790 Broadway
New York, NY 10019
$17.94, 15, Rust Hills

event
Douglas College
P.O. Box 2503
New Westminster
British Columbia
V3L 5B2 Canada
$9, 15, Maurice Hodgson

Fantasy & Science Fiction
Box 56
Cornwall, CT 06753
$17.50, 75, Edward L. Ferman

Farmer's Market
P.O. Box 1272
Galesburg, IL 61402
$7, 10, Jean C. Lee

Fiction
Fiction, Inc.
Department of English

The City College of New York
New York, NY 10031
$7, Mark Mirsky

Fiction International
Department of English &
    Comparative Literature
San Diego State University
San Diego, CA 92182
$14, 35, Roger Cunniff, Edwin Gordon

Fiction Network
P.O. Box 5651
San Francisco, CA 94101
$8, 25, Jay Schaefer

Fiction Review
P.O. Box 12268
Seattle, WA 98102
$15, 25, S. P. Stressman

Fiddlehead
Room 317, Old Arts Building
University of New Brunswick
Fredericton, New Brunswick
E3B 5A3 Canada
$14, 20, Kent Thompsen

Florida Review
Department of English, Box 25000
University of Central Florida
Orlando, FL 32816
$6, 16, Pat Rushin

Folio
Department of Literature
The American University
Washington, D.C. 20016
$8, 12, Carol Eron

Formations
P.O. Box 327
Wilmette, IL 60091
$15, 4, Jonathan and Frances Brent

Forum
Bay State University
Muncie, IN 47306
$15, 40, Bruce W. Hozeski

Four Quarters
LaSalle College
20th and Olney Avenues
Philadelphia, PA 19141
$8, 10, John J. Keenan

Gargoyle
Paycock Press
P.O. Box 30906
Bethesda, MD 20814
$15, 25, Richard Peabody

Georgia Review
University of Georgia
Athens, GA 30602
$12, 15, Stanley W. Lindberg

Gettysburg Review
Gettysburg College
Gettysburg, PA 17325
$12, 20, Peter Stitt

Good Housekeeping
959 Eighth Avenue
New York, NY 10019
$14.97, 24, Naomi Lewis

GQ
350 Madison Avenue
New York, NY 10017
$19.97, 12, Tom Jenks

Grain
Box 3986
Regina, Saskatchewan
S4P 3R9 Canada
$12, 20, Mick Burrs

Grand Street
50 Riverside Drive
New York, NY 10024
$20, 20, Ben Sonnenberg

Granta
250 West 57th Street, suite 1316
New York, NY 10107
$28, NY editor: Anne Kinard

Gray's Sporting Journal
205 Willow Street

South Hamilton, MA 01982
$26.50, 20, Edward E. Gray

Great River Review
211 West 7th
Winona, MN 55987
$9, 6, Ruth Forsyth

Greensboro Review
Department of English
University of North Carolina
Greensboro, NC 27412
$5, 16, Jim Clark

Harper's Magazine
666 Broadway
New York, NY 10012
$18, 15, Lewis H. Lapham

Hawaii Review
University of Hawaii
Department of English
1733 Donaghho Road
Honolulu, HI 96822
$6, 12, Jeannie Thompson

Helicon Nine
P.O. Box 22412
Kansas City, MO 64113
$18, 8, Gloria Vando Hickock

High Plains Literary Review
180 Adams Street, suite 250
Denver, CO 80206
$20, 10, Robert O. Greer, Jr.

Hudson Review
684 Park Avenue
New York, NY 10021
$18, 8, Paula Deitz, Frederick Morgan

Indiana Review
316 North Jordan Avenue
Bloomington, IN 47405
$10, 20, Elizabeth Dodd

In Earnest
P.O. Box 4177
James Madison University
Harrisonburg, VA 22807
6, Greg Barrett

Iowa Review
Department of English
University of Iowa, 308 EPB
Iowa City, IA 52242
$15, 10, David Hamilton

Iowa Woman
P.O. Box 680
Iowa City, IA 52244
$10, 12, Carolyn Hardesty

Isaac Asimov's Science Fiction
  Magazine
380 Lexington Avenue
New York, NY 10017
$19.50, 100, Gardner Dozois

Jewish Currents
22 East 17th Street
New York, NY 10003
$15, 20, editorial board

Jewish Monthly
1640 Rhode Island Avenue NW
Washington, DC 20036
$8, 3, Marc Silver

The Journal
Department of English
Ohio State University
164 West 17th Avenue
Columbus, OH 43210
$5, 2, David Citino

Kansas Quarterly
Department of English
Denison Hall
Kansas State University
Manhattan, KS 66506
$15, 20, Ben Nyberg

Karamu
English Department
Eastern Illinois University
Charleston, IL 61920
John Guzlowski

Kenyon Review
Kenyon College
Gambier, OH 43022

*$15, 15, Philip D. Church, Galbraith M.
  Crump*

Lilith
The Jewish Women's Magazine
250 West 57th Street
New York, NY 10107
$14, 5, Julia Wolf Mazow

Literary Review
Fairleigh Dickinson University
285 Madison Avenue
Madison, NJ 07940
$12, 25, Walter Cummins

Little Magazine
Dragon Press
P.O. Box 78
Pleasantville, NY 10570
$16, 5

McCall's
230 Park Avenue
New York, NY 10169
$13.95, 20, Helen DelMonte

Mademoiselle
350 Madison Avenue
New York, NY 10017
$15, 14, Eileen Schnurr

Madison Review
University of Wisconsin
Department of English
H. C. White Hall
600 North Park Street
Madison, WI 53706
$5, 8, Craig Alexander

Malahat Review
University of Victoria
P.O. Box 1700
Victoria, British Columbia
V8W 2Y2 Canada
$15, 25, Constance Rooke

Massachusetts Review
Memorial Hall
University of Massachusetts
Amherst, MA 01003
$12, 15, Mary Heath

Michigan Quarterly Review
3032 Rackham Building
University of Michigan
Ann Arbor, MI 48109
$13, 10, Laurence Goldstein

Mid-American Review
106 Hanna Hall
Department of English
Bowling Green State University
Bowling Green, OH 48109
$6, 10, Robert Early

Minnesota Review
Department of English
State University of New York
Stony Brook, NY 11794-5350
$7, Helen Cooper

Mississippi Review
University of Southern Mississippi
Southern Station, Box 5144
Hattiesburg, MS 39406-5144
$10, 25, Frederick Barthelme

Missouri Review
Department of English
231 Arts and Sciences
University of Missouri
Columbia, MO 65211
$12, 15, Speer Morgan

MSS
P.O. Box 530
State University of New York
Binghamton, NY 13901
$10, 30, L. M. Rosenberg

Nebraska Review
Writers' Workshop, ASH 212
University of Nebraska
Omaha, NE 68182-0324
$6, 10, Art Homer, Richard Duggin

Negative Capability
62 Ridgelawn Drive East
Mobile, AL 36605
$12, 15, Sue Walker

New Directions
New Directions Publishing

80 Eighth Avenue
New York, NY 10011
$11.95, 4, James Laughlin

New England Review and Bread Loaf
  Quarterly
Middlebury College
Middlebury, VT 05753
$12, 15, Sydney Lea

New Laurel Review
828 Lesseps Street
New Orleans, LA 70117
$8, 2, Lee Meitzer Grue

New Letters
University of Missouri
5216 Rockhill Road
Kansas City, MO 64110
$15, 10, Trish Reeves

New Mexico Humanities Review
P.O. Box A
New Mexico Tech
Socorro, NM 87801
$8, 15, John Rothfork

New Orleans Review
P.O. Box 195
Loyola University
New Orleans, LA 70118
$25, 4, John Biguenet, John Master

New Quarterly
English Language Proficiency
  Programme
University of Waterloo
Waterloo, Ontario
N2L 3G1 Canada
$13, 15, Peter Hinchcliffe

New Renaissance
9 Heath Road
Arlington, MA 02174
$11.50, 10, Louise T. Reynolds

New Virginia Review
1306 East Cary Street, 2A
Richmond, VA 23219
$13.50, 12, Mary Flinn

The New Yorker
25 West 43rd Street
New York, NY 10036
$32, 100

Nimrod
Arts and Humanities Council of
    Tulsa
2210 South Main Street
Tulsa, OK 74114
$10, 10, Francine Ringold

North American Review
University of Northern Iowa
Cedar Falls, IA 50614
$11, 35, Robley Wilson, Jr.

North Dakota Quarterly
University of North Dakota
P.O. Box 8237
Grand Forks, ND 58202
$10, 10, Robert W. Lewis

Northwest Review
369 PLC
University of Oregon
Eugene, OR 97403
$11, 10, John Witte

Oak Square
Box 1238
Allston, MA 02134
$10, 20, Anne E. Pluto

Ohio Journal
Department of English
Ohio State University
164 West 17th Avenue
Columbus, OH 43210
$5, 4, Don Citino

Ohio Review
Ellis Hall
Ohio University
Athens, OH 45701-2979
$12, 10, Wayne Dodd

Old Hickory Review
P.O. Box 1178
Jackson, TN 38301
$4, 5, Dorothy Starfill

Omni
1965 Broadway
New York, NY 10023-5965
$24, 20, Ellen Datlow

Ontario Review
9 Honey Brook Drive
Princeton, NJ 08540
$10, 8, Raymond J. Smith

Other Voices
820 Ridge Road
Highland Park, IL 60035
*$16, 30, Dolores Weinberg, Lois
    Hauselman*

Paris Review
541 East 72nd Street
New York, NY 10021
$20, 15, George Plimpton

Passages North
William Boniface Fine Arts Center
7th Street and 1st Avenue South
Escanaba, MI 49829
$2, 12, Elinor Benedict

Plainswoman
P.O. Box 8027
Grand Forks, ND 58202
$10, 10, Emily Johnson

Playboy
Playboy Building
919 North Michigan Avenue
Chicago, IL 60611
$24, 20, Alice K. Turner

Playgirl
Box 3710
Escondido, CA 92025
$35, 15, Mary Ellen Strote

Ploughshares
P.O. Box 529
Cambridge, MA 02139-0529
$15, 25, DeWitt Henry

Prairie Schooner
201 Andrews Hall
University of Nebraska

Lincoln, NE 68588-0334
$15, 20, Hugh J. Lake

Primavera
1212 East 59th Street
Chicago, IL 60637
$5, 10, Ann Gearen

Prism International
Department of Creative Writing
University of British Columbia
Vancouver, British Columbia
V6T 1W5 Canada
$12, 20, Jennifer Milton

Puerto del Sol
Department of English
New Mexico State University
Las Cruces, NM 88003
$7.75, 12, Kevin McIlvoy

Quarry Magazine
P.O. Box 1061
Kingston, Ontario
K7L 4Y5 Canada
$18, 20, Barry Grills

The Quarterly
Vintage Books
201 East 50th Street
New York, NY 10022
$28, 10, Bernie Wood

RE:AL
School of Liberal Arts
Stephen F. Austin State University
Nacogdoches, TX 75962
$4, 5, Neal B. Houston

River City Review
P.O. Box 34275
Louisville, KY 40232
$5, 10, Richard L. Neumayer

River Styx
Big River Association
14 South Euclid
St. Louis, MO 63108
$14, 10, Carol J. Pierman

A Room of One's Own
P.O. Box 46160
Station G
Vancouver, British Columbia
V6R 4G5 Canada
$11, 12, Gayla Reid

St. Andrews Review
St. Andrews Presbyterian College
Laurinsburg, NC 28352
$12, 10, Ronald H. Bayes

Salmagundi
Skidmore College
Saratoga Springs, NY 12866
$12, 2, Robert Boyers

San Jose Studies
English Department
San Jose State University
One Washington Square
San Jose, CA 95192
$12, 5, Fauneil J. Rinn

Santa Monica Review
Center for the Humanities
Santa Monica College
1900 Pico Boulevard
Santa Monica, CA 90405
$12, 16, Jim Krusoe

Saturday Night
511 King Street West, suite 100
Toronto, Ontario
M5V 2Z4 Canada
Robert Fulford

Seattle Review
Padelford Hall, GN-30
University of Washington
Seattle, WA 98195
$8, 10, Charles Johnson

Seventeen
850 Third Avenue
New York, NY 10022
$13.95, 12, Adrian Nicole LeBlanc

Sewanee Review
University of the South

Sewanee, TN 37375-4009
$18, 10, George Core

Shenandoah
Washington and Lee University
Box 722
Lexington, VA 24450
$11, 10, Dabney Stuart

Short Story Review
P.O. Box 882108
San Francisco, CA 94188-2108
$9, 8, Dwight Gabbard

Sinister Wisdom
P.O. Box 3252
Berkeley, CA 94703
$17, 25, Elana Dykewoman

Sonora Review
Department of English
University of Arizona
Tucson, AZ 85721
$5, 10, Tom Unger

South Carolina Review
Department of English
Clemson University
Clemson, SC 29634-1503
$5, 2, Richard J. Calhoun

South Dakota Review
University of South Dakota
P.O. Box 111 University Exchange
Vermillion, SD 57069
$10, 15, John R. Milton

Southern California Anthology
% Master of Professional Writing
   Program, WPH 404
University of Southern California
Los Angeles, CA 90089
$5.95, 6, Suzanne Harper

Southern Humanities Review
9088 Haley Center
Auburn University
Auburn, AL 36849
*$12, 5, Dan R. Latimer, Thomas L.
   Wright*

Southern Magazine
201 East Markham Street, suite 200
Little Rock, AR 72201
$15, 6, James Morgan

Southern Review
43 Allen Hall
Louisiana State University
Baton Rouge, LA 70803
$12, 20, Fred Hobson, James Olney

Southwest Review
Southern Methodist University
P.O. Box 4374
Dallas, TX 75275
$16, 15, Willard Spiegelman

Sou'wester
School of Humanities
Department of English
Southern Illinois University
Edwardsville, IL 62026-1438
$4, 10, Donald Gilbert

Special Report: Fiction
Whittle Communications L.P.
505 Market Street
Knoxville, TN 37902
$14, 28, Elise Nakhnikian

Stories
14 Beacon Street
Boston, MA 02108
$16, 12, Amy R. Kaufman

Story Quarterly
P.O. Box 1416
Northbrook, IL 60065
$12, 20, Anne Brashler, Diane Williams

The Sun
412 Rosemary Street
Chapel Hill, NC 27514
$28, 12, Sy Safransky

Tampa Review
P.O. Box 19F
University of Tampa
401 West Kennedy Boulevard

Tampa, FL 33606-1490
$7, 12, *Andy Solomon*

Threepenny Review
P.O. Box 9131
Berkeley, CA 94709
$10, 10, *Wendy Lesser*

Tikkun
5100 Leona Street
Oakland, CA 94619
$30, 2, *Rosellen Brown*

Timbuktu
P.O. Box 469
Charlottesville, VA 22902
$6, 6, *Molly Turner*

TriQuarterly
2020 Ridge Avenue
Northwestern University
Evanston, IL 60208
$18, 15, *Reginald Gibbons*

Turnstile
175 Fifth Avenue, suite 2348
New York, NY 10010
$13, 12, *Jill Benz*

University of Windsor Review
Department of English
University of Windsor
Windsor, Ontario
N9B 3P4 Canada
$10, 6, *Joseph A. Quinn*

Virginia Quarterly Review
One West Range
Charlottesville, VA 22903
$15, 12, *Staige D. Blackford*

Voice Literary Supplement
842 Broadway
New York, NY 10003
$12, 8, *M. Mark*

Weber Studies
Weber State College
Ogden, UT 84408
$5, 2, *Neila Seshachari*

Webster Review
Webster University
470 East Lockwood
Webster Groves, MO 63119
$5, 5, *Nancy Schapiro*

West Branch
Department of English
Bucknell University
Lewisburg, PA 17837
$5, 10, *Robert Love Taylor*

Western Humanities Review
University of Utah
Salt Lake City, UT 84112
$15, 10, *Barry Weller*

William and Mary Review
College of William and Mary
Williamsburg, VA 23185
$4.50, 5, *William Clark*

Willow Springs
PUB P.O. Box 1063
Eastern Washington University
Cheney, WA 99004
$7, 8, *Dennis Medina*

Wind
RFD Route 1, P.O. Box 809K
Pikeville, KY 41501
$6, 20, *Quentin R. Howard*

Witness
31000 Northwestern Highway
P.O. Box 9079
Farmington Hills, MI 48333-9079
$16, 15, *Peter Stine*

Worcester Review
6 Chatham Street
Worcester, MA 01609
$10, 8, *Rodger Martin*

Writers Forum
University of Colorado
P.O. Box 7150
Colorado Springs, CO 80933-7150
$8.95, 15, *Alexander Blackburn*

Xavier Review
Xavier University
Box 110C
New Orleans, LA 70125
Rainulf A. Steizmann

Yale Review
1902A Yale Station
New Haven, CT 06520
$16, 12, Mr. Kai Erikson

Yankee
Yankee Publishing, Inc.
Dublin, NH 03444
$18, 10, Edie Clark

Yellow Silk
P.O. Box 6374
Albany, CA 94706
$15, 10, Lily Pond

Z Miscellaneous
P.O. Box 20041
New York, NY 10028
$9, 73, Charles Fabrizio

Zyzzyva
41 Sutter Street, suite 1400
San Francisco, CA 94104
$20, 12, Howard Junker